"No other guide has as much to offer . . . these books are a pleasure to read." Gene Shalit on the *Today Show*

". . . Excellently organized for the casual traveler who is looking for a mix of recreation and cultural insight."
Washington Post

★ ★ ★ ★ ★ (5-star rating) "Crisply written and remarkably personable. Cleverly organized so you can pluck out the minutest fact in a moment. Satisfyingly thorough."
Réalités

"The information they offer is up-to-date, crisply presented but far from exhaustive, the judgments knowledgeable but not opinionated." *New York Times*

"The individual volumes are compact, the prose succinct, and the coverage up-to-date and knowledgeable . . . The format is portable and the index admirably detailed."
John Barkham Syndicate

". . . An abundance of excellent directions, diversions, and facts, including perspectives and getting-ready-to-go advice — succinct, detailed, and well organized in an easy-to-follow style." *Los Angeles Times*

"They contain an amount of information that is truly staggering, besides being surprisingly current."
Detroit News

"These guides address themselves to the needs of the modern traveler demanding precise, qualitative information . . . Upbeat, slick, and well put together."
Dallas Morning News

". . . Attractive to look at, refreshingly easy to read, and generously packed with information." *Miami Herald*

"These guides are as good as any published, and much better than most." *Louisville* (Kentucky) *Times*

Stephen Birnbaum Travel Guides

Acapulco
Bahamas, and Turks & Caicos
Barcelona .
Bermuda
Boston
Canada
Cancun, Cozumel, & Isla Mujeres
Caribbean
Chicago
Disneyland
Eastern Europe
Europe
Europe for Business Travelers
Florence
France
Great Britain
Hawaii
Honolulu
Ireland
Italy
Ixtapa & Zihuatanejo
Las Vegas

London
Los Angeles
Mexico
Miami & Ft. Lauderdale
Montreal & Quebec City
New Orleans
New York
Paris
Portugal
Puerto Vallarta
Rome
San Francisco
South America
Spain
Toronto
United States
USA for Business Travelers
Vancouver
Venice
Walt Disney World
Washington, DC
Western Europe

CONTRIBUTING EDITORS

Laura Hambleton
Laura Kelly
Molly Arost Staub
Melinda Tang

MAPS Mark Carlson
       Susan Carlson
SYMBOLS Gloria McKeown

Birnbaum's
MIAMI &
FT. LAUDERDALE
1993

Alexandra Mayes Birnbaum
EDITORS

Lois Spritzer
EXECUTIVE EDITOR

Laura L. Brengelman
Managing Editor

Mary Callahan
Jill Kadetsky
Susan McClung
Beth Schlau
Dana Margaret Schwartz
Associate Editors

Gene Gold
Assistant Editor

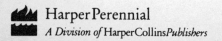

HarperPerennial
A Division of HarperCollins*Publishers*

To Stephen, who merely made all this possible.

FIRST EDITION

ISSN 0749-2561 (Stephen Birnbaum Travel Guides)
ISSN 1056-4454 (Miami & Ft. Lauderdale)
ISBN 0-06-278065-4 (pbk.)

92 93 94 95 96 CC/WP 10 9 8 7 6 5 4 3 2 1

Contents

Sources and Resources

THE CITIES

Thorough, qualitative guides to Miami and Ft. Lauderdale. These are comprehensive reports on the most compelling attractions and amenities, designed to be used on the spot.

DIVERSIONS

A selective guide to more than 15 active and/or cerebral theme vacations, including the best places in Miami and Ft. Lauderdale to pursue them.

For the Experience

For the Body

For the Mind

DIRECTIONS

Nine of the best walks and drives through Miami and Ft. Lauderdale.

A Word from the Editor

Miami Beach — and to a lesser degree, Miami and Ft. Lauderdale — are good object lessons of how not to run towns that depend on tourists.

For a couple of decades after World War II, southeastern Florida had only to exist to attract more than its fair share of northerners seeking the sun during the winter. The temperature alone was a powerful lure, and the existence of glitzy hotels, a beckoning beach, and other such attractions was just frosting (actually, thawing) on the cake. Each year, as the final leaf fell from the last tree in the northeast, huge hordes of heat-seeking sun worshipers — not unlike lemmings determined to reach the sea — headed for Miami.

The vendors of travel services in southeastern Florida, long accustomed to the regular arrival of their traditional clientele, did absolutely the worst possible thing to assure their own continued prosperity: nothing! By taking their customers for granted, they let hotels run down, they allowed shops and restaurants to grow stale, and generally did little to keep the appeal of Miami/Miami Beach very high.

You can say lots of things about travelers, but most of them ain't dumb. Soon tales of equally appealing beaches in the Caribbean, Mexico, and even Hawaii began to reach the ears of longtime Miami visitors, and promotional airfares and discounted package programs made these new destinations delightfully affordable. So it wasn't too long before hotel occupancy levels in southeastern Florida began to fall precipitously.

The decline in tourist traffic meant an absence of cash with which to maintain and refurbish tourism facilities, and the erection of *Walt Disney World* in Orlando in 1971 — followed by important attractions on both the east and west coasts of central Florida — created a "wall" across the Sunshine State that stopped traffic several hundred miles north of Miami Beach. Quite a lot of tourism experts thought they heard the death knell of Miami for tourists.

This conclusion was unshaken by the desperate acts tried by a lot of the folks who had gotten Miami in trouble in the first place. Typical of the grand designs that the fast-buck promoters suggested was the legalization of gambling — despite the fact that it had done little good in the Bahamas, just 50 miles away. Fortunately, the local citizens saw through this self-serving wagering proposal, and the referendum was defeated.

But Miami and Miami Beach were still suffering; travel and tourism habits had dramatically changed, and aside from the appeal that the local climate continued to have for retirees, the bulk of sun-seeking winter travelers tanned elsewhere. A less vital and vibrant community would have packed it in and given up.

The impetus for the turnaround in Miami's fortunes came from an unexpected direction — the south instead of the north. The influx of ambitious, energetic Cubans jump-started the city of Miami — for a long time just a poor relation to the glamour and glitz of Miami Beach. The sharpening of focus on the southern tier of the United States brought new development — commercial, industrial, and residential — to Florida, and Miami got its fair share of the new projects. Finally, Miami became the natural headquarters for virtually all financial and commercial activities relating to Latin America — whether domestic or foreign. Suddenly, Miami was a throbbing force in the expansion of the entire US economy.

Even tourism was a beneficiary of this growth; money earned in everything from banking to sugarcane trickled down to hotel building and restoration, and a new sense of civic pride caused the citizenry to re-examine local assets. It wasn't long before blocks of mostly run-down hotels occupied by pensioners became one of this nation's most compelling areas of Art Deco architecture. Concurrently came the city's emergence as an important art center. Similar development followed.

It also wasn't too long before the troubled tourists started coming back, although they are no longer the sole foundation on which the local economy depends. It made some of us — who had glibly predicted Miami's demise — gladly rethink our conclusions.

My husband Stephen Birnbaum had a particular affinity for Florida — admittedly not always shared by me. He was a golfer (his game was his handicap) and a sun worshiper. I am an indoors woman: no fairways or swaths of sand for me. And until Miami's relatively recent renaissance, for me, this "moon over" city meant sitting under a palm tree, my head protected by a broad-brimmed straw hat, my face slathered with zinc oxide. Steve and I did, however, share one major Miami passion: dinner at *Joe's Stone Crab*.

Our own evolution as travelers (which happily continues for me) is mirrored by the evolution of our guidebook series. When we began our series of modern travel guides, we logically began with "area" books, attempting to publish guides that would include the widest possible number of attractive destinations. When the public seemed to accept our new way of delivering travel data, we added titles covering only a single country, and when these became popular we began our newest expansion phase, which centers on a group of books that deal with only a single city. Now we can not only highlight our favorite urban destinations, but really describe how to get the very most out of a visit.

Such treatment of travel information only mirrors an increasingly pervasive trend among travelers — the frequent return to a treasured travel spot. Once upon a time, even the most dedicated travelers would visit distant parts of the world no more than once in a lifetime — usually as part of that fabled Grand Tour. But greater numbers of would-be sojourners are now availing themselves of the opportunity to visit a favored part of the world over and over again.

So where once it was routine to say you'd "seen" a particular city or country after a very superficial, once-over-lightly encounter, the more perceptive travelers of today recognize that it's entirely possible to have only skimmed the surface of a specific travel destination even after having visited that place more than a dozen times. Similarly, repeated visits to a single site permit true exploration of special interests, whether they be sporting, artistic, or intellectual.

For those of us who now have spent the last several years working out the special system under which we present information in this series, the luxury of being able to devote nearly as much space as we'd like to just a single city is as close to paradise for guide writers and editors as any of us expects to come. But clearly this is not the first guide to the glories of Miami — one suspects that guides of one sort or another have existed at least since the day when Mr. Flagler decided to run his railroad down the full length of the Florida peninsula — so a traveler might logically ask why a new one is suddenly necessary.

Our answer is that the nature of travel to Miami — and even of the travelers who now routinely make the trip — has changed dramatically of late. For the past 200 years or so, travel to even a town within our own country was considered an elaborate undertaking, one that required extensive advance planning. But with the advent of jet air travel in the late 1950s and of increased-capacity, wide-body aircraft during the late 1960s, travel to and around once distant destinations became extremely common. Attitudes as well as costs have changed significantly in the last couple of decades.

Obviously, any new guidebook to Miami must keep pace with and answer the real needs of today's travelers. That's why we've tried to create a guide that's specifically organized, written, and edited for the more demanding modern traveler, one for whom qualitative information is infinitely more desirable than mere quantities of unappraised data. We think that this book, along with all the other guides in our series, represents a new generation of travel guides — one that is especially responsive to modern needs and interests.

For years, dating back as far as Herr Baedeker, travel guides have tended to be encyclopedic, seemingly much more concerned with demonstrating expertise in geography and history than with a real analysis of the sorts of things that actually concern a typical modern tourist. But today, when it is hardly necessary to tell a traveler where Miami is (in many cases, the traveler has been there nearly as often as the guidebook editors), it becomes the responsibility of those editors to provide new perspectives and to suggest new directions in order to make the guide genuinely valuable.

That's exactly what we've tried to do in this series. I think you'll notice a different, more contemporary tone to the text, as well as an organization and focus that are distinctive and more functional. And even a random reading of what follows will demonstrate a substantial departure from the standard guidebook orientation, for we've not only attempted to provide information of a more compelling sort, but we also have tried to present the data in a format that makes it particularly accessible.

Needless to say, it's difficult to decide just what to include in a guidebook of this size — and what to omit. Early on, we realized that giving up the encyclopedic approach precluded our listing every single route and restaurant, a realization that helped define our overall editorial focus. Similarly, when we discussed the possibility of presenting certain information in other than strict geographic order, we found that the new format enabled us to arrange data in a way that we feel best answers the questions travelers typically ask.

Large numbers of specific questions have provided the real editorial skeleton for this book. The volume of mail we regularly receive emphasizes that modern travelers want very precise information, so we've tried to organize our material in the most responsive way possible. Readers who want to know the best restaurants or the least crowded beach in Miami will have no trouble extracting that data from this guide.

Travel guides are, understandably, reflections of personal taste, and putting one's name on a title page obviously puts one's preferences on the line. But I think I ought to amplify just what "personal" means. Like Steve, I don't believe in the sort of personal guidebook that's a palpable misrepresentation on its face. It is, for example, hardly possible for any single travel writer to visit thousands of restaurants (and nearly as many hotels) in any given year and provide accurate appraisals of each. And even if it were physically possible for one human being to survive such an itinerary, it would of necessity have to be done at a dead sprint, and the perceptions derived therefrom would probably be less valid than those of any other intelligent individual visiting the same establishments. It is, therefore, impossible (especially in a large, annually revised and updated guidebook *series* such as we offer) to have only one person provide all the data on the entire world.

I also happen to think that such individual orientation is of substantially less value to readers. Visiting a single hotel for just one night or eating one hasty meal in a random restaurant hardly equips anyone to provide appraisals that are of more than passing interest. No amount of doggedly alliterative or oppressively onomatopoeic text can camouflage a technique that is essentially specious. We have, therefore, chosen what I like to describe as the "thee and me" approach to restaurant and hotel evaluation and, to a somewhat more limited degree, to the sites and sights we have included in the other sections of our text. What this really reflects is a personal sampling tempered by intelligent counsel from informed local sources, and these additional friends-of-the-editor are almost always residents of the city and/or area about which they are consulted.

Despite the presence of several editors, writers, researchers, and local contributors, very precise editing and tailoring keep our text fiercely subjective. So what follows is the gospel according to Birnbaum, and it represents as much of our own taste and instincts as we can manage. It is probable, therefore, that if you like your cities stylish and prefer small hotels with personality to huge high-rise anonymities, we're likely to have a long and meaningful relationship. Readers with dissimilar tastes may be less enraptured.

I also should point out something about the person to whom this guidebook is directed. Above all, he or she is a "visitor." This means that such elements as restaurants have been specifically picked to provide the visitor with a representative, enlightening, stimulating, and above all pleasant experience. Since so many extraneous considerations can affect the reception and service accorded a regular restaurant patron, our choices can in no way be construed as an exhaustive guide to resident dining. We think we've listed all the best places, in various price ranges, but they were chosen with a visitor's enjoyment in mind.

Other evidence of how we've tried to tailor our text to reflect modern travel habits is most apparent in the section we call DIVERSIONS. Where once it was common for travelers to spend an urban visit in a determinedly passive state, the emphasis is far more active today. So we've organized every activity we could reasonably evaluate and arranged the material in a way that is especially accessible to activists of either athletic or cerebral bent. It is no longer necessary, therefore, to wade through a pound or two of superfluous prose just to find the very best stone crabs to nibble or the most architecturally compelling neighborhood within the city limits.

If there is a single thing that best characterizes the revolution in and evolution of current holiday habits, it is that most travelers now consider travel a right rather than a privilege. No longer is a family trip to the far corners of the world necessarily a once-in-a-lifetime thing; nor is the idea of visiting exotic, faraway places in the least worrisome. Travel today translates as the enthusiastic desire to sample all of the world's opportunities, to find that elusive quality of experience that is not only enriching but comfortable. For that reason, we've tried to make what follows not only helpful and enlightening, but the sort of welcome companion of which every traveler dreams.

Finally, I also should point out that every good travel guide is a living enterprise; that is, no part of this text is carved in stone. In our annual revisions, we refine, expand, and further hone all our material to serve your travel needs better. To this end, no contribution is of greater value to us than your personal reaction to what we have written, as well as information reflecting your own experiences while using the book. We earnestly and enthusiastically solicit your comments about this guide *and* your opinions and perceptions about places you have recently visited. In this way, we will be able to provide the most current information — including the actual experiences of recent travelers — and to make those experiences more readily available to others. Please write to us at 10 E. 53rd St., New York, NY 10022.

We sincerely hope to hear from you.

ALEXANDRA MAYES BIRNBAUM

How to Use This Guide

A great deal of care has gone into the special organization of this guidebook, and we believe it represents a real breakthrough in the presentation of travel material. Our aim is to create a new, more modern generation of travel books, and to make this guide the most useful and practical travel tool available today.

Our text is divided into four basic sections in order to present information in the best way on every possible aspect of a vacation to Miami. This organization itself should alert you to the vast and varied opportunities available, as well as indicate all the specific data necessary to plan a successful visit. You won't find much of the conventional "swaying palms and shimmering sands" text here; we've chosen instead to deliver more useful and practical information. Prospective itineraries tend to speak for themselves, and with so many diverse travel opportunities, we feel our main job is to highlight what's where and to provide basic information — how, when, where, how much, and what's best — to assist you in making the most intelligent choices possible.

Here is a brief summary of the four sections of this book, and what you can expect to find in each. We believe that you will find both your travel planning and en route enjoyment enhanced by having this book at your side.

GETTING READY TO GO

This mini-encyclopedia of practical travel facts is a sort of know-it-all companion with all the precise information necessary to create a successful journey to Miami. There are entries on more than 25 separate topics, including how to get where you're going, what preparations to make before leaving, what your trip is likely to cost, and how to avoid prospective problems. The individual entries are specific, realistic, and, where appropriate, cost-oriented.

We expect you to use this section most in the course of planning your trip, for its ideas and suggestions are intended to simplify this often confusing period. Entries are intentionally concise, in an effort to get to the meat of the matter with the least extraneous prose. These entries are augmented by extensive lists of specific sources from which to obtain even more specialized data, plus some suggestions for obtaining travel information on your own.

THE CITIES

Individual reports on Miami and Ft. Lauderdale, prepared with the aid of researchers, contributors, professional journalists, and experts on the spot. Although useful at the planning stage, THE CITIES is really designed to be taken along and used on the spot. The reports offer a short-stay guide, including an essay introducing each city as a contemporary place to visit.

At-a-Glance material is actually a site-by-site survey of the most important, interesting, and sometimes most eclectic sights to see and things to do. *Sources and Resources* is a concise listing of pertinent tourism information, meant to answer myriad potentially pressing questions as they arise — from simple things such as the address of the local tourism office, how to get around, which sightseeing tours to take, and when special events occur, to something more difficult like where to find the best nightspot, which are the shops that have the finest merchandise and/or the most irresistible bargains, and where the best museums and theaters are to be found. *Best in Town* lists our collection of cost-and-quality choices of the best places to eat and sleep on a variety of budgets.

DIVERSIONS

This section is designed to help travelers find the best places in which to pursue a wide range of physical and cerebral activities, without having to wade through endless pages of unrelated text. This very selective guide lists the broadest possible range of activities, including all the best places to pursue them.

We start with a list of special places to stay and eat, move to activities that require some perspiration — sports preferences and other rigorous pursuits — and go on to report on a number of more cerebral and spiritual vacation opportunities. In every case, our suggestion of a particular location — and often our recommendation of a specific resort — is intended to guide you to that special place where the quality of experience is likely to be highest. Whether you seek a hotel built in the Art Deco style or the best place to shop or swim, each category is the equivalent of a comprehensive checklist of the absolute best in the area.

DIRECTIONS

Here are seven walks and drives that cover the city, along its main thoroughfares and side streets, past its most spectacular landmarks and lovely parks, and the most compelling tours in the areas nearby. This is the only section of the book that is organized geographically; itineraries can be connected for longer sojourns or used individually for short, intensive explorations. We also suggest two 1-day or overnight drives: to the Florida Keys and Everglades National Park.

Although each of the book's sections has a distinct format and a special function, they have all been designed to be used together to provide a complete inventory of travel information. To use this book to full advantage, take a few minutes to read the table of contents and random entries in each section to get a firsthand feel for how it all fits together.

Pick and choose needed information. Assume, for example, that you have always wanted to visit Miami and sample its spectacular seafood — but never really knew how to organize such a gastronomic excursion. Choose specific restaurants from the selections offered in "Eating Out" in THE CITIES, add some of those noted in each walking tour in DIRECTIONS, then cross-reference with those in the roundup of the best in the city in the *Miami's Best Restaurants* section in DIVERSIONS.

In other words, the sections of this book are building blocks designed to help you put together the best possible trip. Use them selectively as a tool, a source of ideas, a reference work for accurate facts, and a guidebook to the best buys, the most exciting sights, the most pleasant accommodations, the tastiest foods — *the best travel experience* that you can possibly have in Miami.

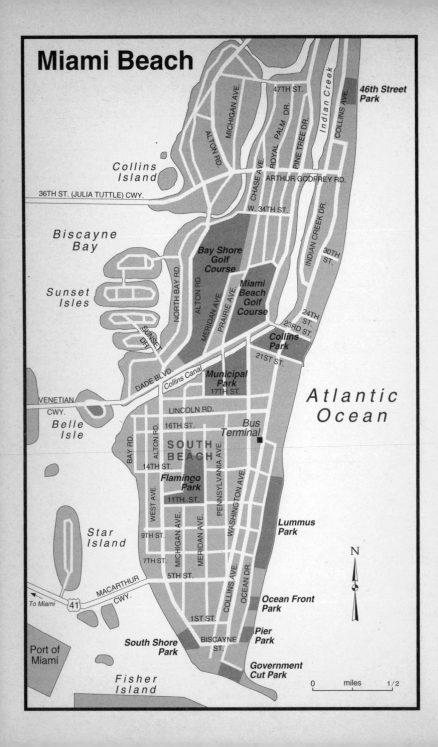

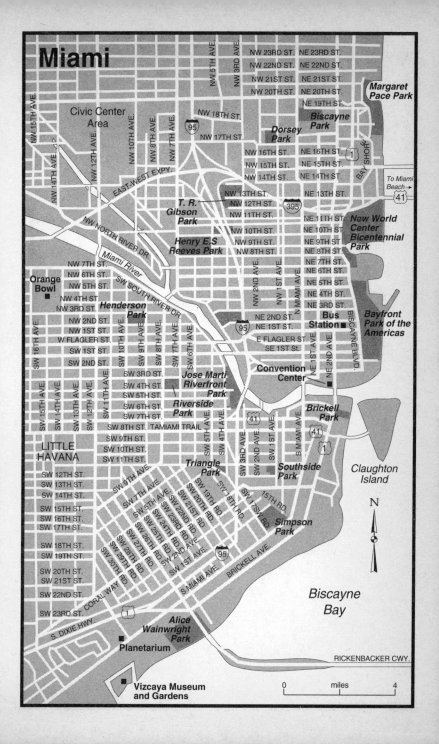

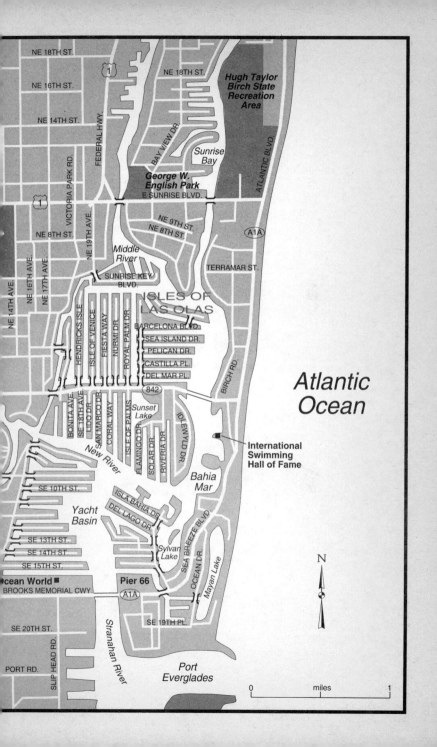

GETTING READY TO GO

When and How to Go

When to Go

 There isn't really a best time to visit Miami and Ft. Lauderdale, although the most popular vacation time traditionally is in winter. Both cities enjoy tropical weather, with an average temperature in the 80s in the summer and mid 70s in the winter. Temperatures rarely drop below the 60s. Showers and occasional heavy downpours can be expected in the summer, so be prepared with rain gear if you are visiting during that season.

There are good reasons for visiting Miami and Ft. Lauderdale any time of the year. There are no real off-season periods when attractions are closed, so you aren't risking the disappointment of arriving at an attraction and finding the gates locked. However, you can benefit from lower room rates if you visit during the less busy summer months and what's known as the "shoulder season" (May through September).

■**Note:** When planning the timing of your visit, there is one period during which you must be careful. In the winter, especially during the *Christmas* holidays, hotels are packed and most bargains disappear. This is also the prime meeting and convention season. During this period, make your bookings extra early — preferably 2 to 3 months ahead.

WEATHER: Travelers can get current readings and extended forecasts through the *Weather Channel Connection,* the worldwide weather report center of the *Weather Channel,* a cable TV station. By dialing 900-WEATHER and punching in either the first four letters of the city name or the area code (MIAM or 305 for Miami; FTLA or 305 for Ft. Lauderdale) for over 600 cities in the US (including Puerto Rico and the US Virgin Islands), an up-to-date recording will provide such information as current temperature, barometric pressure, relative humidity, and wind speed, as well as a general 2-day forecast. Beach, boating, and highway reports are also provided for some locations. This 24-hour service can be accessed from any touch-tone phone in the US, and costs 95¢ per minute. The charge will show up on your phone bill. For additional information, contact the *Weather Channel Connection,* 2600 Cumberland Pkwy., Atlanta, GA 30339 (phone: 404-434-6800).

CULTURAL EVENTS: Autumn signals the beginning of the year's cultural calendar. The Ft. Lauderdale–based *Philharmonic Orchestra of Florida* starts its season in October. It also has a pop series in the summer. This major orchestra performs in several cities, including Ft. Lauderdale and Miami. For a calendar of its scheduled performances, call 800-226-1812. The 51-year-old *Greater Miami Opera* performs each year in Miami from January through April. It also tours occasionally in Ft. Lauderdale. Reggae, Latin, jazz, and rock groups of all types add to the area's musical mix. Miami native Gloria Estefan and her *Miami Sound Machine* give occasional local concerts between national tours.

The *Miami City Ballet* performs both modern jazz and classical ballet from September through March in Miami and Ft. Lauderdale. The Spanish dance company, *Ballet Flamenco La Rosa,* performs regularly in Miami. For a schedule of their performances, call 305-672-0552. Current Broadway hits as well as modern experimental plays can be seen at almost a dozen major theaters in Miami and Ft. Lauderdale. Ft. Lauderdale's new $56-million *Broward Center for the Performing Arts* showcases Broadway productions and top name talent.

With more than 20 museums combined, including the *Center for the Fine Arts, Bass Museum of Art, Lowe Art Museum,* and *The Cuban Museum of Arts and Culture* in Miami, and the *Fort Lauderdale Historical Museum* and *Museum of Art* in Ft. Lauderdale, the two cities draw visitors from all over the world.

FESTIVALS: In January, the *Art Deco Weekend Festival* highlights Miami's famed Art Deco district. The *Miami International Boat Show,* one of the largest boat shows in the US, showcases the latest sailing vessels in February. The *Miami Beach Film Festival* also is held in February. In March *Carnaval Miami/Calle Ocho* re-creates the goings-on in Rio for 9 days. Also in Miami, the annual *International Hispanic Theater Festival* in May features theater companies from around the world that perform award-winning productions by Hispanic playwrights. The *Miami/Bahamas Goombay Festival* in June brings the flavor of the islands to the city, while American Indian heritage is celebrated at the *Everglades/Miccosukee 18th Annual International Music and Crafts Festival* in July. *Festival Miami* in September and October presents internationally acclaimed musicians, who perform at the University of Miami's *Gusman Concert Hall.* October's 21st annual month-long *Hispanic Heritage Festival* features Spanish and Latin arts and crafts, folk dances, and live entertainment at various locations in the Greater Miami area. The *Miami Book Fair,* one of the top literary events in the country, takes place in November and is open to the public.

In Ft. Lauderdale, more than 200 artists exhibit their original works, including jewelry, paintings, and sculpture, during the *Las Olas Art Festival* in March. The *Orange Blossom Festival and Rodeo* also is held in March. The *Pompano Beach Seafood Festival* in April features the fare of more than 40 local restaurants with live music and arts and crafts. On *July 4,* sand sculpture artists from all over the country participate in the *Sandblast.* Together they create one large sand sculpture for exhibition and also compete with their individual creations along the Ft. Lauderdale beach. In October, the Ft. Lauderdale *International Boat Show,* said to be the largest in-water boat show in the world, is held at the Bahia Mar marina. The *Hollywood Jazz Festival,* also in October, provides the best opportunity to hear the country's greatest jazz musicians at *Hollywood Young Circle.* In November, the *Greater Ft. Lauderdale Film Festival* features over 80 independent films, while the *Broward County Fair* and the *Sunshine State Championship Rodeo* draw crowds to outdoor venues. The *Winterfest Boat Parade* is the city's annual *Christmas* celebration; over 100 boats decorated with eye-catching lights parade along the inland waterway.

Traveling by Plane

Flying is the quickest, most convenient means of travel between different parts of the country. It *sounds* expensive to travel across the US by air, but when all costs are taken into account for traveling any substantial distance, plane travel usually is less expensive per mile than traveling by car. It also is the most economical way to go in terms of time. Although touring by car, bus, or train certainly is a more scenic way to travel, air travel is far faster and more direct — and the less time spent in transit, the more time spent in Miami and Ft. Lauderdale.

SCHEDULED FLIGHTS: Numerous airlines offer regularly scheduled flights to

Miami and Ft. Lauderdale. Miami International Airport is located just 8 miles from downtown and Ft. Lauderdale/Hollywood International Airport is about 12 miles from downtown. They both handle international and domestic traffic.

Listed below are the major national air carriers serving the two cities and their toll-free telephone numbers.

American (both airports) *and American Eagle* (Miami only)*:* 800-433-7300.
America West: 800-247-5692.
Braniff: 800-BRANIFF.
Continental and Continental Express: 800-525-0280.
Delta and Delta Connection: 800-221-1212.
Northwest and NW Airlink: 800-225-2525.
TWA (both airports) *and Trans World Exppress* (Miami only)*:* 800-221-2000.
United: 800-241-6522.
USAir and USAir Express: 800-428-4322.

Among the international carriers that serve Miami and Ft. Lauderdale are *Air Canada, Air France, Alitalia, Bahamasair, British Airways, BWIA, El Al,* and *Lufthansa.*

Tickets – When traveling on regularly scheduled flights, a full-fare ticket provides maximum travel flexibility. There are no advance booking or other ticketing requirements — except seat availability — although cancellation restrictions vary. It pays to check *before* booking your flight. It also is advisable to reserve well in advance during popular vacation periods and around holiday times.

Fares – Full-fare tickets are followed by a wide variety of discount fares, which even experts find hard to keep current. With these fares, the less you pay for your ticket, the more restrictions and qualifications are likely to be attached to the ticket purchase, including the months (and the days of the week) during which you must travel, how far in advance you must purchase your ticket, the minimum and maximum amount of time you may or must remain away, and your willingness to decide and stick with a return date at the time of booking. It is not uncommon for passengers sitting side by side on the same plane to have paid fares varying by hundreds of dollars.

In general, domestic airfares break down to four basic categories — first class, business class, coach (also called economy or tourist class), and excursion or discount fares. In addition, Advance Purchase Excursion (APEX) fares offer savings under certain conditions.

A **first class** ticket admits you to the special section of the aircraft with larger seats, more legroom, better (or more elaborately served) food, free drinks, free headsets for movies and music channels, and above all, personal attention. First class fares cost about twice those of full-fare (often called "regular") economy.

Behind first class often lies **business class,** usually a separate cabin or cabins. While standards of comfort and service are not as high as in first class, they represent a considerable improvement over conditions in the rear of the plane, with roomier seats, more leg and shoulder space between passengers, and fewer seats abreast. Free liquor and headsets, a choice of meal entrées, and a separate counter for speedier check-in are other inducements. Note that airlines often have their own names for their business class service — such as Ambassador Class on *TWA* and Medallion Class on *Delta.*

The terms of the **coach** or **economy** fare may vary slightly from airline to airline, and in fact from time to time airlines may be selling more than one type of economy fare. Coach or economy passengers sit more snugly, as many as 10 in a single row on a wide-body jet, behind the first class and business class sections. Normally, alcoholic drinks are not free, nor are the headsets.

In first, business class, and regular economy, passengers are entitled to reserve seats and are sold tickets on an open reservation system. They may travel on any scheduled flight they wish, buy a one-way or round-trip ticket, and have the ticket remain valid for a year. There are no requirements for a minimum or maximum stay or for advance booking and (often) no cancellation penalties — but beware, the rules regarding cancellation vary from carrier to carrier. The fare also allows free stopover privileges, although these can be limited in economy.

Excursion and other **discount** fares are the airlines' equivalent of a special sale and usually apply to round-trip bookings only. These fares generally differ according to the season and the number of travel days permitted. They are only a bit less flexible than full-fare economy tickets, and are, therefore, often useful for both business and holiday travelers. Most round-trip excursion tickets include strict minimum and maximum stay requirements and can be changed only within the specified time limits. So don't count on extending a ticket beyond the specified time of return or staying less time than required. Different airlines may have different regulations concerning the number of stopovers permitted, and sometimes excursion fares are less expensive during midweek. The availability of these reduced-rate seats is most limited at busy times such as holidays. Discount or excursion fare ticket holders sit with the coach passengers and, for all intents and purposes, are indistinguishable from them. They receive all the same basic services, even though they may have paid anywhere between 30% and 55% less for the trip. Obviously, it's wise to make plans early enough to qualify for this less expensive transportation if possible.

These discount or excursion fares may masquerade under a variety of names and invariably have strings attached. A common requirement is that the ticket be purchased a certain number of days — usually between 7 and 21 days — in advance of departure, though it may be booked weeks or months in advance (it has to be "ticketed," or paid for, shortly after booking, however). The return reservation usually has to be made at the time of the original ticketing and often cannot be changed later than a certain number of days (again, usually 7 to 21) before the return flight. If events force a change in the return reservation after the date allowed, the passenger may have to pay the difference between the round-trip excursion rate and the round-trip coach rate, although some carriers permit such scheduling changes for a nominal fee. In addition, some airlines may allow passengers to use their discounted fares by standing by for an empty seat, even if the carrier doesn't otherwise have standby fares. Another common condition is the minimum and maximum stay requirement; for example, 1 to 6 days or 6 to 14 days (but including at least a Saturday night). Last, cancellation penalties of up to 50% of the full price of the ticket have been assessed — if a refund is offered at all — so check the specific penalty in effect when you purchase your discount/excursion ticket.

On some airlines, the ticket bearing the lowest price of all the current discount fares is the ticket where no change at all in departure and/or return flights is permitted, and where the ticket price is totally nonrefundable. If you do buy such a nonrefundable ticket, you should be aware of a policy followed by some airlines that may make it easier to change your plans if necessary. For a fee — set by each airline and payable at the airport when checking in — you *may* be able to change the time or date of a return flight on a nonrefundable ticket. However, if the nonrefundable ticket price for the replacement flight is higher than that of the original (as often is the case when trading in a weekday for a weekend flight), you also will have to pay the difference. Any such change must be made a certain number of days in advance — in some cases as little as 2 days — of either the original or the replacement flight, whichever is earlier; restrictions are set by the individual carrier. (Travelers holding a nonrefundable or other restricted ticket who must change their plans due to a family emergency should know that some carriers may make special allowances in such situations.)

■ **Note:** Due to recent changes in many US airlines' policies, nonrefundable tickets are now available that carry none of the above restrictions. Although passengers still may *not* be able to obtain a refund for the price paid, the time or date of a departing or return flight may be changed at any time (assuming seats are available) for a nominal service charge.

There also is a newer, often less expensive, type of excursion fare, the **APEX**, or **Advanced Purchase Excursion**, fare. As with traditional excursion fares, passengers paying an APEX fare sit with and receive the same basic services as any other coach or economy passengers, even though they may have paid 50% less for their seats. In return, they are subject to certain restrictions. In the case of domestic flights, the ticket usually is good for a minimum of 1 to 3 days away (including a Saturday) and a maximum, currently, of 1 to 6 months (depending on the airline and the destination); and as its name implies, it must be "ticketed," or paid for in its entirety, a certain period of time before departure — usually 21 days.

The drawback to some APEX fares is that they penalize travelers who change their minds — and travel plans. Usually the return reservation must be made at the time of the original ticketing, and if for some reason you change your schedule, you will have to pay a penalty of $100 or 10% of the ticket value, whichever is greater, as long as you travel within the valid period of your ticket. More flexible APEX fares recently have been introduced, which allow travelers to make changes in the date or time of their flights for a nominal charge (as low as $25).

With either type of APEX fare, if you change your return to a date less than the minimum stay or more than the maximum stay, the difference between the round-trip APEX fare and the full round-trip coach rate will have to be paid. There also is a penalty of anywhere from $50 to $100 or more for canceling or changing a reservation *before* travel begins — check the specific penalty in effect when you purchase your ticket.

In addition, most airlines also offer package deals that may include a car rental, accommodations, and dining and/or sightseeing features along with the basic airfare, and the combined cost of packaged elements usually is considerably less than the cost of the exact same elements when purchased separately.

When you're satisfied that you've found the lowest price for which you can conveniently qualify, make your booking. You may have to call the airline more than once, because different airline reservations clerks have been known to quote different prices, and different fares will be available at different times for the same flight because of a relatively new computerized airline practice called yield management, which adds or subtracts low-fare seats to a given flight depending on how well it is selling.

To protect yourself against fare increases, purchase and pay for your ticket as soon as possible after you've received a confirmed reservation. Airlines generally will honor their tickets, even if the price at the time of your flight is higher than the price you paid. If fares go up between the time you *reserve* a flight and the time you *pay* for it, however, you likely will be out of luck. Finally, with excursion or discount fares, it is important to remember that when a reservations clerk says that you must purchase a ticket by a specific date, this is an absolute deadline. Miss the deadline and the airline usually will automatically cancel your reservation without telling you.

Frequent Flyers – Most of the leading carriers serving Miami and Ft. Lauderdale — including *American, Delta, Northwest, United,* and *USAir* — offer a bonus system to frequent travelers. After the first 10,000 miles, for example, a passenger might be eligible for a first class seat for the coach fare; after another 10,000 miles, he or she might receive a discount on his or her next ticket purchase. The value of the bonuses continues to increase as more miles are logged.

Bonus miles also may be earned by patronizing affiliated car rental companies or hotel chains, or by using one of the credit cards that now offers this reward. In deciding whether to accept such a credit card from one of the issuing organizations that tempt you with frequent flyer mileage bonuses on a specific airline, first determine whether the interest rate charged on the unpaid balance is the same as (or less than) possible alternate credit cards, and whether the annual "membership" fee also is equal or lower. If these charges are slightly higher than those of competing cards, weigh the difference against the potential value in airfare savings. Also ask about any bonus miles awarded just for signing up — 1,000 is common, 5,000 generally the maximum.

For the most up-to-date information on frequent flyer bonus options, you may want to send for the monthly *Frequent* newsletter. Issued by Frequent Publications, it provides current information about frequent flyer plans in general, as well as specific data about promotions, awards, and combination deals to help you keep track of the profusion — and confusion — of current and upcoming availabilities. For a year's subscription, send $33 to Frequent Publications, 4715-C Town Center Dr., Colorado Springs, CO 80916 (phone: 800-333-5937).

There also is a monthly magazine called *Frequent Flyer,* but unlike the newsletter mentioned above, its focus is primarily on newsy articles of interest to business travelers and other frequent flyers. Published by Official Airline Guides (PO Box 58543, Boulder, CO 80322-8543; phone: 800-323-3537), *Frequent Flyer* is available for $24 for a 1-year subscription.

Low-Fare Airlines – Increasingly, the stimulus for special fares is the appearance of airlines associated with bargain rates. On these airlines, all seats generally sell for the same price, which tends to be somewhat below the lowest discount fare offered by the larger, more established airlines. It is important to note that tickets offered by these smaller companies frequently are not subject to the same restrictions as some of the discounted fares offered by the more established carriers. They may not require advance purchase or minimum and maximum stays, may involve no cancellation penalties, and may be available one way or round trip. A disadvantage to some low-fare airlines, however, is that when something goes wrong, such as delayed baggage or a flight cancellation due to equipment breakdown, their smaller fleets and fewer flights mean that passengers may have to wait longer for a solution than they would on one of the equipment-rich major carriers.

Taxes and Other Fees – Travelers who have shopped for the best possible flight at the lowest possible price should be warned that a number of extras will be added to that price and collected by the airline or travel agent who issues the ticket. The 10% federal US Transportation Tax applies to travel within the US or US territories. Another fee is charged by some airlines to cover more stringent security procedures, prompted by recent terrorist incidents. Note that these taxes *usually* (but not always) are included in advertised fares and in the prices quoted by airlines reservations clerks.

Reservations – For those who don't have the time or patience to investigate personally all possible air departures and connections for a proposed trip, a travel agent can be of inestimable help. A good agent should have all the information on which flights go where and when, and which categories of tickets are available on each. Most have computerized reservation links with the major carriers, so that a seat can be reserved and confirmed in minutes. An increasing number of agents also possess fare-comparison computer programs, so they often are very reliable sources of detailed competitive price data. (For more information, see *How to Use a Travel Agent,* in this section.)

If making plane reservations through a travel agent, ask the agent to give the airline your home phone number, as well as your daytime business phone number. All too often the agent uses his or her agency's number as the official contact for changes in flight plans. Especially during the winter, weather conditions hundreds or even thousands of miles away can wreak havoc with flight schedules. The airlines are fairly reliable about getting this sort of information to passengers if they can reach them;

diligence does little good at 10 PM if the airline has only the agency's or an office number.

Reconfirmation is not generally required on domestic flights. However, it always is wise to call ahead to make sure that the airline did not slip up in entering your original reservation, or in registering any changes you may have made since, and that it has your seat reservation and/or special meal request in the computer.

If you plan not to take a flight on which you hold a confirmed reservation, by all means inform the airline. Because the problem of "no-shows" is a constant expense for airlines, they are allowed to overbook flights, a practice that often contributes to the threat of denied boarding for a certain number of passengers (see "Getting Bumped," below).

Seating – For most types of tickets, airline seats usually are assigned on a first-come, first-served basis at check-in, although some airlines make it possible to reserve a seat at the time of ticket purchase. Always check in early for your flight, even with advance seat assignments. A good rule of thumb for domestic flights is to arrive at the airport *at least* 1 hour before the scheduled departure to give yourself plenty of time in case there are long lines.

Most airlines furnish seating charts, which make choosing a seat much easier, but there are a few basics to consider. You must decide whether you prefer a window, aisle, or middle seat. On those few domestic flights where smoking is permitted (see "Smoking," below), you also should indicate if you prefer the smoking or nonsmoking section.

The amount of legroom provided (as well as chest room, especially when the seat in front of you is in a reclining position) is determined by something called "pitch," a measure of the distance between the back of the seat in front of you and the front of the back of your seat. The amount of pitch is a matter of airline policy, not the type of plane you fly. First class and business class seats have the greatest pitch, a fact that figures prominently in airline advertising. In economy class or coach, the standard pitch ranges from 33 to as little as 31 inches — downright cramped.

The number of seats abreast, another factor determining comfort, depends on a combination of airline policy and airplane dimensions. First class and business class have the fewest seats per row. Economy generally has 9 seats per row on a DC-10 or an L-1011, making either one slightly more comfortable than a 747, on which there normally are 10 seats per row. A 727 has 6 seats per row.

Airline representatives claim that most craft are more stable toward the front and midsections, while the seats farthest from the engines are quietest. Passengers who have long legs and are traveling on a wide-body aircraft might request a seat directly behind a door or emergency exit, since these seats often have greater than average pitch, or a seat in the first row of a given section, which offers extra legroom — although these seats are increasingly being reserved for passengers who are willing (and able) to perform certain tasks in the event of emergency evacuation. It often is impossible, however, to see the movie from seats that are directly behind the plane's exits. Be aware that the first row of the economy section (called a "bulkhead" seat) on a conventional aircraft (not a widebody) does *not* offer extra legroom, since the fixed partition will not permit passengers to slide their feet under it, and that watching a movie from this first-row seat also can be difficult and uncomfortable. These bulkhead seats do, however, provide ample room to use a bassinet or safety seat and often are reserved for families traveling with small children.

A window seat protects you from aisle traffic and clumsy serving carts and also provides a view, while an aisle seat enables you to get up and stretch your legs without disturbing your fellow travelers. Middle seats are the least desirable, and seats in the last row are the worst of all, since they seldom recline fully. If you wish to avoid children on your flight or if you find that you are sitting in an especially noisy section, you usually are free to move to any unoccupied seat — if there is one.

If you are large, you may face the prospect of a long flight with special trepidation. Center seats in the alignments of wide-body 747s, L-1011s, and DC-10s are about 1½ inches wider than those on either side, so larger travelers tend to be more comfortable there.

Despite all these rules of thumb, finding out which specific rows are near emergency exits or at the front of a wide-body cabin can be difficult because seating arrangements on any two same-model planes usually vary from airline to airline. There is, however, a quarterly publication called the *Airline Seating Guide* that publishes seating charts for most major US airlines and many foreign carriers as well. Your travel agent should have a copy, or you can buy the US edition for $39.95 per year. Order from Carlson Publishing Co., Box 888, Los Alamitos, CA 90720 (phone: 800-728-4877 or 310-493-4877).

Simply reserving an airline seat in advance, however, actually may guarantee very little. Most airlines require that passengers arrive at the departure gate at least 45 minutes (sometimes more) ahead of time to hold a seat reservation. It pays to read the fine print on your ticket carefully and follow its requirements.

A far better strategy is to visit an airline ticket office (or one of a select group of travel agents) to secure an actual boarding pass for your specific flight. Once this has been issued, airline computers show you as checked in, and you effectively own the seat you have selected (although some carriers may not honor boarding passes of passengers arriving at the gate less than 10 minutes before departure). This also is good — but not foolproof — insurance against getting bumped from an overbooked flight and is, therefore, an especially valuable tactic at peak travel times.

Smoking – One decision regarding choosing a seat has been taken out of the hands of most domestic travelers who smoke. Effective February 25, 1990, the US government imposed a ban that prohibits smoking on all flights scheduled for 6 hours or less within the US and its territories. The new regulation applies to both domestic and international carriers serving these routes.

Only flights with a *continuous* flying time of over 6 hours between stops in the US or its territories are exempt. Even if the total flying time is longer, smoking is not permitted on segments of domestic flights where the time between US landings is under 6 hours — for instance, flights that include a stopover (even with no change of plane), or connecting flights. To further complicate the situation, several individual carriers ban smoking altogether on certain routes.

On those flights that do permit smoking, the US Department of Transportation has determined that nonsmoking sections must be enlarged to accommodate all passengers who wish to sit in one. The airline does not, however, have to shift seating to accommodate nonsmokers who arrive late for a flight or travelers flying standby. Cigar and pipe smoking are prohibited on all flights, even in the smoking sections.

For a wallet-size guide, which notes in detail the rights of nonsmokers according to these regulations, send a self-addressed, stamped envelope to *ASH (Action on Smoking and Health),* Airline Card, 2013 H St. NW, Washington, DC 20006 (phone: 202-659-4310).

Meals – If you have specific dietary requirements, be sure to let the airline know well before departure time. The available meals include vegetarian, seafood, kosher, Muslim, Hindu, high-protein, low-calorie, low-cholesterol, low-fat, low-sodium, diabetic, bland, and children's menus (not all of these may be available on every carrier). There is no extra charge for this option. It usually is necessary to request special meals when you make your reservations — check-in time is too late. It's also wise to reconfirm that your request for a special meal has made its way into the airline's computer — the time to do this is 24 hours before departure. (Note that special meals generally are not available on shorter domestic flights, particularly on small local carriers. If this poses a problem, try to eat before you board, or bring a snack with you.)

Baggage – Though airline baggage allowances vary slightly, in general all passengers are allowed to carry on board, without charge, one piece of luggage that will fit easily under a seat of the plane or in an overhead bin, and whose combined dimensions (length, width, and depth) do not exceed 45 inches. A reasonable amount of reading material, camera equipment, and a handbag also are allowed. In addition, all passengers are allowed to check two bags in the cargo hold: one usually not to exceed 62 inches when length, width, and depth are combined, the other not to exceed 55 inches in combined dimensions. Generally no single bag may weigh more than 70 pounds.

Charges for additional, oversize, or overweight bags usually are made at a flat rate; the actual dollar amount varies from carrier to carrier. If you plan to travel with any special equipment or sporting gear, be sure to check with the airline beforehand. Most have specific procedures for handling such baggage, and you may have to pay for transport regardless of how much other baggage you have checked. Golf clubs may be checked through as luggage (most airlines are accustomed to handling them), but tennis rackets should be carried onto the plane. Aqualung tanks, depressurized and appropriately packed with padding, and surfboards (minus the fin and padded) also may go as baggage. Snorkeling gear should be packed in a suitcase, duffel or tote bag.

To reduce the chances of your luggage going astray, remove all airline tags from previous trips, label each bag inside and out — with your business address, rather than your home address, on the outside, to prevent thieves from knowing whose house might be unguarded. Lock everything and double-check the tag that the airline attaches to make sure that it is correctly coded — MIA or FLL — for Miami and Ft. Lauderdale/Hollywood International airports, respectively.

If your bags are not in the baggage claim area after your flight or if they're damaged, report the problem to airline personnel immediately. Keep in mind that policies regarding the specific time limit within which you have to make your claim vary from carrier to carrier. Fill out a report form on your lost or damaged luggage and keep a copy of it and your original baggage claim check. If you must surrender the check to claim a damaged bag, get a receipt for it to prove that you did, indeed, check your baggage on the flight. If luggage is missing, be sure to give the airline your destination and/or the telephone number where you can be reached. Also take the name and number of the person in charge of recovering lost luggage.

Most airlines have emergency funds for passengers stranded away from home without their luggage, but if it turns out that your bags are truly lost and not simply delayed, do not then and there sign any paper indicating you'll accept an offered settlement. Since the airline is responsible for the value of your bags within certain statutory limits ($1,250 per passenger for lost baggage on a US domestic flight) you should take the time to assess the extent of your loss (see *Insurance,* in this section). It's a good idea to keep records the value of the contents of your luggage. A wise alternative is to take a Polaroid picture of the most valuable of your packed items just after putting them in your suitcase.

Considering the increased incidence of damage to baggage, now more than ever it's advisable to keep the sales slips that confirm how much you paid for your bags. These are invaluable in establishing the value of damaged luggage and eliminate any arguments. A better way to protect your precious gear from the luggage-eating conveyers is to try to carry it on board whenever possible.

Getting Bumped – A special air travel problem is the possibility that an airline will accept more reservations (and sell more tickets) than there are seats on a given flight. This is entirely legal and is done to make up for "no-shows," passengers who don't show up for a flight for which they have made reservations and bought tickets. If the airline has oversold the flight and everyone does show up, there simply aren't enough seats. When this happens, the airline is subject to stringent rules designed to protect travelers. In such cases, the airline first seeks ticket holders willing to give up their seats voluntarily in return for a negotiable sum of money or some other inducement, such as an offer of upgraded seating on the next flight or a voucher for a free trip at some other time. If there are not enough volunteers, the airline may bump passengers against their wishes.

Anyone inconvenienced in this way, however, is entitled to an explanation of the criteria used to determine who does and does not get on the flight, as well as compensation if the resulting delay exceeds certain limits. If the airline can put the bumped passengers on an alternate flight that is *scheduled to arrive* at their original destination within 1 hour of their originally scheduled arrival time, no compensation is owed. If the delay is more than 1 hour but less than 2 hours on a domestic US flight, they must be paid denied-boarding compensation equivalent to the one-way fare to their destination (but not more than $200). If the delay is more than 2 hours after the original arrival time on a domestic flight, the compensation must be doubled (not more than $400). The airline also may offer bumped travelers a voucher for a free flight instead of the denied-boarding compensation. The passenger may be given the choice of either the money or the voucher, the dollar value of which may be no less than the monetary compensation to which the passenger would be entitled. The voucher is not a substitute for the bumped passenger's original ticket; the airline continues to honor that as well. Keep in mind that the above regulations and policies are for US flights only.

To protect yourself as best you can against getting bumped, arrive at the airport early, allowing plenty of time to check in and get to the gate. If the flight is oversold, ask immediately for the written statement explaining the airline's policy on denied-boarding compensation and its boarding priorities. If the airline refuses to give you this information, or if you feel they have not handled the situation properly, file a complaint with both the airline and the appropriate government agency (see "Consumer Protection," below).

Delays and Cancellations – The above compensation rules also do not apply if the flight is canceled or delayed, or if a smaller aircraft is substituted due to mechanical problems. Each airline has its own policy for assisting passengers whose flights are delayed or canceled or who must wait for another flight because their original one was overbooked. Most airline personnel will make new travel arrangements if necessary. If the delay is longer than 4 hours, the airline may pay for a phone call or telegram, a meal, and in some cases, a hotel room and transportation to it.

■**Caution:** If you are bumped or miss a flight, be sure to ask the airline to notify other airlines on which you have reservations or connecting flights. When your name is taken off the passenger list of your initial flight, the computer usually cancels all of your reservations automatically, unless *you* take steps to preserve them.

CHARTER FLIGHTS: By booking a block of seats on a specially arranged flight, charter tour operators offer travelers air transportation for a substantial reduction over the full coach or economy fare. These operators may offer air-only charters (selling transportation alone) or charter packages (the flight plus a combination of land arrangements such as accommodations, meals, tours, or car rentals). Charters are especially attractive to people living in smaller cities or out-of-the-way places, because they frequently take off from nearby airports, saving travelers the inconvenience and expense of getting to a major gateway.

From the consumer's standpoint, charters differ from scheduled airlines in two main respects: You generally need to book and pay in advance, and you can't change the itinerary or the departure and return dates once you've booked the flight. In practice, however, these restrictions don't always apply. Today, although most domestic charter flights still require advance reservations, some permit last-minute bookings (when there are unsold seats available), and some even offer seats on a standby basis. Though charters almost always are round trip, and it is unlikely that you would be sold a one-way seat on a round-trip flight, on rare occasions one-way tickets on charters are offered.

Things to keep in mind about the charter game:

1. It cannot be repeated often enough that if you are forced to cancel your trip, you can lose much (and possibly all) of your money unless you have cancellation insurance, which is a *must* (see *Insurance,* in this section). Frequently, if the cancellation occurs far enough in advance (often 6 weeks or more), you may forfeit only a $25 or $50 penalty. If you cancel only 2 or 3 weeks before the flight, there may be no refund at all unless you or the operator can provide a substitute passenger.

2. Charter flights may be canceled by the operator up to 10 days before departure for any reason, usually underbooking. Your money is returned in this event, but there may be too little time for you to make new arrangements.

3. Most charters have little of the flexibility of regularly scheduled flights regarding refunds and the changing of flight dates; if you book a return flight, you must be on it or lose your money.

4. Charter operators are permitted to assess a surcharge, if fuel or other costs warrant it, of up to 10% of the airfare up to 10 days before departure.

5. Because of the economics of charter flights, your plane almost always will be full, so you will be crowded, though not necessarily uncomfortable. (There is, however, a new movement among charter airlines to provide flight accommodations that are more comfort-oriented, so this situation may change in the near future.)

To avoid problems, *always* choose charter flights with care. When you consider a charter, ask your travel agent who runs it and carefully check the company. The Better Business Bureau in the company's home city can report on how many complaints, if any, have been lodged against it in the past. Protect yourself with trip cancellation and interruption insurance, which can help safeguard your investment if you, or a traveling companion, are unable to make the trip and must cancel too late to receive a full refund from the company providing your travel services. (This is advisable whether you're buying a charter flight alone or a tour package for which the airfare is provided by charter or scheduled flight.)

Bookings – If you do fly on a charter, read the contract's fine print carefully and pay particular attention to the following:

Instructions concerning the payment of the deposit and its balance and to whom the check is to be made payable. Ordinarily, checks are made out to an escrow account, which means the charter company can't spend your money until your flight has safely returned. This provides some protection for you. To ensure the safe handling of your money, make out your check to the escrow account, the number of which must appear by law on the brochure, though all too often it is on the back in fine print. Write the details of the charter, including the destination and dates, on the face of the check; on the back, print "For Deposit Only." Your travel agent may prefer that you make out your check to the agency, saying that it will then pay the tour operator the fee minus commission. It is perfectly legal to write the check as we suggest, however, and if your agent objects too vociferously (he or she should trust the tour operator to send the proper commission), consider taking your business elsewhere. If you don't make your check out to the escrow account, you lose the protection of that escrow should the trip be canceled. Furthermore, recent bankruptcies in the travel industry have served to point out that even the protection of escrow may not be enough to safeguard a traveler's investment. More and more, insurance is becoming a necessity. The charter company should be bonded (usually by an insurance company), and if you want to file a claim against it, the claim should be sent to the bonding agent. The contract will set a time limit within which a claim must be filed.

Specific stipulations and penalties for cancellations. Most charters allow you to cancel up to 45 days in advance without major penalty, but some cancellation dates are 50 to 60 days before departure.

Stipulations regarding cancellation and major changes made by the charterer. US rules say that charter flights may not be canceled within 10 days of departure except when circumstances — such as natural disasters or political upheavals — make it physically impossible to fly. Charterers may make "major changes," however, such as in the date or place of departure or return, but you are entitled to cancel and receive a full refund if you don't wish to accept these changes. A price increase of more than 10% at any time up to 10 days before departure is considered a major change; no price increase at all is allowed during the last 10 days immediately before departure.

At the time of this writing, the following companies regularly offered charter flights to or from Miami and/or Ft. Lauderdale:

> *Amber Tours* (7337 W. Washington St., Indianapolis, IN 46251; phone: 800-225-9920). Goes to Ft. Lauderdale. Retails to the general public.
>
> *Apple Vacations East* (7 Campus Blvd., Newtown Sq., PA 19073; phone: 800-727-3400). Goes to Orlando area. This agency is a wholesaler, so use a travel agent.
>
> *MLT Vacations* (5130 Hwy. 101, Minnetonka, MN 55345; phone: 800-328-0025). Goes to Orlando area. This agency is a wholesaler, so use a travel agent.
>
> *Morris Air Service* (260 E. Morris Ave., Salt Lake City, UT 84115-3200; phone: 800-444-5660). Goes to Orlando area. Retails to the general public.
>
> *MTI Vacations* (1220 Kensington, Oak Brook, IL 60521; phone: 800-323-7285). This agency is a wholesaler, so use a travel agent.

You also may want to subscribe to the travel newsletter *Jax Fax,* which regularly features a list of charter companies and packagers offering seats on US charter flights. For a year's subscription send a check or money order for $12 to *Jax Fax,* 397 Post Rd., Darien, CT 06820 (phone: 203-655-8746).

DISCOUNTS ON SCHEDULED FLIGHTS: Promotional fares often are called discount fares because they cost less than what used to be the standard airline fare — full-fare economy. Nevertheless, they cost the traveler the same whether they are bought through a travel agent or directly from the airline. Tickets that cost less if bought from some outlet other than the airline do exist, however. While it is likely that the vast majority of travelers flying within the US in the near future will be doing so on a promotional fare or charter rather than on a "discount" air ticket of this sort, it still is a good idea for cost-conscious consumers to be aware of the latest developments in the budget airfare scene. Note that the following discussion makes clear-cut distinctions among the types of discounts available based on how they reach the consumer; in actual practice, the distinctions are not nearly so precise.

Net Fare Sources – The newest notion for reducing the costs of travel services comes from travel agents who offer individual travelers "net" fares. Defined simply, a net fare is the bare minimum amount at which an airline or tour operator will carry a prospective traveler. It doesn't include the amount that normally would be paid to the travel agent as a commission. Traditionally, such commissions amount to about 10% on domestic fares — not counting significant additions to these commission levels that are paid retroactively when agents sell more than a specific volume of tickets or trips for a single supplier. At press time, at least one travel agency in the US was offering travelers the opportunity to purchase tickets and/or tours for a net price. Instead of earning its income from individual commissions, this agency assesses a fixed fee that may or may not provide a bargain for travelers; it requires a little arithmetic to determine whether to use the services of a net travel agent or those of one who accepts conventional commissions. One of the potential drawbacks of buying from agencies selling travel services at net fares is that some airlines refuse to do business with them, thus possibly limiting your flight options.

Travel Avenue is a fee-based agency that rebates its ordinary agency commission to the customer. They will find the lowest retail fare, then rebate 7% to 10% (depending on the airline) of that price, minus a ticket-writing charge of $10 for domestic flights. The ticket-writing charge is imposed per ticket; if the ticket includes more than eight separate flights, an additional $10 fee is charged. Customers using free flight coupons pay the ticket-writing charge, plus an additional $5 coupon-processing fee.

Travel Avenue will rebate its commissions on all tickets, including heavily discounted fares and senior citizen passes. Available 7 days a week, reservations should be made far enough in advance to allow the tickets to be sent by first class mail, since extra charges accrue for special handling. It's possible to economize further by making your own airline reservation, then asking *Travel Avenue* only to write/issue your ticket. For travelers outside the Chicago area, business may be transacted by phone and purchases charged to a credit card. For information, contact *Travel Avenue* at 641 W. Lake, Suite 201, Chicago, IL 60606-1012 (phone: 312-876-1116 in Illinois; 800-333-3335 elsewhere in the US).

Consolidators and Bucket Shops – Other vendors of travel services can afford to sell tickets to their customers at an even greater discount because the airline has sold the tickets to them at a substantial discount (usually accomplished by sharply increasing commissions to that vendor), a practice in which many airlines indulge, albeit discreetly, preferring that the general public not know they are undercutting their own "list" prices. Airlines anticipating a slow period on a particular route sometimes sell off a certain portion of their capacity at a very great discount to a wholesaler or consolidator. The wholesaler sometimes is a charter operator who resells the seats to the public as though they were charter seats, which is why prospective travelers perusing the brochures of charter operators with large programs frequently see a number of flights designated as "scheduled service." As often as not, however, the consolidator, in turn, sells the seats to a travel agency specializing in discounting. Airlines also can sell seats directly to such an agency, which thus acts as its own consolidator. The airline offers the seats either at a net wholesale price, but without the volume-purchase requirement that would be difficult for a modest retail travel agency to fulfill, or at the standard price, but with a commission override large enough (as high as 50%) to allow both a profit and a price reduction to the public.

Travel agencies specializing in discounting sometimes are called "bucket shops," a term fraught with connotations of unreliability in this country. But in today's highly competitive travel marketplace, more and more conventional travel agencies are selling consolidator-supplied tickets, and the old bucket shops' image is becoming respectable. Agencies that specialize in discounted tickets exist in most large cities, and usually can be found by studying the smaller ads in the travel sections of local Sunday newspapers.

Before buying a discounted ticket, whether from a bucket shop or a conventional, full-service travel agency, keep the following considerations in mind: To be in a position to judge how much you'll be saving, first find out the "list" prices of tickets to your destination. Then do some comparison shopping among agencies. Also bear in mind that a ticket that may not differ much in price from one available directly from the airline may, however, allow the circumvention of such things as the advance-purchase requirement. If your plans are less than final, be sure to find out about any other restrictions, such as penalties for canceling a flight or changing a reservation. Most discount tickets are non-endorsable, meaning that they can be used only on the airline that issued them, and they usually are marked "nonrefundable" to prevent their being cashed in for a list-price refund.

A great many bucket shops are small businesses operating on a thin margin, so it's a good idea to check the local Better Business Bureau for any complaints registered against the one with which you're dealing — before parting with any money. If you still do not feel reassured, consider buying discounted tickets only through a conventional travel agency, which can be expected to have found its own reliable source of consolidator tickets — some of the largest consolidators, in fact, sell only to travel agencies.

A few bucket shops require payment in cash or by certified check or money order, but if credit cards are accepted, use that option. Note, however, if buying from a charter operator selling both scheduled and charter flights, that the scheduled seats are not protected by the regulations — including the use of escrow accounts — governing the charter seats. Well-established charter operators, nevertheless, may extend the same protections to their scheduled flights and, when this is the case, consumers should be sure that the payment option selected directs their money into the escrow account.

Listed below are some of the consolidators frequently offering discounted domestic fares:

> *Bargain Air* (655 Deep Valley Dr., Suite 355, Rolling Hills, CA 90274; phone: 800-347-2345 or 213-377-2919).
>
> *Maharaja/Travel Consumer Wholesale* (34 W. 33rd St., Suite 1014, New York, NY 10001; phone: 212-213-2020 in New York; 800-223-6862 elsewhere in the US).
>
> *TFI Tours International* (34 W. 37th St., 12th Floor, New York, NY 10001; phone: 212-736-1140 in New York State; 800-825-3834 elsewhere in the US).
>
> *25 West Tours* (2490 Coral Way, Miami, FL 33145; phone: 305-856-0810 in Florida; 800-252-5052 elsewhere in the US).
>
> *Unitravel* (1177 N. Warson Rd., St. Louis, MO 63132; phone: 314-569-2501 in Missouri; 800-325-2222 elsewhere in the US).

Check with your travel agent for other sources of consolidator-supplied tickets.

■ **Note:** Although rebating and discounting are becoming increasingly common, there is some legal ambiguity concerning them. Strictly speaking, it is legal to discount domestic tickets but not international tickets. On the other hand, the law that prohibits discounting, the Federal Aviation Act of 1958, is consistently ignored these days, in part because consumers benefit from the practice and in part because many illegal arrangements are indistinguishable from legal ones. Since the line separating the two is so fine that even the authorities can't always tell the difference, it is unlikely that most consumers would be able to do so, and in fact it is not illegal to *buy* a discounted ticket. If the issue of legality bothers you, ask the agency whether any ticket you're about to buy would be permissible under the above-mentioned act.

Last-Minute Travel Clubs – Still another way to take advantage of bargain airfares is open to those who have a flexible schedule. A number of organizations, usually set up as last-minute travel clubs and functioning on a membership basis, routinely keep in touch with travel suppliers to help them dispose of unsold inventory at discounts of between 15% and 60%. A great deal of the inventory consists of complete package tours and cruises, but some clubs offer air-only charter seats and, occasionally, seats on scheduled flights.

Members generally pay an annual fee and receive a toll-free hotline telephone number to call for information on imminent trips. In some cases, they also receive periodic mailings with information on bargain travel opportunities for which there is more advance notice. Despite the suggestive names of the clubs providing these services, last-minute travel does not necessarily mean that you cannot make plans until literally the last minute. Trips can be announced as little as a few days or as much as 2 months before departure, but the average is from 1 to 4 weeks' notice.

Among the organizations regularly offering such discounted travel opportunities in the US are the following:

Discount Club of America (61-33 Woodhaven Blvd., Rego Park, NY 11374; phone: 800-321-9587 or 718-335-9612). Annual fee: $39 per person.

Discount Travel International (Ives Building, 114 Forrest Ave., Suite 205, Narberth, PA 19072; phone: 800-334-9294 or 215-668-7184). Annual fee: $45 per household.

Encore/Short Notice (4501 Forbes Blvd., Lanham, MD 20706; phone: 301-459-8020; 800-638-0930 for customer service). Annual fee: $48 per family for Encore (main discount travel program), $36 per family for Short Notice program.

Last Minute Travel (1249 Boylston St., Boston MA 02215; phone: 800-LAST-MIN or 617-267-9800). No fee.

Moment's Notice (425 Madison Ave., New York, NY 10017; phone: 212-486-0503). Annual fee: $45 per family.

Traveler's Advantage (3033 S. Parker Rd., Suite 1000, Aurora, CO 80014; phone: 800-548-1116). Annual fee: $49 per family.

Vacations to Go (2411 Fountain View, Suite 201, Houston, TX 77057; phone: 800-338-4962). Annual fee: $19.95 per family.

Worldwide Discount Travel Club (1674 Meridian Ave., Miami Beach, FL 33139; phone: 305-534-2082). Annual fee: $40 per person; $50 per family.

Generic Air Travel – Organizations that apply the same flexible-schedule idea to air travel only and arrange for flights at literally the last minute also exist. Their service sometimes is known as "generic" air travel, and it operates somewhat like an ordinary airline standby service, except that the organizations running it do not guarantee flights to a specific destination, but only to a general region, and offer seats on not one but several scheduled and charter airlines.

One pioneer of generic flights is *Airhitch* (2790 Broadway, Suite 100, New York, NY 10025; phone: 212-864-2000). Prospective travelers stipulate a range of at least 5 consecutive departure dates and their desired destination, along with alternate choices, and pay the fare in advance. They are then sent a voucher good for travel *on a space-available basis* on flights to their destination region (i.e., not necessarily the specific destination requested) during this time period. The week before this range of departure dates begins, travelers must contact *Airhitch* for specific information about flights on which seats may be available and instructions on how to proceed for check-in. (Return fights are arranged in the same manner as the outbound flights — a specified period of travel is decided upon, and a few days before this date range begins, prospective passengers contact *Airhitch* for details about flights that may be available.) If the client does not accept any of the suggested flights or cancels his or her travel plans after selecting a flight, the amount paid may be applied toward a future fare or the flight arrangements can be transferred to another individual (although, in both cases, an additional fee may be charged). No refunds are offered unless the prospective passenger does not ultimately get on any flight in the specified date range; in such a case, the full fare is refunded. (Note that *Airhitch*'s slightly more expensive Target program, which provides confirmed reservations on specific dates to specific destinations, offers passengers greater — but not guaranteed — certainty regarding destinations and other flight arrangements.) At press time, *Airhitch* did not serve the Florida area, but it might be worthwhile to call when planning a trip to see if it has expanded its service.

Bartered Travel Sources – Suppose a hotel buys advertising space in a newspaper. As payment, the hotel gives the publishing company the use of a number of hotel rooms in lieu of cash. This is barter, a common means of exchange among hotels, airlines, car rental companies, cruise lines, tour operators, restaurants, and other travel service companies. When a bartering company finds itself with empty airline seats (or excess hotel rooms, or cruise ship cabin space, and so on) and offers them to the public, considerable savings can be enjoyed.

Bartered travel clubs often can give discounts of up to 50% to members, who pay an annual fee (approximately $50 at press time), which entitles them to select from the flights, cruises, hotel rooms, or other travel services that the club obtained by barter. Members usually present a voucher, club credit card, or scrip (a dollar-denomination voucher negotiable only for the bartered product) to the hotel, which in turn subtracts the dollar amount from the bartering company's account.

Selling bartered travel is a perfectly legitimate means of retailing. One advantage to club members is that they don't have to wait until the last minute to obtain flight or room reservations.

Among the companies specializing in bartered travel, several that frequently offer members travel services throughout the US include the following:

> *Travel Guild* (18210 Redmond Way, Redmond, WA 98052; phone: 206-861-1900). Annual fee: $48 per family.
>
> *Travel World Leisure Club* (225 W. 34th St., Suite 2203, New York, NY 10122; phone: 800-444-TWLC or 212-239-4855). Annual fee: $50 per person; $20 for each additional member of a family.

OTHER DISCOUNT TRAVEL SOURCES: An excellent source of information on economical travel opportunities is the *Consumer Reports Travel Letter,* published monthly by Consumers Union. It keeps abreast of the scene on a wide variety of fronts, including package tours, rental cars, insurance, and more, but it is especially helpful for its comprehensive coverage of airfares, offering guidance on all the options, from scheduled flights on major or low-fare airlines to charters and discount sources. For a year's subscription, send $37 ($57 for 2 years) to *Consumer Reports Travel Letter* (PO Box 53629, Boulder, CO 80322-3629; phone: 800-999-7959). For information on other travel newsletters, see *Books, Magazines, and Newsletters,* in this section.

CONSUMER PROTECTION: Consumers who feel that they have not been dealt with fairly by an airline should make their complaints known. Begin with the customer service representative at the airport where the problem occurred. If your complaint cannot be resolved there to your satisfaction, write to the airline's consumer office. In a businesslike, typed letter, explain what reservations you held, what happened, the names of the employees involved, and what you expect the airline to do to remedy the situation. Send copies (never the originals) of the tickets, receipts, and other documents that back your claims. Ideally, all correspondence should be sent via certified mail, return receipt requested. This provides proof that your complaint was received.

Passengers with consumer complaints — lost baggage, compensation for getting bumped, violation of smoking and nonsmoking rules, deceptive practices by an airline — who are not satisfied with the airline's response should contact the Department of Transportation (DOT), Consumer Affairs Division (400 Seventh St. SW, Room 10405, Washington, DC 20590; phone: 202-366-2220). DOT personnel stress, however, that consumers initially should direct their complaints to the airline that provoked them.

Remember, too, that the federal Fair Credit Billing Act permits purchasers to refuse to pay for credit card charges for services which have not been delivered, so the onus of dealing with the receiver for a bankrupt airline, for example, falls on the credit card company. Do not rely on another airline to honor any ticket you're holding from a failed airline, since the days when virtually all major carriers subscribed to a default protection program that bound them to do so are long gone. Some airlines may voluntarily step forward to accommodate the stranded passengers of a fellow carrier, but this is now an entirely altruistic act.

The deregulation of US airlines has meant that travelers must find out for themselves what they are entitled to receive. The Department of Transportation's informative consumer booklet, *Fly Rights,* is a good place to start. To receive a copy, send $1 to the Superintendent of Documents (US Government Printing Office, Washington, DC 20402-9325; phone: 202-783-3238). Specify its stock number, 050-000-00513-5, and allow 3 to 4 weeks for delivery.

On Arrival

 FROM THE AIRPORT TO THE CITY: Miami International Airport is usually a 15-minute drive from downtown and about a half hour from Miami Beach, longer during rush periods (8:30 to 9:30 AM and 4:30 to 6PM). Taxi fares average $12 to downtown, $16 to mid–Miami Beach. The *Supershuttle* (phone: 871-2000) has van service to and from Miami International Airport for $7 to $15.

Ft. Lauderdale/Hollywood International Airport is a 10- to 15-minute drive from downtown; taxi fare should run about $10 to $15. *Broward County Transit* (phone: 357-8400) runs a No. 1 bus between the airport (pick-ups at the *Delta* Dash pull-in area and next to terminal 3, both Lower Level) and the downtown bus terminal at NW 1st Street and 1st Avenue; the fare is 85¢. *Airport Express* (phone: 527-8690) offers round-trip transportation from the airport to anywhere in Broward County for $6 to $13. Sedans stop at the service desks outside the major terminals, beyond the baggage claim area.

Tri-Rail (phone: 800-TRI-RAIL in Florida or 728-8445), the commuter rail system connecting Dade (Miami), Broward (Ft. Lauderdale), and Palm Beach counties, operates shuttle bus–rail connections between Miami International (shuttle bus pick-up at Concourse E, lower level) and downtown Miami and between Ft. Lauderdale/Hollywood International (pick-up at Terminals 1 and 3) and downtown Ft. Lauderdale. The service in each case costs $2 and operates every day but Sunday.

CAR RENTAL: Unless planning to drive round trip from home, most travelers who want to drive while on vacation simply rent a car. They can rent a car through a travel agent or national rental firm before leaving home, or from a local company once they arrive in Miami or Ft. Lauderdale. Another possibility, also arranged before departure, is to rent the car as part of a larger travel package.

It's tempting to wait until arrival to scout out the lowest-priced rental from the company located the farthest from the airport high-rent district and offering no pick-up services. But if your arrival coincides with a holiday or a peak travel period, you may be disappointed to find that even the most expensive car in the city was reserved months ago. Whenever possible, it is best to reserve in advance, anywhere from a few days in slack periods to a month or more during the busier seasons.

Often, the easiest place to rent (or at least pick up) the car is at the airport on arrival. The majority of the national car rental companies have locations at Miami and Ft. Lauderdale/Hollywood International Airports, where shuttle buses from each company pick up clients from the terminals and take them to the car rental locations. Travel agents can arrange rentals for clients, but it is just as easy to call and rent a car yourself. Listed below are the nationwide, toll-free telephone numbers of the major national rental companies that have locations in Miami and Ft. Lauderdale.

Alamo: 800-327-9633
American International Rent-A-Car: 800-527-0202
Avis: 800-331-1212
Budget Rent-A-Car: 800-527-0700

Dollar Rent-A-Car: 800-800-4000
Hertz: 800-654-3131
National Car Rental: 800-CAR-RENT
Sears Rent-A-Car: 800-527-0770
Thrifty Rent-A-Car: 800-367-2277

If you decide to wait until after you arrive, you'll often find a surprising number of small companies listed in the local yellow pages. (All of the following companies are in the 305 area code.) Local companies that serve the Miami area include *A-Jiffy Rent-A-Car* (phone: 621-5566), *Delta Auto Rental* (phone: 526-8755), *Exchange Car Rental* (phone: 800-777-2836), *Fiesta Rent-A-Car* (phone: 871-7777), *General Rent-A-Car* (phone: 800-327-7607 or 871-3573), *Inter-American Car Rental* (phone: 800-327-1278 or 871-3030), *Pass Rent-A-Car* (phone: 871-6262), *Superior Rent-A-Car* (phone: 800-237-8106 or 649-7012), and *Unidas* (phone: 530-9513).

Companies that serve the Ft. Lauderdale area include *Air & Sea Rent-A-Car, Inc.* (phone: 359-4747), *Arrow Car Rental* (phone: 776-4500), *Enterprise Rent-A-Car* (phone: 764-3144), *Lauderdale-by-the-Sea Rent-A-Car* (phone: 776-4950), *Riteway Car & Truck Rental* (phone: 987-4085), *Slaton Rent-A-Car* (phone: 561-5222), and *USA Rent A Car* (phone: 635-7800).

To economize on a car rental, also consider one of the firms that rents 3- to 5-year-old cars that are well-worn but (presumably) mechanically sound; one such company is *Rent-a-Wreck* (10045 S. Dixie Hwy.; phone: 666-9817), whose local office is located 15 minutes away from the Miami International Airport. Currently the company does not have a location in Ft. Lauderdale.

At the other extreme, for those who feel like splurging, *Prestige Auto Rental and Leasing* (1946 NE 123 St., Miami; phone: 895-0854), which rents Corvettes, Jaguars, and Mercedes, among other exotic cars, can deliver one to your hotel in Miami or Ft. Lauderdale.

Requirements – Whether you decide to rent a car in advance from a large national rental company or wait to rent from a local company, you should know that renting a car is rarely as simple as signing on the dotted line and roaring off into the night. If you are renting for personal use, you must have a valid driver's license and will have to convince the renting agency that (1) you are personally creditworthy, and (2) you will bring the car back at the stated time. This will be easy if you have a major credit card; most rental companies accept credit cards in lieu of a cash deposit, as well as for payment of your final bill. If you prefer to pay in cash, leave your credit card imprint as a "deposit," then pay your bill in cash when you return the car.

Note that *Avis, Budget, Hertz,* and other national companies usually *will* rent to travelers paying in cash and leaving either a credit card imprint or a substantial amount of cash as a deposit. This is not necessarily standard policy, however, as other national chains and a number of local companies will *not* rent to an individual who doesn't have a valid credit card. In this case, you will have to call around to find a company that accepts cash.

Also, keep in mind that although the minimum age to drive in most states is 16, the minimum age to rent a car is set by the rental company. (Restrictions vary from company to company, as well as at different locations.) Many firms have a minimum age requirement of 21 years, some raise that to 23 or 25 years, and for some models of cars it rises to 30 years. The upper age limit at many companies is between 69 and 75; others have no upper limit or may make drivers above a certain age subject to special conditions.

Costs – Finding the most economical car rental will require some telephone shopping on your part. As a *general* rule, expect to hear lower prices quoted by the smaller, strictly local companies than by the well-known international names.

Comparison shopping always is advisable, however. Even the international giants offer discount plans whose conditions are easy for most travelers to fulfill. For instance, *Budget* and *National* sometimes offer discounts of anywhere from 10% to 30% off their usual rates (according to the size of the car and the duration of the rental), provided that the car is reserved a certain number of days before departure (usually 7 to 14 days, but it can be less), is rented for a minimum period (5 days or, more often, a week), is paid for at the time of booking, and, in most cases, is returned to the same location that supplied it or to another in the same area. Similar discount plans include *Hertz*'s Leisure Rates and *Avis*'s Supervalue Rates.

If driving short distances for only a day or two, the best deal may be a per-day, per-mile rate: You pay a flat fee for each day you keep the car, plus a per-mile charge. An increasingly common alternative is to be granted a certain number of free miles each day and then be charged on a per-mile basis over that number.

Most companies also offer a flat per-day rate with unlimited free mileage; this certainly is the most economical rate if you plan to drive over 100 miles. Make sure that the low, flat daily rate that catches your eye, however, is indeed a per-day rate: Often the lowest price advertised by a company turns out to be available only with a minimum 3-day rental — fine if you want the car that long, but it's not the bargain it appears if you really intend to use it no more than 24 hours. Flat weekly rates also are available, as are some flat monthly rates that represent a further saving over the daily rate.

Another factor influencing the cost is the type of car you rent. Rentals are based on a tiered price system, with different sizes of cars — variations of budget, economy, regular, and luxury — often listed as A (the smallest and least expensive) through F, G, or H, and sometimes even higher. Charges may increase by only a few dollars a day through several categories of subcompact and compact cars — where most of the competition is — then increase by great leaps through the remaining classes of full-size and luxury cars and passenger vans. The larger the car, the more it costs to rent and the more gas it consumes, but for some people the greater comfort and extra luggage space of a larger car (in which bags and sporting gear can be safely locked out of sight) may make it worth the additional expense. Also more expensive are sleek sports cars, but again, for some people the thrill of driving such a car — for a week or a day — may be worth it.

Electing to pay for collision damage waiver (CDW) protection will add considerably to the cost of renting a car. (Some companies, such as *Hertz* and *Avis,* now call the option a loss damage waiver, or LDW.) You may be responsible for the *full value* of the vehicle being rented if it is damaged or stolen, but you can dispense with all of the possible liability by buying the offered waiver at a cost of around $5 to $13 a day. Before making any decisions about optional collision damage waivers, however, check with your own insurance agent and determine whether your personal automobile insurance policy covers rented vehicles; if it does, you probably won't need to pay for the waiver. Be aware, too, that increasing numbers of credit cards automatically provide CDW coverage if the car rental is charged to the appropriate credit card. However, the specific terms of such credit card coverage differ sharply among individual card companies, so check with the credit card company for information on the nature and amount of coverage provided. Business travelers also should be aware that, at the time of this writing, *American Express* had withdrawn its automatic CDW coverage from some corporate *Green* card accounts and limited the length of coverage — watch for similar cutbacks by other credit card companies.

When inquiring about CDW or LDW coverage and costs, be aware that a number of car rental companies now are automatically including the cost of this waiver in their quoted prices. This does not mean that they are absorbing this cost and you are receiving free coverage — in many cases total rental prices have increased to include the former CDW charge. The disadvantage of this inclusion is that you probably will not have the option to refuse this coverage, and will end up paying the added charge — even if you already are adequately covered by your own insurance policy or through a credit card company.

Another cost to be added to the price tag is drop-off charges or one-way service fees. The lowest price quoted by any given company may apply only to a car that is returned to the same location from which it was rented. A slightly higher rate may be charged if the car is to be returned to a different location (even within the same city).

■**Note:** Drivers should be aware that the latest fad among local thieves is "smash and grab" robbery — where windows are smashed and valuables grabbed while cars are stopped in traffic. Forewarned is forearmed.

Package Tours

 If the mere thought of buying a package for your visit to Miami or Ft. Lauderdale conjures up visions of a trip spent marching in lockstep through the city's attractions with a horde of frazzled fellow travelers, remember that packages have come a long way. For one thing, not all packages necessarily are escorted tours, and the one you buy does not have to include any organized touring at all — nor will it necessarily include traveling companions. If it does, however, you'll find that people of all sorts — many just like yourself — are taking advantage of packages today because they are economical and convenient and save an immense amount of planning time. Given the high cost of travel these days, packages have emerged as a particularly wise buy.

In essence, a package is just an amalgam of travel services that can be purchased in a single transaction. A package (tour or otherwise) may include any or all of the following: round-trip transportation, local transportation (and/or car rentals), accommodations, some or all meals, sightseeing, entertainment, transfers to and from the hotel, taxes, tips, escort service, and a variety of incidental features that might be offered as options at additional cost. In other words, a package can be any combination of travel elements, from a fully escorted tour offered at an all-inclusive price to a simple fly/drive booking that allows you to move about totally on your own. Its principal advantage is that it saves money: The cost of the combined arrangements invariably is well below the price of all of the same elements if bought separately, and, particularly if transportation is provided by discount flight, the whole package could cost less than just a round-trip economy airline ticket on a regularly scheduled flight. A package provides more than economy and convenience: It releases the traveler from having to make individual arrangements for each separate element of a trip.

Tour programs generally can be divided into two categories — "escorted" (or locally hosted) and "independent." An escorted tour means that a guide will accompany the group from the beginning of the tour through to the return flight; a locally hosted tour means that the group will be met upon arrival at each location by a different local host. On independent tours, there generally is a choice of hotels, meal plans, and sightseeing trips, as well as a variety of special excursions. The independent plan is for travelers who do not want a totally set itinerary, but who do prefer confirmed hotel reservations. Whether choosing an escorted or an independent tour, always bring along complete contact information for your tour operator in case a problem arises, although tour operators often have local affiliates who can give additional assistance or make other arrangements on the spot.

To determine whether a package — or more specifically, *which* package — fits your travel plans, start by evaluating your interests and needs, deciding how much and what you want to spend, see, and do. Gather brochures on Miami and Ft. Lauderdale tours. Be sure that you take the time to read each brochure *carefully* to determine precisely what is included. Keep in mind that they are written to entice you into signing up for a package tour. Often the language is deceptive and devious. For example, a brochure may quote the lowest prices for a package tour based on facilities that are unavailable during the off-season, undesirable at any season, or just plain nonexistent. Information such as "breakfast included" or "plus tax" (which can add up) should be taken into account. Note, too, that the prices quoted in brochures almost always are based on double occupancy: The rate listed is for each of two people sharing a double room, and if you travel alone, the supplement for single accommodations can raise the price considerably (see *Hints for Single Travelers,* in this section).

In this age of erratic airfares, the brochure most often will *not* include the price of an airline ticket in the price of the package, though sample fares from various gateway cities usually will be listed separately, as extras to be added to the price of the ground arrangements. Before figuring your actual costs, check the latest fares with the airlines, because the samples invariably are out of date by the time you read them. If the brochure gives more than one category of sample fares per gateway city — such as an individual tour-basing fare, a group fare, an excursion, APEX, or other discount ticket — your travel agent or airline tour desk will be able to tell you which one applies to the package you choose, depending on when you travel, how far in advance you book, and other factors. (An individual tour-basing fare is a fare computed as part of a package that includes land arrangements, thereby entitling a carrier to reduce the air portion almost to the absolute minimum. Though it always represents a saving over full-fare coach or economy, lately the individual tour-basing fare has not been as inexpensive as the excursion and other discount fares that also are available to individuals. The group fare usually is the least expensive fare, and it is the tour operator, not you, who makes up the group.) When the brochure does include round-trip transportation in the package price, don't forget to add the cost of round-trip transportation from your home to the departure city to come up with the total cost of the package.

Finally, read the general information regarding terms and conditions and the responsibility clause (usually in fine print at the end of the descriptive literature) to determine the precise elements for which the tour operator is — and is not — liable. Here the tour operator frequently expresses the right to change services or schedules as long as equivalent arrangements are offered. This clause also absolves the operator of responsibility for circumstances beyond human control, such as avalanches, earthquakes, or floods, or injury to you or your property. While reading, ask the following questions:

1. Does the tour include airfare or other transportation, sightseeing, meals, transfers, taxes, baggage handling, tips, or any other services? Do you want all these services?
2. If the brochure indicates that "some meals" are included, does this mean a welcoming and farewell dinner, two breakfasts, or every evening meal?
3. What classes of hotels are offered? If you will be traveling alone, what is the single supplement?
4. Does the tour itinerary or price vary according to the season?
5. Are the prices guaranteed; that is, if costs increase between the time you book and the time you depart, can surcharges unilaterally be added?
6. Do you get a full refund if you cancel? If not, be sure to obtain cancellation insurance.
7. Can the operator cancel if too few people join? At what point?

One of the consumer's biggest problems is finding enough information to judge the reliability of a tour packager, since individual travelers seldom have direct contact with the firm putting the package together. Usually, a retail travel agent is interposed between customer and tour operator, and much depends on his or her candor and cooperation. So ask a number of questions about the tour you are considering. For example:

- Has the travel agent ever used a package provided by this tour operator?
- How long has the tour operator been in business? Check the Better Business Bureau in the area where the tour operator is based to see if any complaints have been filed against it.
- Is the tour operator a member of the *United States Tour Operators Association* (*USTOA;* 211 E. 51st St., Suite 12B, New York, NY 10022; phone: 212-944-5727). *USTOA* will provide a list of its members on request; it also offers a useful brochure called *How to Select a Package Tour.*
- How many and which companies are involved in the package?

■ **A word of advice:** Purchasers of vacation packages who feel they're not getting their money's worth are more likely to get a refund if they complain in writing to the operator — and bail out of the whole package immediately. Alert the tour operator to the fact that you are dissatisfied, that you will be leaving for home as soon as transportation can be arranged, and that you expect a refund. They may have forms to fill out detailing your complaint; otherwise, state your case in a letter. Even if difficulty in arranging immediate transportation home detains you, your dated, written complaint should help in procuring a refund from the operator.

SAMPLE PACKAGES TO MIAMI AND FT. LAUDERDALE: Following is a list of some of the major tour operators that offer Miami and Ft. Lauderdale packages. Some operators offer flexible city stays that start with 1 hotel night — with a choice of locations and prices available — to which may be added more nights and a wide variety of options, such as sightseeing, transfers, car rental, and, in some cases, dine-around plans. As indicated, some operators are wholesalers only, and will deal only with a travel agent.

Adventure Tours (9818 Liberty Rd., Randallstown, MD 21133; phone: 301-922-7000 in Baltimore; 800-638-9040 elsewhere in the US). Offers flexible city stays. This company is a wholesaler; consult a travel agent.

American Express Travel Related Services (offices throughout the US; phone: 800-241-1700 for information and local branch offices). Offers independent Miami and Ft. Lauderdale packages, as well as independent and escorted tours throughout the US. The tour operator is a wholesaler, so use a travel agent.

Dailey-Thorp (315 W. 57th St., New York, NY 10019; phone: 212-307-1555). Luxury tours focusing on opera and other music-related themes.

Domenico Tours (751 Broadway, Bayonne, NJ 07002; phone: 201-823-8687, 212-757-8687, or 800-554-8687). Offers a 17-day Miami Beach Getaway motorcoach tour from the New York area, which includes sightseeing and leisure time, as well as an 8-day sightseeing-only program.

Funway Holidays Funjet Inc. (8907 N. Port Washington Rd., PO Box 1460, Milwaukee, WI 53201-1460; phone: 414-351-3553). This tour company, which is also a charter operator, offers packages for a minimum of 3 nights, including scheduled air transport, car rentals, and sightseeing; a 5-night land-only program also is available. The tour operator is a wholesaler, so use a travel agent.

GoGo Tours (69 Spring St., Ramsey, NJ 07446-0507; phone: 201-934-3500, or call any of the 75 local GoGo offices). Offers 2- to 7-night packages, including air transportation and car.

MTI Vacations, Inc. (1220 Kensington Ct., Oak Brook, IL 60521; phone: 708-990-8028). This charter operator also offers city packages, including air transporta-

tion and use of a car for a minimum of 2 nights. It is a wholesaler, so use a travel
agent.

Saga Holidays (120 Boylston St., Boston, MA 02116; phone: 800-343-0273). Offers
southern Florida tours.

Travel Tours International (250 W. 49th St., Suite 600, New York, NY 10019;
phone: 800-767-8777 or 212-262-0700). Offers air/hotel city packages to Miami
and Ft. Lauderdale. The tour operator is a wholesaler, so use a travel agent.

Many of the major air carriers maintain their own tour departments or subsidiaries
to stimulate vacation travel to the cities they serve. In all cases, the arrangements may
be booked through a travel agent or directly with the company. Air/hotel Miami and
Ft. Lauderdale packages are offered by the following airlines serving the two cities.

American Airlines FlyAAway Vacations (Southern Reservation Center, Mail Drop
1000, Box 619619, Dallas/Ft. Worth Airport, TX 75261-9619; phone: 800-321-
2121).

Continental's Grand Destinations (PO Box 1460, Milwaukee, WI 53201-1460;
phone: 800-634-5555).

TWA Getaway (10 E. Stow Rd., Marlton, NJ 08053; phone: 800-GETAWAY).

Whether visiting Florida independently or on one of the above packages, if you would
like to include some organized touring, *Eagle Tours and Travel* (6261 Collins Ave.,
Miami, FL 33140; phone 305-864-6204) offers various half- and 1-day tours of major
city attractions. *Art Deco Tours/Miami Design Preservation League* (1244 Ocean Ave.,
Miami Beach, FL 33139; phone: 305-672-2014) offers short walking tours that explore
the historic Art Deco district of South Miami beach. On Saturdays, *Water Taxi of Ft.
Lauderdale* (phone: 305-564-5507) operates 2-hour historic cruises of the New River.
Call the Historic Society (phone: 305-463-4431) for reservations.

■ **Note:** Frequently, the best city packages are offered by the hotels, which are trying
to attract guests during the weekends, when business travel drops off, and during
other slow periods. These packages are sometimes advertised in local newspapers
and in the Sunday travel sections of major metropolitan papers, such as *The New
York Times,* which has a national edition available in most parts of the US. It's
worth asking about packages, especially family and special-occasion offerings,
when you call to make a hotel reservation. Calling several hotels can garner you
a variety of options from which to choose.

Preparing

Calculating Costs

$ **DETERMINING A BUDGET:** A realistic appraisal of travel expenses is the most crucial bit of planning before any trip. It also is, unfortunately, one for which it is most difficult to give precise practical advice.

Estimating travel expenses for a vacation in Miami and Ft. Lauderdale depends on the mode of transportation you choose and how long you will stay, as well as the kind of trip you are planning.

When calculating costs, start with the basics, the major expenses being transportation, accommodations, and food. For Miami and Ft. Lauderdale, that will mean $140 or more a night for a double at an expensive hotel, $95 to $135 for a moderate property, and somewhat under $90 for an inexpensive one. Dinner for two without wine runs to over $70 at an expensive restaurant, $50 to $70 at a moderate one, and under $50 at an inexpensive one. Then there are breakfast and lunch to consider.

Don't forget such extras as local transportation, shopping, and such miscellaneous items as laundry and tips. The reasonable cost of these items often is a positive surprise to your budget. Ask about special discount passes that provide unlimited or cut-rate travel by the day or the week on regular city or local transportation. For example, a public transit weekly pass (for information, call 305-357-8400) provides 7 days of unlimited travel on all county buses in Ft. Lauderdale for $8. If you plan to travel along the South Florida coast, consider a 7-day *Tri-Rail* pass (phone: 800-TRI-RAIL in Florida or 305-728-8445) for $17. It includes transportation in the area between West Palm Beach and Miami, as well as Ft. Lauderdale.

Other expenses, such as the cost of local sightseeing tours and other excursions, should be included. Tourist information offices and most of the better hotels will have someone at the front desk to provide a rundown on the cost of local tours and full-day excursions in and out of Miami and Ft. Lauderdale. Travel agents also can provide this information.

In planning any travel budget, it also is wise to allow a realistic amount for both entertainment and recreation. Are you planning to spend time sightseeing and visiting local tourist attractions? Is tennis or golf a part of your plan? Are you traveling with children who want to visit every site? Finally, allow for the extra cost of nightlife, if such is your pleasure. This one item alone can add a great deal to your daily expenditures.

If at any point in the planning process it appears impossible to estimate expenses, consider this suggestion: The easiest way to put a ceiling on the price of all these elements is to buy a package tour with transportation, rooms, meals, sightseeing, local travel, tips, and a dinner show or two included and prepaid. This provides a pretty exact total of what the trip will cost beforehand, and the only surprise will be the one you spring on yourself by succumbing to some irresistible souvenir.

Planning a Trip

123 Travelers fall into two categories: those who make lists and those who do not. Some people prefer to plot the course of their trip to the finest detail, with contingency plans and alternatives at the ready. For others, the joy of a voyage is its spontaneity; exhaustive planning only lessens the thrill of anticipation and the sense of freedom.

For most travelers, however, a week-plus trip can be too expensive for an "I'll take my chances" attitude. At least some planning is crucial. This is not to suggest that you work out your itinerary in minute detail before you go, but it's still wise to decide certain basics at the very start: where to go, what to do, and how much to spend. These decisions require a certain amount of consideration. So before rigorously planning specific details, you might want to establish your general travel objectives:

1. How much time will you have for the entire trip, and how much of it are you willing to spend getting where you're going?
2. What interests and/or activities do you want to pursue while on vacation?
3. At what time of year do you want to go?
4. Do you want peace and privacy or lots of activity and company?
5. How much money can you afford to spend for the entire vacation?

You now can make almost all of your own travel arrangements if you have time to follow through with hotels, airlines, tour operators, and so on. But you'll probably save considerable time and energy if you have a travel agent make arrangements for you. The agent also should be able to advise you of alternative arrangements of which you may not be aware. Only rarely will a travel agent's services cost a traveler any money, and they may even save you some (see *How to Use a Travel Agent,* below).

Make plans early. During the winter months and holidays, make hotel reservations at least a month in advance. If you are flying at these times and want to benefit from savings offered through discount fares, purchase tickets as far ahead as possible. Many hotels require deposits before they will guarantee reservations, and this most often is the case during peak travel periods. (Be sure to get a receipt for any deposit or, better yet, charge the deposit to a credit card.)

When packing, make a list of any valuable items you are carrying with you, including credit card numbers and the serial numbers of your traveler's checks. Put copies in your purse or pocket, and leave other copies at home. Put a label with your name and home address on the inside of your luggage for identification in case of loss. Put your name and business address — *never your home address* — on a label on the outside of your luggage. (Those who run businesses from home should use the office address of a friend or relative.)

Review your travel documents. If you are traveling by air, check that your ticket has been filled in correctly. The left side of the ticket should have a list of each stop you will make (even if you are stopping only to change planes), beginning with your departure point. Be sure that the list is correct, and count the number of copies to see that you have one for each plane you will take. If you have confirmed reservations, be sure that the column marked "status" says "OK" beside each flight. Have in hand vouchers or proof of payment for any reservation for which you've paid in advance; this includes hotels, transfers to and from the airport, sightseeing tours, car rentals, and tickets to special events.

Although policies vary from carrier to carrier, it's still smart to reconfirm your flight 48 to 72 hours before departure, both going and returning. If you are traveling by car, bring your driver's license, car registration, and proof of insurance, as well as gasoline credit cards and auto service card (if you have them).

Finally, you always should bear in mind that despite the most careful plans, things do not always occur on schedule. If you maintain a flexible attitude and try to accept minor disruptions as less than cataclysmic, you will enjoy yourself a lot more.

How to Use a Travel Agent

 A reliable travel agent remains the best source of service and information for planning a trip, whether you have a specific itinerary and require an agent only to make reservations or you need extensive help in sorting through the maze of airfares, tour offerings, hotel packages, and the scores of other arrangements that may be involved in your trip.

Know what you want from a travel agent so that you can evaluate what you are getting. It is perfectly reasonable to expect your travel agent to be a thoroughly knowledgeable travel specialist, with information about your destination and, even more crucial, a command of current airfares, ground arrangements, and other wrinkles in the travel scene.

Most travel agents work through computer reservations systems (CRS). These are used to assess the availability and cost of flights, hotels, and car rentals, and through them they can book reservations. Despite reports of "computer bias," in which a computer may favor one airline over another, the CRS should provide agents with the entire spectrum of flights available to a given destination and the complete range of fares in considerably less time than it takes to telephone the airlines individually — and at no extra cost to the client.

Make the most intelligent use of a travel agent's time and expertise; understand the economics of the industry. As a client, traditionally you pay nothing for the agent's services; with few exceptions it's all free, from hotel bookings to advice on package tours. Any money the travel agent makes on the time spent arranging your itinerary — booking hotels, resorts, or flights, or suggesting activities — comes from commissions paid by the suppliers of these services — the airlines, hotels, and so on. These commissions generally run from 10% to 15% of the total cost of the service, although suppliers often reward agencies that sell their services in volume with an increased commission called an override.

A travel agent sometimes may charge a fee for special services. These chargeable items may include long-distance telephone costs incurred in making a booking, for reserving a room in a place that does not pay a commission (such as a small, out-of-the way hotel), or for a special attention such as planning a highly personalized itinerary. A fee also may be assessed in instances of deeply discounted airfares.

Choose a travel agent with the same care with which you would choose a doctor or lawyer. You will be spending a good deal of money on the basis of the agent's judgment, so you have a right to expect that judgment to be mature, informed, and interested. At the moment, unfortunately, there aren't many standards within the travel agent industry to help you gauge competence, and the quality of individual agents varies enormously.

At present, only nine states have registration, licensing, or other forms of travel agent–related legislation on their books. Rhode Island licenses travel agents; Florida, Hawaii, Iowa, and Ohio register them; and California, Illinois, Oregon, and Washington have laws governing the sale of transportation or related services. While state licensing of agents cannot absolutely guarantee competence, it can at least ensure that an agent has met some minimum requirements.

Perhaps the best-prepared agents are those who have completed the CTC Travel Management program offered by the *Institute of Certified Travel Agents (ICTA)* and carry the initials CTC (Certified Travel Counselor) after their names. This indicates a relatively high level of expertise. For a free listing of CTCs in your area, send a self-addressed, stamped, #10 envelope to *ICTA*, 148 Linden St., Box 56, Wellesley, MA 02181 (phone: 617-237-0280 in Massachusetts; 800-542-4282 elsewhere in the US).

An agent's membership in the *American Society of Travel Agents (ASTA)* can be a useful guideline in making a selection. But keep in mind that *ASTA* is an industry organization, requiring only that its members be licensed in those states where required; be accredited to represent the suppliers whose products they sell, including airline and cruise tickets; and adhere to its Principles of Professional Conduct and Ethics code. *ASTA* does not guarantee the competence, ethics, or financial soundness of its members, but it does offer some recourse if you feel you have been dealt with unfairly. Complaints may be registered with *ASTA* (Consumer Affairs Dept., 1101 King St., Alexandria, VA 22314; phone: 703-739-2782). First try to resolve the complaint directly with the supplier. For a list of *ASTA* members in your area, send a self-addressed, stamped, #10 envelope to *ASTA* (Public Relations Dept.) at the address above.

There also is the *Association of Retail Travel Agents (ARTA)*, a smaller but highly respected trade organization similar to *ASTA*. Its member agencies and agents similarly agree to abide by a code of ethics, and complaints about a member can be made to *ARTA*'s Grievance Committee, 1745 Jefferson Davis Hwy., Arlington, VA 22202-3402 (phone: 800-969-6069 or 703-553-7777).

Perhaps the best way to find a travel agent is by word of mouth. If the agent (or agency) has done a good job for your friends over a period of time, it probably indicates a certain level of commitment and competence. Always ask for the name of the company *and* for the name of the specific agent with whom your friends dealt, for it is that individual who will serve you, and quality can vary widely within a single agency.

Insurance

 It is unfortunate that most decisions to buy travel insurance are impulsive and usually are made without any real consideration of the traveler's existing policies. Therefore, the first person with whom you should discuss travel insurance is your own insurance broker, not a travel agent or the clerk behind the airport insurance counter. You may discover that the insurance you already carry — homeowner's policies and/or accident, health, and life insurance — protects you adequately while you travel and that your real needs are in the more mundane areas of excess value insurance for baggage or trip cancellation insurance.

TYPES OF INSURANCE: To make insurance decisions intelligently, however, you first should understand the basic categories of travel insurance and what they cover. Then you can decide what you should have in the broader context of your personal insurance needs, and you can choose the most economical way of getting the desired protection: through riders on existing policies; with onetime, short-term policies; through a special program put together for the frequent traveler; through coverage that's part of a travel club's benefits; or with a combination policy sold by insurance companies through brokers, automobile clubs, tour operators, and travel agents.

There are seven basic categories of travel insurance:

1. Baggage and personal effects insurance
2. Personal accident and sickness insurance
3. Trip cancellation and interruption insurance
4. Default and/or bankruptcy insurance
5. Flight insurance (to cover injury or death)

6. Automobile insurance (for driving your own or a rented car)
7. Combination policies

Baggage and Personal Effects Insurance – Ask your insurance agent if baggage and personal effects are included in your current homeowner's policy, or if you will need a special floater to cover you for the duration of a trip. The object is to protect your bags and their contents in case of damage or theft anytime during your travels, not just while you're in flight, where only limited protection is provided by the airline. Baggage liability varies from carrier to carrier, but generally speaking, on domestic flights, luggage is insured to $1,250 — that's per passenger, not per bag. This limit should be specified on your airline ticket, but to be awarded any amount, you'll have to provide an itemized list of lost property, and if you're including new and/or expensive items, be prepared for a request that you back up your claim with sales receipts or other proof of purchase.

If you are carrying goods worth more than the maximum protection offered by the airlines, consider excess value insurance. Additional coverage is available from airlines at an average, currently, of $1 to $2 per $100 worth of coverage, up to a maximum of $5,000. This insurance can be purchased at the airline counter when you check in, though you should arrive early to fill out the necessary forms and to avoid holding up other passengers.

Major credit card companies provide coverage for lost or delayed baggage — and this coverage often also is over and above what the airline will pay. The basic coverage usually is automatic for all cardholders who use the credit card to purchase tickets, but to qualify for additional coverage, cardholders generally must enroll.

> *American Express:* Provides $500 coverage for checked baggage; $1,250 for carry-on baggage; and $250 for valuables, such as cameras and jewelry.
>
> *Carte Blanche and Diners Club:* Provide $1,250 free insurance for checked or carry-on baggage that's lost or damaged.
>
> *Discover Card:* Offers $500 insurance for checked baggage and $1,250 for carry-on baggage — but to qualify for this coverage cardholders first must purchase additional flight insurance (see "Flight Insurance," below).
>
> *MasterCard and Visa:* Baggage insurance coverage set by the issuing institution.

Additional baggage and personal effects insurance also is included in certain of the combination travel insurance policies discussed below.

> ■ **A note of warning:** Be sure to read the fine print of any excess value insurance policy; there often are specific exclusions, such as cash, tickets, furs, gold and silver objects, art, and antiques. Insurance companies ordinarily will pay only the depreciated value of the goods rather than their replacement value. The best way to protect your property is to take photos of your valuables, and keep a record of the serial numbers of such items as cameras, typewriters, laptop computers, radios, and so on. If an airline loses your luggage, you will be asked to fill out a Property Irregularity Report before you leave the airport. Also, report the loss to the police (since the insurance company will check with the police when processing the claim).

Personal Accident and Sickness Insurance – This covers you in case of illness during your trip or death in an accident. Most policies insure you for hospital and doctors' expenses, lost income, and so on. In most cases, it is a standard part of existing health insurance policies (especially where domestic travel is concerned), though you should check with your insurance broker to be sure of the conditions for which your policy will pay. If your coverage is insufficient, take out a separate vacation accident policy or an entire vacation insurance policy that includes health and life coverage.

Trip Cancellation and Interruption Insurance – Most package tour passengers pay for their travel well before departure. The disappointment of having to miss a vacation because of illness or any other reason pales before the awful prospect that not all (and sometimes none) of the money paid in advance might be returned. So cancellation insurance for any package tour is a must.

Although cancellation penalties vary (they are listed in the fine print of every tour brochure, and before you purchase a package tour you should know exactly what they are), rarely will a passenger get more than 50% of this money back if forced to cancel within a few weeks of scheduled departure. Therefore, if you book a package tour, you should have trip cancellation insurance to guarantee full reimbursement or refund should you, a traveling companion, or a member of your immediate family get sick, forcing you to cancel your trip or *return home early.*

The key here is *not* to buy just enough insurance to guarantee full reimbursement for the cost of the package in case of cancellation. The proper amount of coverage should include reimbursement for the cost of having to catch up with a tour after its departure or having to travel home at the full economy airfare if you have to forgo the return flight tied to the package. There usually is quite a discrepancy between an excursion or other special airfare and the amount charged to travel the same distance on a regularly scheduled flight at full economy fare.

Trip cancellation insurance is available from travel agents and tour operators in two forms: as part of a short-term, all-purpose travel insurance package (sold by the travel agent); or as specific cancellation insurance designed by the operator for a specific tour. Generally, tour operators' policies are less expensive, but also less inclusive. Cancellation insurance also is available directly from insurance companies or their agents as part of a short-term, all-inclusive travel insurance policy.

Before you decide on a policy, read each one carefully. (Either type can be purchased from a travel agent when you book the package tour.) Be sure to check the fine print for stipulations concerning "family members" and "pre-existing medical conditions," as well as allowances for living expenses if you must delay your return due to injury or illness.

Default and/or Bankruptcy Insurance – Although trip cancellation insurance usually protects you if *you* are unable to complete — or begin — your trip, a fairly recent innovation is coverage in the event of default and/or bankruptcy on the part of the tour operator, airline, or other travel supplier. In some travel insurance packages, this contingency is included in the trip cancellation portion of the coverage; in others, it is a separate feature. Either way, it is becoming increasingly important. Whereas sophisticated travelers have long known to beware of the possibility of default or bankruptcy when buying a tour package, in recent years more than a few respected airlines have unexpectedly revealed their shaky financial condition, sometimes leaving hordes of stranded ticket holders in their wake. While default/bankruptcy insurance will not ordinarily result in reimbursement in time to pay for new arrangements, it can ensure that you will get your money back, and even independent travelers buying no more than an airplane ticket may want to consider it.

Flight Insurance – US airlines' liability for injury or death to passengers on domestic flights currently is determined on a case-by-case basis in court — this means potentially unlimited liability. But remember, this liability is not the same thing as an insurance policy; every penny that an airline eventually pays in the case of death or injury likely will be subject to a legal battle.

But before you buy last-minute flight insurance from an airport vending machine, consider the purchase in light of your total existing insurance coverage. A careful review of your current policies may reveal that you already are amply covered for accidental death. Be aware that airport insurance, the kind typically bought at a counter or from a vending machine, is among the most expensive forms of life insurance coverage, and that even within a single airport, rates for approximately the same coverage vary widely.

If you buy your plane ticket with a major credit card, you generally receive automatic insurance coverage at no extra cost. Additional coverage usually can be obtained at extremely reasonable prices, but a cardholder must sign up for it in advance.

Automobile Insurance – If you have an accident in a state that has "no fault" insurance, each party's insurance company pays his or her expenses up to certain specified limits. When you rent a car, the rental company is required to provide you with collision protection.

In your car rental contract, you'll see that for about $5 to $13 a day you may buy an optional collision damage waiver (CDW) protection. Some companies, such as *Hertz* and *Avis,* call the option a loss damage waiver (LDW). (If partial coverage with a deductible is included in the rental contract, the CDW will cover the deductible in the event of an accident, and can cost as much as $25 per day.) If you do not accept the CDW coverage, you may be liable for as much as the full retail value of the rental car if it is damaged or stolen; by paying for the CDW, you are relieved of all responsibility for any damage to the car. Before agreeing to this coverage, however, check with your own broker about your own existing personal automobile insurance policy. It very well may cover your entire liability exposure without any additional cost, or you automatically may be covered by the credit card company to which you are charging the cost of your rental. To find out the amount of rental car insurance provided by major credit cards, contact the issuing institutions.

Combination Policies – Short-term insurance policies, which may include a combination of any or all of the types of insurance discussed above, are available through retail insurance agencies, automobile clubs, and many travel agents. These combination policies are designed to cover you for the duration of a single trip.

The following companies provide such coverage for the insurance needs discussed above:

Access America International: A subsidiary of the Blue Cross/Blue Shield plans of New York and Washington, DC, now available nationwide. Contact *Access America,* PO Box 90310, Richmond, VA 23230 (phone: 800-284-8300 or 804-285-3300).

Carefree: Underwritten by The Hartford. Contact *Carefree Travel Insurance,* Arm Coverage, PO Box 310, Mineola, NY 11501 (phone: 800-645-2424 or 516-294-0220).

NEAR Services: In addition to a full range of travel services, this organization offers a comprehensive travel insurance package. An added feature is coverage for lost or stolen airline tickets. Contact *NEAR Services,* 450 Prairie Ave., Suite 101, Calumet City, IL 60409 (phone: 708-868-6700 in the Chicago area; 800-654-6700 elsewhere in the US and Canada).

Tele-Trip: Underwritten by the Mutual of Omaha Companies. Contact *Tele-Trip Co.,* PO Box 31685, 3201 Farnam St., Omaha, NE 68131 (phone: 402-345-2400 in Nebraska; 800-228-9792 elsewhere in the US).

Travel Assistance International: Provided by Europ Assistance Worldwide Services, and underwritten by Transamerica Occidental Life Insurance Company. Contact *Travel Assistance International,* 1133 15th St. NW, Suite 400, Washington, DC 20005 (phone: 202-331-1609 in Washington, DC; 800-821-2828 elsewhere in the US).

Travel Guard International: Underwritten by the Insurance Company of North America, it is available through authorized travel agents; or contact *Travel Guard International,* 1145 Clark St., Stevens Point, WI 54481 (phone: 715-345-0505 in Wisconsin; 800-826-1300 elsewhere in the US).

Travel Insurance PAK: Underwritten by The Travelers. Contact *The Travelers Companies,* Ticket and Travel Plans, One Tower Sq., Hartford, CT 06183-5040 (phone: 203-277-2319 in Connecticut; 800-243-3174 elsewhere in the US).

Wallach & Co.: This organization offers two health insurance plans as well as other coverage. Contact *Wallach & Co.,* 243 Church St. NW, Suite 100-D, Vienna, VA 22180 (phone: 703-281-9500 in Virginia, 800-237-6615 elsewhere in the US).

Hints for Handicapped Travelers

From 40 to 50 million people in the US alone have some sort of disability, and over half this number are physically handicapped. Like everyone else today, they — and the uncounted disabled millions around the world — are on the move. More than ever before, they are demanding facilities they can use comfortably, and they are being heard.

PLANNING A TRIP: Collect as much information as you can about your specific disability and facilities for the disabled in Miami and Ft. Lauderdale. Make your travel arrangements well in advance and specify to services involved the exact nature of your condition or restricted mobility, as your trip will be much more comfortable if you know that there are accommodations and facilities to suit your needs.

It also is advisable to call the hotel you are considering and ask specific questions. If you require a corridor of a certain width to maneuver a wheelchair or if you need handles on the bathroom walls for support, ask the manager (many large hotels have rooms especially designed for the handicapped). A travel agent or the local chapter or national office of the organization that deals with your particular disability — for example, the *American Foundation for the Blind* or the *American Heart Association* — will supply the most up-to-date information on the subject.

The following organizations also offer general information on access:

ACCENT on Living (PO Box 700, Bloomington, IL 61702; phone: 309-378-2961). This information service for persons with disabilities provides a free list of travel agencies specializing in arranging trips for the disabled; for a copy send a self-addressed, stamped envelope. It also offers a wide range of publications, including a quarterly magazine ($10 per year; $17.50 for 2 years) for persons with disabilities.

Direct Link (PO Box 1036, Solvang, CA 93463; phone: 805-688-1603). This company provides an on-line computer service and links the disabled and their families with a wide range of information, including accessibility, attendant care, transportation, and travel necessities.

Disabled Individuals Assistance Line (*DIAL;* 100 W. Randolph St., Suite 8-100, Chicago, IL 60601; 800-233-DIAL; both voice and TDD). This toll-free hotline provides information about public and private resources available to people with disabilities.*Information Center for Individuals with Disabilities* (Ft. Point Pl., 1st Floor, 27-43 Wormwood St., Boston, MA 02210; phone: 800-462-5015 in Massachusetts; 617-727-5540/1 elsewhere in the US; both numbers provide voice and TDD). The center offers information on accessibility of the transportation system, cultural sites, and other attractions. Also provides referral services on disability-related issues, publishes fact sheets on travel agents, tour operators, and other travel resources, and can otherwise help you research your trip.

Mobility International USA (*MIUSA;* PO Box 3551, Eugene, OR 97403; phone: 503-343-1284; both voice and TDD). This US branch of *Mobility International* (the main office is at 228 Borough High St., London SE1 1JX, England; phone: 011-44-71-403-5688), a nonprofit British organization with affiliates worldwide, offers members advice and assistance — including information on accommodations and other travel services, and publications applicable to the traveler's disability. *Mobility International* also offers a quarterly newsletter and a comprehensive sourcebook, *A World of Options for the 90s: A Guide to International Education Exchange, Community Service and Travel for Persons with Disabilities* ($14 for members; $16 for non-members). Membership includes the newsletter and is $20 a year; subscription to the newsletter alone is $10 annually.

National Rehabilitation Information Center (8455 Colesville Rd., Suite 935, Silver Spring, MD 20910; phone: 301-588-9284). A general information, resource, research, and referral service.

Paralyzed Veterans of America (PVA; PVA/ATTS Program, 801 18th St. NW, Washington, DC 20006; phone: 202-416-7708 in Washington, DC; 800-424-8200 elsewhere in the US). The members of this national service organization all are veterans who have suffered spinal cord injuries, but it offers advocacy services and information to all persons with a disability. *PVA* also sponsors Access to the Skies (ATTS), a program that coordinates the efforts of the national and international air travel industry in providing airport and airplane access for the disabled. Members receive several helpful publications, as well as regular notification of conferences on subjects of interest to the disabled traveler.

Society for the Advancement of Travel for the Handicapped (SATH; 347 Fifth Ave., Suite 610, New York, NY 10016; phone 212-447-7284). To keep abreast of developments in travel for the handicapped as they occur, you may want to join *SATH,* a nonprofit organization whose members include consumers, as well as travel service professionals who have experience (or an interest) in travel for the handicapped. For an annual fee of $45 ($25 for students and travelers who are 65 and older), members receive a quarterly newsletter and have access to extensive information and referral services. *SATH* also offers two useful publications: *Travel Tips for the Handicapped* (a series of informative fact sheets) and *The United States Welcomes Handicapped Visitors* (a 48-page book covering domestic transportation and accommodations, as well as useful hints for travelers with disabilities); to order, send a self-addressed, #10 envelope and $1 per title for postage.

Travel Information Service (Moss Rehabilitation Hospital, 1200 W. Tabor Rd., Philadelphia, PA 19141-3099; phone: 215-456-9600 for voice; 215-456-9602 for TDD). This service assists physically handicapped people in planning trips and supplies detailed information on accessibility, for a nominal fee.

Blind travelers should contact the *American Foundation for the Blind* (15 W. 16th St., New York, NY 10011; phone: 800-829-0500 or 212-620-2147) and *The Seeing Eye* (Box 375, Morristown, NJ 07963-0375; phone: 201-539-4425); both provide useful information on resources for the visually impaired.

In addition, there are a number of publications — from travel guides to magazines — of interest to handicapped travelers. Among these are the following:

Access to the World, by Louise Weiss, offers sound tips for the disabled traveler. Published by Facts on File (460 Park Ave. S., New York, NY 10016; phone: 212-683-2244 in New York State; 800-322-8755 elsewhere in the US; 800-443-8323 in Canada), it costs $16.95 and is available only in paperback. Check with your local bookstore; it also can be ordered by phone with a credit card.

The Diabetic Traveler (PO Box 8223 RW, Stamford, CT 06905; phone: 203-327-5832) is a useful quarterly newsletter for travelers with diabetes. Each issue highlights a single destination or type of travel and includes information on general resources and hints for diabetics. A 1-year subscription costs $18.95. When subscribing, ask for the free fact sheet including an index of special articles; back issues are available for $4 each.

Guide to Traveling with Arthritis, a free brochure available by writing to the Upjohn Company (PO Box 307-B, Coventry, CT 06238), provides lots of good, commonsense tips on planning your trip and how to be as comfortable as possible when traveling by car, bus, train, cruise ship, or plane.

Handicapped Travel Newsletter is regarded as one of the best sources of information for the disabled traveler. It is edited by wheelchair-bound Vietnam veteran Michael Quigley, who has traveled to 93 countries around the world. Issued every 2 months (plus special issues), a subscription is $10 per year. Write to *Handicapped Travel Newsletter,* PO Box 269, Athens, TX 75751 (phone: 903-677-1260).

Handi-Travel: A Resource Book for Disabled and Elderly Travellers, by Cinnie Noble, is a comprehensive travel guide full of practical tips for those with disabilities affecting mobility, hearing, or sight. To order this book, send $12.95, plus shipping and handling, to the *Canadian Rehabilitation Council for the Disabled,* 45 Sheppard Ave. E., Suite 801, Toronto, Ontario M2N 5W9, Canada (phone: 416-250-7490; both voice and TDD).

The Itinerary (PO Box 2012, Bayonne, NJ 07002-2012; phone: 201-858-3400). This bimonthly travel magazine for people with disabilities includes information on accessibility, listings of tours, news of adaptive devices, travel aids, and special services, as well as numerous general travel hints. A subscription costs $10 a year.

The Physically Disabled Traveler's Guide, by Rod W. Durgin and Norene Lindsay, rates accessibility of a number of travel services and includes a list of organizations specializing in travel for the disabled. It is available for $9.95, plus shipping and handling, from Resource Directories, 3361 Executive Pkwy., Suite 302, Toledo, OH 43606 (phone: 419-536-5353 in the Toledo area; 800-274-8515 elsewhere in the US).

Ticket to Safe Travel offers useful information for travelers with diabetes. A reprint of this article is available free from local chapters of the *American Diabetes Association.* For the nearest branch, contact the central office at 505 Eighth Ave., 21st Floor, New York, NY 10018 (phone: 212-947-9707 in New York State; 800-232-3472 elsewhere in the US).

Travel for the Patient with Chronic Obstructive Pulmonary Disease, a publication of the George Washington University Medical Center, provides some sound practical suggestions for those with emphysema, chronic bronchitis, asthma, or other lung ailments. To order, send $2 to Dr. Harold Silver, 1601 18th St. NW, Washington, DC 20009 (phone: 202-667-0134).

Traveling Like Everybody Else: A Practical Guide for Disabled Travelers, by Jacqueline Freedman and Susan Gersten, offers the disabled tips on traveling by car, cruise ship, and plane, as well as lists of accessible accommodations, tour operators specializing in tours for disabled travelers, and other resources. It is available for $11.95, plus postage and handling, from Modan Publishing, PO Box 1202, Bellmore, NY 11710 (phone: 516-679-1380).

Travel Tips for Hearing-Impaired People, a free pamphlet for deaf and hearing-impaired travelers, is available from the *American Academy of Otolaryngology* (One Prince St., Alexandria, VA 22314; phone: 703-836-4444). For a copy, send a self-addressed, stamped, business-size envelope to the academy.

Travel Tips for People with Arthritis, a free 31-page booklet published by the *Arthritis Foundation,* provides helpful information regarding travel by car, bus, train, cruise ship, or plane, planning your trip, medical considerations, and ways to conserve your energy while traveling. It also includes listings of helpful resources, such as associations and travel agencies that operate tours for disabled travelers. For a copy, contact your local *Arthritis Foundation* chapter, or send $1 to the national office, PO Box 19000, Atlanta, GA 30326 (phone: 404-872-7100).

The Wheelchair Traveler, by Douglass R. Annand, lists accessible hotels, motels, restaurants, and other sites by state throughout the US. This valuable resource is available directly from the author. For the price of the most recent edition, contact Douglass R. Annand, 123 Ball Hill Rd., Milford, NH 03055 (phone: 603-673-4539).

A few more basic resources to look for are *Travel for the Disabled,* by Helen Hecker ($19.95), and by the same author, *Directory of Travel Agencies for the Disabled* ($19.95). *Wheelchair Vagabond,* by John G. Nelson, is another useful guide for travelers confined to a wheelchair (hardcover, $14.95; paperback, $9.95). All three titles are published by Twin Peaks Press, PO Box 129, Vancouver, WA 98666 (phone: 800-637-CALM or 206-694-2462). The publisher also offers a catalogue of 26 other books on travel for the disabled for $2.

PLANE: The US Department of Transportation (DOT) has ruled that US airlines must accept all passengers with disabilities. As a matter of course, US airlines were pretty good about accommodating handicapped passengers even before the ruling, although each airline has somewhat different procedures. Ask for specifics when you book your flight.

Disabled passengers always should make reservations well in advance and should provide the airline with all relevant details of their conditions. These details include information on mobility and equipment that you will need the airline to supply — such as a wheelchair for boarding or portable oxygen for in-flight use. Be sure that the person to whom you speak fully understands the degree of your disability — the more details provided, the more effective help the airline can give you.

On the day before the flight, call back to make sure that all arrangements have been prepared, and arrive early on the day of the flight so that you can board before the rest of the passengers. It's a good idea to bring a medical certificate with you, stating your specific disability or the need to carry particular medicine.

Because most airports have jetways (corridors connecting the terminal with the door of the plane), a disabled passenger usually can be taken as far as the plane, and sometimes right onto it, in a wheelchair. If not, a narrow boarding chair may be used to take you to your seat. Your own wheelchair, which will be folded and put in the baggage compartment, should be tagged as escort luggage to assure that it's available at planeside upon landing rather than in the baggage claim area. Travel is not quite as simple if your wheelchair is battery-operated: Unless it has non-spillable batteries, it might not be accepted on board, and you will have to check with the airline ahead of time to find out how the batteries and the chair should be packaged for the flight. Usually people in wheelchairs are asked to wait until other passengers have disembarked. If you are making a tight connection, be sure to tell the attendant.

Passengers who use oxygen may not use their personal supply in the cabin, though it may be carried on the plane as cargo (the tank must be emptied) when properly packed and labeled. If you will need oxygen during the flight, the airline will supply it to you (there is a charge) provided you have given advance notice — 24 hours to a few days, depending on the carrier.

The free booklet *Air Transportation of Handicapped Persons* explains the general guidelines that govern air carrier policies. For a copy, write to the US Department of

Transportation (Distribution Unit, Publications Section, M-443-2, Washington, DC 20590) and ask for "Free Advisory Circular #AC-120-32." *Access Travel: A Guide to the Accessibility of Airport Terminals,* a free publication of the *Airport Operators Council International,* provides information on more than 500 airports worldwide and offers ratings of 70 features, such as accessibility to bathrooms, corridor width, and parking spaces. For a copy, contact the Consumer Information Center (Dept. 563W, Pueblo, CO 81009; phone: 719-948-3334).

The following airlines serving Miami/Ft. Lauderdale have TDD toll-free lines in the US for the hearing-impaired:

American: 800-582-1573 in Ohio; 800-543-1586 elsewhere in the US
America West: 800-526-8077
Continental: 800-343-9195
Delta: 800-831-4488
Northwest: 800-328-2298
TWA: 800-252-0622 in California; 800-421-8480 elsewhere in the US
United: 800-942-8819 in Illinois; 800-323-0170 elsewhere in the US
USAir: 800-242-1713 in Pennsylvania; 800-245-2966 elsewhere in the US

GROUND TRANSPORTATION: Perhaps the simplest solution to getting around is to travel with an able-bodied companion who can drive. If you are accustomed to driving your own hand-controlled car and want to rent one, you are in luck. Some rental companies will fit cars with hand controls. *Avis* (phone: 800-331-1212) can convert a car to hand controls with as little as 24 hours' notice, though it's a good idea to arrange for one more than a day in advance. *Hertz* (phone: 800-654-3131) requires 2 days to install the controls. Neither company charges extra for hand controls, but *Avis* will fit them only on a full-size car, and both request that you bring your handicapped driver's permit with you. Other car rental companies provide hand-control cars at some locations; however, as there usually are only a limited number available, call well in advance.

A relatively new company, *Wheelchair Getaways,* rents vans accommodating one or two wheelchairs and up to 5 passengers. Each vehicle has four-point straps to secure wheelchairs, air conditioning, and stereo. The renter provides the driver. The Pennsylvania-based company (PO Box 819, Newtown, PA 18940; phone: 800-642-2042 or 215-579-9120) has franchises in a number of US cities, including one serving Miami and Ft. Lauderdale (PO Box 20126, West Palm Beach, FL 33416; phone: 800-637-7577 or 407-967-9488; fax: 407-641-3658).

The *American Automobile Association (AAA)* publishes a useful booklet, *The Handicapped Driver's Mobility Guide.* Contact the central office of your local *AAA* club for availability and pricing, which may vary at different branch offices.

TOURS: Programs designed for the physically impaired are run by specialists who have researched hotels, restaurants, and sites to be sure they present no insurmountable obstacles. The following travel agencies and tour operators specialize in making group and individual arrangements for travelers with physical or other disabilities:

Access: The Foundation for Accessibility by the Disabled (PO Box 356, Malverne, NY 11565; phone: 516-887-5798). A travelers' referral service that acts as an intermediary with tour operators and agents worldwide, and provides information on accessibility at various locations.

Accessible Journeys (412 S. 45th St., Philadelphia, PA 19104; phone: 215-747-0171). Arranges for traveling companions who are medical professionals — registered or licensed practical nurses, therapists, or doctors (all are experienced travelers). Several prospective companions' profiles and photos are sent to the client for perusal, and if one is acceptable, the "match" is made. The client usually pays all travel expenses for the companion, plus a certain amount in "earnings" to replace wages the companion would be making at his or her usual job.

Accessible Tours/Directions Unlimited (720 N. Bedford Rd., Bedford Hills, NY 10507; phone: 914-241-1700 in New York State; 800-533-5343 elsewhere in the continental US). Arranges group or individual tours for disabled persons traveling in the company of able-bodied friends or family members. Accepts the unaccompanied traveler if completely self-sufficient.

Evergreen Travel Service (4114 198th St. SW, Suite 13, Lynnwood, WA 98036-6742; phone: 800-435-2288 or 206-776-1184 throughout the continental US and Canada). Offers worldwide tours, including to Ft. Lauderdale, for the disabled (Wings on Wheels Tours), sight impaired/blind (White Cane Tours), and hearing impaired/deaf (Flying Fingers Tours). Most programs are first class or deluxe, and include a trained escort.

First National Travel Ltd. (Thornhill Sq., 300 John St., Suite 302, Thornhill, Ontario L3T 5W4, Canada; phone: 416-731-4714). Handles individual arrangements.

Flying Wheels Travel (143 W. Bridge St., Box 382, Owatonna, MN 55060; phone: 507-451-5005 or 800-535-6790). Handles both tours and individual arrangements.

Guided Tour (613 W. Cheltenham Ave., Suite 200, Melrose Park, PA 19126-2414; phone: 215-782-1370). Arranges tours, including to Miami and Ft. Lauderdale, for people with developmental and learning disabilities and sponsors separate tours for members of the same population who also are physically disabled or who simply need a slower pace.

Handi-Travel (First National Travel Ltd., Thornhill Sq., 300 John St., Suite 405, Thornhill, Ontario L3T 5W4, Canada; phone: 416-731-4714). Handles tours and individual arrangements.

Prestige World Travel (5710X High Point Rd., Greensboro, NC 27407; phone: 800-476-7737 or 919-292-6690). Owner Kay Jones arranges for the handicapped — including the wheelchair-bound — to travel on her regular tour programs; she also will design independent travel programs.

USTS Travel Horizons (11 E. 44th St., New York, NY 10017; phone: 800-487-8787 or 212-687-5121). Travel agent and registered nurse Mary Ann Hamm designs trips for individual travelers requiring all types of kidney dialysis and handles arrangements for the dialysis.

Whole Person Tours (PO Box 1084, Bayonne, NJ 07002-1084; phone: 201-858-3400). Handicapped owner Bob Zywicki travels the world with his wheelchair and offers a lineup of escorted tours (many conducted by him) for the disabled. *Whole Person Tours* also publishes *The Itinerary,* a bimonthly newsletter for disabled travelers (see the publication source list above).

Travelers who would benefit from being accompanied by a nurse or physical therapist also can hire a companion through *Traveling Nurses' Network,* a service provided by Twin Peaks Press (PO Box 129, Vancouver, WA 98666; phone: 800-637-CALM or 206-694-2462). For a $10 fee, clients receive the names of three nurses, whom they can then contact directly; for a $125 fee, the agency will make all the hiring arrangements for the client. Travel arrangements also may be made in some cases — the fee for this further service is determined on an individual basis.

A similar service is offered by *MedEscort International* (ABE International Airport, PO Box 8766, Allentown, PA 18105; phone: 800-255-7182 in the continental US; elsewhere, call 215-791-3111). Clients can arrange to be accompanied by a nurse, paramedic, respiratory therapist, or physician through *MedEscort.* The fees are based on the disabled traveler's needs. This service also can assist in making travel arrangements.

Hints for Single Travelers

 Just about the last trip in human history on which the participants were neatly paired was the voyage of Noah's Ark. Ever since, passenger lists and tour groups have reflected the same kind of asymmetry that occurs in real life, as countless individuals set forth to see the world unaccompanied (or unencumbered, depending on your outlook) by spouse, lover, friend, companion, or relative.

The truth is that the travel industry is not very fair to people who vacation by themselves. People traveling alone almost invariably end up paying more than individuals traveling in pairs. Most travel bargains, including package tours, accommodations, resort packages, and cruises, are based on *double occupancy* rates. This means that the per-person price is offered on the basis of two people traveling together and sharing a double room (which means they each will spend a good deal more on meals and extras). The single traveler will have to pay a surcharge, called a single supplement, for exactly the same package. In extreme cases, this can add as much as 35% to the basic per-person rate.

Don't despair, however. Throughout the US, there are scores of smaller hotels and other hostelries where, in addition to a cozier atmosphere, prices still are quite reasonable for the single traveler.

The obvious, most effective alternative is to find a traveling companion. Even special "singles' tours" that promise no supplements usually are based on people sharing double rooms. Perhaps the most recent innovation along these lines is the creation of organizations that "introduce" the single traveler to other single travelers. Some charge fees, while others are free, but the basic service offered is the same: to match an unattached person with a compatible travel mate. Among such organizations are the following:

> *Jane's International* (2603 Bath Ave., Brooklyn, NY 11214; phone: 718-266-2045). This service puts potential traveling companions in touch with one another. It has started a new organization, *Sophisticated Women Travelers,* to create groups for single women to travel together. No age limit, no fee for either.
>
> *Partners-in-Travel* (PO Box 491145, Los Angeles, CA 90049; phone: 213-476-4869). Members receive a list of singles seeking traveling companions; prospective companions make contact through the agency. The membership fee is $40 per year and includes a chatty newsletter (6 issues per year).
>
> *Travel Companion Exchange* (PO Box 833, Amityville, NY 11701; phone: 516-454-0880). This group publishes a newsletter for singles and a directory of individuals looking for travel companions. On joining, members fill out a lengthy questionnaire and write a small listing (much like an ad in a personal column). Based on these listings, members can request copies of profiles and contact prospective traveling companions. It is wise to join well in advance of your planned vacation so that there's enough time to determine compatibility and plan a joint trip. Membership fees, including the newsletter, are $30 for 6 months or $60 a year for a single-sex listing; $66 and $120, respectively, for a complete listing. Subscription to the newsletter alone costs $24 for 6 months or $36 per year.

In addition, a number of tour packagers cater to single travelers. These companies offer packages designed for individuals interested in vacationing with a group of single travelers or in being matched with a traveling companion. Among the better established of these agencies are the following:

Gallivanting (515 East 79 St., Suite 20F, New York, NY 10021; phone: 800-933-9699 or 212-988-0617). Offers matching service for singles ages 25 through 55 willing to share accommodations in order to avoid paying single supplement charges, with the agency guaranteeing this arrangement if bookings are paid for at least 75 days in advance.

Marion Smith Singles (611 Prescott Pl., N. Woodmere, NY 11581; phone: 516-791-4852, 516-791-4865, or 212-944-2112). Specializes in tours for singles ages 20 to 50, who can choose to share accommodations to avoid paying single supplement charges.

Odyssey Network (118 Cedar St., Wellesley, MA 02181; phone: 800-487-6059 or 617-237-2400). Originally founded to match single female travelers, this company now includes men in its enrollment. *Odyssey* offers a quarterly newsletter for members who are seeking a travel companion and makes independent arrangements for them. A $50 membership fee includes the newsletter.

Saga International Holidays (120 Boylston St., Boston MA 02116; phone: 800-343-0273 or 617-451-6808). A subsidiary of a British company specializing in older travelers, many of them single, *Saga* offers a broad selection of packages for people age 60 and over or those 50 to 59 traveling with someone 60 or older. Recent offerings included a Florida's Golden Coast program. Although anyone can book a *Saga* trip, a $15 club membership includes a subscription to their newsletter, as well as other publications and travel services — such as a matching service for single travelers.

Singles in Motion (545 W. 236th St., Suite 1D, Riverdale, NY 10463; phone: 718-884-4464). Offers a program for singles in Ft. Lauderdale.

Travel in Two's (239 N. Broadway, Suite 3, N. Tarrytown, NY 10591; phone: 914-631-8409). For city programs, this company matches up solo travelers and then customizes programs for them. The firm also puts out a quarterly *Singles Vacation Newsletter,* which costs $7.50 per issue or $20 per year.

A good book for single travelers is *Traveling On Your Own,* by Eleanor Berman, which offers tips on traveling solo and includes information on trips for singles. Available in bookstores, it also can be ordered by sending $12.95, plus postage and handling, to Random House, Order Dept., 400 Hahn Rd., Westminster, MD 21157 (phone: 800-733-3000).

Single travelers also may want to subscribe to *Going Solo,* a newsletter that offers helpful information on going on your own. Issued eight times a year, a subscription costs $36. Contact Doerfer Communications, PO Box 1035, Cambridge, MA 02238 (phone: 617-876-2764).

Those interested in a particularly cozy type of accommodation should consider going the bed and breakfast route. Though a single person will likely pay more than half of the rate quoted for a couple even at a bed and breakfast establishment, the prices still are quite reasonable, and the homey atmosphere will make you feel less conspicuously alone.

Another possibility is the *United States Servas Committee* (11 John St., Room 407, New York, NY 10038; phone: 212-267-0252), which maintains a list of hosts around the world, including Miami and Ft. Lauderdale, who are willing to take visitors into their homes as guests. *Servas* will send an application form and a list of interviewers at the nearest locations for you to contact. After the interview, if you are accepted as a *Servas* traveler, you'll receive a membership certificate. The membership fee is $45 per year for an individual, with a $15 deposit to receive the host list, refunded upon its return.

Hints for Older Travelers

 Special discounts and more free time are just two factors that have given Americans over age 65 a chance to see the world at affordable prices. Senior citizens make up an ever-growing segment of the travel population, and the trend among them is to travel more frequently and for longer periods of time.

PLANNING: When planning a vacation, prepare your itinerary with one eye on your own physical condition and the other on your interests. One important factor to keep in mind is not to overdo anything and to be aware of the effects that the weather may have on your capabilities.

Older travelers may find the following publications of interest:

Discount Guide for Travelers Over 55, by Caroline and Walter Weintz, is an excellent book for budget-conscious older travelers. Published by Penguin USA, it is currently out of print; check your local library.

International Health Guide for Senior Citizen Travelers, by Dr. W. Robert Lange, covers such topics as trip preparations, food and water precautions, adjusting to weather and climate conditions, finding a doctor, motion sickness, jet lag, and so on. Also includes a list of resource organizations that provide medical assistance for travelers. It is available for $4.95 postpaid from Pilot Books, 103 Cooper St., Babylon, NY 11702 (phone: 516-422-2225).

Mature Traveler is a monthly newsletter that provides information on travel discounts, places of interest, useful tips, and other topics of interest for travelers 49 and up. To subscribe, send $24.50 to GEM Publishing Group, PO Box 50820, Reno, NV 89513 (phone: 702-786-7419).

Senior Citizen's Guide to Budget Travel in the US and Canada, by Paige Palmer, provides specific information on economical travel options for senior citizens. To order, send $4.95, plus $1 for postage and handling, to Pilot Books (address above).

Take a Camel to Lunch and Other Adventures for Mature Travelers, by Nancy O'Connell, offers offbeat and unusual adventures for travelers over 50. Available for $8.95 at bookstores or directly from Bristol Publishing Enterprises (include $2.75 for shipping and handling), PO Box 1737, San Leandro, CA 94577 (phone: 800-346-4889 or 510-895-4461).

Travel Easy: The Practical Guide for People Over 50, by Rosalind Massow, discusses a wide range of subjects — from trip planning, transportation options, and preparing for departure to avoiding and handling medical problems en route. The book is out of print, so check your local library.

Unbelievably Good Deals & Great Adventures That You Absolutely Can't Get Unless You're Over 50, by Joan Rattner Heilman, offers travel tips for older travelers, including discounts on accommodations and transportation, as well as a list of organizations for seniors. It is available for $7.95, plus shipping and handling, from Contemporary Books, 180 N. Michigan Ave., Chicago, IL 60601 (phone: 312-782-9181).

HEALTH: Pre-trip medical and dental checkups are strongly recommended. In addition, be sure to take along any prescription medication you need, enough to last *without a new prescription* for the duration of your trip; pack all medications with a note from your doctor for the benefit of airport authorities. If you have specific medical problems, bring prescriptions and a "medical file" composed of the following:

1. A summary of your medical history and current diagnosis.
2. A list of drugs to which you are allergic.
3. Your most recent electrocardiogram, if you have heart problems.
4. Your doctor's name, address, and telephone number.

DISCOUNTS AND PACKAGES: Since guidelines change from place to place, it is a good idea to inquire in advance about discounts on transportation, hotels, concerts, movies, museums, and other activities. For instance, the National Park Service has a Golden Age Passport, which entitles people over 62 (and those in the car with them) to free entrance to all national parks and monuments (available by showing a Medicare card or driver's license as proof of age at any national park).

Many hotel chains, airlines, cruise lines, bus companies, car rental companies, and other travel suppliers offer discounts to older travelers. For instance, *United* offers senior citizen coupon books — with either four or eight coupons each — that can be exchanged for tickets on domestic flights of up to 2,000 miles. These coupons are good 7 days a week for travel in all 50 states, although some peak travel periods are omitted. Other airlines also offer discounts for passengers age 60 (or 62) and over, which may be applicable to one traveling companion per senior. Among the airlines that often offer such discounted airfares are *America West, Continental,* and *TWA.* Given the continuing changes in the airline industry, however, these discounted fares may not be available when you purchase your tickets. For information on current prices and applicable restrictions, contact the individual carriers.

In order to take advantage of these discounts, you should carry proof of your age (or eligibility). A driver's license, membership card in a recognized senior citizens organization, or a Medicare card should be adequate. Among the organizations dedicated to helping older travelers see the world are the following:

American Association of Retired Persons (*AARP;* 601 E St. NW, Washington, DC 20049; phone: 202-434-2277). The largest and best known of these organizations. Membership is open to anyone 50 or over, whether retired or not; dues are $8 a year, $20 for 3 years, or $45 for 10 years, and include spouse. The *AARP* Travel Experience Worldwide program, available through *American Express Travel Related Services,* offers members tours and other travel programs designed exclusively for older travelers. Members can book these services by calling *American Express* at 800-927-0111 for land and air travel.

Mature Outlook (Customer Service Center, 6001 N. Clark St., Chicago, IL 60660; phone: 800-336-6330). Through its *Travel Alert,* tours, cruises, and other vacation packages are available to members at special savings. Hotel and car rental discounts and travel accident insurance also are available. Membership is open to anyone 50 years of age or older, costs $9.95 a year, and includes a bimonthly newsletter and magazine, as well as information on package tours.

National Council of Senior Citizens (1331 F St., Washington, DC 20005; phone: 202-347-8800). Here, too, the emphasis is on keeping costs low. This nonprofit organization offers members a different roster of package tours each year, as well as individual arrangements through its affiliated travel agency *(Vantage Travel Service).* Although most members are over 50, membership is open to anyone (regardless of age) for an annual fee of $12 per person or couple. Lifetime membership costs $150.

Certain travel agencies and tour operators offer special trips geared to older travelers. Among them are the following:

Evergreen Travel Service (4114 198th St. SW, Suite 13, Lynnwood, WA 98036-6742; phone: 800-435-2288 or 206-776-1184 throughout the continental US and Canada). This specialist in trips for persons with disabilities recently introduced Lazybones Tours, a program offering leisurely tours for older travelers, including to Ft. Lauderdale. Most programs are first class or deluxe, and include an escort.

Saga International Holidays (120 Boylston St., Boston MA 02116; phone: 800-343-0273 or 617-451-6808). A subsidiary of a British company catering to older travelers, *Saga* offers a broad selection of packages for people age 60 and over or those 50 to 59 traveling with someone 60 or older. Recent offerings included a Florida's South Coast package. Although anyone can book a *Saga* trip, a $15 club membership includes a subscription to their newsletter, as well as other publications and travel services.

Many travel agencies, particularly the larger ones, are delighted to make presentations to help a group of senior citizens select destinations. A local chamber of commerce should be able to provide the names of such agencies. Once a time and place are determined, an organization member or travel agent can obtain group quotations for transportation, accommodations, meal plans, and sightseeing. Larger groups usually get the best breaks.

Another choice open to older travelers is a trip that includes an educational element. *Elderhostel,* a nonprofit organization, offers programs at educational institutions in the US, including Miami and Ft. Lauderdale, and worldwide. The domestic programs generally last 1 week, and include double-occupancy accommodations in hotels or student residence halls and all meals. Travel to the programs usually is by designated scheduled flights, and participants can arrange to extend their stay at the end of the program. Elderhostelers must be at least 60 years old (younger if a spouse or companion qualifies), in good health, and not in need of special diets. For a free catalogue describing the program and current offerings, write to *Elderhostel* (75 Federal St., Boston, MA 02110; phone: 617-426-7788). Those interested in the program also can borrow slides at no charge or purchase an informational videotape for $5.

Hints for Traveling with Children

What better way to enjoy Miami and Ft. Lauderdale's wide array of family-oriented attractions than in the company of the young, wide-eyed members of your family? Their presence does not have to be a burden or an excessive expense. The current generation of discounts for children and family package deals can make a trip together quite reasonable.

A family trip to Miami and Ft. Lauderdale can be a fun-filled educational experience for your children while visiting the various zoos, nature parks, aquariums, children's museums, and science and space planetariums, one that will leave a sure memory that will be among the fondest you will share with them someday. Their insights will be refreshing to you; their impulses may take you to unexpected places with unexpected dividends. The experience will be invaluable to them at any age.

PLANNING: Here are several hints for making a trip with children easy and fun:

1. Children, like everyone else, will derive more pleasure from a trip if they know something about their destination before they arrive. Begin their education about a month before you leave. Using maps, travel magazines, and books, give children a clear idea of where you are going and how far away it is.
2. Children should help to plan the itinerary, and where you go and what you do

should reflect some of their ideas. If they already know something about the city and the sites they will visit, they will have the excitement of recognition when they arrive.

3. Give children specific responsibilities: The job of carrying their own flight bags and looking after their personal things, along with some other light chores, will give them a stake in the journey.

4. Give each child a travel diary or scrapbook to take along.

Children's books about Miami and Ft. Lauderdale and its place in the history of our country provide an excellent introduction and can be found at children's bookstores (see "Books and Bookstores"), many general bookstores, and in libraries.

And for parents, *Travel With Your Children* (*TWYCH;* 80 Eighth Ave., New York, NY 10011; phone: 212-206-0688) publishes a newsletter, *Family Travel Times,* that focuses on families with young travelers and offers helpful hints. An annual subscription (10 issues) is $35 and includes a copy of the "Airline Guide" issue (updated every other year), which focuses on the subject of flying with children. This special issue is available separately for $10.

Another newsletter devoted to family travel is *Getaways.* This quarterly publication provides reviews of family-oriented literature, activities, and useful travel tips. To subscribe, send $25 to *Getaways,* Att. Ms. Brooke Kane, PO Box 8282, McLean, VA 22107 (phone: 703-534-8747).

Also of interest to parents traveling with their children is *How to Take Great Trips With Your Kids,* by psychologist Sanford Portnoy and his wife, Joan Flynn Portnoy. The book includes helpful tips from fellow family travelers, tips on economical accommodations and touring by car, as well as over 50 games to play with your children en route. It is available for $8.95, plus shipping and handling, from Harvard Common Press, 535 Albany St., Boston, MA 02118 (phone: 617-423-5803). Another title worth looking for is *Great Vacations with Your Kids,* by Dorothy Jordan (Dutton: $12.95).

Another book on family travel, *Travel with Children* by Maureen Wheeler, offers a wide range of practical tips on traveling with children. It is available for $10.95, plus shipping and handling, from Lonely Planet Publications, Embarcadero West, 112 Linden St., Oakland, CA 94607 (phone: 510-893-8555).

Finally, parents arranging a trip with their children may want to deal with an agency specializing in family travel such as *Let's Take the Kids* (1268 Devon Ave., Los Angeles, CA 90024; phone: 800-726-4349 or 213-274-7088). In addition to arranging and booking trips for individual families, this group occasionally organizes trips for single-parent families traveling together. They also offer a parent travel network, whereby parents who have been to a particular destination can evaluate it for others.

PLANE: Begin early to investigate all available family discount flights, as well as any package deals and special rates offered by the major airlines. When you make your reservations, tell the airline that you are traveling with a child. Children ages 2 through 11 generally travel at about a 20% to 30% discount off regular full-fare adult ticket prices on domestic flights. This children's fare, however, usually is much higher than the excursion fare, which may be used by any traveler, regardless of age. An infant under 2 years of age usually can travel free if it sits on an adult's lap. A second infant without a second adult would pay the fare applicable to children ages 2 through 11.

Although some airlines will, on request, supply bassinets for infants, most carriers encourage parents to bring their own safety seat on board, which then is strapped into the airline seat with a regular seat belt. This is much safer — and certainly more comfortable — than holding the child in your lap. If you do not purchase a seat for your baby, you have the option of bringing the infant restraint along on the off-chance that there might be an empty seat next to yours — in which case some airlines will let you use that seat at no charge for your baby and infant seat. However, if there is no empty seat available, the infant seat no doubt will have to be checked as baggage (and you may have to pay an additional charge), since it generally does not fit under the airplane seats or in the overhead racks. The safest bet is to pay for a seat.

Be forewarned: Some safety seats designed primarily for use in cars do not fit into plane seats properly. Although nearly all seats manufactured since 1985 carry labels indicating whether they meet federal standards for use aboard planes, actual seat sizes may vary from carrier to carrier. At the time of this writing, the FAA was in the process of reviewing and revising the federal regulations regarding infant travel and safety devices — it was still to be determined if children should be *required* to sit in safety seats and whether the airlines will have to provide them.

If using one of these infant restraints, you should try to get bulkhead seats, which will provide extra room to care for your child during the flight. You also should request a bulkhead seat when using a bassinet — again, this is not as safe as strapping the child in. On some planes the bassinet hooks into a bulkhead wall; on others it is placed on the floor in front of you. (Note that bulkhead seats often are reserved for families traveling with small children.) As a general rule, babies should be held during takeoff and landing.

Request seats on the aisle if you have a toddler or if you think you will need to use the bathroom frequently. Carry onto the plane all you will need to care for and occupy your children during the flight — formula, diapers, a sweater, books, favorite stuffed animals, and so on. Dress your baby simply, with a minimum of buttons and snaps, because the only place you may have to change a diaper is at your seat or in a small lavatory.

You also can ask for a hot dog or hamburger instead of the airline's regular dinner if you give at least 24 hours' notice. Some, but not all, airlines have baby food aboard, and the flight attendant can warm a bottle for you. While you should bring along toys from home, also ask about children's diversions. Some carriers have terrific free packages of games, coloring books, and puzzles.

When the plane takes off and lands, make sure your baby is nursing or has a bottle, pacifier, or thumb in its mouth. This sucking will make the child swallow and help to clear stopped ears. A piece of hard candy will do the same for an older child.

Parents traveling by plane with toddlers, children, or teenagers may want to consult *When Kids Fly,* a free booklet published by Massport (Public Affairs Dept., 10 Park Plaza, Boston, MA 02116-3971; phone: 617-973-5600), which includes helpful information on airfares for children, infant seats, what to do in the event of overbooked or canceled flights, and so on.

■ **Note:** Newborn babies, whose lungs may not be able to adjust to the altitude, should not be taken aboard an airplane. And some airlines may refuse to allow a pregnant woman in her 8th or 9th month to fly. Check with the airline ahead of time, and carry a letter from your doctor stating that you are fit to travel — and indicating the estimated date of birth.

Things to Remember

1. If you are visiting many sites, pace the days with children in mind. Break the trip into half-day segments, with running around or "doing" time built in.
2. Don't forget that a child's attention span is far shorter than an adult's. Children don't have to see every sight or all of any sight to learn something from their trip; watching, playing with, and talking to other children can be equally enlightening.
3. Let your children lead the way sometimes; their perspective is different from yours, and they may lead you to things you would never have noticed on your own.

4. Remember the places that children love to visit: aquariums, zoos, amusement parks, beaches, nature trails, and so on. Among the activities that may pique their interest are bicycling, boat trips, visiting planetariums and children's museums, and viewing natural habitat exhibits. The perennial Miami and Ft. Lauderdale attractions for children include the *Miami Metrozoo, Miami Seaquarium, Monkey Jungle, Miami Museum of Science & Space Transit Planetarium, Atlantis the Water Kingdom,* and the *Discovery Center.*

On the Road

Credit Cards and Traveler's Checks

 It may seem hard to believe, but one of the greatest (and least understood) costs of travel is money itself. Your one single objective in relation to the care and retention of your travel funds is to make them stretch as far as possible. When you do spend money, it should be on things that expand and enhance your travel experience, with no buying power lost due to carelessness or lack of knowledge. This requires more than merely ferreting out the best airfare or the most charming budget hotel. It means being canny about the management of money itself. Herewith, a primer on making money go as far as possible while traveling.

TRAVELER'S CHECKS: It's wise to carry traveler's checks while on the road instead of (or in addition to) cash, since it's possible to replace them if they are stolen or lost; in the US, you usually can receive partial or full replacement funds the same day if you have your purchase receipt and proper identification. Issued in various denominations, with adequate proof of identification (credit cards, driver's license, passport), traveler's checks are as good as cash in most hotels, restaurants, stores, and banks. Don't assume, however, that restaurants, small shops, and other establishments are going to be able to change checks of large denominations. More and more establishments are beginning to restrict the face amount of traveler's checks they will accept or cash, so it is wise to purchase at least some of your checks in small denominations — say, $10 and $20.

Every type of traveler's check is legal tender in banks around the world, and each company guarantees full replacement if checks are lost or stolen. After that the similarity ends. Some charge a fee for purchase, while others are free; you can buy traveler's checks at almost any bank, and some are available by mail. Most important, each traveler's check issuer differs slightly in its refund policy — the amount refunded immediately, the accessibility of refund locations, the availability of a 24-hour refund service, and the time it will take you to receive replacement checks. For instance, *American Express* offers a 3-hour replacement of lost or stolen traveler's checks at any *American Express* office; other companies may not be as prompt. (Note that *American Express*'s 3-hour policy is based on the traveler's being able to provide the serial numbers of the lost checks. Without numbers, refunds can take much longer.) *American Express*'s offices in Miami are located at 330 Biscayne Blvd. (phone: 358-7353) and 9700 Collins Ave. (phone: 865-5959). In Ft. Lauderdale, you can contact their offices at 777 American Express Way (phone: 473-3513) and 3312 NE 32 St. (phone: 565-9481).

We cannot overemphasize the importance of knowing how to replace lost or stolen checks. All of the traveler's check companies have agents throughout the US, both in their own name and at associated agencies (usually, but not necessarily, banks), where refunds can be obtained during business hours. Most of them also have 24-hour toll-free telephone lines, and some even will provide emergency funds to tide you over on a Sunday.

Be sure to make a photocopy of the refund instructions that will be given to you by the issuing institution at the time of purchase. To avoid complications should you need to redeem lost checks (and to speed up the replacement process), keep the purchase receipt and an accurate list, by serial number, of the checks that have been spent or cashed. You may want to incorporate this information in an "emergency packet," also including the numbers of the credit cards you are carrying, and any other bits of information you shouldn't be without. Always keep these records separate from the checks and the original records themselves (you may want to give them to a traveling companion to hold).

Several of the major traveler's check companies charge 1% for the acquisition of their checks; others don't. To receive fee-free traveler's checks you may have to meet certain qualifications — for instance, *Thomas Cook*'s checks issued in US currency are free if you make your travel arrangements through its travel agency. *American Express* traveler's checks are available without charge to members of the *American Automobile Association (AAA)*. Holders of some credit cards (such as the *American Express Platinum* card) also may be entitled to free traveler's checks. The issuing institution (e.g., the particular bank at which you purchase them) may itself charge a fee. If you purchase traveler's checks at a bank in which you or your company maintains significant accounts (especially commercial accounts of some size), the bank may absorb the 1% fee as a courtesy.

American Express, Bank of America, Citicorp, MasterCard, Thomas Cook, and *Visa* all offer traveler's checks. Here is a list of the major companies issuing traveler's checks and the numbers to call to report lost or stolen checks throughout the US:

American Express: 800-221-7282
Bank of America: 800-227-3460
Citicorp: 800-645-6556
MasterCard: Note that *Thomas Cook MasterCard* (below) is now handling all *MasterCard* traveler's check inquiries and refunds (see below).
Thomas Cook MasterCard: 800-223-7373
Visa: 800-227-6811

CREDIT CARDS: Some establishments you may encounter during the course of your travels may not honor any credit cards and some may not honor all cards, so there is a practical reason to carry more than one. The following is a list of credit cards that enjoy wide domestic and international acceptance:

American Express: Cardholders can cash personal checks for traveler's checks and cash at *American Express* or its representatives' offices in the US up to the following limits (within any single 21-day period): $1,000 for *Green* and *Optima* cardholders; $5,000 for *Gold* cardholders; and $10,000 for *Platinum* cardholders. Check cashing also is available to cardholders who are guests at participating hotels (up to $250), and for holders of airline tickets at participating airlines (up to $50). Free travel accident, baggage, and car rental insurance is provided if the ticket or rental is charged to the card; additional insurance also is available for additional cost. For further information or to report a lost or stolen *American Express* card, call 800-528-4800 throughout the continental US.

Carte Blanche: Free travel accident, baggage, and car rental insurance if ticket or rental is charged to card; additional insurance also is available at additional cost. For medical, legal, and travel assistance, call 800-356-3448 throughout the US. For further information or to report a lost or stolen *Carte Blanche* card, call 800-525-9135 throughout the US.

Diners Club: Emergency personal check cashing for cardholders staying at participating hotels and motels (up to $250 per stay). Free travel accident, baggage, and car rental insurance if ticket or rental is charged to card; additional insurance also is available for an additional fee. For medical, legal, and travel assistance worldwide, call 800-356-3448 throughout the US. For further information or to report a lost or stolen *Diners Club* card, call 800-525-9135.

Discover Card: Offered by a subsidiary of Sears, Roebuck & Co., it provides cardholders with cash advances at numerous automatic teller machines and *Sears* stores throughout the US. For further information or to report a lost or stolen *Discover* card, call 800-DISCOVER throughout the US.

MasterCard: Cash advances are available at participating banks worldwide. Check with your issuing bank for information. *MasterCard* also offers a 24-hour emergency lost card service; call 800-826-2181 throughout the US.

Visa: Cash advances are available at participating banks worldwide. Check with your issuing bank for information. *Visa* also offers a 24-hour emergency lost card service; call 800-336-8472 throughout the US.

SENDING MONEY: If you have used up your traveler's checks, cashed as many emergency personal checks as your credit card allows, drawn on your cash advance line to the fullest extent, and still need money, have it sent to you via one of the following services:

American Express (phone: 800-543-4080). Offers a service called "Moneygram," completing money transfers in as little as 15 minutes. The sender can go to any *American Express* office in the US and transfer money by presenting cash, a personal check, money order, or credit card — *Discover, MasterCard, Visa,* or *American Express Optima* (no other *American Express* or other credit cards are accepted). *American Express Optima* cardholders also can arrange for this transfer over the phone. The minimum transfer charge is $12, which rises with the amount of the transaction; the sender can forward funds of up to $10,000 per transaction (credit card users are limited to the amount of their pre-established credit line). To collect at the other end, the receiver must show identification (driver's license or other picture ID) at an *American Express* branch office. The company's offices in Miami and Ft. Lauderdale are listed above in the "Traveler's Checks" section.

Western Union Telegraph Company (phone: 800-325-4176 throughout the US). A friend or relative can go, cash in hand, to any *Western Union* office in the US, where, for a *minimum* charge of $13 (it rises with the amount of the transaction), the funds will be transferred to a centralized *Western Union* account. When the transaction is fully processed — generally within 30 minutes — you can go to any *Western Union* branch office to pick up the transferred funds; for an additional fee of $2.95 you will be notified by phone when the money is available. For a higher fee, the sender may call *Western Union* with a *Master-Card* or *Visa* number to send up to $2,000, although larger transfers will be sent to a predesignated location. *Western Union* has about 50 branches in the Ft. Lauderdale/Miami area. Downtown offices include: in Miami, 256 SW 8th St. (phone: 379-8373) and 18127 Biscayne Blvd. (phone: (937-4702); in Ft. Lauderdale, 513 NE 3rd St. (phone: 462-2852) and 1007 N. Federal Hwy. (phone: 764-6245).

CASH MACHINES: Automatic teller machines (ATMs) are increasingly common throughout the US. If your bank participates in one of the international ATM networks (most do), the bank will issue you a "cash card" along with a personal identification code or number (also called a PIC or PIN). You can use this card at any ATM in the same electronic network to check your account balances, transfer monies between checking and savings accounts, and — most important for a traveler — withdraw cash instantly. Network ATMs generally are located in banks, commercial and transportation centers, and near major tourist attractions.

Some financial institutions offer exclusive automatic teller machines for their own customers only at bank branches. At the time of this writing, ATMs that *are* connected generally belong to one of the following two international networks:

Cirrus: Has over 70,000 ATMs in more than 45 countries, including over 65,000 locations in the US — nearly 140 in Miami and around 50 in Ft. Lauderdale. *MasterCard* holders also may use their cards to draw cash against their credit lines. For further information on the *Cirrus* network, call 800-4-CIRRUS.

Plus System: Has over 70,000 automatic teller machines worldwide, including over 50,000 locations in the US — about 110 of them in Miami and close to 45 in Ft. Lauderdale. *MasterCard* and *Visa* cardholders also may use their cards to draw cash against their credit lines. For further information on the *Plus System* network, call 800-THE-PLUS.

Information about the *Cirrus* and *Plus* systems also is available at member bank branches, where you can obtain free booklets listing the locations worldwide. Note that a recent change in banking regulations permits financial institutions to subscribe to *both* the *Cirrus* and *Plus* systems, allowing users of either network to withdraw funds from ATMs at participating banks.

Time Zone and Business Hours

TIME ZONE: Miami and Ft. Lauderdale are in the eastern standard time zone and observe daylight saving time beginning on the first Sunday in April and continuing until the last Sunday in October.

BUSINESS HOURS: Miami and Ft. Lauderdale maintain business hours that are fairly standard throughout the country: 9 AM to 5 PM, Mondays through Fridays.

Banks generally are open weekdays from 9 AM to 3 PM, and 24-hour "automatic tellers" or "cash machines" are increasingly common (for information on national networks, see *Credit Cards and Traveler's Checks,* in this section).

In Miami and Ft. Lauderdale, retail stores and department stores usually are open from 10 AM to 9 PM, Mondays through Saturdays. Most of the larger stores and malls are open on Sundays from noon to 6 PM. The giant and renowned Ft. Lauderdale *Swap Shop* is open every day of the year.

Mail, Telephone, and Electricity

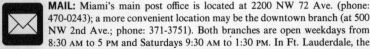

MAIL: Miami's main post office is located at 2200 NW 72 Ave. (phone: 470-0243); a more convenient location may be the downtown branch (at 500 NW 2nd Ave.; phone: 371-3751). Both branches are open weekdays from 8:30 AM to 5 PM and Saturdays 9:30 AM to 1:30 PM. In Ft. Lauderdale, the main post office, at 1900 W. Oakland Park Blvd. (phone: 527-2009), is open weekdays from 7:30 AM to 7 PM and Saturdays from 8:30 AM to 2:30 PM. A downtown branch (at 330 SW 2nd St.; phone: 761-1172), is open weekdays from 8:30 AM to 5 PM and Saturdays from 8:30 AM until 12:30 PM. Other post offices are located conveniently throughout these cities; consult the yellow pages.

Stamps also are available at most hotel desks. There are vending machines for stamps in drugstores, transportation terminals, and other public places. Stamps cost more from these machines than they do at the post office. One convenient post office for visitors in Miami is at One Biscayne Tower, 2 S. Biscayne Blvd. (phone: 372-9473) and in Ft. Lauderdale at the intersection of Sunrise Blvd. and Federal Hwy. (phone: 463-6776).

For rapid, overnight delivery to other cities, *Federal Express* can be useful. The phone number to call for pick-up in Miami is 371-8500, while convenient drop-off addresses include Courthouse Center Lobby, 175 NW First Ave.; One Biscayne Tower, 2 S. Biscayne Blvd.; and Southeast Financial Center Lobby, 200 S. Biscayne Blvd. In Ft. Lauderdale, call 484-4811 for pick-up. Drop-off locations include the NCNB Bank Building at 100 E. Broward and Three Lakes Plaza, 4641 NW 31st Ave.

Another useful overnight service is *DHL Worldwide Courier Express.* In the Miami area, call 471-0491 for pick-up; drop-off locations include 30 SW 8th St. In Ft. Lauderdale, call 791-7400 for pick-up; drop-off locations include 500 E. Broward Blvd., 4th Floor.

 TELEPHONE: Public telephones are available just about everywhere — including transportation terminals, hotel lobbies, restaurants, drugstores, libraries, post offices, and other municipal buildings, as well as major tourist centers.

The area code for both Miami and Ft. Lauderdale is 305.

Although you can use a telephone company credit card number on any phone, pay phones that take major credit cards (*American Express, MasterCard, Visa,* and so on) are increasingly common, particularly in transportation and tourism centers. Also now available is the "affinity card," a combined telephone calling card/bank credit card that can be used for domestic and international calls. Cards of this type include the following:

> *AT&T/Universal* (phone: 800-662-7759).
> *Executive Telecard International* (phone: 800-950-3800).

Similarly, *MCI VisaPhone* (phone: 800-866-0099) can add phone card privileges to the services available through your existing *Visa* card. This service allows you to use your *Visa* account number, plus an additional code, to charge calls on any touch-tone phone.

You must first dial 1 to indicate that you are making a long-distance call. The nationwide number for information is 555-1212. If you need a number in another area code, dial 1 + the area code + 555-1212. (If you don't know the area code, simply dial 0 for an operator who will tell you.)

Long-distance rates are charged according to when the call is placed: weekday daytime; weekday evenings; and nights, weekends, and holidays. Least expensive are the calls you dial yourself from a private phone at night and on weekends and major holidays. It generally is more expensive to call from a pay phone than it is to call from a private phone, and you must pay for a minimum 3-minute call. If the operator assists you, calls are more expensive. This includes credit card, bill-to-a-third-number, collect, and time-and-charge calls, as well as person-to-person calls, which are the most expensive. Rates are fully explained in the front of the white pages of every telephone directory.

Hotel Surcharges – Before calling from any hotel room, inquire about any surcharges the hotel may impose. These can be excessive, but are avoidable by calling collect, using a telephone credit card (see above), or calling from a public pay phone. (Note that when calling from your hotel room, even if the call is made collect or charged to a credit card number, some establishments still may add on a nominal line usage charge — so ask before you call.)

Emergency Number – As in most cities, 911 is the number to dial· in the event of an emergency in Miami or Ft. Lauderdale. Operators at this number will get you the help you need from the police, fire department, or ambulance service. It is, however, a number that should be used for real emergencies only.

■**Note:** An excellent resource for planning your trip is *AT&T's Toll-Free 800 Directory,* which lists thousands of companies with 800 numbers, both alphabetically (white pages) and by category (yellow pages), including a wide range of travel services — from travel agents to transportation and accommodations. Issued in a consumer edition for $9.95 and a business edition for $14.95, both are available from *AT&T Phone Centers* or by calling 800-426-8686. Other useful directories for use before you leave and on the road include the *Toll-Free Travel & Vacation Information Directory* ($4.95 postpaid from Pilot Books, 103 Cooper St., Babylon, NY 11702; phone: 516-422-2225) and *The Phone Booklet,* which lists the nationwide, toll-free (800) numbers of travel information sources and suppliers — such as major airlines, hotel and motel chains, car rental companies, and tourist information offices (send $2 to Scott American Corp., Box 88, West Redding, CT 06896).

ELECTRICITY: All 50 US states have the same electrical current system: 110 volts, 60 cycles, alternating current (AC). Appliances running on standard current can be used throughout the US without adapters or converters.

Staying Healthy

The surest way to return home in good health is to be prepared for medical problems that might occur en route. Below, we've outlined everything about which you need to think before you go.

BEFORE YOU GO: Older travelers or anyone suffering from a chronic medical condition, such as diabetes, high blood pressure, cardiopulmonary disease, asthma, or ear, eye, or sinus trouble, should consult a physician before leaving home. Those with conditions requiring special consideration when traveling should consider seeing, in addition to their regular physician, a specialist in travel medicine. For a referral in a particular community, contact the nearest medical school or ask a local doctor to recommend such a specialist. Dr. Leonard Marcus, a member of the *American Committee on Clinical Tropical Medicine and Travelers' Health,* provides a directory of more than 100 travel doctors across the country. For a copy, send a 9x12-inch, addressed, stamped envelope, to Dr. Marcus at 148 Highland Ave., Newton, MA 02165 (phone: 617-527-4003).

Also be sure to check with your insurance company ahead of time about the applicability of your hospitalization and major medical policies while you're away. If your medical policy does not protect you while you're traveling, there are comprehensive combination policies specifically designed to fill the gap. (For a discussion of medical insurance and a list of inclusive combination policies, see *Insurance,* in this section.)

FIRST AID: Put together a compact, personal medical kit including Band-Aids, first-aid cream, antiseptic, nose drops, insect repellent, aspirin or non-aspirin pain reliever, an extra pair of prescription glasses or contact lenses (and a copy of your prescription for glasses or contact lenses), sunglasses, over-the-counter remedies for diarrhea, indigestion, and motion sickness, a thermometer, and a supply of those prescription medicines you take regularly.

In a corner of your kit, keep a list of all the drugs you have brought and their purpose, as well as duplicate copies of your doctor's prescriptions (or a note from your doctor). As brand names may vary in different parts of the US, it's a good idea to ask your doctor for the generic name of any drugs you use so that you can ask for their equivalent should you need a refill.

It also is a good idea to ask your doctor to prepare a medical identification card that includes such information as your blood type, your social security number, any allergies or chronic health problems you have, and your medical insurance information. Considering the essential contents of your medical kit, keep it with you, rather than in your checked luggage.

MEDICAL ASSISTANCE: If a bona fide emergency occurs, dial 911, the emergency number, and immediately state the nature of your problem and your location. If you are able to, another alternative is to go directly to the emergency room of the nearest hospital.

In Miami, the *Cedars Medical Center* (1400 NW 12th Ave.; phone: 800-327-7386 or 325-5511) provides first-rate emergency service. *Mercy Hospital* (3663 S. Miami Ave., Coconut Grove; phone: 854-4400) also has a 24-hour emergency room. Other major hospitals include *Jackson Memorial Hospital* (1611 NW 12th Ave., Miami; phone: 325-7429) and *Mt. Sinai Medical Center* (4300 Alton Rd., Miami Beach; phone: 674-2200).

In the Ft. Lauderdale area, major hospitals with emergency facilities include *Holy Cross Hospital* (4725 N. Federal Hwy., Ft. Lauderdale; phone: 771-8000), *Hollywood Memorial Hospital* (3501 Johnson St., Hollywood; phone: 987-2000), and *North Beach Hospital* (2835 N. Ocean Blvd.; phone: 568-1000).

For other medical emergencies, in Miami, 24-hour, 7-day-a-week *Eckerd Drug Stores* are in two convenient locations (9031 SW 107 Ave.; phone: 274-6776 and 182 NE 185 St., North Miami Beach; phone: 932-5740). In Ft. Lauderdale, there is a 24-hour *Eckerd* pharmacy (154 N. University Dr.; phone: 432-5510). *Walgreen's* (3101 N. Ocean Blvd.; phone: 564-8424) also is open 24 hours a day, but the prescription section is only open on weekdays from 8 AM to 10 PM, on Saturdays from 9 AM to 9PM, and on Sundays from 9 AM to 6PM.

If a doctor is needed for something less than an emergency, there are several ways to find one. If you are staying in a hotel, ask for help in reaching a doctor or other emergency services, or for the house physician, who may visit you in your room or ask you to visit an office. When you check in at a hotel, it's not a bad idea to include your home address and telephone number; this will facilitate the process of notifying friends, relatives, or your own doctor in case of an emergency.

Medical assistance also is available for travelers who have chronic ailments or whose illness requires them to return home. If you have a health condition that may not be readily perceptible to the casual observer — one that might result in a tragic error in an emergency situation — *Medic Alert Foundation* (2323 N. Colorado, Turlock, CA 95380; phone: 800-ID-ALERT or 209-668-3333) offers identification emblems specifying such conditions. The foundation also maintains a computerized central file from which your complete medical history is available 24 hours a day by phone (the telephone number is clearly inscribed on the emblem). The onetime membership fee (between $25 and $45) is based on the type of metal from which the emblem is made — the choices range from stainless steel to 10K gold-filled.

■ **Note:** Those who are unable to take a reserved flight due to personal illness or who must fly home unexpectedly due to a family emergency should be aware that airlines may offer a discounted airfare (or arrange a partial refund) if the traveler can demonstrate that his or her situation is indeed a legitimate emergency. Your inability to fly or the illness or death of an immediate family member usually must be substantiated by a doctor's note or the name, relationship, and funeral home where the deceased will be buried. In such cases, airlines often will waive certain advance purchase restrictions or you may receive a refund check or voucher for future travel at a later date. Be aware, however, that this bereavement fare may not necessarily be the least expensive fare available and, if possible, it is best to have a travel agent check all possible flights through a computer reservations system (CRS).

HELPFUL PUBLICATIONS: Practically every phase of health care — before, during, and after a trip — is covered in *The New Traveler's Health Guide* by Drs. Patrick J. Doyle and James E. Banta. It is available for $4.95, plus postage and handling, from Acropolis Books Ltd., 13950 Park Center Rd., Herndon, VA 22071 (phone: 800-451-7771 or 703-709-0006).

The *Traveling Healthy Newsletter,* which is published six times a year, also is brimming with healthful travel tips. For an annual subscription, which costs $24, contact Dr. Karl Neumann (108-48 70th Rd., Forest Hills, NY 11375; phone: 718-268-7290). Dr. Neumann also is the editor of the useful free booklet, *Traveling Healthy,* which is available by writing to the *Travel Healthy Program* (PO Box 10208, New Brunswick, NJ 08906-9910; phone: 908-732-4100).

Legal Aid

LEGAL AID: The best way to begin looking for legal aid in an unfamiliar area is to call your own lawyer. If you don't have, or cannot reach, your own attorney, most cities offer legal referral services (sometimes called attorney referral services) maintained by county bar associations. Such referral services see that anyone in need of legal representation gets it. (Attorneys also are listed in the yellow pages.) In Miami, a lawyer referral service is run by the Florida Bar Association (phone: 800-342-8011 in Florida or 904-561-5600). In Ft. Lauderdale, contact the Broward County Bar Association (phone: 764-8040). They can match you with an attorney and set up an appointment for you. If your case goes to court, you are entitled to court-appointed representation if you can't get a lawyer or can't afford one.

In the case of minor traffic accidents (such as fender benders), it is often most expedient to settle the matter before the police get involved. If you get a traffic or parking ticket, pay it. For most violations, you will receive a citation at most, and be required to appear in court on a specified date.

Drinking and Drugs

DRINKING: As in all 50 states, the legal drinking age in Florida is 21. Liquor generally cannot be served in Florida restaurants, bars, and lounges from 2 AM until 6 AM, however, the hours may differ slightly from county to county. On Sundays, no liquor may be served before noon.

For retail purchases, liquor, wine, and beer are sold at liquor stores. Beer and wine also can be bought at supermarkets. No liquor or wine can be purchased on Sunday mornings.

DRUGS: Despite the US government's intensified and concerted effort to stamp out drugs, illegal narcotics still are prevalent in the US, as elsewhere. Enforcement of drug laws is becoming increasingly strict throughout the nation, however, and local narcotics officers are renowned for their absence of understanding and lack of a sense of humor.

Possession of marijuana is a misdemeanor in Florida, while being caught with cocaine or heroin brings exposure to a felony charge, with conviction leading to up to 2 years in jail for possession and up to 10 years for selling the drugs. It is important to bear in mind that the quantity of drugs involved is of minor importance. The best advice we can offer is this: Don't carry, use, buy, or sell illegal drugs.

To avoid difficulties during spot luggage inspections at the airport, if you carry medicines that contain such controlled drugs as codeine or codeine derivatives, be sure to bring along a current doctor's prescription.

Tipping

 While tipping is at the discretion of the person receiving the service, 50¢ is the rock-bottom tip for anything, and $1 is the current customary minimum for small services. In restaurants, tip between 10% and 20% of the bill. For average service in an average restaurant, a 15% tip to the waiter is reasonable, although one should never hesitate to penalize poor service or reward excellent and efficient attention by leaving less or more.

Although it's not necessary to tip the maître d' of most restaurants — unless he has been especially helpful in arranging a special party or providing a table (slipping him something *may*, however, get you seated sooner or procure a preferred table) — when tipping is desirable or appropriate, the least amount should be $5. In the finest restaurants, where a multiplicity of servers are present, plan to tip 5% to the captain in addition to the gratuity left for the waiter. The sommelier (wine waiter) is tipped approximately 10% of the price of the bottle of wine.

In allocating gratuities at a restaurant, pay particular attention to what has become the standard credit card charge form, which now includes separate places for gratuities for waiters and/or captains. If these separate boxes are not on the charge slip, simply ask the waiter or captain how these separate tips should be indicated. In some establishments, tips indicated on credit card receipts may not be given to the help, so you may want to leave tips in cash.

In a large hotel, where it is difficult to determine just who out of a horde of attendants actually performed particular services, it is perfectly proper for guests to ask to have an extra 10% to 15% added to their bill. For those who prefer to distribute tips themselves, a chambermaid generally is tipped at the rate of around $1 a day. Tip the concierge or hall porter for specific services only, with the amount of such gratuities dependent on the level of service provided. For any special service you receive in a hotel, a tip is expected — $1 being the minimum for a small service.

Bellhops, doormen, and porters at hotels and transportation centers generally are tipped at the rate of $1 per piece of luggage, along with a small additional amount if a doorman helps with a cab or car. Taxi drivers should get about 15% of the total fare.

Miscellaneous tips: Sightseeing tour guides should be tipped. If you are traveling in a group, decide together what you want to give the guide and present it from the group at the end of the tour ($1 per person is a reasonable tip). If you have been individually escorted, the amount paid should depend on the degree of your satisfaction, but it should not be less than 10% of the tour price. Museum and monument guides also are usually tipped a few dollars. Coat checks are worth about 50¢ to $1 a coat, and washroom attendants are tipped — there usually is a little plate with a coin already in it suggesting the expected amount. In barbershops and beauty parlors, tips also are expected, but the percentages vary according to the type of establishment — 10% in the most expensive salons; 15% to 20% in less expensive establishments. (As a general rule, the person who washes your hair should get a small additional tip.)

Tipping always is a matter of personal preference. In the situations covered above, as well as in any others that arise where you feel a tip is expected or due, feel free to express your pleasure or displeasure. Again, never hesitate to reward excellent and efficient attention and to penalize poor service. Give an extra gratuity and a word of thanks when someone has gone out of his or her way for you. Either way, the more personal the act of tipping, the more appropriate it seems. And if you didn't like the service — or the attitude — don't tip.

Religion on the Road

The surest source of information on religious services in an unfamiliar community is the desk clerk of the hotel or resort in which you are staying; the local tourist information office or a church of another religious affiliation also may be able to provide this information. For a full range of options, joint religious councils often provide circulars with the addresses and times of services of other houses of worship in the area. These often are printed as part of general tourist guides provided by the local tourist and convention center, or as part of a "what's going on" guide to the city. Many newspapers also offer a listing of religious services in their area in weekend editions.

You may want to use your vacation to broaden your religious experience by joining an unfamiliar faith in its service. This can be a moving experience, especially if the service is held in a church, synagogue, or temple that is historically significant or architecturally notable. You almost always will find yourself made welcome and comfortable.

Sources and Resources

Tourist Information

The Greater Miami Convention and Visitors Bureau is located at 701 Brickell Ave., Suite 2700, Miami, FL 33131 (phone: 539-3000). The Greater Ft. Lauderdale Convention and Visitors Bureau is located at 200 E. Las Olas Blvd., Ft. Lauderdale, FL 33301 (phone: 765-4466). For other local tourist information, see *Local Sources and Resources* in THE CITIES.

For More Information

BOOKS AND BOOKSTORES: The variety and scope of books and other travel information in and on the United States today is astounding. Every city and region is represented, so before you leave on your journey you can prepare by perusing books relevant to your special travel interests. These can usually be found in bookshops devoted to travel, among them the following:

Book Passage (51 Tamal Vista Blvd., Corte Madera, CA 94925; phone: 415-927-0960 in California; 800-321-9785 elsewhere in the US). Travel guides and maps to all areas of the world. A free catalogue is available.

The Complete Traveller (199 Madison Ave., New York, NY 10016; phone: 212-685-9007). Travel guides and maps. A catalogue is available for $2.

Forsyth Travel Library (PO Box 2975, Shawnee Mission, KS 66201-1375; phone: 800-367-7984 or 913-384-3440). Travel guides and maps, old and new, to all parts of the world. Ask for the "Worldwide Travel Books and Maps" catalogue.

Gourmet Guides (2801 Leavenworth Ave., San Francisco, CA 94133; phone: 415-771-9948). Travel guides and maps, along with cookbooks. Mail-order lists available on request.

Phileas Fogg's Books and Maps (87 *Stanford Shopping Center,* Palo Alto, CA 94304; phone: 800-533-FOGG or 415-327-1754). Travel guides, maps, and language aids.

Powell's Travel Store (Pioneer Courthouse Sq., 701 SW 6th Ave., Portland, OR 97204; phone: 503-228-1108). A wealth of travel-related books (over 15,000 titles) and reference materials (globes, an extensive selection of maps, language aids, for example), as well as luggage and travel accessories (travel irons, electrical converters, and the like). There is even a travel agency on the premises.

Tattered Cover (2955 E. First Ave., Denver, CO 80206; phone: 800-833-9327 or 303-322-7727). The travel department alone of this enormous bookstore carries over 7,000 books, as well as maps and atlases. No catalogue is offered (the list is too extensive), but a newsletter, issued three times a year, is available on request.

Thomas Brothers Maps & Travel Books (603 W. Seventh St., Los Angeles, CA 90017; phone: 213-627-4018). Maps (including road atlases, street guides, and wall maps), guidebooks, and travel accessories.

Traveller's Bookstore (22 W. 52nd St., New York, NY 10019; phone: 212-664-0995). Travel guides, maps, literature, and accessories. A catalogue is available for $2.

MAGAZINES: As sampling the regional fare is likely to be one of the highlights of any visit, you will find reading about local edibles worthwhile before you go or after you return. *Gourmet,* a magazine specializing in food, frequently features mouthwatering articles on food and restaurants in the US, although its scope is much broader than domestic fare alone. It is available at newsstands nationwide for $2.50 an issue or for $18 a year from *Gourmet,* PO Box 53780, Boulder, CO 80322 (phone: 800-365-2454).

There are numerous additional magazines for every special interest available; check at your library information desk for a directory of such publications, or look over the selection offered at a well-stocked newsstand.

NEWSLETTERS: One of the very best sources of detailed travel information is *Consumer Reports Travel Letter.* Published monthly by Consumers Union (PO Box 53629, Boulder, CO 80322-3629; phone: 800-999-7959), it offers comprehensive coverage of the travel scene on a wide variety of fronts. A year's subscription costs $37; 2 years, $57.

In addition, the following travel newsletters provide useful up-to-date information on travel services and bargains:

Entree (PO Box 5148, Santa Barbara, CA 93150; phone: 805-969-5848). Monthly; a year's subscription costs $59. Subscribers also have access to a 24-hour hotline providing information on restaurants and accommodations around the world. This newsletter caters to a sophisticated, discriminating traveler with the means to explore the places mentioned.

The Hideaway Report (Harper Associates, Subscription Office: PO Box 300, Whitefish, MO 59937; phone: 406-862-3480; Editorial Office: PO Box 50, Sun Valley, ID 83353; phone: 208-622-3193). This monthly source highlights retreats — including domestic idylls — for sophisticated travelers. A year's subscription costs $90.

Romantic Hideaways (217 E. 86th St., Suite 258, New York, NY 10028; phone: 212-969-8682). This newsletter leans toward those special places made for those traveling in twos. A year's subscription to this monthly publication costs $65.

Travel Smart (Communications House, 40 Beechdale Rd., Dobbs Ferry, NY 10522; phone: 914-693-8300 in New York; 800-327-3633 elsewhere in the US). This monthly newsletter covers a wide variety of trips and travel discounts. A year's subscription costs $44.

COMPUTER SERVICES: Anyone who owns a personal computer and a modem can subscribe to a database service providing everything from airline schedules and fares to restaurant listings. Two such services to try:

CompuServe (5000 Arlington Center Blvd., Columbus, OH 43220; phone: 800-848-8199 or 614-457-8600). It costs $39.95 to join, plus hourly usage fees of $6 to $12.50.

Prodigy Services (445 Hamilton Ave., White Plains, NY 10601; phone: 800-822-6922 or 914-993-8000). A month's subscription costs $12.95, plus variable phone charges.

■**Note:** Before using any computer bulletin-board services, be sure to take precautions to prevent downloading of a computer "virus." First install one of the programs designed to screen out such nuisances.

Cameras and Equipment

 Vacations (and even some business trips) are everybody's favorite time for taking pictures and home movies. After all, most of us want to remember the places we visit — and to show them off to others. Here are a few suggestions to help you get the best results from your travel photography or videography.

BEFORE THE TRIP

If you're taking your camera or camcorder out after a long period in mothballs, or have just bought a new one, check it thoroughly before you leave to prevent unexpected breakdowns or disappointing pictures.

1. Still cameras should be cleaned carefully and thoroughly, inside and out. If using a camcorder, run a head cleaner through it. You also may want to have your camcorder professionally serviced (opening the casing yourself will violate the manufacturer's warranty). Always use filters to protect your lens while traveling.
2. Check the batteries for your camera's light meter and flash, and take along extras just in case yours wear out during the trip. For camcorders, bring along extra Nickel-Cadmium (Ni-Cad) batteries; if you use rechargeable batteries, a recharger will cut down on the extras.
3. Using all the settings and features, shoot at least one test roll of film or one videocassette, using the type you plan to take along with you.

EQUIPMENT TO TAKE ALONG

Keep your gear light and compact. Items that are too heavy or bulky to be carried comfortably on a full-day excursion will likely remain in your hotel room.

1. Invest in a broad camera or camcorder strap if you now have a thin one. It will make carrying the camera much more comfortable.
2. A sturdy canvas, vinyl, or leather camera or camcorder bag, preferably with padded pockets (not an airline bag), will keep your equipment organized and easy to find. If you will be doing much shooting around the water, a waterproof case is best.
3. For cleaning, bring along a camel's hair brush that retracts into a rubber squeeze bulb. Also take plenty of lens tissue, soft cloths, and plastic bags to protect equipment from dust and moisture.

FILM AND TAPES: If you are concerned about airport security X-rays damaging rolls of undeveloped still film (X-rays do not affect processed film) or tapes, store them in one of the lead-lined bags sold in camera shops. This possibility is not as much of a threat as it used to be, however. In the US, incidents of X-ray damage to unprocessed film (exposed or unexposed) are few because low-dosage X-ray equipment is used virtually everywhere. If you're traveling without a protective bag, you may want to ask to have your photo equipment inspected by hand. One type of film that should never be subjected to X-rays is the very high speed ASA 1000 film; there are lead-lined bags made especially for it — and, in the event that you are refused a hand inspection, this is the only way to save your film. The walk-through metal detector devices at airports do not affect film, though the film cartridges may set them off.

You should have no problem finding film or tapes in Florida. When buying film, tapes, or photo accessories the best rule of thumb is to stick to name brands with which you are familiar. The availability of film processing labs and equipment repair shops will vary.

For tips on some of Miami and Ft. Lauderdale's most photogenic spots, see *A Shutterbug's View* in DIVERSIONS.

THE CITIES

MIAMI–
MIAMI BEACH

Difficult as it is to find adults over 30 who actually were born in Miami, practically all residents regard themselves — somehow — as natives. The year-round population of the greater Miami area is 1.8 million. Although visitors often consider Miami a haven for seniors, residents over age 65 constitute only 15% of the population in Dade County, and 20% in Broward County.

Newcomers escaping economic woes and harsh winters elsewhere arrive in droves daily. This figure swells tremendously during the winter months, when millions of "snowbirds" arrive. "Snowbird" is a tricky term as used in Miami. It refers primarily to tourists escaping the northeastern freeze, but just as easily could describe South Americans in town for a midsummer shopping spree. Some even distinguish between "snowbirds," who stay for the winter, and "snowflakes," who own homes here but fly back and forth to another home for short stays. Sprawling across 2,054 square miles of land (the metropolitan area also encompasses 354 square miles of water), Miami is a huge and cosmopolitan metropolis; however, it has managed to maintain a provincial quality in spite of commercialized efforts to identify it as a tropical New York City.

This is due in part to the way in which the metropolitan area is organized. Greater Miami — actually metropolitan Dade County — comprises almost 3 dozen municipalities and a scattering of totally unincorporated areas. This breeds something of a small-town attitude in residents who have a chauvinistic interest in their own enclaves. They identify with the whole city — it is, after all, all Miami. But their particular neighborhood is where they live.

In even larger part, this attitude is due to a deeply rooted tradition of hospitality and neighborliness that can only be described as somehow "Southern" — even while admitting that a large number of the residents who display it most openly are either recent arrivals or part-time snowbirds.

From an early, small settlement consisting primarily of Indians around the government's Fort Dallas, Miami's growth was slow until one Julia Tuttle tickled the fancy of a railroad tycoon with some orange blossoms. Tuttle was an early settler who was eager to see Miami become part of a railroad hookup with the rest of the state. She petitioned railroad magnate Henry M. Flagler to extend his *Florida East Coast Railroad* south from Palm Beach to Miami. He seemed in no great hurry to do so until the Big Freeze of 1894–95 devastated most of Florida's fruit and vegetable crops. Most, but not all. When he received a box of frost-free orange blossoms from Tuttle, he suddenly got her point. Soon enough Miami had rail access to the rest of the world.

Flagler's railroad didn't stop here. On January 22, 1912, he rode his own special car into Key West on a trackbed constructed at great hardship over 156 miles of water and marshy land from Miami. Hurricanes brought an end to Key West rail service in 1935, but 3 years later Flagler's trackbed was used to build the Overseas Highway, which still connects the mainland to Key West. Flagler always dreamed big. At his death in 1913, at age 83, he was still hoping to extend the line from Key West to Cuba.

It wasn't long until the rest of the world was glad of access to South Florida. Attracted by year-round warmth and sunshine, thousands of new residents began pouring into the area, only one step behind hundreds of shrewd (and even occasionally honest) entrepreneurs. Miami and Miami Beach became glittering wintertime destinations and later began drawing vacationers in summer, as well. While Miami Beach still remains tourist-oriented, the city of Miami has developed into a flourishing international business hub. Together they are an attractive combination that lures a wide variety of visitors.

Jolted into the realization that their fun-and-sun city had begun to lose its good reputation about 10 years ago, the local government began implementing a series of major programs dedicated to restoration and redevelopment. They began by renewing the beaches, sprucing up oceanfront hotels, and dressing up the historic hotel district in Miami Beach. The improvements weren't just for tourists. The Miami River was cleaned up and the city expanded its park system. Ecologists have pushed for strict enforcement of environmental laws to protect the delicate marine ecology, reflecting a determination to keep the good life good in South Florida. The result is truly a new Miami, attractive to residents and to visitors, clean, beautiful, and gleaming in the bright Florida sunlight.

That Miami still has the image of offering the good life is attested to by the waves of new residents who continue to settle in one or another of Miami's municipalities each year. Today, many of these new residents are Spanish-speaking, a large number of them coming from the steady flow of refugees from Cuba. Others have fled recent violence in Central America and poverty in the Caribbean; still others are affluent Venezuelans and Colombians who occupy their homes only part of the year. The current mayor of the city, Xavier Suarez, is of Cuban origin.

This Latin immigration has turned metropolitan Miami into a city where you can buy anything from fried bananas to Chilean wine, and where Spanish is the first language of more than 60% of the year-round residents. More recently, the Latin influence has been felt in Miami's art world, as an appreciation of and growing demand for the works of such renowned Latin American artists as Rufino Tamayo, Wilfredo Lam, Roberto Matta, and Armando Morales have made the the the city the undisputed center of Latin American art in the US. A group of newly opened galleries — most featuring the works of Latin American artists and sculptors — has had an extraordinary impact on the once-struggling Miami art community (see *Shopping*). Together with the higher-priced works of their famous colleagues, the affordably priced art of some up-and-coming Latins is drawing a loyal following of collectors and investors alike.

There also is an only slightly smaller tide of newcomers and regular visitors from the Caribbean, Britain, and Europe, bringing Miami an even more international aspect with additions like Jamaican-Chinese restaurants, Haitian grocery stores, and elegant French cuisine. Miami today is a tropical melange of cultures, languages, ethnic eateries, and ambiences.

Coral Gables is Miami's prestigious planned community, conceived and built by entrepreneur George Merrick in the 1920s. Elegant gates to the city still are standing in various spots around the Gables, relics of Merrick's grand scheme to build "a place where castles in Spain are made real." Strict building codes prevail, and woe to the newcomer who tries to put a flat roof on his home. In a county where almost all the streets are laid out in a simple north-south-east-west numbered grid, Coral Gables sticks to its Spanish and Italian street names and layout; for those unfamiliar with its winding ways, it's easy to get lost here. Just 10 minutes from the airport, it also has become one of the favored locales for multinational corporations doing business in Latin America. For more information see *Tour 4: Cruising through Coral Gables* in DIRECTIONS.

South Miami, adjacent to the Gables, is reminiscent of an Anywhere, USA, crossroads town. Farther south, in an unincorporated part of Dade County called Kendall, lie expensive estates with pools and tennis courts, where not so long ago there were only extensive mango and avocado groves.

Closer to downtown Miami is the area known as Coconut Grove, a base for wealthy year-round and winter residents and not so wealthy colonies of artists and writers. Here crafts shops stand next to expensive boutiques; health food stores sit alongside posh restaurants; and old Florida houses of coral rock nestle close to modern high-rises. Luxurious yachts and sailboats lie in Biscayne Bay, and the Grove's younger generation lies all over Peacock Park. (For more information, see *Tour 3: Coconut Grove* in DIRECTIONS.) The area known as Little Havana is part of the center city, but is really a small world unto itself, with its Latin culture intact. Increasingly, it dominates Miami's political and commercial life (see below and *Tour 5: Little Havana* in DIRECTIONS.).

Also in a class by themselves are the communities of Miami Beach and Key Biscayne. Besides its glittering hotel row, the Beach and the small manmade islands between it and the mainland house some of the most luxurious waterfront homes in Greater Miami. The South Beach section has undergone a tremendous renaissance, with the rehabilitation of many classic Art Deco apartment buildings and hotels, as well as the construction of new high-rise condominiums. Key Biscayne has rows of luxury high-rises, simple bungalows, expensive houses, and excellent parks and beaches.

In fact, Miami's Art Deco district has recently replaced Manhattan's posh Hampton beach havens as the escape of choice for such luminaries as Lauren Hutton, resident Floridian Gloria Estefan, Anne Bancroft and Mel Brooks, and John F. Kennedy, Jr. Attracted by the climate and good buys in real estate, celebrities, wanna-bes, and just plain folks have become the area's newest snowbirds.

With a mean annual temperature of 75F, 85,000-plus registered boats, miles of improved beaches, 61 marinas, 11,829 acres of parks, 354 square miles of protected waters, and 3,200 more of sheltered waters, Miami's vital statistics support its reputation as a sunny, water-oriented resort. Yet in recent years, the city has become a major urban area, with an economic diversity associated with cities of comparable size. To a large extent, this is a result of the Latin American–Caribbean connection. The population has grown by 54% since the early 1970s, and employment has doubled in local business and industry. Indeed, the export trade is expected soon to overtake tourism as the number one local industry.

Traditional tourist migration from the Northeast has slowed, due in great measure to the growing attractions of the Tampa–*Walt Disney World*–Orlando–Daytona axis; nevertheless, increased numbers of travelers from Europe and the Orient have taken up the slack. The drug problems and race-related flare-ups that have brought Miami unwanted national headlines in the past have largely been defused — though they remain very much alive in the public consciousness. With the city's new appearance and a calming of tensions, promoters anticipate encouraging increases in tourism.

Still, this area once was a small village stuck on the side of a swamp. In spite of its unappealing natural setting, Miami — and after it, other parts of South Florida — has evolved into America's single greatest tourist magnet. It's probably not true, as an old Florida legend claims, that a race of giants once lived here, but it surely is true that Miami today possesses a gigantic will that wants more than anything else to grow — and grow and grow and grow. It's hard to believe the new, revitalized Miami will not have its way.

MIAMI–MIAMI BEACH AT-A-GLANCE

SEEING THE CITY: The *Rusty Pelican* (3201 Rickenbacker Cswy., Key Biscayne) looks across Biscayne Bay at the spectacular Miami skyline; the *Roof Garden* restaurant atop the *Doral-on-the-Ocean* hotel (4833 Collins Ave., Miami Beach) offers vistas of the bay and the Atlantic; *Crawdaddy's* restaurant (1 Washington Ave.), on the southernmost tip of Miami Beach, affords spectacular views of Government Cut, the throughway for the dozens of cruise ships that dock at the Port of Miami; and the *Bayside* restaurant (3501 Rickenbacker Cswy., Key Biscayne) has an outdoor seating area with good views of downtown Miami.

Miami is largely a waterfront city, and one of the best ways to get to know it is by boat. Besides the *Island Queen,* which leaves from Miamarina (see *Special Places,* below), *Nikko's Gold Coast* cruises set sail out of Haulover Marina (10800 Collins Ave.; phone: 945-5461); the *Spirit* — with lunch, dinner, and "moonlight party" cruises at 2:30, 7, and 10:30 PM, respectively — departs from the *Fontainebleau Hilton* hotel (4441 Collins Ave.; phone: 458-4999); and *Harrah's Belle,* a replica of a paddle-wheel boat, offers sightseeing and dining cruises from the *Miami Beach Eden Roc* hotel (4525 Collins Ave.; phone: 672-5911). *The Heritage of Miami* is a dramatic tall ship that offers 2-hour tours of Biscayne Bay. It docks behind *Bayside Marketplace* (phone: 442-9697) and is available for charters.

Popular narrated sightseeing trips are offered by *Old Town Trolley* for $14. The

90-minute tour provides on-and-off-again access at no extra charge for those wishing to spend time at different spots along the route. Tours leave every half hour, boarding at seven locations (phone: 374-TOUR).

Knowledgeable and folksy narrated walking tours are offered by Dr. Paul S. George, a local history professor. Itineraries include Little Havana, the Art Deco District, Coconut Grove, and Coral Gables (phone: 858-6021).

For a different view of the city, take *Miami Helicopter*'s flight over Miami Beach from Opa-Locka Airport. Open year-round (phone: 685-8223). On the south side of MacArthur Causeway, between downtown Miami and Miami Beach, try *Dade Helicopter Rides* (phone: 374-3737) or *Chalk's International Flights* (phone: 371-8628 or 800-4-CHALKS). Flights cost about $49 (for 10 minutes) to $98 (for 25 minutes) for 1 or 2 passengers.

Tropical Balloons (phone: 666-6645) offers an hour-long balloon tour of downtown Miami, Biscayne Bay, and the Everglades for $110 per person.

SPECIAL PLACES: The best way to see Greater Miami is by car.

Port of Miami – Every week thousands of people depart from here on Caribbean cruises, making Miami the world's largest cruise port. Cruises aren't free, but watching the tourist-laden ocean liners turn around in the narrow channel that leads to the open sea is. With the rise of terrorism a few years back, increased security measures were taken that now prevent non-cruising visitors from boarding ships. However, you can park your car on the MacArthur Causeway between downtown Miami and Miami Beach and watch them maneuver. Or have a cool drink at an outdoor café in the Art Deco district and watch the behemoths glide out to sea. Most ships leave Fridays, Saturdays, Sundays, and Mondays from 4 to 7 PM, but you'll spot the largest outbound fleets on Saturdays and Sundays around 4 to 5 PM.

The Port of Miami is not only the world's largest; it also is the world's busiest cruise-ship port, serving the largest number of cruise-ship passengers. About 3 million passengers embark annually; 17 cruise ships make it their home port, primarily offering 3- and 4-day Bahamas-bound trips and 1-week eastern or western Caribbean itineraries. Many vacationers combine a cruise with a stay before or after a Miami visit. Several day cruises also are offered (see *Day Cruises* in DIVERSIONS). Among the cruise lines serving the port are *Carnival Cruise Lines* (phone: 800-432-5424), *Chandris Fantasy Cruises* (phone: 800-437-3111), *Commodore Cruise Line* (phone: 800-432-6793), *Dolphin Cruise Line* (phone: 800-222-1003), *Ivaran Line* (phone: 800-451-1639), *Majesty Cruise Line* (phone: 536-0000 or 800-532-7788), *Norwegian Cruise Line* (phone: 800-262-4625), *Royal Caribbean Cruise Line* (phone: 800-432-6559), *SeaEscape* (phone: 800-432-0900), and *Starlite Cruises* (phone: 800-354-5005). For port information, call 371-PORT.

Bass Museum – Its Art Deco motif complements an outstanding collection of Renaissance, baroque, and rococo works, plus a recently expanded architectural collection. There also are readings, concerts, and showings of classic films. Open from 10 AM to 5 PM Tuesday through Saturday, and from 1 to 5 PM Sunday. Admission charge, except for children under 16. 2121 Park Ave., Miami Beach (phone: 673-7533).

Art Deco District – A drive or stroll through this area will convince you that you're in a decidedly different Miami, and will forever banish images of the city as a geriatric center. New and restored buildings, hotels, and cafés gleam with façades of shocking pink, bright turquoise, palpitating peach, and Day-Glo yellow. During the mid-1980s, local preservationists decided to upgrade the South Beach area, from Ocean Drive to Lenox Court, which was in a state of complete ruin. Over 800 buildings were rehabilitated and redecorated in a combination of Bauhaus and Art Moderne styles, which was dubbed — though not all architecturally authentic — "'Art Deco." The latest large-scale renovation is along Española Way, between 14th and 15th Streets, from Drexel to Washington Avenues. The Spanish Renaissance–style buildings — many have funky shops and art galleries on the ground floors — have been painted in warm coral tones with gaily striped awnings flapping in the breeze; gaslight lamps lend a romantic glow. For more information see *Quintessential Miami* in DIVERSIONS, and *Tour 1: Art Deco District* in DIRECTIONS.

Bill Baggs Cape Florida State Park – This 406-acre spread of bike paths, woodlands, picnic areas, and a mile-long beach is the perfect place to get away from it all without actually leaving the city. The 45-foot lighthouse here is South Florida's oldest landmark, dating from 1825. Tours of the lighthouse and a reconstructed lightkeeper's house are offered. Open daily from 8 AM to sunset. Admission charge. 1200 Crandon Blvd. (phone: 361-5811).

Miamarina – Sightseeing and charter boats berth in this downtown marina adjacent to the *Bayside* complex (see below). Board the *Island Queen* (phone: 379-5119) for a daily 2-hour circle cruise of Biscayne Bay, viewing waterfront estates and residential islands. Marina open daily from 7 AM to 11 PM. Admission charge. 400 SE 2nd Ave. (phone: 579-6955).

Bayside Marketplace – On 20 acres of Biscayne Bay shoreline, this newly renovated complex includes 160 shops and more than 30 eating establishments. Among the jumping spots is *Dick Clark's American Bandstand Grill,* with TV sets showing old "American Bandstand" clips; the perennial teenager himself sometimes makes an appearance. Entertainment areas provide the setting for strolling jugglers and cartoon-costumed characters, and a life-size reproduction of the HMS *Bounty.* Built for the 1960 film *Mutiny on the Bounty,* the ship docks here from April to October. The *Marketplace* is open daily from 10 AM to 10 PM, Sundays noon to 8 PM. Admission charge to the *Bounty.* Entrance at NE 4th St. and Biscayne Blvd. (phone: 577-3344).

Charles Deering Estate – Undisturbed native mangroves and hardwood hammocks add to the appeal of the 358-acre estate built by the half brother and business partner of James Deering, the International Harvester magnate. Tours of the 1923 Spanish Renaissance winter home leave every hour on weekends. A frame homestead, Indian mounds, and a canoe trip on Biscayne Bay to the estate's Chicken Key add interest to the site. Open Saturdays and Sundays only, 9 AM to 5 PM. Admission charge and extra fee for the canoe trip. 16700 Old Cutler Rd. (phone: 235-1668).

Ichimura Miami Japan Garden – Presented as a gift to the city in 1961 by Kiyoshi Ichimura, a founder of Japan's Ricoh Company, this small (only 1-acre) garden on the north side of Watson Island boasts an 8-ton, 8-foot-high granite statue of Hotei (the Japanese god of prosperity) and a 300-year-old stone lantern. Open Tuesdays from 9 AM to 1 PM, Thursdays and Sundays 1 to 5 PM, and Saturdays 11 AM to 3 PM. No admission charge. Off MacArthur Cswy., Miami Beach (phone: 538-2121).

Little Havana, Calle Ocho (8th Street) – The real Latin flame burns in this community (see *Quintessential Miami* in DIVERSIONS, and *Tour 5: Little Havana* in DIRECTIONS), founded by Cubans who left the island after Castro's takeover. Shops feature handmade jewelry, dolls, and works of art. Fruit stands, bakeries, restaurants, and coffee stalls offer authentic Latin food. Try *Málaga* (740 SW 8th St.; phone: 858-4224) or *Versailles* (3555 SW 8th St.; phone: 444-0240) for lunch or dinner — roast pork with rice and black-bean sauce, then flan (a custard covered with caramel syrup) for dessert, followed by a cup of espresso at a sidewalk stall. Watch cigars being hand-rolled by Cuban experts in exile at *Padrón Cigars,* but never on Sunday (1566 W. Flagler St.; phone: 643-2117).

Caribbean Marketplace – Designed by Haitian architect Charles Harrison Pawley, this vividly colored marketplace in Little Haiti — influenced by the tin roof and yellow-and-orange walls of the *Iron Marketplace* in Haiti's capital city of Port-au-Prince — recently received national recognition from the American Institute of Architects.

Housed here are 2 dozen shops offering fresh produce, fish, Caribbean arts and crafts, records, and tapes. 59th St. and NE 2nd Ave. (phone: 758-8708).

Metro-Dade Cultural Center – This huge, $25-million downtown complex, designed by Philip Johnson, provides a tranquil Spanish-style oasis in the midst of dingy commercial buildings. It houses the *Center for the Fine Arts* (open from 10 AM to 5 PM Tuesday, Wednesday, Friday, and Saturday, 10 AM to 9 PM on Thursday, and noon to 5 PM Sunday; admission charge; phone: 375-1700), which features traveling exhibitions. The *Historical Museum of South Florida* (open from 10 AM to 5 PM Monday through Wednesday, Friday, and Saturday, 10 AM to 9 PM Thursday, and noon to 5 PM on Sunday; admission charge; phone: 375-1492) has excellent exhibitions on Spanish exploration, Indian civilization, and maritime history — it's almost a microcosm of the groups that have settled here, with contributions by the Cubans, Jews, blacks, and others who make up Miami's unique ethnic tapestry. The Miami-Dade Public Library also is here (open 9 AM to 6 PM Monday through Wednesday, Friday, and Saturday, 9 AM to 9 PM Thursday, and 1 to 5 PM Sunday; phone: 375-BOOK). The cultural center is at 101 W. Flagler St. (phone: 375-1700).

Metrozoo – Here, in Miami's cageless zoo, Bengal tigers lounge before a replica of a Cambodian temple; and the mountains, streams, and bridges inside the free-flight aviary evoke the natural habitat of the Asian birds inside. Miami's zoo has been hailed for its excellent design and focus on animal rights. An air conditioned monorail whisks visitors through the aviary. There's a special combined fare with the *Metrorail* on weekends. Open daily. Admission charge. 12400 SW 152nd St. (phone: 251-0401).

Miami Seaquarium – You can see the creatures who live in the oceans at South Florida's largest tropical marine aquarium. Among the 10,000 creatures swimming around the tidepools, jungle islands, and tanks (under a geodesic dome) are killer whales, sharks, sea lions, and performing seals and dolphins. The real stars, though, are Lolita, a killer whale, and Flipper, of TV fame (no longer the original dolphin, who starred in many episodes filmed here many years ago), who performs in a new stadium; there's also a film set, where a new series — with audience members appearing alongside the dolphins — is being filmed. Established in 1955, the *Seaquarium* has expanded in size. Open daily from 9:30 AM to 6 PM. Admission charge. 4400 Rickenbacker Cswy., Key Biscayne (phone: 361-5705).

Miami Marine Stadium – This 6,500-seat roofed grandstand on Biscayne Bay hosts Miami's big shows, as well as powerboat races such as the *Budweiser Unlimited Hydroplane Regatta,* water shows, outdoor concerts, and fireworks displays. Check newspapers for details. 3601 Rickenbacker Cswy., Key Biscayne (phone: 361-6732 or 361-6730).

Miccosukee Indian Village – Just 25 miles west of Miami, descendants of Florida's original settlers are maintaining the lifestyle of their forebears. Among the attractions are alligator wrestling, crafts demonstrations, and airboat rides. Open daily from 9 AM to 5 PM. Admission charge. US 41 (Tamiami Trail) West (phone: 223-8380 weekdays or 223-8388 weekends).

Vizcaya Museum and Gardens – A palatial estate, where James Deering, the International Harvester magnate, reaped his personal harvest. The 70-room Venetian palazzo, with 34 rooms open to the public, is furnished with European antiques, precious china, and artworks from the 15th to the 19th century, and is surrounded by 10 acres of formal gardens. Open from 9:30 AM to 4:30 PM daily except *Christmas Day.* Admission charge. 3251 S. Miami Ave., just off US 1 (phone: 579-2708 or 579-4626).

Museum of Science and Space Transit Planetarium – Exhibitions on a coral reef and the Everglades are enlightening, and there's a participatory science arcade, a wildlife center housing 180 live animals, and a history of cartography display. The planetarium has several shows daily, and really inspired visitors can search for the stars themselves, in the evenings, with the Southern Cross Observatory telescope atop the building. Open daily from 10 AM to 6 PM; closed *Christmas* and *Thanksgiving*. Admission charge. 3280 S. Miami Ave. (phone: 854-4247).

Fairchild Tropical Gardens – Founded by a tax attorney with a touch of the poet in him, this might just be one of the most lyrical tax shelters imaginable — 83 acres of paradise with tropical and subtropical plants and trees (something's always blooming), lakes, and a rare plant house with an extensive collection of unusual tropical flora. Tram rides are available through the grounds, complete with intelligent commentary. Closed *Christmas Day.* Admission charge. 10901 Old Cutler Rd. (phone: 667-1651).

Parrot Jungle – More of the tropics, but this time, screaming, colorful, and talented. Not only do these parrots, macaws, and cockatoos fly, but they also ride bicycles, roller skate, and solve math problems. If you don't believe it, just wait till you see the flamingos on parade — all amid a jungle of huge cypress and live oaks. Don't miss the photo opportunity to pose with brilliantly plumaged red, turquoise, and yellow parrots poised on your arms and head. The coffee shop here is a great breakfast stop. Open daily. Admission charge. Two miles south of US 1 at 11000 SW 57th Ave. (Red Rd.) and Killian Dr. (phone: 666-7834).

Monkey Jungle – The monkeys wander, run free, go swimming, and swing from trees while visitors watch from inside a wire cage. Naturally, some chimp stars perform, and there also are orangutans, gibbons, and an Amazonian rain forest with South American monkeys in natural habitats. Open daily. Admission charge. 14805 SW 216th St. (phone: 235-1611).

Orchid Jungle – Jungle trails wind through this huge orchid display, showing more species and colors than you thought existed. Open daily. Admission charge. South of Miami off US 1 in Homestead, 26715 SW 157th Ave. (phone: 247-4824).

Fruit and Spice Park – Some 20 tropical acres feature over 500 species of fruit, nut, and spice trees and plants. Guided tours by Parks Department naturalists include samplings of seasonal fruits, and you're free to eat anything that's fallen to the ground. Appropriately, this also is the site of the *Tropical Agricultural Fiesta* each July. Tours are conducted Saturday and Sunday afternoons for a nominal charge. Closed *Thanksgiving, Christmas Day,* and *New Year's Day.* Admission charge weekends and holidays. Thirty-five miles southwest of Miami, at 24801 SW 187th Ave., Homestead (phone: 247-5727).

Miami Beach – At one time, this 8-mile-long island east of the mainland was renowned for its glittering seaside resorts, until the beaches and hotels fell into decline. That old reputation, however, has been largely restored, along with the unique architecture. Recent efforts at renewal and redevelopment have brought tourists to the flashy *Fontainebleau Hilton* and the other big hotels that line Collins Avenue, the main drag. A $64-million beach renourishment program has created a 300-foot strand extending from Government Cut to Haulover Inlet, and a beach boardwalk runs 1.8 miles from 21st to 46th Streets (see *Quintessential Miami* in DIVERSIONS). The southern end of the island, between 5th and 20th Streets, known locally as South Beach, has been designated a National Historic District because of its many Art Deco buildings (see *Quintessential Miami* in DIVERSIONS and *Tour 1: Art Deco District* in DIRECTIONS). Ocean Drive recently has been widened and spruced up. Today, the street is lined with outdoor cafés, shops, galleries, and plenty of pedestrian traffic.

Spanish Monastery – The oldest building in the Western Hemisphere, this charming monastery, which today houses artworks, was first built in 1141 in Spain, dismantled, shipped, and rebuilt in Miami in 1954. Open daily 10 AM to 5 PM, Sundays noon to 5 PM. Admission charge. 16711 W. Dixie Hwy., North Miami (phone: 945-1461).

Coral Castle – This is testimony to lost love. Hand-built by a man who was jilted the day before his wedding, this unusual home required more than 1,000 tons of coral rock to be dug by hand and fashioned into a mansion that's a maze of rooms, complete with outdoor furniture and solar-heated bathtubs. Open daily. Admission charge. 28655 US 1, Homestead (phone: 248-6344).

Holocaust Memorial – A $3-million memorial park dedicated to the survivors of the Holocaust in Europe during World War II. At the center of the park is the sculpture *Love and Anguish,* a 42-foot bronze outstretched hand that seems to grow from the ground, symbolic of the concentration camp victims' struggle for survival. A walk surrounding the reflecting pool features touching photographs etched into a granite wall by a special chemical process. Open daily. No admission charge. Meridian Ave. and Dade Blvd., Miami Beach (phone: 538-1663).

Venetian Pool – Once a rock quarry that provided material for many of the stately coral rock homes in Coral Gables, the Venetian Pool has undergone an extensive face-lift. A free-form lagoon with varying levels and waterfalls, and surrounded by lush vegetation, it's a place for Esther Williams fantasies. It's crowded with camp children in summertime, but the rest of the year provides plenty of swimming space and the opportunity to view photographs of former swimming greats. Open daily. Admission charge. 2701 DeSoto Blvd., Coral Gables (phone: 442-6483).

■**EXTRA SPECIAL:** For a refreshing change, drive south along US 27 through miles of Miami's little-known farmland. Stock up on fresh fruit and vegetables at numerous stands, or go right out into the U-Pic fields and choose your own. There's such an abundance of locally grown produce that during harvest time you'll see tables outside mango orchards selling a 2-foot-high stack for a dollar. Forty miles south of Miami (turn off on US 1) is Everglades National Park, a unique and extremely diverse subtropical wilderness with some of the best naturalist-oriented activities anywhere in the world. This 1½-million-acre preserve features alligators, raccoons, manatees, mangroves, and thousands of rare birds, all in their natural habitats. (For more information see *Tour 9: The Everglades National Park* in DIRECTIONS.) Farther south along US 1 stretch the Florida Keys, a chain of islands connected by the Overseas Highway. Key Largo is the site of the only living coral reef in the continental United States, which you can see in all its glory only by skin diving or snorkeling, or in a glass-bottom boat at John Pennekamp State Park, the only underwater park in this country. As you drive down the highway, you'll pass great fishing possibilities and even better food and drink: conch chowder, Key lime pie, and colorful tropical concoctions with romantic names to enjoy, appropriately, in a tropical sunset. The 7-mile bridge is a spectacular part of the drive, and you'll pass through a series of little islands, or keys, with intriguing names like Little Torch and Big Coppitt. The road finally reaches Marathon and Key West, where you'll find reminders of Ernest Hemingway, a museum of Mel Fisher's Spanish galleon treasure hunting, and a hotel built by Henry M. Flagler that's still operating. There's lots to do in Key West, most of it involving the sun and the water, and keeping your body full of good things to eat and drink. For more information see *Tour 8: Florida Keys* in DIRECTIONS.

LOCAL SOURCES AND RESOURCES

TOURIST INFORMATION: The Greater Miami Convention and Visitors Bureau (701 Brickell Ave., Suite 2700, Miami, FL 33131; phone: 539-3000; fax: 305-539-3113) is best for brochures, maps, and general tourist information. For information on fairs, art shows, and events in the area's parks, call the Parks and Recreation Department's information line (phone: 579-2568). Contact the Florida state hotline (904-487-1462) for maps, calendars of events, health updates, and travel advisories.

Local Coverage – *Miami Herald,* a morning daily, publishes its Weekend section on Fridays, full of a schedule of upcoming events; *South Florida* magazine, a monthly; *New Times,* an alternative weekly — Miami's answer to New York City's *Village Voice* — includes "The Wave," a listing of weekly happenings; and *New Miami,* a monthly business magazine. Spanish coverage includes the dailies *El Nuevo Herald* and *El Diario las Américas,* and monthly magazines *Miami Mensual* and *Selecta.*

Television Stations – WPBT Channel 2–PBS; WTVJ Channel 4–NBC; WCIX Channel 6–CBS; WPLG Channel 10–ABC.

Radio Stations – AM: WIOD 610 (news); WEAT 850 (easy listening); WINZ 940 (news/talk). FM: WTMI 93.1 (classical music); WKIS 99.9 (country); WMXJ 102.7 (oldies); WJQY 106.7 (easy listening).

TELEPHONE: The area code for Miami is 305.

SALES TAX: There is a 6% statewide sales tax and a 12.5% hotel tax.

GETTING AROUND: Bus – *Metrobus* serves downtown Miami, Collins Avenue in Miami Beach, Coral Gables, and Coconut Grove fairly well, but service to other areas tends to be slow and complicated. For information on routes, schedules, and fares, call 638-6700.

Car Rental – Miami is served by the large national firms; intensive competition makes rates here among the least expensive in the country, but if you want to drive a convertible during peak season, be sure to reserve one well in advance. *General Rent-A-Car* has corporate headquarters in nearby Hollywood, with several offices locally (phone: 871-3573). For more information about car rental see GETTING READY TO GO.

Metrorail – *Metrorail,* an elevated rail system, operates from the *Dadeland* shopping mall in the Kendall area to downtown Miami, beyond to the Civic Center and Hialeah; fare, $1. The *Metromover* rail system is a 1.9-mile downtown loop; fare, 25¢ (the line is being expanded to cover 4.3 miles by next year). For information, call 638-6700.

Taxi – You sometimes can hail a cab in the street, but it's better to order one on the phone or pick one up in front of any of the big hotels. Major cab companies are *Central Cab* (phone: 532-5555), *Metro Taxi* (phone: 888-8888), *Super Yellow Cab* (phone: 888-7777), and *Yellow Cab* (phone: 444-4444).

Tri-Rail – The 67-mile commuter railroad system began operating in 1989, connecting Dade, Broward, and Palm Beach counties with increasingly frequent routes, Mondays through Saturdays. The fare is $2, with discounts for seniors, students, and the disabled. Passengers board the double-decker trains at any of 14 stops, with free connecting passes to *Metrorail/Metromover* and to county and shuttle buses. The train provides access to major sights and to Miami, Ft. Lauderdale/Hollywood, and Palm Beach airports. Extra trains are scheduled for games at *Joe Robbie* and *Orange Bowl* stadiums, special events, and guided tours to *Bayside Marketplace* and other attractions. Accessible to the handicapped (phone: 800-TRI-RAIL).

LOCAL SERVICES: Accountants – *Accountants on Call,* 800 Douglas Entrance, Coral Gables (phone: 443-9333).

Audiovisual Equipment – *Spire Audio-Visual,* 24 NW 36th St., Miami (phone: 576-5736).

Business Services – *Ad Staff Temporary Service,* 273 Alhambra Circle, Coral Gables (phone: 443-2122).

Convention Facilities – *Stephen Muss Convention Center* (1901 Convention Center Dr., Miami Beach; phone: 673-7311), *Miami Convention Center* (400 SE 2nd Ave., Miami; phone: 579-6341), and *Coconut Grove Convention Center* (2700 S. Bayshore Dr., Coconut Grove; phone: 579-3310).

Copiers and Equipment – *Kinko's* makes standard and color copies, provides hourly rentals of typewriters and computers. Open 24 hours daily. Two locations: 1309 SW 107th Ave., Miami (phone: 220-8172) and 1212 S. Dixie Hwy., Coral Gables (phone: 662-6716).

Dental Emergency – *American Dental Association* maintains a 24-hour daily referral service (phone: 667-3647).

Dry Cleaner/Tailor – *La Salle Cleaners* (2341 LeJeune Rd., Coral Gables; phone: 444-7376); *Mark's* (1201 20th St., Miami Beach; phone: 538-6104).

Limousine – *Red Top Sedan Service* (11077 NW 36th Ave.; phone: 688-7700); *Club Limousine Service* (11055 Biscayne Blvd.; phone: 893-9850).

Mechanics – *Dave's Car Clinic* (5800 Commerce La.; phone: 661-7711); *Martino,* for foreign and American cars (7145 SW 8th St.; phone: 261-6071).

Medical Emergency – *Jackson Memorial Hospital* (1611 NW 12th Ave., Miami; phone: 325-7429); *Mt. Sinai Medical Center* (4300 Alton Rd., Miami Beach; phone: 674-2200). For further information, see *Staying Healthy* in GETTING READY TO GO.

Messenger Services – *Sunshine State Messenger Service,* open 24 hours daily (phone: 944-6363); *Metro Messenger Service* (phone: 757-7777).

National/International Courier – *Federal Express* (phone: 371-8500 or 800-238-5355); *DHL Worldwide Courier Express* (phone: 471-0490). For further information, see *Mail, Telephone, and Electricity* in GETTING READY TO GO.

Pharmacy – *Eckerd Drug Stores* are open 24 hours; locations include 9031 SW 107 Ave. (phone: 274-6776) and 1825 NE 185 St., North Miami Beach (phone: 932-5740).

Photocopies – *Sir Speedy* (locations include 1659 James Ave., Miami Beach; phone: 531-5858); *Ace Industries* (54 NW 11th St.; phone: 358-2571).

Post Office – The downtown office is located at 500 NW 2nd Ave. (phone: 371-2911); the office in Miami Beach is located at 1300 Washington Ave. (phone: 531-3763).

Professional Photographer – *Convention Photographers International* (1630 Cleveland Rd., Miami; phone: 865-5628); *Pelham Photographic* (665 Mokena Dr., Miami Springs; phone: 885-2006).

Secretary/Stenographer – *Abacus Business Center,* English/Spanish (12000 Biscayne Blvd., Miami; phone: 892-8644); *Girl Friday* (25 SE 2nd Ave., Miami; phone: 379-3461).

Teleconference Facilities – *Inter-Continental* hotel (100 Chopin Plaza, Miami; phone: 577-1000); *Miami Convention Center* (400 SE 2nd Ave., Miami; phone: 579-6341); *Omni International* (1601 Biscayne Blvd., Miami; phone: 374-0000); *Stephen Muss Convention Center* (1901 Convention Center Dr., Miami Beach; phone: 673-7311).

Translator – *Berlitz* (phone: 371-3686 or 800-523-7548); *Professional Translating Services* (phone: 371-7887).

Typewriter Rental – *Beach Typewriter,* 1-week minimum (phone: 538-6272); *A-1 Etron,* 2-week minimum (phone: 264-4652); see also *Kinko's* above ("Copiers and Equipment").

Western Union/Telex – Many offices are located around the city (phone: 223-8000 or 800-325-4045).

Other – *ABC Office Equipment* (phone: 891-5090); *Florida Tent Rental,* tent pavilions for conferences or receptions, often set up at *Vizcaya Museum and Gardens* (phone: 633-0199); *Florida Convention Services,* meeting and conference planners (phone: 758-7868); *Pearl's and Jessie's Catering* (20160 W. Dixie Hwy.; phone: 937-1511); *US Passport Agency,* open Mondays through Fridays 8:30 AM to 4:30 PM; closed federal holidays (51 SW 1st Ave., Miami; phone: 536-5395).

SPECIAL EVENTS: Miami is the site of the annual *King Orange Jamboree Parade* (phone: 371-4600), nationally televised from Biscayne Boulevard each *New Year's Eve* as a prelude to the *Orange Bowl* football classic (phone: 371-3351), which is played on *New Year's* night. (The *King Mango Strut* parade, held a few days earlier, pokes fun at the lavish *Orange Bowl* festivities.) *New Year's Day* also heralds the *Kwanzaa Festival;* a fairly new celebration for Miami, it recalls black African traditions, celebrated with food, music, and arts and crafts (phone: 573-8981). Two of the country's largest boat shows are held here each year, the *Boat Show in the Grove* (phone: 696-6100) at the Coconut Grove Convention Center in October, and the *International Boat Show* (phone: 531-8410) at the Stephen Muss Convention Center in February. Miami Beach hosts the *Art Deco Weekend* every January on Ocean Drive, in the historic Art Deco district on South Beach (phone: 672-2014), as well as the *Festival of the Arts* each February (phone: 673-7733) and the *Coconut Grove Art Festival* (phone: 447-0401) during the same month. These festivals draw many folks away from the beach to stroll the shady lanes of this artists' haven. February also hosts the *Miami Film Festival,* 10 days of premieres of national and international films with visiting directors, producers, and stars (phone: 377-3456). In late March or early April is the *Miami Grand Prix,* attracting top racing drivers to the downtown "track" (Biscayne Blvd. between Flagler and NE 8th Sts.; phone: 665-RACE). In March, in Little Havana, natives and visitors alike head for Calle Ocho (8th St.) for *Carnaval Miami* (phone: 644-8888), a 9-day festival featuring a 23-block-long street party and the largest conga line in the world. In April, the *Greater Miami Billfish Tournament* attracts more than 500 anglers in pursuit of marlin and sailfish, vying for South Florida's richest fishing purse (phone: 598-8127 or 754-0710). *Taste of Miami* offers tidbits from area restaurants, cooking demonstrations, and wine tastings in May at Bayfront Park (phone: 375-8480). May also brings the *Haitian Festival* at Miami-Dade Community College (phone: 347-1320). Coconut Grove is the site of the *Miami/Bahamas Goombay Festival* in June, celebrating the area's Bahamian heritage and considered the country's largest black heritage festival, with *junkanoo* groups (local citizens who form bands and play calypso and reggae music on homemade instruments), continuous music, and lots of conch chowder and fritters (phone: 372-9966).

For sailboat enthusiasts, the 2-day *Columbus Day Regatta,* held in June, attracts more than 600 entrants. July brings the *Tropical Agricultural Fiesta* at the Fruit and Spice Park (phone: 247-5727) and the *Miccosukee Music and Crafts Festival* at the Miccosukee Indian Village in the Everglades (phone: 223-8388). Chocoholics won't want to miss the *Chocolate Festival* in September at the *Fontainebleau Hilton* (phone: 535-3240). The *Miami Mile,* a world class run, is held the third week of September. In November, the *Miami Book Fair International* welcomes authors, publishers, book-sellers, and street vendors to one of the world's largest week-long celebrations of the printed word, considered the country's premier literary event by *The New York Times* and *Publisher's Weekly* (phone: 347-3258). The *Christmas* season gets off to an enchanting start in early December with the *Greater Miami Boat Parade,* when hundreds of brightly lighted and gaily decorated boats sail along the Intracoastal Waterway (phone: 935-9959). The *Florida Indian Arts Festival* in late December draws members from 40 tribes who exhibit song, dance, and other skills at the *Miccosukee Indian Village* (phone: 223-8380 weekdays or -8388 weekends). And the year ends as it begins with the *Blockbuster Bowl,* a top-ranked collegiate football classic, which takes place between *Christmas* and *New Year's* (phone: 564-5000).

MUSEUMS: The *Bass Museum of Art,* the museums in the *Metro-Dade Cultural Center,* the *Museum of Science and Space Transit Planetarium,* and the *Vizcaya Museum and Gardens* are described in *Special Places.* Other museums to see include the following. (For more information, see *Memorable Museums* in DIVERSIONS.)

American Police Hall of Fame and Museum – Exhibits of law enforcement vehicles — there's even an electric chair. 3801 Biscayne Blvd., Miami (phone: 573-0070).

Art Museum at Florida International University – Collection of the works of contemporary North and South American artists. University Park, SW 107th Ave. and 8th St. (phone: 348-2890).

Cuban Museum of Arts and Culture – The cultural heritage of Miami's Cuban community. 1300 SW 12th Ave. (phone: 858-8006).

Lowe Art Museum – Displaying contemporary art, on the University of Miami campus in Coral Gables. 1301 Stanford Dr. (phone: 284-3536).

Miami Youth Museum – Hands-on exhibits, including "Kidscape," a miniature neighborhood for kids from 18 months to 8 years, complete with a supermarket, dental office, and fire station. Bakery Centre, 5701 Sunset Dr., Suite 313, South Miami (phone: 661-3046).

Weeks Air Museum – Dedicated to aircraft. 14710 SW 128th St., Kendall-Tamiami Airport (phone: 233-5197).

 MAJOR COLLEGES AND UNIVERSITIES: The University of Miami in Coral Gables, a 4-year college with highly regarded graduate schools, has an enrollment of 17,000 (1200 San Amaro Dr.; phone: 284-2211). Florida International University is a 4-year college with two separate campuses (SW 8th St. and 107th Ave., and NE 151st St. and Biscayne Blvd.; phone: 554-2363). Miami Dade Community College, with three campuses, is the largest junior college in the country (11380 NW 27th Ave., 11011 SW 104th St., and 300 NE 2nd Ave.; phone: 347-3135).

 SHOPPING: In addition to sparkling blue waters and powdery white beaches, Miami also offers some sand-free sports, and the best of them is shopping. For a change of pace, the many shopping malls in the area provide an alternative to sand and surf. Those listed below carry a wide variety of items, and many have lovely restaurants and scenic views as well.

Aventura Mall – One of South Florida's largest malls, with 200 shops and stores on 2 levels. Anchors are *Lord & Taylor, Macy's, JC Penney,* and *Sears.* Open daily from 10 AM to 9:30 PM. 19501 Biscayne Blvd., North Miami Beach (phone: 935-1110).

Bal Harbour Shops – Lovely open-air shopping amid gardens and fountains. The 97 upscale stores include *Saks Fifth Avenue, Neiman Marcus, Martha, Cartier, Gucci, Brooks Brothers,* and *F.A.O. Schwarz.* Open Mondays, Thursdays, and Fridays 10 AM to 9 PM, Tuesdays, Wednesdays, and Saturdays 10 AM to 6 PM, and Sundays noon to 5 PM. 9700 Collins Ave., Bal Harbour (phone: 866-0311).

Bayside Marketplace – Open-air marketplace overlooking the water. A wide variety of shopping options, from *Victoria's Secret* and *The Gap* to *B. Dalton's.* There also are pushcarts where you can buy arts and crafts items from South America, Central America, and the Caribbean. The International Food Court with its enclosed restaurants satisfy hunger cravings. Open from 10 AM to 10 PM Mondays through Saturdays and noon to 8 PM on Sundays. 401 Biscayne Blvd. (phone: 577-3344).

Books & Books – Two locations, one in Coral Gables and the other in Miami Beach. Both offer frequent readings by authors such as Carlos Fuentes and Susan Sontag. The

Coral Gables store features a sizable selection of used and out-of-print books. The Coral Gables shop is open from 10 AM to 8 PM weekdays, 10 AM to 7 PM Saturdays, and noon to 5 PM Sundays; the Miami Beach store is open from 10 AM to 9 PM Mondays through Thursdays, 10 AM to midnight Fridays and Saturdays, and noon to 5 PM Sundays. 296 Aragon Ave., Coral Gables (phone: 442-4408); 933 Lincoln Rd., Miami Beach (phone: 532-3222).

CocoWalk – An exciting new open-air, Spanish-style shopping complex in the heart of Coconut Grove, it boasts 3 dozen shops, several eateries, and entertainment for the young and young-at-heart. Stores include *The Limited Express, The Gap, Banana Republic, Victoria's Secret,* and a *B. Dalton's* that remains open until 1 AM Fridays and Saturdays. There's also *Café Tu Tu Tango* and *Big City Fish* (see *Eating Out*). Stores are open from 11 AM to 10 PM daily except holidays. 3015 Grand Ave., Coconut Grove (phone: 444-0777).

Couler Square – Antiques, glassware, jewelry, art, and vintage clothing are sold in this 20-shop complex in a 10-acre shopping area. Open from 10 AM to 4:30 PM Mondays through Saturdays. 22400 Old Dixie Hwy., Goulds (phone: 258-3543).

Dadeland Mall – This large mall in southern Miami claims Florida's largest *Burdine's,* along with *Saks Fifth Avenue, Lord & Taylor,* and 170 other shops. Open Mondays through Saturdays 10 AM to 9 PM, Sundays noon to 6 PM. 7535 N. Kendall Dr. (phone: 665-6226).

Elite Fine Art – Latin American art by masters and emerging artists. Includes paintings, drawings, and sculpture by artists such as the Brazilian Antonio Amaral, Cuban Mario Bencomo, and Panamanian Guillermo Trujillo. Open Tuesdays through Saturdays 11 AM to 6 PM. 3140 Ponce de León Blvd., Coral Gables (phone: 448-3800; 800-USA-ELITE outside Florida).

Epicure Market – *The* place on the Beach for unusual grocery items and take-out goodies for sand or sea, including three types of smoked salmon, imported caviar, fresh-ground coffee, large cooked shrimp, and prepared meals. Open Mondays through Fridays from 9 AM to 7 PM and Saturdays and Sundays 9 AM to 6 PM. 1656 Alton Rd., Miami Beach (phone: 672-1861).

Falls Shopping Center – Upscale stores and restaurants set among splashing waterfalls. The 60 shops include Miami's only *Bloomingdale's.* Open Mondays through Saturdays from 10 AM to 9 PM, Sundays noon to 5 PM. 8888 Howard Dr. (phone: 255-4570).

Fashion Row – Known as "Shmatte Row" (Yiddish for garments or rags), it offers discounts, discounts, and more discounts. One section of discount dress and handbag shops is located off Hallandale Beach Boulevard on NE 1st Avenue (dubbed "Fashion Row" on street signs); the other is on NE 2nd Avenue between NE 3rd and NE 4th Streets. Open daily 10 AM to 5 PM between December and March 30th, closed on Sundays other times. Stop at *Barnett's,* chock-full of everything for the home at discount prices; it stays open on Sundays year-round. 100 E. Hallandale Beach Blvd., Hallandale (phone: 456-0566). Or, still in the home mode, try the *Dansk Factory Outlet* for discounts on seconds and overstocks of these fine Danish designs. Open Mondays through Saturdays from 10 AM to 5:30 PM, Sundays noon to 5 PM. 27 W. Hallandale Beach Blvd., Hallandale (phone: 454-3900).

A Likely Story – Children's books and imported educational toys, including easels, games, and specialized items. Open from 10 AM to 6 PM Mondays through Saturdays, and noon to 5 PM Sundays. 5740 Sunset Dr. (phone: 667-3730).

Mayfair Shops in the Grove – High-fashion shops predominate, including *Polo/Ralph Lauren, Ann Taylor,* and *Benetton.* Open from 10 AM to 8 PM Mondays and Thursdays, 10 AM to 7 PM Tuesdays, Wednesdays, Fridays, and Saturdays, and noon to 5 PM Sundays. Grand Ave., Coconut Grove (phone: 448-1700).

Miami Duty Free – Travelers planning to leave the country, even for a short cruise, may buy items at duty-free prices right in Miami, in clean, uncluttered surroundings. Drive into the highly secure parking lot and present either your cruise or flight ticket to the security guard. Select and pay for your goods. *MDF* will deliver your purchases to your plane or ship on the day of departure. Items include Givenchy and Calvin Klein scents, Absolut and Dewar's liquor, Fendi purses, Wedgwood china, Waterford crystal, Rolex watches, and Nina Ricci scarves. Salespeople speak seven languages. Prices are 20% to 40% below retail, and no Florida tax is levied. Open daily from 9 AM to 10 PM. 125 NE 8th St. (phone: 358-9774).

Spy Shops International – Fortunately, Miami is no longer at the top of every crime list. But just for protection, customers here may purchase high-tech security systems, anti-kidnapping devices, and electric surveillance gadgets, or arrange to have a vehicle armored. Open Mondays through Fridays 9:30 AM to 6 PM, Saturdays until 3 PM. 2900 Biscayne Blvd. (phone: 573-4779) and 350 Biscayne Blvd. (phone: 374-4779).

Unicorn Village Marketplace – This large, immaculate shop associated with the *Unicorn Village* restaurant features enormous displays of organically grown produce, prepared Pritikin Diet items, and wines produced without pesticides or added sulphites. At *The Shops at the Waterways,* 3595 NE 207th St., North Miami Beach (phone: 933-8829).

Virginia Miller Galleries – Features contemporary artworks by Latin Americans, including Carlos Loarca, South American and European artists, including Karel Appel of the Netherlands, and US artists Larry Gerber, Tom Hopkins, and the late Alice Neel, plus Australian aboriginal paintings of the Turkey Creek art community. Open Mondays through Saturdays from 10 AM to 6 PM. 169 Madeira Ave., Coral Gables (phone: 444-4493).

 SPORTS AND FITNESS: Baseball – The University of Miami *Hurricanes* play at *Mark Light Stadium* (on campus at 1 Hurricane Dr., corner of Ponce de León and San Amaro; phone: 284-2655). Miami is all aflutter at being named the home of the National League's Florida *Marlins.* They'll be playing baseball at *Joe Robbie Stadium* (2269 NW 199th St.; phone: 620-2578 or 623-6100) starting this spring. Fans also can watch pre-season games of the Baltimore *Orioles,* whose spring training camp is in Miami; they often play the New York *Yankees,* who train in nearby Ft. Lauderdale. And the new *Homestead Sports Complex* (SW 152nd St.; phone: 230-0212 or 246-8721) is the spring training site for the Cleveland *Indians.*

Basketball – The *Heat,* Miami's NBA entry, burns up the court at the *Miami Arena,* 721 NW 1st Ave. (phone: 530-4400, 577-HEAT). The *Harlem Globetrotters* occasionally present their frantic antics here, too.

Bicycling – Rent from *Dade Cycle Shop* (3216 Grand Ave., Coconut Grove; phone: 443-6075) or *Cycles on the Beach* (713 Fifth St., Miami Beach; phone: 673-2055). Rentals cost $3 per hour or $15 per day. There are more than 100 miles of bicycle paths in the Miami area, including tree-shaded lanes through Coconut Grove and Coral Gables. A self-guided bicycle tour of Key Biscayne originates in Crandon Park. Dade County Parks & Recreation Department has information (phone: 579-2676). For more information see *Biking* in DIVERSIONS.

Boating – Greater Miami is laced with navigable canals and has many private and public marinas with all kinds of boats for rent. Sailboats are available from *Dinner Key Marina* (Pan American Dr., Coconut Grove; phone: 579-6980). Windsurfer and Hobie Cat rentals, some with free instruction, are available from *Easy Sailing* shops on Key Biscayne (phone: 858-4001 or 800-780-4001) or *Sailboats Miami* (phone: 361-SAIL or 361-3870); *Beachsport International* (phone: 538-0752) also rents wave runners and glass-bottom powerboats. Rentals cost from $15 to $35. The *Cat Ppalu* and *Pauhana,* two 49-passenger catamarans, are available for charter or sunset tours (phone: 888-

3002). Charter boats for sport fishing are available at *Crandon Park Marina* (phone: 361-1281), *Castaways Dock* (phone: 949-2278), *Miami Beach Marina* (phone: 673-6000), and *Miami Marina* downtown (phone: 374-6260). For 18-footers, try *Beach Boat Rentals* (2380 Collins Ave., Miami Beach; phone: 534-4307). The ubiquitous *Club Nautico* has docks in Miami (phone: 371-4252), Miami Beach (phone: 673-2502), Coconut Grove (phone: 858-6258), and North Miami Beach (phone: 945-3232).

Dog Racing – Greyhound racing is held at *Flagler* (NW 37th Ave. at 7th St.; phone 649-3000) and at *Biscayne* (320 NW 115th St.; phone: 754-3484 or 800-432-0232). Check the racing dates before heading to the track.

Fishing – Surf and offshore saltwater fishing are available year-round. The boardwalks on the Rickenbacker, MacArthur, and Venetian causeways are popular land-based fishing spots; the Haulover Beach Fishing Pier (10800 Collins Ave., Miami Beach; phone: 947-6767) and *Holiday Inn* Newport Pier (16701 Collins Ave., Miami; phone: 949-1300) are open 24 hours daily and provide equipment rental (admission charge). There's also plenty of freshwater action in canals and backwaters, including the Everglades and Florida Bay. Charter boats offer a choice of half-day or full-day deep-sea fishing for snapper, grouper, yellowtail, pompano, and mackerel trips from *Crandon Park Marina* (on Key Biscayne; phone: 361-1281) and *Haulover Marina* (10800 Collins Ave., Miami Beach; phone: 945-3934). Or try *Castaways Dock* (16485 Collins Ave., Miami Beach; phone: 949-2278), with such standbys as *Therapy IV* (phone: 945-1578) and the *Kelley Fleet* (phone: 949-1173). For more information see *Fishing* in DIVERSIONS.

Fitness Centers – Staying in shape is no problem in Dade County. Try the *YMCA* (at the downtown World Trade Center; phone: 577-3091); out-of-town visitors who are members of a *Y* back home (more than 50 miles away) are welcome without charge. The *Downtown Athletic Club* (atop the Southeast Bank Building; phone: 358-9988) and *Body and Soul* (355 Greco Ave., Coral Gables; phone: 443-8688) also are good places.

Football – The NFL *Dolphins* and *Dolphin*-mania infect the entire city during the pro football season, so for good seats call the *Joe Robbie Stadium* in North Dade in advance (2269 NW 199th St.; phone: 620-2578). The University of Miami *Hurricanes* play at the *Orange Bowl;* for tickets, contact the University of Miami ticket office (1 Hurricane Dr., Coral Gables; phone: 284-2655), or go to the *Orange Bowl* (1501 NW 3rd St.).

Golf – More than 35 golf courses are open to the public. Some of the best are *Kendale Lakes* (6401 Kendale Lakes Dr.; phone: 382-3930); *Miami Springs* (650 Curtiss Pkwy., Miami Springs; phone: 888-2377); *Bayshore* (2301 Alton Rd., Miami Beach; phone: 532-3350); *Palmetto* (9300 SW 152nd St., Miami; phone: 238-2922); and *Key Biscayne* (6700 Crandon Blvd., Key Biscayne; phone: 361-9129). There also are major courses at several resorts (see *Great Golf* in DIVERSIONS).

Horse Racing – Betting is big in Miami. The *Hialeah Race Track* (2200 E. 4th Ave., Hialeah; phone: 885-8000 or 800-442-5324), listed on the National Register of Historic Places, is worth a visit just to see the beautiful grounds and clubhouse and the famous flock of pink flamingos. After a 2-year lay-off, the elegant equines are off and running again, daily except Mondays in late autumn. Dining is available in the *Citation Room, Flamingo Pavilion,* and *Turf Club.* There also is thoroughbred horse racing at *Gulf-stream Park* (901 S. Federal Hwy., Hallandale; phone: 944-1242) and at *Calder* (21001 NW 27th Ave.; phone: 625-1311), where recent additions include dining in the *Turf Club,* 2 other dining rooms, and snack bars.

Jai Alai – From December through April, there's jai alai (a Basque game resembling a combination of lacrosse, handball, and tennis), and betting action nightly at the *Miami Jai-Alai Fronton,* the country's largest. You can pick up tickets at the gate or reserve them in advance. 3500 NW 37th Ave. (phone: 633-6400).

Jogging – Run along South Bayshore Drive to David Kennedy Park, at 22nd

Avenue, and jog the Vita Path; or jog in Bayfront Park, at Biscayne and NE 4th Street. On Miami Beach, run on a wooden boardwalk that extends along the ocean from 21st to 51st Street, or run toward the parcourse on the southern tip of South Beach. The *Miami Mile,* a world class event planned after New York's *Fifth Avenue Mile* and San Francisco's *California Mile,* is off and running the third week of September. For more information, contact Bob Rodriguez (phone: 756-8600).

Nature Walks – There are nature walks at Fairchild Tropical Gardens and the Fruit and Spice Park, but the Parks & Recreation Department offers frequent guided tours through natural hammocks, tree forests, bird rookeries, and even through water (a marine walk, nature lesson, and dousing are at Bear Cut, Key Biscayne). For information contact the Parks Department office (phone: 662-4124).

Parasailing – To fly through the air with the greatest of ease, contact *Beachsport International* (2401 Collins Ave., Miami Beach; phone: 538-0752). Cost is $42 for a 10-minute flight.

Skating – Hard-hit snowbirds can head south to Homestead for ice skating at the *Ice Castle Skating Arena* (255 NE 2nd Dr.; phone: 255-4144) or north to Broward County for year-round nightly ice skating at the *Sunrise Ice Skating Center* (3363 Pine Island Rd., Sunrise; phone: 741-2366). Roller-skating to a computerized light show — 2 million lights, synchronized to music — takes place at *Hot Wheels Roller Skating Center* (12265 SW 112th St.; phone: 255-4144). At the *Miami Arena* (721 NW 1st Ave.; phone: 530-4400), *Disney on Ice* appears in April, and the *Tour of World Figure Skating Champions* is in June.

Swimming – With an average daily temperature of 75F, and miles of ocean beach on the Atlantic, Miami Beach and Key Biscayne offer some great places for swimming, all water sports, and another prime activity: sedentary sun worshiping. Some of the best beaches include the following:

> *Bill Baggs Cape Florida State Park:* This long beach with sand dunes, picnic areas, fishing, a boat basin, a restored old lighthouse, and a museum is a favorite of residents. Open from 8 AM to sundown daily. Admission charge. At Cape Florida, the far south end of Key Biscayne (phone: 361-5811).
>
> *Crandon Park Beach:* A 2-mile stretch lined with shade trees, picnic tables, barbecue pits, and ample parking. Drive to the far end for private cabañas rented by the day or week. Open from 9:15 AM to 8 PM daily. Admission charge. Rickenbacker Cswy. to Key Biscayne (phone: 361-5421).
>
> *Haulover Beach* is a long stretch of beautiful beach, good for surfing and popular with families. Marina, sightseeing boats, charter fishing fleets, restaurants, and a fishing pier. Open from 7 AM to 10 PM daily. No admission charge. A1A north of Bal Harbour (phone: 947-3525).
>
> *Miami Beach:* Several long stretches of public beach at various places, including South Beach for surfers (5th St. and Collins Ave.), Lummus Park with lots of shaded beaches (South Beach on Ocean Ave.), and North Shore Beach with landscaped dunes and an oceanfront walkway (71st St. and Collins Ave.). There also are small public beaches at the east ends of streets near major hotels.

Tennis – Many hotels have courts for the use of their guests, and there also are public facilities throughout the county. Some of the best are the *Abel Holtz Tennis Stadium* in Flamingo Park in Miami Beach with hard and clay courts (1200 12th St.; phone: 673-7761); *International Tennis Center* on Key Biscayne with 17 hard and clay courts, rentals and lessons (7200 Crandon Blvd.; phone: 361-8633); *Tamiami* (10901 Coral Way; phone: 223-7076); *North Shore Center* (350 73rd St., Miami Beach; phone: 993-2022); and *Tropical Park* (7900 SW 40th St., Miami; phone: 223-8710). Some hotels offer outstanding tennis facilities and programs (see *Tennis* in DIVERSIONS).

Windsurfing – Major beachfront hotels rent equipment, but the best spot is arguably

Windsurfer Beach at Key Biscayne. Bring your own board or rent from *Sailboats Miami* (Rickenbacker Cswy; phone: 361-SAIL or 361-3870) at $15 an hour or $39 for a 2-hour lesson guaranteed to teach any novice. Or try *Beachsports International* (2401 Collins Ave., Miami Beach; phone: 538-0752), which charges $12 an hour.

THEATER: For current offerings, check the publications listed above. The *Coconut Grove Playhouse* (3500 Main Hwy.; phone: 442-4000) imports New York stars for its season of classics that runs from October to May. The *Jackie Gleason Theater of the Performing Arts,* referred to locally as *TOPA,* offers touring plays and musicals, including some pre- and post-Broadway shows (1700 Washington Ave., Miami Beach; phone: 673-8300). The *Gusman Cultural Center* (174 E. Flagler St., Miami; phone: 374-2444) and the *Dade County Auditorium* (2901 W. Flagler St., Miami; phone: 545-3395) book theatrical and cultural events year-round. The *Miami City Ballet* (905 Lincoln Rd., Miami Beach; phone: 532-7713), headed by Edward Villella, is one of the country's best young companies and performs a full season beginning each fall.

MUSIC: Visiting orchestras and artists perform in Miami at the *Gusman Cultural Center* (174 E. Flagler St.; phone: 374-2444) and at *Dade County Auditorium* (2901 W. Flagler St.; phone: 545-3395), or in Miami Beach at the *Theater of the Performing Arts* (1700 Washington Ave.; phone: 673-8300). The *Greater Miami Opera Association* (1200 Coral Way; phone: 854-7890) stages a full complement of major productions during the winter season, as does the *New World Symphony* (101 E. Flagler St., Miami; phone: 371-3005). Gloria Estefan and the *Miami Sound Machine* perform at the *Miami Arena* (721 NW 1st Ave.; phone: 530-4444) and Bicentennial Park (1075 Biscayne Blvd.; phone: 575-5256 or 579-6909).

NIGHTCLUBS AND NIGHTLIFE: Miami's nightlife runs the gamut. For a Vegas-style "flesh and feathers" revue, head for the *Sheraton Bal Harbour* (9701 Collins Ave., Miami Beach; phone: 865-7511), the *Club Tropigala* at the *Fontainebleau Hilton* (4441 Collins Ave., Miami Beach; phone: 672-7469), or to *Les Violins* for a flashy show with a Cuban twist (1751 Biscayne Blvd.; phone: 371-8668). Shout *olé* to flamenco shows in Little Havana at *Málaga* (740 SW 8th St., Miami; phone: 858-4224) and *Centro Vasco* (2235 SW 8th St., Miami; phone: 643-9606). For live blues and a bit of history, stop in at *Tobacco Road* (626 S. Miami Ave.; phone: 374-1198), Miami's oldest bar. If jazz is your bag, try *Greenstreet's* (2051 LeJeune Rd., Coral Gables; phone: 445-2131) or *Semper's* in Miami Beach (860 Ocean Dr.; phone: 673-6730). For a gigantic nightclub experience complete with 10-piece band, enormous video, and 6 bars, head for *Facade* (3509 NE 163rd St., North Miami Beach; phone: 948-6868). For tunes from the 1950s and 1960s (as well as the present), a popular spot is *Studebaker's* in Kendall (8505 Mills Dr.; phone: 598-1021). The *Village Inn* (3131 Commodore Plaza, Miami; phone: 445-8721) features mellow rock. The south end of Miami Beach is the latest "in" spot for nightlife. Disco hot spots are the *Alcazaba* in the *Hyatt Regency Coral Gables* (50 Alhambra Plaza, Coral Gables; phone: 441-1234; see *Checking In*), the *English Pub* (320 Crandon Blvd., Key Biscayne; phone: 361-8877), and *Club Boomerang* (323 23rd St.; phone: 532-1666). Head to the *Island Club* for hip-hop dancing (the latest rage in Miami) on Mondays, rock 'n' roll Fridays, and reggae Saturdays (701 Washington Ave.; phone: 538-1213). *Egoist* (455 Ocean Dr.; phone: 534-7436), a late-night dance bistro, features reggae on Sundays. Clubs favored by gays include *Warsaw* (1450 Collins Ave.; phone: 531-4555), *Torpedo* (634 Collins Ave.; phone: 538-2500), and *Hombre* (925 Washington Ave.; phone: 538-7883). And, just for laughs, hit the *Improv,* where dinner is served at several shows nightly (*CocoWalk,* 3015 Grand Ave., Coconut Grove; phone: 441-8200). For authentic Haitian music, head for the *Chateau Club* (8267 NE 2nd Ave.; 751-0212) where Haitians, locals, and visitors listen and dance to the *compas* (pronounced *con*-pah), an ear-splitting mix of synthesizers, bongo drums, horns, and cowbells.

BEST IN TOWN

CHECKING IN: Winter is the busy season, and reservations should be made well in advance. In winter, a double room in the very expensive range will run $195 and up per night; $140 to $180 in expensive; $95 to $135 in moderate; and about $50 to $90 in inexpensive. Besides the hotels listed below, hundreds of others abound, including branches of chains such as Howard Johnson or Holiday Inn; check the yellow pages or call the hotel toll-free 800 numbers. In summer, most hotels cut their rates, so shop around. For information about bed and breakfast accommodations, contact the Greater Miami Convention and Visitors Bureau (701 Brickell Ave., Miami FL 33131; phone: 539-3000; fax: 305-539-3113). All telephone numbers are in the 305 area code unless otherwise indicated.

Alexander – An elegant, yet surprisingly homey place metamorphosed from former luxury apartments, with some units now selling as condominiums. A chandeliered portico, a grand lobby with a curving stairway and antiques from the Cornelius Vanderbilt mansion in New York, and 211 spacious, antique-filled suites are all impressive, as is *Dominique's* restaurant (see *Eating Out*), with a main dining room overlooking the ocean. Roasted rack of lamb and exotic appetizers such as rattlesnake salad, alligator tails, and buffalo sausage are specialties. A $15-million expansion added a second restaurant and a ballroom. The grounds include an acre of tropical gardens, 2 lagoon swimming pools — 1 with its own waterfall — and 4 soothing whirlpool baths; a private marina and golf and tennis facilities are nearby. The cost is actually lower per person for a family staying in a suite here than in several rooms in other hotels. Room service is available until 11 PM; other amenities include a concierge desk and secretarial services. There are 8 meeting rooms to serve business needs. 5225 Collins Ave., Miami Beach (phone: 865-6500, 861-5252, or 800-327-6121; fax: 305-864-8525). Very expensive.

Colonnade – Still sporting its original façade, this 1920s hostelry has 157 luxury rooms and suites, 2 restaurants, and a rooftop pool and Jacuzzi overlooking Coral Gables. The intimate lobby boasts dark paneling, overstuffed sofas, and Oriental rugs. The hotel's ballrooms often are the settings for lavish banquets. The *Aragon Café* is one of Miami's best hotel restaurants (see *Eating Out*). *Doc Dammers Saloon* is an informal eatery with interesting early photos of the region. Live jazz Tuesdays to Thursdays, 7 to 11 PM, and Saturdays from 9 PM. There's a piano player at other times. Amenities include 2-line computer-compatible telephones, 6 meeting rooms, and a small health club. Guests also have complimentary use of the *Scandinavian Health Club,* 3 blocks away. 180 Aragon Ave., Coral Gables (phone: 441-2600 or 800-533-1337; fax: 305-445-3929). Very expensive.

Doral Country Club – One of a trio of Doral facilities, 14 miles west of the ocean and the site of the annual *Doral-Ryder Open* (February/March), the resort features 5 championship golf courses and a par 3 executive's course (see *Great Golf* in DIVERSIONS) serving guests in its 650 rooms and suites. Other athletic facilities include 15 tennis courts (4 lighted), a heated Olympic-size pool, volleyball, a jogging trail, and a 24-stall equestrian center. Professional golf and tennis workshops are available. Dozens of meeting and reception rooms. Dining options include the *Provare* Italian restaurant, featuring grilled meat and fish plus pasta,

Sandpiper for steaks and seafood, a coffee shop, outdoor grill, and a lounge featuring nightly live entertainment. Access to *Doral Ocean Beach* (see below) and *Doral Saturnia Spa* (see below). 4400 NW 87th Ave., Miami (phone: 592-2000, 800-327-6334, or 800-22DORAL; fax: 305-594-4682). Very expensive.

Doral Ocean Beach – On the 18th floor of this 420-room high-rise is *Alfredo, the Original of Rome* restaurant (see *Eating Out*), known worldwide for its pasta dishes, but also heralded here for such entrées as veal stuffed with mushrooms. Not to be overlooked is the stunning view of the ocean, the Intracoastal Waterway, downtown Miami, and the cruise ships at the Port of Miami. The lobby's European-style gold mosaics, marble, and crystal chandelier have been retained, but other details have been spruced up. Other highlights include a presidential suite, exclusive shops, Olympic-size pool, numerous water sports, 2 outdoor Jacuzzis, a disco, a lounge with a piano player, fitness center, poolside activities such as bingo, day camp during holidays, a video gameroom, 2 lighted tennis courts, an 80-foot executive yacht available for meetings, and an FAA-licensed helipad. All meals are served indoors and out daily at the *Doral Café* in the hotel and the *Sandbar* at the ocean — more than just another beach bar. There's courtesy shuttle service to the country club (see above) and the spa; *Doral* guests may use the facilities at these two locations at the normal guest rates. Relaxed elegance and friendly staff. In addition to 18 meeting rooms, there are concierge and secretarial services, and room service can be summoned around the clock. 4833 Collins Ave., Miami Beach (phone: 532-3600, 800-327-6334, 800-22DORAL, or 800-FORATAN in Florida; fax: 305-534-7409). Very expensive.

Doral Saturnia Spa – Adjacent to the *Doral Country Club,* the spa evokes the feeling of its ancient namesake in Tuscany through clay tile roofs and Roman arches, yet the equipment is thoroughly 20th century. Each of its 48 suites has its own whirlpool bath, but that's only the beginning. There's everything needed by those in search of enhanced fitness, health, and stress management (see *Sybaritic Spas* in DIVERSIONS). The Tuscan menu, based on the spa's Fat Point System of Nutrition, is served in the informal *Ristorante di Saturnia* or the luxurious *Villa Montepaldi.* All the facilities at the two previously mentioned Doral resorts are available to guests here. 8755 NW 36th St., Miami (phone: 593-6030, 800-331-7768, or 800-22DORAL; fax: 305-591-9266). Very expensive.

Fisher Island – Just off the southern tip of Miami Beach, this exclusive 216-acre island was once the Spanish-style private winter playground of William Vanderbilt. Now a private club and elite residential resort refuge, the island has extravagantly furnished apartments, villas, and a couple of historic cottages surrounded by manicured gardens with strolling peacocks. Though the cost for transient rental is significant, it's worth it to many for the island's unique serenity and distance from "the outside world." A 40-person security force ensures that privacy. Facilities include a 9-hole golf course designed by P. B. Dye — plus clubhouse and complimentary golf cart — superb tennis courts (including grass ones; see *Tennis* in DIVERSIONS), croquet, basketball, paddle tennis, elaborate European-style spa (see *Sybaritic Spas* in DIVERSIONS), an oceanfront beach, 2 marinas harboring enormous yachts, 7 restaurants (1 housed in the original Vanderbilt mansion, with marble floors and mahogany paneling), and several shops. Secretarial services are available. Accessible only by private ferry; special treatment begins as drivers exit the ferry, when cars are hosed off to remove salt spray (phone: 535-6030 or 800-624-3251; fax: 305-535-6008). Very expensive.

Grand Bay – Run by the Aga Khan's CIGA chain and done in truly high style, this 181-room property overlooks Biscayne Bay and is Miami's most elite hotel. There are 3 restaurants, including the famed *Grand Café,* open daily from 7AM to 11PM (see *Eating Out*); 2 lounges; and an outdoor pool and hot tub. There's 24-hour room service, as well as 3 meeting rooms, a concierge desk (where check-in begins with a mimosa cocktail of champagne and fresh-squeezed orange juice), and afternoon tea served in the elegantly furnished lobby. There also are secretarial services. The health club is open 24 hours daily, and the hotel provides limo service to the *Mayfair Health Club.* 2669 S. Bayshore Dr., Coconut Grove (phone: 858-9600 or 800-327-2788, 800-341-0809 in Florida; fax: 305-859-2026). Very expensive.

Mayfair House – This all-suite hotel, part of the *Mayfair Mall* complex in the heart of Coconut Grove, has 182 suites, each with a Jacuzzi (in some cases on a terrace), and a small dining area where a complimentary continental breakfast (with lots of tropical fruit) is served each morning. Suites are beautifully decorated in dark woods and calming tones that accentuate eye-appealing angles of the architectural design; 50 boast antique pianos and all include VCRs, marble bathrooms, and 2 phones. The lobby boasts two original Tiffany windows. Dining and/or drinking options include the highly regarded *Mayfair Grill* (see *Eating Out*), 2 lounges, and a bar at the rooftop pool with view of the bay. Other conveniences include a concierge and secretarial services, 3 meeting rooms, and express checkout. 3000 Florida Ave., Coconut Grove (phone: 441-0000, 800-433-4555, or 800-341-0809 in Florida; fax: 305-447-9173). Very expensive.

Sheraton Bal Harbour – Located in the exclusive Bal Harbour area, this 650-room property sits within a lushly landscaped 10-acre garden leading directly to the ocean. Enticements include 2 outdoor pools, 2 tennis courts, a jogging path along the beach, exercise equipment, volleyball, a vita exercise course on the beach, water sports, and a gameroom. For sipping and supping, there are *The Twenties,* a steak and seafood restaurant with open-hearth kitchen, an enlarged coffee shop that's open all day, an oceanside snack and drink bar, 3 lounges, and the *Brown Bag,* a 24-hour take-out deli. The *Crystal Ballroom* no longer offers Vegas-style reviews, but often spotlights big-name entertainers. For the business-minded, there's a concierge and business center with copy and facsimile machines, plus computer hookups, and 23 meeting rooms. Directly across the street are the elegant *Bal Harbour Shops,* with tenants such as *Neiman Marcus, Saks Fifth Avenue, Martha, Cartier, Brooks Brothers,* and *F.A.O. Schwarz.* 9701 Collins Ave., Bal Harbour (phone: 865-7511 or 800-325-3535; fax: 305-864-2601). Very expensive.

Sonesta Beach – On the beach at Key Biscayne, this top class resort's facilities include a tennis club with 10 Laykold courts (3 lighted) and instruction by two pros, an Olympic-size swimming pool, a fitness center, outdoor whirlpool bath, bike rentals, and "Just Us Kids," an extensive children's program for ages 5 to 13. In addition to the 300 rooms, there also are 4 restaurants, including the double-headed Oriental *Two Dragons* (see *Eating Out*), 4 lounges (*Desires* features live entertainment), and villas with 2 to 5 bedrooms. Included in the amenities are 24-hour room service, secretarial assistance, 12 meeting rooms, and express checkout. 350 Ocean Dr., Key Biscayne (phone: 361-2021 or 800-SONESTA; fax: 305-361-3096). Very expensive.

Hyatt Regency Coral Gables – A smaller property than its sister *Hyatt* and much more beautiful, this one has 242 rooms (half are nonsmoking) in Spanish-Mediterranean style influenced by the Alhambra Palace, an outdoor pool, a Jacuzzi, and health club. The *Two Sisters* restaurant features Spanish-Mediterranean cuisine, with a landscaped courtyard for outdoor dining (see *Eating Out*), and the *Alcazaba* disco swings. Meeting rooms and express checkout accommodate business types who flock here. 50 Alhambra Plaza, Coral Gables (phone: 441-1234 or 800-233-1234; fax: 305-441-0520). Very expensive to expensive.

Miami Airport Hilton – Located on a lagoon at the airport (natch), the 500-room hostelry offers a pool, a Jacuzzi, a sauna, jet- and water-ski rentals, and 24-hour free use of 3 lighted tennis courts; they'll even lend you a racquet. There's also a café and a bar. 5101 Blue Lagoon Dr., Miami (phone: 262-1000 or 800-445-8667; fax: 305-267-0038). Very expensive to expensive.

Sheraton Royal Biscayne Beach – Reminiscent of early Bahamian hotels and a favorite among Europeans, this pink low-rise complex (2 to 4 stories) focuses on its quarter-mile oceanfront and water sports. Besides the 192 rooms, there are 17 lanai suites with full kitchens. Amenities include 2 pools with bars and musical entertainment, a lounge, a semi-enclosed informal eatery, and the *Caribbean Room,* featuring seafood, especially at its Friday night buffet. There also are 10 Laykold tennis courts, 4 night-lit, and free tennis clinics. 555 Ocean Dr., Key Biscayne (phone: 361-5775 or 800-325-3535; fax: 305-361-0360). Very expensive to expensive.

Turnberry Isle – On the Intracoastal Waterway in North Miami, this 300-acre island resort complex offers superb marina facilities, along with major golf, tennis, and spa attractions. The country club, marina, and yacht hotels boast a combined 361 rooms and suites. The marina moors up to 117 boats at a maximum of 150 feet, including the new 140-foot *Miss Turnberry,* available for charter at $12,000 per day! There are 5 pools and a beach, which is reachable by complimentary shuttle, plus 2 championship golf courses and 24 tennis courts. The *Veranda* restaurant is open only to members and registered guests (see *Eating Out*); there also are 4 other restaurants and 5 lounges, one of which is a disco. For business guests, there is a helipad, 24-hour room service, expanded meeting facilities, in-room whirlpool baths, and dual-line phones to meet most guests' communications needs. 19999 W. Country Club Dr., Aventura (phone: 932-6200 or 800-327-7028; fax: 305-937-0528). Very expensive to expensive.

Biscayne Bay Marriott – On the marina, it offers 623 rooms on 31 floors; half the rooms have a view of the bay. The brass and marble lobby is comfortably welcoming, and the 2 restaurants serve fresh seafood. A third-floor skybridge connects the building to the *Omni International* shopping and hotel complex. Room service is available until midnight. In addition, there's a concierge desk, 4 meeting rooms, secretarial services, and express checkout. 1633 N. Bayshore Dr., Key Biscayne (phone: 374-3900 or 800-228-9290; fax: 305-375-0597). Expensive.

Don Shula's – Miami *Dolphins* head coach Don Shula is a partner in this newly opened property on the former site of the *Miami Lakes Inn* in northwest Dade County. There are 200 rooms and 100 suites in a contemporary decor; the *Don Shula Golf Course* is a mile away. A nonsmoking floor and a hospitality floor, both offering complimentary breakfast, are available. As you might expect, sports are featured here: For golfers, there's an 18-hole championship course, an 18-hole executive course, and a lighted driving range; tennis buffs can play on 5 clay and 4 hard-surface courts, all lighted, and 7 racquetball courts. Basketball, volleyball, and aerobics classes provide more perspiration prospects. Add 2 pools, 3 Jacuzzis, and 5 restaurants (including *Shula's Steak House*) and lounges to fill out the scorecard. Main St., Miami Lakes (phone: 821-1150 or 800-24-SHULA for reservations; fax: 305-821-1150). Expensive.

Fontainebleau Hilton – This famous Miami Beach landmark, on 18 acres of beachfront real estate, is far more glitzy than glamorous. The lagoon-like pool has a grotto bar inside a cave, and there are 12 restaurants and lounges, as well as a kosher kitchen. The *Dining Galleries* restaurant is especially popular for Sunday brunch and continental dinner (see *Eating Out*). Amenities include a fully equipped spa (see *Sybaritic Spas* in DIVERSIONS); 1,206 rooms; and 7 tennis courts. Twenty-four-hour room service, concierge and secretarial services, and express checkout also are offered. 4441 Collins Ave., Miami Beach (phone: 538-2000, 800-HILTONS, or 800-548-8886 in Florida; fax: 305-534-7821). Expensive.

Inter-Continental Miami – Built in the grand old hotel tradition, this property is in the city center, near the Brickell Avenue financial district and *Bayside Market-place*. The 646 rooms in the soaring 34-floor travertine triangle have marble baths and Oriental furniture, along with other luxurious appointments. President George Bush and actor Eddie Murphy have stayed in the 2-story Royal Suite. The lobby, with its 18-foot Henry Moore sculpture, is done in beige and bone travertine marble, accented with green rattan furniture and area rugs. Facilities include the highly regarded *Le Pavillon Grill* (see *Eating Out*) and 2 other restaurants, a lounge, a swimming pool, 2 lighted tennis courts, and 2 air conditioned racquetball courts, plus a quarter-mile outdoor jogging trail that takes advantage of the stunning views of Biscayne Bay. Stores include a duty-free shop. There are 3 nonsmoking floors, 25 meeting rooms, and a 200-seat auditorium. There's also a concierge desk, secretarial services, and 24-hour room service. Parking arrangements are less than ideal; guests have been known to wait as long as an hour for their cars to be tracked down in the garage and delivered to them. 100 Chopin Plaza, Miami (phone: 577-1000, or 800-327-0200; fax: 305-577-0384). Expensive.

Marlin – This recently renovated addition to the Art Deco district combines 1930s architecture with 1990s amenities in 11 units, which include central air conditioning, TV sets with VCRs, and kitchens. The *Shabeen* restaurant serves West Indian food. 1200 Collins Ave., Miami Beach (phone: 673-8770). Expensive.

Miami Mariott Dadeland – New at this 303-room South Miami establishment are 38 rooms equipped with state-of-the-art systems purifying the air and water (especially popular among guests suffering from allergies). Facilities include an outdoor pool with sauna, a whirlpool bath, exercise and gamerooms, meeting rooms, and complimentary shuttle service to Miami International Airport and the *Dadeland Mall*. There's a restaurant, a lounge, and *Coconut's Comedy Club* (Wednesday through Saturday nights). Concierge floor includes complimentary breakfast. 9090 S. Dadeland Blvd., Miami (phone: 663-1035 or 800-228-9290; fax: 305-666-7124). Expensive.

Sheraton Brickell Point – This comfortable hostelry overlooks Biscayne Bay, with a view of the cruise ships docked at Port Miami. Located in the financial district, it has 613 rooms and suites, an executive floor, an outdoor pool with a tiki bar, and 8 meeting rooms. *Ashley's* restaurant serves moderately priced food, open daily from 6:30AM to 11PM, and the *Coco Loco* lounge features live Latin music on Friday nights. 495 Brickell Ave., Miami (phone: 373-6000 or 800-325-3535; fax: 305-374-2279). Expensive.

Doubletree – Formerly the *Coconut Grove* hotel, it is within walking distance of Coconut Grove's attractions and within view of *Monty's,* a major marina. With 190 rooms and suites, it offers 2 lighted tennis courts, a café, complimentary shuttle service to downtown and shopping, and a pool with a bar that's a weekend hangout for local young singles. 2649 S. Bayshore Dr., Coconut Grove (phone: 858-2500 or 800-528-0444; fax: 305-858-5776). Expensive to moderate.

Occidental Parc Suite – In the heart of the Brickell Avenue business district, this 135-all-suite establishment in the former home of the *River Parc* hotel overlooks the Miami River. The Spain-based Occidental chain has invested $4 million in renovations of the lobby and guestrooms. There's an executive business center, meeting rooms, and an outdoor swimming pool. A Spanish restaurant and café in a glass-atrium setting complete the amenities. 100 SE 4th St., Miami (phone: 374-5100 or 800-521-5100; fax: 305-381-9826). Expensive to moderate.

Cavalier – Built back in 1937, this 40-room, hostelry offers TV sets, free parking, complimentary continental breakfast, with a restaurant at the nearby (and under the same ownership) *Cardozo* hotel (see *Eating Out*). 1320 Ocean Dr., Miami Beach (phone: 534-2135 or 800-338-9076; fax: 305-531-5543). Moderate.

Crown – With 250 centrally air conditioned rooms set on 500 feet of beach, this *glatt* kosher place has an Olympic-size pool, an outdoor Jacuzzi, a dining room plus a dairy bar, nightly entertainment (except on the Sabbath), a card room, a sauna, and shops. Rates include 2 meals daily, 3 on the Sabbath. There's a synagogue on the premises. 4041 Collins Ave., Miami Beach (phone: 531-5771 or 800-327 8163, 800-541-6874 in Florida; fax: 305-673-1612). Moderate.

Hyatt Regency – In the heart of downtown, this 615-room riverside hostelry is part of Miami's convention and conference complex. The top 2 floors feature Hyatt's Regency Club service, with complimentary continental breakfast, a private lounge, and other extras. Certain special rooms are reserved for the handicapped and for nonsmokers. There are 2 restaurants, the more elegant *Esplanade* featuring a continental menu. Among the business services are 24-hour room service, 30 meeting rooms, secretarial and concierge service, and express checkout. There's a small outdoor pool and guests can use the *Downtown Athletic Club* for a daily fee. An on-premises ticket office has tickets for concerts and ball games, and there's direct access to the 5,000-seat *James Knight Convention Center.* 400 SE 2nd Ave., Miami (phone: 358-1234, 800-233-1234, or 800-228-9000 in Florida; fax: 305-358-0529). Moderate.

Omni International – With 535 rooms, it's part of a 10½-acre downtown complex that includes 165 shops, 10 movie theaters, 21 restaurants, an amusement area, a sun deck, and a rooftop pool. Amenities include its outstanding *The Fish Market* (see *Eating Out*) and a less formal restaurant, 30 meeting rooms, and 24-hour room service, as well as concierge and secretarial assistance. 1601 Biscayne Blvd., Miami (phone: 374-0000 or 800-THE-OMNI; fax: 305-374-0020). Moderate.

Park Central – Located in the heart of where the action is in South Beach, this 85-room property has a pool, a restaurant, and a lounge. There's also cable TV, room service, and complimentary continental breakfast. 640 Ocean Dr., Miami Beach (phone: 538-1611; fax: 305-534-7520). Moderate.

Sofitel – A member of the French hotel chain located near the airport, this sleek property is strictly international business in flavor. It offers 285 rooms, 2 French restaurants, a French bakery, a lobby bar, a health club, a pool, a Jacuzzi, and boating on a 100-acre freshwater lake. Other amenities include 24-hour room service, a concierge desk, 8 meeting rooms, secretarial services, and express checkout. 5800 Blue Lagoon Dr., Miami (phone: 264-4888, 800-258-8888 or 800-SOFI-TEL in Florida; fax: 305-262-9079). Moderate.

Place St. Michel – Charming, cozy, and elegant describe this small European-style bed and breakfast establishment built in 1926. In the heart of Coral Gables, it's favored by international architects who appreciate its Deco details and antique furnishings. On the premises are *Stuart's,* a jazz bar, an excellent dining spot, *Restaurant St. Michel* (see *Eating Out*), and a charcuterie that's popular with the local lunch crowd. All 27 rooms are air conditioned and have TV sets. Breakfast is included; room service is available until 11 PM, and there's an obliging concierge desk. 162 Alcazar Ave., Coral Gables (phone: 444-1666 or 800-247-8526; fax: 305-529-0074). Moderate to inexpensive.

Ritz Plaza – This 1940s-style hostelry, with its much-photographed Art Deco squared finial, has been restored to its early splendor, with a soaring lobby featuring the original 4-color terrazo floor and a front desk made of coral — one of the few such pieces extant. (Protection of reefs now prohibits this kind of use.) The 133 recently redecorated rooms and suites feature central air conditioning, television sets, and modernized original cast-iron tubs. An Olympic-size pool overlooks the ocean, with water sports available a few feet away. The *Ritz Café,* a high-ceilinged dining room with a huge crystal chandelier and a round window wall facing the ocean, is open for dinner from 6:30 PM, offering standard fare; other meals are served on the terrace. *Harry's Bar* has a 1940s–1950s look, with a glass brick bar, lots of chrome, and a juke box playing 1950s music. Guests often include photography crews shooting fashion assignments nearby. 1701 Collins Ave. (near the Convention Center), Miami Beach (phone: 534-3500 or 800-522-6400; fax: 305-531-6928). Moderate to inexpensive.

Beach Paradise – This recently renovated 1929-era hostelry sits across from the beach on Ocean Drive in the Art Deco district, (see "Art Deco District" in *Quintessential Miami,* DIVERSIONS) and boasts 50 spacious rooms and suites, central air conditioning, television sets, modern plumbing, and a new sprinkler system. Corner suites offer ocean views and colorful street scenes. The *Paradise Café,* choice of many Miami power brokers, features informal indoor and outdoor dining, from breakfast to late-night snacks, while the glamorous *Beach Villa* Chinese restaurant, with 7 regional Chinese chefs imported from New York, offers daily lunch and dinner, plus weekend dim sum brunch; a take-out menu also is available. The *Underground* nightclub features music and dancing till 5 AM. 600 Ocean Dr., Miami Beach (phone: 531-0021 or 800-258-8886; fax: 305-674-0206). Inexpensive.

EATING OUT: Much of Miami socializing centers around restaurant dining, so beware long lines during the winter season (December through April), when snowbirds swell the ranks of resident regulars. Residents always make reservations. Expect to pay $85 or more for a dinner for two in the very expensive range; $70 to $80 in the expensive; $50 to $70 in the moderate; and under $50 in the inexpensive range. Prices do not include drinks, wine, or tips. Many establishments in the very expensive and expensive categories require that men wear jackets; it's wise to call ahead to inquire. All telephone numbers are in the 305 area code unless otherwise indicated.

Aragon Café – This fine hotel dining room boasts elegant Old World decor, and a menu that includes everything from exquisitely prepared Muscovy duck to humble, but oh so delicious, polenta. Don't miss the pistachio soufflé. Open for dinner 6 to 11 PM Tuesdays through Saturdays. Reservations necessary. Major credit cards accepted. 180 Aragon Ave., Coral Gables (phone: 441-2600 or 800-533-1337). Very expensive.

Café Chauveron – Transplanted many years ago from New York City to Bay Harbor without the slightest disturbance of its famous mile-high soufflés, this is an elegant French dining place in the grand manner. Everything is beautifully prepared, from *coquille de fruits de mer au champagne* (scallops in champagne) to *pompano papillote* (local fish cooked in parchment paper) to the Grand Marnier soufflé. Docking space is provided if you arrive by boat. Open daily 6 to 10:30 PM, but closed from June through early October. Reservations necessary. Major credit cards accepted. 9561 E. Bay Harbor Dr., Bay Harbor Island, Miami Beach (phone: 866-8779). Very expensive.

Dining Galleries – Frequently chosen as one of Miami's top restaurants, the Old World ambience features antiques, statues, and candelabra. Continental food includes veal and salmon scallops in a champagne-mustard sauce and Florida pompano filled with shrimp, crab, and wild mushrooms. Jackets are required for men. Open daily for dinner 6 PM to midnight, and for Sunday brunch 10 AM to 3 PM. Reservations necessary. Major credit cards accepted. 4441 Collins Ave. in the *Fontainebleau Hilton,* Miami Beach (phone: 538-2000). Very expensive.

Dominique's – Known for its exotic dishes, such as rattlesnake and alligator, it also offers excellent rack of lamb and filet of beef or veal, done in a classic manner. For dessert, try the pistachio soufflé with sabayon sauce, named for a famous patron, actor Don Johnson. Or the wonderful cheese mousse in passion-fruit sauce. The rich, gleaming wood-paneled setting is considered by many to be Miami's most romantic, especially the window table. Open from 5:30 to 11 PM Sundays through Thursdays; until midnight Fridays and Saturdays. Reservations necessary weekends and advised weekdays. Major credit cards accepted. In the *Alexander Hotel,* 5225 Collins Ave., Miami Beach (phone: 861-5252). Very expensive.

Forge – Despite a devastating fire ($20 million in damages), this elegant dining place is again open; happily, its famous 300,000-bottle wine collection was undamaged (a recently purchased 1822 Lafitte Rothschild bottle sells for $75,000!). Though smaller (now seating 175), the ornately decorated restaurant is still filled with antique furnishings, stained glass, carved ceilings, and crystal chandeliers galore. The kitchen has ditched its stodgy steaks and chops offerings for more imaginative fare. The blackened duck is not what diners might expect: free-range duck roasted with a fantastic currant and raspberry sauce. The menu also contains spa choices, such as roasted tuna with citrus and shiitake mushroom sauce. For dessert, regulars love the famed blacksmith pie — alternating layers of chocolate cake, French vanilla custard, and whipped cream — but don't bypass the apple killer — an ethereal experience. There's also a lounge with entertainment, but fortunately the noisy disco has vanished. Open daily 5 to 11:30 PM. Reservations necessary. Major credit cards accepted. 432 Arthur Godfrey Rd., Miami Beach (phone: 538-8533). Very expensive.

Grand Café – This place oozes good taste, from its European elegance and attentive service to beautifully presented dishes like rack of lamb, she-crab soup, and black linguine (made with squid ink). Follow it up with chocolate raspberry truffle cake. Famed chef Katsuo Sugiura (known as "Suki") has returned after a brief stint at Atlantic City's *Taj Mahal.* Foodies are relieved that the dining room's creations are back on track. Jackets are required for men. Open daily for breakfast 7 to 11 AM, for Sunday brunch 11:30 AM to 3 PM, and for lunch 11:30 AM to 3 PM Mondays through Saturdays; dinner daily 6 to 11 PM. Reservations are necessary for dinner, advised for breakfast and lunch. Major credit cards accepted. In the *Grand Bay Hotel,* 2669 S. Bayshore Dr., Coconut Grove (phone: 858-9600). Very expensive.

Pavillon Grill – Among the most elegant hotel dining rooms in town, featuring American dishes with a continental flavor. From lamb chops (grilled over mesquite) to *crème brûlée* with berries, it's far more than down-home cooking. The ambience complements the cuisine. Dinner from 6 to 10 PM Mondays through Thursdays, until 11 PM Fridays and Saturdays. Reservations necessary. Major credit cards accepted. In the *Inter-Continental Hotel,* 100 Chopin Plaza, Miami (phone: 577-1000). Very expensive.

Veranda – The premier dining spot at the *Turnberry Isle Yacht & Country Club* is open only to members and registered guests. In this elegant Mediterranean setting, with soft pink and gray decor, Chef Robbin Haas combines classical techniques with tropical overtones, like excellent lobster medallion salad with tiny cubes of Kent mango. His twists include Caesar salad croutons made from *foccacia* and a Key lime pie that is actually a tart. Open Mondays through Saturdays 6 to 10 PM. Reservations advised. Major credit cards accepted. 19999 W. Country Club Dr., Aventura (phone: 932-6200). Very expensive.

A Mano – The Art Deco section along Ocean Drive boasts numerous restaurants, good for informal dining and lots of local color. Most, however, are simply average, but this one, in the *Betsy Ross* hotel, rises far above the others. Award-winning chef Norman Van Aken bills his food as "New World Cooking," the style favored by South Florida's best chefs, who use contemporary American techniques married with local and Caribbean ingredients to create unique dishes. Outstanding examples are the charred venison with sautéed porcini and fried crab cakes with

Peruvian purple potato salad. Open 7 to 10 PM Tuesdays through Sundays. Reservations advised. Major credit cards accepted. 1440 Ocean Dr., Miami Beach (phone: 531-6266). Very expensive to expensive.

Ruth's Chris Steak House – This national chain is known for outstanding prime midwestern beef; seafood also is served. Guests of all ages — in all sorts of attire — dine in the warmth of wood paneling, while viewing the Intracoastal Waterway through the windows. Filet mignon is a favorite dish. Open 5 to 11 PM Mondays through Saturdays, 5 to 10 PM Sundays. Reservations advised. Major credit cards accepted. 3913 NE 163rd St., North Miami Beach (phone: 949-0100). Very expensive to expensive.

Barocco – Located in the lobby of the *Park Central* hotel, the Art Deco background provides the ambience for 1990s cookery, featuring pasta and fish dishes. Most popular are spinach ravioli and the ubiquitous tiramisu for dessert. Open sometimes for a breakfast buffet (call first to check), with lunch served daily from noon to 4:30 PM and dinner from 6:30 to 11 PM weekdays; until midnight Fridays and Saturdays. Reservations advised for dinner. Major credit cards accepted. 640 Ocean Dr., Miami Beach (phone: 538-7700). Expensive.

Brasserie Le Coze – Created by Gilbert and Maguy Le Coze, brother and sister owners of New York's *Le Bernardin,* this new French bistro has leather booths, hand-painted French and Portuguese tiles, and terrace doors that open to sidewalk tables. The menu features oysters, clams, and shrimp priced by the piece, plus stone-crab appetizers, shrimp *beignets,* grouper with aioli (garlic) sauce, and several non-aqueous-based dishes — such as duck *confit* cassoulet. Open Tuesdays through Sundays, serving lunch noon to 2:30 PM and dinner from 6 PM to midnight. Reservations advised. Major credit cards accepted. 2901 Florida Ave., Coconut Grove (phone: 444-9697). Expensive.

Cardozo – Newly reopened in the Art Deco district, the specialties of this hotel dining room include grilled tuna steaks and *penne pasta pomidoro* (quill-shape pasta with tomatoes). Eat on the broad pillared porch to people watch, or, for atmosphere, inside the former lobby, with its original aqua-and-pink terrazzo floor, mauve marble fireplace and long bar. A portrait of Supreme Court Justice Benjamin Cardozo, for whom the hotel was named, dominates the room. Open daily. Lunch is served from 11 AM to 2:30 PM; dinner, 5 PM to midnight. Reservations unnecessary. Major credit cards accepted. 1300 Ocean Dr., Miami Beach (phone: 672-5565). Expensive.

Chef Allen's – Regional South Florida cooking in a recently expanded and refurbished setting of lacquered furniture and bright neon lights, using local produce and fish like yellowtail, tuna, and snapper. Specials on the daily changing menu may include whole-wheat linguine with lobster and Florida bay scallop ceviche with cilantro. Chef Allen Susser's white chocolate bombe is as good to look at as it is to eat. There also are several spa cuisine dishes on the menu. Open daily for dinner 6 to 11 PM. Reservations advised. Major credit cards accepted. 19088 NE 29th Ave., North Miami Beach (phone: 935-2900). Expensive.

Christine Lee's Gaslight – Like the Tamarac branch near Ft. Lauderdale, the offerings here are of Szechuan, Mandarin, and Cantonese origin — and some of the best steaks in South Florida. Open daily 5 to 11 PM. Reservations advised. Major credit cards accepted. 18401 Collins Ave., Miami Beach (phone: 931-7700 or 932-1145). Expensive.

Fish Market – This is possibly South Florida's best seafood restaurant, in a pleasant atmosphere, with courteous, efficient service. Schools of fish are served grilled with a choice of sauces, but the kitchen also performs magic with specialties like the colossal shrimp — Central American crustaceans as large as baby lobster tails, yet succulent and tender. Or try sole filets stuffed with Florida lobster, mussels, and wild mushrooms. The garden of baby vegetables is crowned with an unbelievable fresh corn flan. For a tropical dessert treat, try the pâté of fruits and berries with passion-fruit sauce. Two dining rooms sparkle with marble and mirrors, but the small nonsmoking section seems an afterthought, decor-wise. Businesspeople love the "executive service" lunch, when a 2-course meal is served in less than 30 minutes or there's no charge. Open for lunch 11:30 AM to 2:30 PM Mondays through Fridays and dinner 6:30 to 11 PM Mondays through Saturdays. Reservations advised. Major credit cards accepted. In the *Omni International Hotel,* 1601 Biscayne Blvd., Miami (phone: 374-4399). Expensive.

Gatti – In Miami Beach since 1924, this family-owned place, in its original stucco house, serves Northern Italian fare and offers attentive service. Open for dinner from 5:30 to 10:30 PM; closed Mondays. Reservations advised. Major credit cards accepted. 1427 West Ave., Miami Beach (phone: 673-1717). Expensive.

Mayfair Grill – Located in the *Mayfair House* hotel in Coconut Grove, the new menu has been updated by Joachim Slichal of Los Angeles fame, adding Caribbean influences and local ingredients, including sauce of stone crab and grilled grouper. Dark Honduras mahogany contrasts with pink napery and white lace, not too feminine for many of Miami's high-powered businesspeople. Popular entrées include veal medallions with stone-crab sauce and grilled baby chicken with corn pancakes. Open daily; breakfast served from 7 to 11 AM, lunch 11 AM to 3 PM, and dinner 6 to 11 PM. Reservations advised. Major credit cards accepted. 3000 Florida Ave., Coconut Grove (phone: 441-0000). Expensive.

Mezzanotte – *The* place to see and be seen on South Beach, the action here starts late. Favorite dishes are *lombata Mezzanotte,* a veal chop with vegetables, and *zuppa di pesce* with linguine. Open daily 6 PM to midnight. Reservations accepted for six or more. Major credit cards accepted. 1200 Washington Ave., Miami Beach (phone: 673-4343). Expensive.

Reflections on the Bay – The waterfront setting is spectacular, the glass and beam structure stunning, and the food carefully prepared and artistically presented. The menu changes frequently, but always features fresh ingredients and an intriguing tropical flair. Try the gingered duck breast with Minnesota rice; peppered prawns with callaloo greens and plantains; or spicy crab cakes with lobster sauce and okra. Open daily for dinner from 6 to 11 PM, and for Sunday brunch 11 AM to 3 PM. Reservations advised. Major credit cards accepted. *Bayside Marketplace,* 401 Biscayne Blvd., Miami (phone: 371-6433). Expensive.

St. Michel – Reminiscent of a European bistro in an architecturally distinctive 1926 bed and breakfast establishment, dinner favorites here include blue crab cake on black-pepper linguine and grilled, herb-crusted swordfish. There's also a "light fare" selection. Open for breakfast weekdays, lunch and dinner Mondays through Thursdays 11 AM to 11 PM, until 1 AM Fridays and Saturdays. On Sundays, brunch with live music is served 11 AM to 2:30 PM and dinner 5 to 11 PM. Reservations advised for weekend dinners. Major credit cards accepted. 162 Alcazar Ave., Coral Gables (phone: 446-6572). Expensive.

Sencle's – Located on Lincoln Road, with indoor and terrace dining, it offers such specialties as porcini pasta and pan-seared salmon with passion-fruit glaze. Dishes lower in calories and cholesterol also are highlighted. Open for lunch Wednesdays through Fridays 11:30 AM to 2 PM; dinner daily 6 to 10 PM, Sundays 5 to 9 PM; closed Tuesdays. Reservations advised. MasterCard and Visa accepted. 630 Lincoln Rd., Miami Beach (phone: 538-7484). Expensive.

Stars & Stripes Café – This popular eatery that shares South Beach's *Betsy Ross* hotel with *A Mano* is less formal in tone, although chef Sharon Feldman performs gastronomic feats as well. Excellent creamy risotto with baby Indian River clams and duck breast ravioli accompanying duck *confit.* Open 11:30 AM to 11 PM Sundays through Thursdays and until midnight Fridays and Saturdays. Reservations necessary for dinner. Major credit cards accepted. 1440 Ocean Dr., Miami Beach (phone: 531-3310). Expensive.

Two Dragons – This hotel dining room has a split personality: One section serves Japanese food, with chefs chopping, flipping, and frying hibachi steaks and shrimp at set-in-table grills; the other serves Chinese fare, including steamed red snapper and walnut chicken, to patrons who sit in bamboo booths. Open 6 to 11 PM nightly. Reservations advised. Major credit cards accepted. 350 Ocean Dr., Key Biscayne (phone: 361-2021). Expensive.

Two Sisters – The Moorish design of the *Hyatt Regency Coral Gables* hotel is carried out in its elegant dining room. Specialties from the open kitchen include fresh fish and steaks plus more ambitious dishes, including lobster *farfalle* — lobster medallions and pasta with basil cream sauce. Sunday brunch here may be South Florida's most lavish, with countless hot and cold dishes augmented by freshly wokked Chinese foods and individual servings of duck or scallops. Open daily for breakfast from 7 to 11 AM, lunch from 11 AM until 3 PM, dinner from 6 to 11:30 PM, and Sunday brunch from 11 AM to 3 PM. Reservations advised. Major credit cards accepted. 50 Alhambra Plaza, Coral Gables (phone: 441-1234). Expensive.

Victor's Café – A branch of Manhattan's *Victor's Café 52,* this Cuban eatery has a dramatic 33-foot-high glass ceiling. Specialties include palomia steaks and yuca empanadas (grilled sirloin steaks marinated in bitter Seville orange juice and garlic with yuca-plant croquettes). Strolling guitarists except on Mondays. Open daily for lunch and dinner from noon to midnight. Reservations advised. Major credit cards accepted. 2340 SW 32nd Ave., Miami (phone: 445-1313). Expensive.

Yuca – The name derives from both a Miami acronym for Young Upscale Cuban-Americans and a starchy vegetable that is a staple of Cuban cooking. The bilingual menu features nouvelle twists on Cuban standards: black-bean soup with rice cakes, excellent yellowtail filet in plantain leaves served with crab enchiladas — dishes savored by a sophisticated international clientele. A braille menu is available. This place recently moved across the street from its original location, doubling the capacity and adding an open kitchen. Open for lunch Mondays through Fridays noon to 3 PM, dinner daily 6 to 11:30 PM. Reservations necessary. Major credit cards accepted. 177 Giralda Ave., Coral Gables (phone: 444-4448). Expensive.

Kaleidoscope – Fine dining in the Grove, in a romantic enclosed garden, on a balcony, or in air conditioned dining rooms. Favorites include the grilled swordfish and fresh fruit tarts made on the premises with almond pastry. Open daily for lunch 11:30 AM to 3 PM and for dinner Mondays through Thursdays 6 to 11 PM, Fridays and Saturdays until midnight, and Sundays 5:30 to 10:30 PM. Reservations advised. Major credit cards accepted. 3112 Commodore Plaza, Coconut Grove (phone: 446-5010). Expensive to moderate.

Mark's Place – Chef Mark Militello conjures up rich desserts and imaginative dishes such as rare tuna steaks edged with black and white sesame seeds with *wasabi* (Japanese horseradish), and a veal chop with *crimini* mushrooms. Even something as pedestrian as mozzarella cheese and tomato salad makes a creative statement, cut and stacked in a perfect square. Don't pass up the pear *tarte tatin.* Militello's designation as one of the country's top new chefs by *Food & Wine* magazine, plus a cool, post-modern interior (recently expanded and highlighting stunning contemporary Venetian glass artwork) and an unobtrusive location have made this one of the city's hottest stops. Open for lunch weekdays noon to 2:30 PM, for dinner

Mondays through Thursday 6:30 to 10:30 PM, Fridays and Saturdays 6 to 11 PM, and Sundays 6 to 10:30 PM. Reservations necessary. Major credit cards accepted. 2286 NE 123 St., North Miami Beach (phone: 893-6888). Expensive to moderate.

Beach Villa – For those visiting South Beach who tire of the same old grilled food and salads, this eatery offers fine Chinese fare in a subdued dining room with lacquered furniture. Bird's nest soup with crabmeat and sautéed conch with Chinese vegetables are specialties, along with more traditional dishes. Open 11:30 AM to 11 PM weekdays and until midnight weekends. Reservations advised. Major credit cards accepted. 600 Ocean Dr., Miami Beach (phone: 532-2679). Moderate.

Big City Fish – The Gulf Coast has been transported to South Florida in this seafood warehouse with an open kitchen serving such specialties as Florida stone crabs, shrimp broiled in cane sugar, and Apalachicola oysters — surprisingly good value for the money. The chef is imported from Mississippi, the beer from Louisiana, and the food from the whole region. We recommend the swordfish dip (smoked on the premises), seafood gumbo, and the oyster "po'boy." Open daily for lunch and dinner 11:30 AM to 11 PM, Fridays, Saturdays, and Sundays to midnight. No reservations, except for large groups. Major credit cards accepted. In *CocoWalk*, 3015 Grand Ave., Coconut Grove (phone: 445-CITY). Moderate.

La Bussola – Gleaming with mirrors and Italian Renaissance artwork, this Italian dining spot adds to the ambience with a pianist and a violinist. Selections include black linguine with calamari and roasted peppers and yellowfin tuna with black olive sauce and fried capers. Open daily for lunch from noon to 3 PM and dinner from 6 to 11:30 PM. Reservations advised. Major credit cards accepted. 270 Giralda Ave., Coral Gables (phone: 445-8788). Moderate.

Café Tanino – What with white lights twinkling overhead, mirrors, fresh flowers, and peach and white napery, it's as festive as the Venice *Carnevale* prints on the walls. The food is pan-Italian, with dishes from Sicily and Naples, as well as the north. Try the scampi prepared tableside in a Provençal sauce. Open for lunch 11:30 AM to 2:30 PM Mondays through Fridays and dinner 5 to 11 PM Mondays through Saturdays. Reservations advised. Major credit cards accepted. 2312 Ponce de León Blvd., Coral Gables (phone: 446-1666). Moderate.

Caffè Abbracci – Created by restaurateur Nino Pernetti, who also owns *Caffè Baci* (see below), specialties include tuna carpaccio, porcini risotto, and grilled salmon with a pesto and sun-dried tomato sauce. Open for lunch weekdays from 11:30 AM to 2:30 PM; dinner 6 to 11 PM Sundays through Thursdays and until midnight Fridays and Saturdays. Reservations advised. Major credit cards accepted. 318 Aragon Ave., Coral Gables (phone: 441-0700). Moderate.

Caffè Baci – Northern Italian specialties dominate at this recently redecorated place, with such dishes as jumbo shrimp sautéed with herbs and served on rappini (a leafy green vegetable similar to broccoli), and veal with roasted peppers. In the heart of Coral Gables, this is a favorite lunch spot. Open for lunch weekdays 11:30 AM to 3:30 PM; for dinner 6 to 11 PM Mondays through Thursdays and Sundays, Fridays and Saturdays until 11:30 PM. Reservations advised. Major credit cards accepted. 2522 Ponce de León Blvd., Coral Gables (phone: 442-0600). Moderate.

Casa Juancho – Country hams hang over the bar and troubadours stroll and serenade at this lively Spanish spot, thought by many to offer the best Spanish food in Little Havana's Calle Ocho neighborhood. The *parrillada en marisco* (shrimp, scallops, squid, and lobster cooked on the big open grill) is a house specialty, as are the *tapas* (hors d'oeuvres), served straight from the bar. Open daily, noon to midnight, Fridays and Saturdays until 1 AM. Reservations advised on weekends, but not accepted for after 8 PM. Major credit cards accepted. 2436 SW 8th St., Miami (phone: 642-2452). Moderate.

Charade – Continental food is featured in this charming Coral Gables landmark.

Portions are large, and an oversize salad is included in the price of an entrée. Try the grilled Norwegian salmon in caviar sauce, or the roasted leg of lamb. Open for lunch Sundays through Fridays 11:30 AM to 3 PM and for dinner daily 6 to 11 PM. Reservations advised. Major credit cards accepted. 2900 Ponce de León Blvd., Coral Gables (phone: 448-6077). Moderate.

Christy's – This place feels like a private club, with its leather armchairs, brass sconces, and dark wood — and for the pinstripe-suit types who entertain here, it practically is. The aged Iowa steaks and Caesar salad are tops; lobster, veal, duck, and chicken also are first rate. Open Mondays through Fridays 11:30 AM to 10:45 PM, Saturdays 5 to 11:45 PM, and Sundays 5 to 10:45 PM. Reservations necessary on weekends. Major credit cards accepted. 3101 Ponce de León Blvd., Coral Gables (phone: 446-1400). Moderate.

Crawdaddy's – Standard international fare (primarily seafood) served among Victoriana in 9 dining rooms in a spectacular spot. in South Pointe Park on Government Cut, where cruise ships sail out to sea seemingly within touching distance of every table. Open for lunch 11 AM to 3 PM Mondays through Saturdays, for Sunday brunch 11 AM to 3 PM, for dinner 5 to 11 PM Mondays through Thursdays, to midnight Fridays and Saturdays, and until 10 PM Sundays. Reservations advised. Major credit cards accepted. 1 Washington Ave., Miami Beach (phone: 673-1708). Moderate.

English Pub – Dismantled in England and shipped here, this place is dark, atmospheric, and . . . pubbish. Prime ribs are the specialty, along with the chef's own *tarte tatin* — an apple delight. Open daily for lunch noon to 3 PM and dinner 6 to 11:30 PM. Disco Wednesdays to Saturdays 8 PM until the wee hours. No reservations. Major credit cards accepted. 320 Crandon Blvd., Key Biscayne (phone: 361-8877). Moderate.

Joe's Stone Crab – For years this famous, old (since 1913) South Beach restaurant has been a Miami tradition, big, crowded, noisy, and friendly (get there by 6:30 or you'll have to wait). The stone crabs are brought in by *Joe's* own fishing fleet. People come here for serious eating, ordering tons of the coleslaw, hash brown potatoes, and Key lime pie that can keep dedicated diners waiting in line for up to 2 hours. (See *Quintessential Miami* in DIVERSIONS, too.) Open for lunch Tuesdays through Saturdays 11:30 AM to 2 PM and dinner daily 5 to 10 PM, until 11 PM Fridays and Saturdays; closed from mid-May to mid-October. No reservations. Major credit cards accepted. 227 Biscayne St., Miami Beach (phone: 673-0365 or 800-780-CRAB). Moderate.

Le Manoir – Well-frequented by business executives, this spot serves very good traditional French fare at reasonable prices. The big hit here is the Friday night bouillabaisse. Closed Sundays. Reservations necessary. Major credit cards accepted. 2534 Ponce de León Blvd., Coral Gables (phone: 442-1990). Moderate.

Monty Trainer's – A casual atmosphere pervades this bayside eatery in Coconut Grove. Guests can arrive either by car or boat (100 dock spaces are available for diners), then enjoy a seafood meal on a palm-fringed terrace or indoors in a more formal atmosphere with a view of the bay. Its inside, upstairs section — *Monty's Stone Crab,* serves those delectable crustaceans year-round (they're brought in from Virginia during the local off-season), as well as a wide array of fresh seafood, steaks, and pasta. Both open for lunch Sundays through Thursdays 11:30 AM to 4 PM and Fridays and Saturdays noon to 4 PM; dinner Sundays through Thursdays 5 to 11 PM and Fridays and Saturdays 5 PM to midnight. Reservations advised. Major credit cards accepted. 2550 S. Bayshore Dr., Coconut Grove (phone: 858-1431). Moderate.

Penrod's – Two lively, casual South Beach locations overlook the ocean, serving burgers, fish, chicken, ribs, and salads. Afternoon beach barbecues. Open daily 11

AM to 10 PM. Reservations unnecessary. Major credit cards accepted. 1 Ocean Dr. (phone: 538-1111) and 1001 Ocean Dr., Miami Beach (phone: 538-2604). Moderate.

Salty's – Great Intracoastal location at Haulover Inlet, with indoor and dockside dining. Fresh fish, chicken, and steaks are featured. Open daily 11:30 AM to 1 AM. Reservations advised. Major credit cards accepted. Rte. A1A north of Haulover Inlet, Miami Beach (phone: 945-5115). Moderate.

Shooters – With an Intracoastal Waterway location,. guests often arrive by boat (there's even valet parking service for vessels). Lots of fried pick-up goodies, burgers, or a Philly cheesesteak. A kiddie menu is available. Open Sundays through Thursdays 11:30 AM to midnight, Fridays and Saturdays until 1 AM. No reservations. Major credit cards accepted. 3969 NE 163rd St., North Miami Beach (phone: 949-2855). Moderate.

Strand – This Miami Beach hot spot caters to an artsy, chic clientele, and suffers from uneven service, but is still recommended for the opportunity to glimpse Miami's see-and-be-seen crowd. Try the fried goat cheese with marinara sauce, Caesar salad, and the wonderful meat loaf. Open 6 AM to midnight weekdays and until 2 AM weekends. Reservations advised on weekends. Major credit cards accepted. 671 Washington Ave., Miami Beach (phone: 532-2340). Moderate.

Sundays on the Bay – Steaks, pasta, fresh fish, and chicken head the bill at this bayside location for water watchers on Key Biscayne. Dining is inside or dockside, where lighter dishes also are available. Open Mondays through Saturdays 11:30 AM to 11:30 PM and Sundays noon to 2 AM; Sunday brunch is served 10:30 AM to 3:30 PM. Reservations necessary for dinner. Major credit cards accepted. 5420 Crandon Blvd., Key Biscayne (phone: 361-6777). Moderate.

Toni's – Japanese standards and nouvelle Tokyo fare, such as grilled salmon, chicken, steaks, and shrimp teriyaki. Their sushi is the best on South Beach. Open daily 6 PM to midnight. Reservations necessary on weekends. Major credit cards accepted. 1208 Washington Ave., Miami Beach (phone: 673-9368). Moderate.

Unicorn Village Marketplace – Outstanding natural-food restaurant and marketplace, with tables inside and outside on a marina with dockage for diners arriving by boat. Totally nonsmoking. Creative salads, low-fat and low-sodium dishes, and Tongol tuna (which presents no threat to dolphins) are featured. A large selection of by-the-glass wines includes 7 organically produced choices (with no added sulfites). Open daily for lunch from 11:30 AM to 3:30 PM and dinner from 4:30 to 9:30 PM, Fridays and Saturdays until 10 PM. Reservations advised for parties of six or more. Major credit cards accepted. At *The Shops at the Waterways,* 3595 NE 207th St., North Miami Beach (phone: 933-8829). Moderate.

East Side Mario's – A branch of a national chain located in the *Aventura Mall,* this eatery serves Italian food in an atmosphere of hanging garlic and sausages and stacks of olive-oil and Italian tomato containers. Favorites include linguine *primavera* and *tortellini alla fini,* plus pizza made in a wood-burning oven. Open Mondays through Saturdays 10:30 AM to 1 AM and Sundays until midnight. Reservations accepted for parties of eight or more. Major credit cards accepted. *Aventura Mall,* 19501 Biscayne Blvd., North Miami Beach (phone: 935-3589). Moderate to inexpensive.

Bahamas Fish Market – Fish and seafood are specialties at this "heavy on food, light on ambience" eatery. Try the lobster or fried red snapper. Open daily for lunch and dinner. No reservations. American Express accepted. 7200 SW 8th St., Miami (phone: 262-3035). Inexpensive.

Big Fish – Funky and friendly, this converted gas station on the Miami River is a popular lunchtime stop (dinner is served on Fridays only). The appeal is casual dining, a panoramic view of downtown, and fresh seafood on a menu chalked on a blackboard. Try the grouper sandwich on pita, with collard greens and black-eyed peas as accompaniments, or Portuguese squid in marinara sauce. Open Mondays through Saturdays 11 AM to 3 PM; prix fixe dinner served Fridays from 6:30 to 10 PM. Reservations advised for Friday nights only. No credit cards accepted. 55 SW Miami Ave. Rd., Miami (phone: 372-3725). Inexpensive.

Café Tu Tu Tango – In Coconut Grove's *CocoWalk* complex, this jumping eatery decked out as an artist's loft touts its Italian and Latin American fare as "food for the starving artist." It offers light, multi-ethnic dishes such as frittatas (omelettes), pizza, and kebabs. More ambitious entrées include lobster quesadillas, appetizer-sized so patrons pick and choose. Open Tuesdays through Saturdays 11:30 AM to 1:30 AM, and Sundays until midnight. No reservations. Major credit cards accepted. 3015 Grand Ave., Coconut Grove (phone: 529-2222). Inexpensive.

Centro Vasco – Next to jai alai, this is Miami's favorite Basque import. Specializes in *filet madrilene de Centro Vasco,* seafood paella, and *arroz con mariscos.* A great sangria is made right at your table. Open daily noon to midnight. Flamenco shows from 9 PM until 2 AM Wednesday to Sunday nights in *Cacharrito's Place,* a separate entertainment lounge off the dining room. Reservations advised for dinner, but not accepted for the show. Major credit cards accepted. 2235 SW 8th St., Miami (phone: 643-9606). Inexpensive.

Chez Moy – For food in the Haitian tradition, try this small eatery. Favorite dishes include steamed fish with fried plantains or fresh conch served with rice and beans. The neighborhood is a bit rough; it's a good idea to come with a group if possible. Dinner only. Open daily. Reservations advised. No credit cards accepted. 1 NW 54th St. (phone: 757-5056). Inexpensive.

Habana Viega – Touted to have the best *tostones* in all of Miami, this Spanish-style place also serves paella and, for landlubbers, good lamb shanks. Open daily for lunch and dinner. No reservations. Major credit cards accepted. 3622 SW 22nd St., Miami (phone: 448-6660). Inexpensive.

Islas Canarias – Don't be put off by the coffee-shop ambience: the food here — everything from green plantain soup to fried kingfish or roast pork with yuca — is first-rate. Open daily for lunch and dinner. No reservations. No credit cards accepted. 285 NW 27th Ave., Miami (phone: 649-0440). Inexpensive.

La Lechonera – The best pork dishes in town (the restaurant's name means "the pork place"), this eatery serves porcine parts in countless varieties: roasted, fried, pork ribs, pork steaks, and even a whole roast suckling pig. Open daily for lunch and dinner. No reservations. Major credit cards accepted. 3199 SW 8th St. at 32nd Ave., Miami (phone: 541-1500). Inexpensive.

Málaga – This traditional Cuban eatery in Little Havana is a good place to get acquainted with the island basics. Best are standards like fried whole red snapper, spiced pork, or *arroz con pollo.* A must-try is the fried plantains. Terrific flamenco shows with a young female dancer and an aging male singer start at 8 and 11:30 PM nightly, except Tuesdays. Open daily 11:30 AM to 11 PM. Reservations unnecessary. Major credit cards accepted. 740 SW 8th St., Miami (phone: 858-4224). Inexpensive.

La Mar – Another eatery in the heart of Little Havana, this casual spot specializes in seafood (meat lovers should go elsewhere). Most popular dishes include conch ceviche, octopus vinaigrette, and a super grilled seafood *parrillada.* Open daily for lunch and dinner. Reservations advised. Major credit cards accepted. 2772 SW 8th St., Miami (phone: 649-8973). Inexpensive.

Marshall Major's – Some people refer to Miami as the Bronx with palm trees. In any event, this deli ranks with New York's best — pastrami, corned beef, home-style flanken, boiled chicken and vegetables, all served in huge portions. Open daily 7 AM to 9 PM. Reservations advised on holidays. Major credit cards accepted. 6901 SW 57th Ave., Miami (phone: 665-3661). Inexpensive.

News Café – An international newsstand-cum-bookstore-cum-sidewalk café that's an ideal spot for people watching or a pre-beach breakfast. The menu is light, with sandwiches, salads, and cheeses, and an emphasis on Middle Eastern fare. Located across from the ocean in the heart of South Beach. Open daily 24 hours. Reservations unnecessary. Major credit cards accepted. 800 Ocean Dr., Miami Beach (phone: 538-6397). Inexpensive.

Palace Grill – A popular Deco district eatery serving hamburgers and salads at indoor and outdoor tables. You can get a kosher hot dog or a serving of granola. Open weekdays 8 AM to 1 AM; weekends until 3 AM. No reservations. Major credit cards accepted. 1200 Ocean Dr., Miami Beach (phone: 531-9077). Inexpensive.

Rascal House – One of only two Florida restaurants to make food guru Mimi Sheraton's list of the 50 best US restaurants (the other being *Mark's Place*). Long lines snaking into the parking lot attest to the restaurant's popularity for almost 40 years. Try the pastrami on rye or the *rugelach.* Open daily 7 AM to 2 AM. No reservations or credit cards accepted. 17190 Collins Ave., Miami Beach. (phone: 947-4581). Inexpensive.

Versailles – Authentic Cuban food and a lively ambience characterize this Little Havana landmark. A favorite of Latins and knowledgeable gringos. They make wonderful Cuban sandwiches, and there are black beans and rice. Open daily from 8 PM till the wee hours. No reservations. Major credit cards accepted. 3555 SW 8th St., Miami (phone: 444-7614). Inexpensive.

Wolfie's – A Miami Beach institution since 1947, it might be described as an overgrown deli whose eclectic, 500-item menu carries everything from knishes to chicken parmesan and mountainous desserts. Open 24 hours daily. No reservations or credit cards accepted. 2038 Collins Ave., Miami Beach (phone: 538-6626). Inexpensive.

FT. LAUDERDALE

For many Americans, the mere mention of Ft. Lauderdale immediately conjures up images of the 1960 movie *Where the Boys Are* (or its 1980s rcmake), which immortalized the seasonal migration of the nation's college students to Ft. Lauderdale during spring break in search of sun and fun. The annual migration has diminished, however; city leaders have discouraged that much-reported rite of spring in order to improve Ft. Lauderdale's overall appeal to adults and to expand family tourism — and because of the injuries (and occasional deaths) that occurred because of excessive drinking.

It seems to have worked. Collegians now seem to have set their springtime compasses to Daytona Beach while Mom, Dad, and the kids populate Ft. Lauderdale's beaches. And with good reason: Ft. Lauderdale claims to receive 3,000 hours of sunshine a year — more than anywhere else in the continental US — and the year-round average temperature is in the mid-70s. And the city's public relations people would like it known that Ft. Lauderdale has never ever recorded a 100-degree temperature.

In addition to its benign climate, Ft. Lauderdale's proximity to the water has formed its character as a prime resort area. The city is virtually afloat. It (and surrounding Broward County) is bordered on the east by 23 miles of Atlantic Ocean coastline and beaches, on the west by that "river of grass," the Everglades. Between the two are 300 miles of the navigable Intracoastal Waterway and an intricate network of canals that have led to Ft. Lauderdale's nickname, the "Venice of America." Relaxed and informal, Ft. Lauderdale is best enjoyed in shorts and sandals, except at night, when things are a touch more formal.

While other resort areas count only their visitors, the Ft. Lauderdale area also counts boats. More than 40,000 are permanently registered, and 10,000 or so more join their ranks during the winter months, as the yachting crowd from as far away as Canada cruises down to the area's warm waters. (Author John D. MacDonald's readers will recognize the Bahia Mar Yacht Basin as the place where Travis McGee, the laid-back sleuth moors his houseboat, the *Busted Flush.*) Moreover, thousands of smaller craft — sailboats and power-boats — knife through these waters throughout the year. Even the *Christmas* holiday is celebrated in special Ft. Lauderdale fashion. Hundreds of elaborately decorated and lighted boats and yachts take to the Intracoastal Waterway for the unusual *Winterfest Boat Parade* from Port Everglades to Pompano Beach. Every available waterfront viewing point is packed to watch waving Santas navigate their water-sleighs past crowded bridges, backyards, and hotel balconies.

The city is named after Major William Lauderdale, who arrived in 1838 to quell the Seminole Indians and build a fort on the New River amidst mosquito-infested, inhospitable mangrove swamps. The door for development first opened during the late 1890s, when the entrepreneur Henry Flagler began extending his *Florida East Coast Railroad* south from Palm Beach. (For more information on Palm Beach, see *Tour 7: Palm Beach* in DIRECTIONS.) A swamp drainage and reclamation project was undertaken in 1906, and canals were dug to create "finger islands," thus maximizing the city's waterside real estate. Ft. Lauderdale was incorporated in 1911, and has welcomed millions of visitors ever since.

Today, Ft. Lauderdale is the largest — and by far the best known — of the 28 municipalities that constitute Broward County, the second most populous of Florida's 67 counties. The permanent population of just over 1.2 million swells each winter season as 4.5 million tourists pour in. To these guests, Ft. Lauderdale and vicinity offer a wide choice of places to stay, from tiny motels to huge luxury hotels and sumptuous resorts; more than 30,000 rooms for visitors can be found in the five major oceanfront communities. Even the most demanding diner will find satisfaction in one of the area's more than 2,500 restaurants, while its many nightclubs, discos, and theaters provide diversion of an evening. And in the sun-splashed daytime, those who tire of frolicking on the beach may work out on the approximately 76 golf courses and 550 tennis courts.

But Ft. Lauderdale is not just sunshine and surf. It's also a bustling commercial city, and its pride, Port Everglades, is one of the nation's busiest cargo and passenger ports. Near Port Everglades on the Intracoastal Waterway, the nearly $50-million Greater Ft. Lauderdale/Broward County Convention Center opened in the fall of 1991. The center is part of a proposed 33-acre complex, which will include a hotel, restaurants, and offices to be completed this year.

City leaders also recently undertook a $670-million refurbishment and expansion of Ft. Lauderdale's downtown core, and a number of high-rise office buildings have sprung up, attracting new business. Near those structures, on the New River, sits an impressive $50-million performing arts center, which makes up the heart of the city's arts and science district. Across the street is the newest addition, the $30.6-million *Museum of Discovery and Science,* with everything from hands-on exhibits to a 5-story IMAX theater seating 300. A lushly landscaped path has been constructed along the New River, which connects the arts center to the historic district on Las Olas Boulevard.

Furthermore, the cities that make up the greater Ft. Lauderdale area are a diverse lot: Davie, whose residents prefer jeans and cowboy boots and hats, is one of the most "western" towns this side of the Pecos; it has dozens of farms, stables, saloons, country stores, and even a weekly rodeo. In Hollywood, there's a Seminole Indian Reservation, as well as a French-Canadian flavor on the Broadwalk. Hallandale is the home of the well-known *Gulfstream Race Track.* Dania, whose name reflects its early Danish settlers, is now called "the antiques center of the South," in recognition of its proliferation of antiques shops. Stretching away to the west of Ft. Lauderdale are 3,700 fertile acres of fruit and vegetable farms, adding an agricultural side to the city's personality.

As more and more people discover its enviable lifestyle, the area continues to grow and evolve. Current plans are underway to perform a major face-lift on "The Strip," the formerly popular site for spring break, which is expected to include a blueprint for a beachside promenade, upscale shops, and at least one 500-room hotel. Progress has its price, however, and ecologists already are sounding alarms as developers draw closer and closer to the last available land — the eastern fringe of the Everglades.

FT. LAUDERDALE AT-A-GLANCE

 SEEING THE CITY: The most commanding view of this area is available from the *Pier Top Lounge* of the 17-story *Pier 66* hotel (2301 SE 17th St.; phone: 525-6666). As the lounge makes one complete revolution each 66 minutes, a sweeping panorama unveils vistas of the Atlantic Ocean and its beaches to the east, Port Everglades and Ft. Lauderdale International Airport to the south, the city's many canals, sprawling suburbs, and the Everglades to the west, and more canals and the Intracoastal Waterway, leading north to Palm Beach County.

Walking Tours – The Ft. Lauderdale Historical Society conducts 3-hour walking tours of the historical district, where participants learn about the Seminole Wars and early 19th-century farms and trading posts along the then-inhospitable New River (phone: 463-4431). Individual tours are also offered by history professor Dr. Paul S. George (phone: 858-6021).

Boat Tours – Ft. Lauderdale is most easily and attractively seen by boat. One cruise vessel that plies the canals and river is the *Jungle Queen* (at the Bahia Mar Yacht Basin on Rte. A1A; phone: 462-5596). This boat, which offers 3-hour sightseeing tours twice daily, also takes riders down to Miami twice weekly for shopping sprees. The *Carrie-B* (docked behind the *Pantry Pride* supermarket on Las Olas Blvd. and SE 5th Ave.; phone: 768-9920), runs 1½-hour trips on the New River down to Port Everglades. *Entertainer Cruises* (Port Everglades Convention Center, Port Everglades Berth 1A; phone: 524-2322 or 800-537-2789) offers trips with a theme: sailing and shopping, murder-mystery tours, starlight dining, and Broadway at Sea, plus evening sightseeing trips.

Water taxis (1900 SE 15th St.; phone: 565-5507) are a popular way to travel from restaurant to hotel along the New River. Yellow and green boats operate on demand daily from 10 AM until the wee hours, covering 80 landings. Some taxis are open-air boats; the newer vessels are larger and air conditioned. A guided tour of the historic New River departs every Saturday morning at 10:30 from the *Guest Quarters* hotel (2670 E. Sunrise Blvd.; phone: 565-3800). Weekday 6-hour combination tours (charters only, for groups of 40 or more; make arrangements through *Gray Line* bus company) begin with guest pickup at hotels and proceed to a 1-hour cruise aboard the *Super Taxi* along the New River, where you'll spot the fabulous homes of several well-known personalities, including H. Wayne Huizenga (owner of the new Florida *Marlins* base-ball team) and actor Lee Majors. The tour includes lunch at either the *Chart House* restaurant or the *Riverside* hotel restaurant, a walking tour of the historic area, and delivery of guests back at their hotels. Another tour includes shopping on elegant Las Olas Boulevard. Reservations are required 2 weeks in advance (phone: 587-8080).

Tram Tours – Another wonderful way to sightsee is aboard the open-air *South Florida Trolley Tram Tour*, which winds its way through both the new and older sections of Ft. Lauderdale. Passengers can get on and off all day long, or stay put for the 1½-hour tour. There's a trolley booth on Route A1A, south of Las Olas Boulevard (832 Military Rd.; phone: 426-3044), where you can get tickets for the tram tours and other events as well. Also offered are visits to the *Swap Shop* and *Sawgrass Mills.* For further information call 768-0700. *Trolley World Tours* picks up cruise ship passengers at the pier in Port Everglades, offering shopping excursions and a 2½-hour city tour in conjunction with the *South Florida Trolley Tram* (phone: 463-8550).

Hot-Air Balloon – *Rohr Balloons* literally gives passengers a bird's-eye view of Ft. Lauderdale. The balloons fly twice daily, with boarding at the Ft. Lauderdale Executive Airport, Hangar A-1. Cost is $150 per adult, $125 per child ages 7 to 12 for a 1-hour flight (6000 NW 28th Way; phone: 491-1774 or 371-9410 from Dade County).

SPECIAL PLACES: The best way to get around Ft. Lauderdale is by car. It's a sprawling city and there's a lot to see, in all directions.

Port Everglades – Because it has the deepest water of any port between Norfolk, Virginia, and New Orleans, Port Everglades is a natural magnet for cargo ships and the marine outfitting business, as well as for luxury cruise ships. In fact, it's the world's second-largest cruise port, after Miami. Port Everglades is a convenient gateway to the Caribbean, the Gulf of Mexico, and the Panama Canal. Thanks to the remodeling of former warehouses and to new construction, the port today presents an attractive appearance, with some of its eight passenger terminals painted in a striking, bold design. The $50-million Greater Ft. Lauderdale/Broward County Convention Center occupies the northern end of the grounds, with major expansion planned. The port presently has one restaurant, *Burt & Jack's* (Berth 23, Port Everglades; phone: 522-5225), co-owned by Burt Reynolds. While there are no organized tours, visitors are free to roam around the port (except in the secured areas) from 8 AM to 6 PM. State Rd. 84, east of US 1 (phone: 523-3404).

Business travelers and vacationers often combine an area visit with a cruise. A few ships make Port Everglades their home port, offering several options for day cruises (see DIVERSIONS). Cruise lines offering ships with varied itineraries that sail from Port Everglades include *Admiral Cruises* (phone: 800-327-0271), *Celebrity Cruises* (phone: 800-437-3111), *Costa Cruises* (phone: 358-7330 or 800-462-6782), *Crystal Cruises* (phone: 800-446-6645), *Cunard Line* (phone: 800-221-4770), *Discovery Cruises* (phone: 305-525-7800 or 800-937-4477), *Holland America Line* (phone: 800-426-0327), *Princess Cruises* (phone: 800-344-2626), *Royal Caribbean Cruises* (phone: 800-327-6700 or 800-432-6559 in Florida), *SeaEscape* (phone: 800-432-0900), and *Sun Line* (phone: 800-872-6400).

Museum of Discovery and Science – The features of this new 85,000-square-foot museum include a 5-story IMAX screen and such exhibits as walk-through simulated Florida habitats, a laser pinball, and a human gyroscope. There is a cafeteria and a museum store on the premises. Tours are offered of the nearby *King-Cromartie House,* a restored turn-of-the-century residence replete with antiques and set on the New River. Across from the *Broward Center for the Performing Arts.* Closed Mondays. Admission charge. 431 SW 2nd St. (phone: 462-4115).

Everglades Holiday Park – Savor what the famed ecological area is all about by bird watching — you might even spot some American bald eagles — on a narrated airboat ride. You'll see the gold-colored sawgrass and nesting alligators, as well as some of the most beautiful birds Mother Nature has ever created. Your tour guide will give you a healthy respect for the power of alligator jaws, even on the seemingly cute young ones. Alligators can live up to 100 years if they manage to come out on top of most of their battles. There are special tours offering insights into the lives of Seminole Indians, a group of Native Americans whose history is little known outside this region. If you're feeling adventurous, rent a boat or an RV for a closer experience with nature. There's also a campground here. Open daily 6 AM to 6 PM; airboat rides conducted daily 9 AM to 5 PM. There's no admission charge to the park, but a fee is charged for airboat rides. 21940 Griffin Rd. (phone: 434-8111).

Flamingo Gardens – This 60-acre botanical garden has a flamingo exhibit (natch), a tropical plant house, a museum about the Everglades, orange groves, alligators, crocodiles, and river otters. A guided tram tour takes visitors through the groves and wetlands and through an indigenous hardwood hammock (a raised area of dense tropical vegetation) with stands of oak, gumbo-limbo, and fig trees. A new screened-in aviary re-creates several native settings — including a mangrove swamp and a sawgrass prairie — for those who can't get out to the Everglades; throughout the groves are free-flying local birds, including cormorants and ospreys. There's also a snack bar, a gift shop with nature books and crafts, and a produce stall for purchasing and shipping citrus fruit. Open daily 9 AM to 5 PM. Admission charge. 3750 Flamingo Rd., Davie (phone: 473-0010).

Loxahatchee Everglades Tours – Visitors to northern Broward County again can participate in an easy airboat trip through the Everglades without traveling great distances to the south. These airboats provide overhead protection from the sun, ramps for easy boarding of the handicapped, and improved techniques for muffling the engine noises. Passengers skim over the "river of grass," spotting alligators and their babies in nests, plus myriad wild fowl such as gallinules. There's a snack shop at the park. Open daily 9 AM to 5 PM. Admission charge to the park. Admission charge for airboat rides. From Rte. 441 take Lox Rd. (between Hillsboro Blvd. and Palmetto Park Rd.), then drive 6 miles west to the Everglades (phone: 800-683-5873).

Sawgrass Mills Mall – This 2.2 million-square-foot complex features talking alligators and continuously running videos. Billed as the world's largest outlet mall, this discount shopping complex boasts anchor stores including *Saks Fifth Avenue, Macy's, Sears, Marshalls,* and *Spiegel's* — and 200 specialty shops. Among the temptations are an *Ann Taylor* clearance center and a *Joan & David* shoe outlet. Open Mondays through Saturdays 10 AM to 9:30 PM, Sundays 11 AM to 6 PM. 12801 W. Sunrise Blvd., Sunrise (phone: 846-1000 or 800-FL-MILLS).

Swap Shop – The largest flea market in the South, with 2,000 vendors, this is *the* place to find bargains on everything from electronic equipment to tomatoes. There also are concerts and a circus to amuse the children and to help the mind clear between purchases. There are two locations in Broward: 3291 W. Sunrise Blvd. (phone: 791-SWAP) and 1000 N. State Rd. 7, Margate (phone: 971-SWAP).

Butterfly World – A refuge for butterflies where visitors can walk among the multicolored creatures fluttering freely in a re-created jungle atmosphere. These beauties are seen in all their stages of life, from larvae and pupae to cocoons and full adulthood. Certain species are attracted to light-colored clothing and certain scents; if you've spent a hot morning in traffic or sightseeing, you may find yourself converted into a temporary perch. This 3-acre habitat has butterflies from all over the world, and a spectacular museum of mounted insects. Open daily. Admission charge. 3600 W. Sample Rd., Coconut Creek (phone: 977-4400).

Atlantis the Water Kingdom – This 65-acre water theme park has a 6-story slide tower and 9 water slides, a 500,000 gallon wave pool, and a small golf course. Slide fans claim that one of the slides here is the fastest in Florida. There are 100 lifeguards on duty, and a special kiddie area features small-scale attractions and a game show teaching water safety. Open March through October with varying hours. Reservations necessary 48 hours in advance. Admission charge. 2700 Stirling Rd., Hollywood (phone: 926-1000).

Hugh Taylor Birch State Recreation Area – Just across the street from the beach is this lush, tropical park, with 180 acres ideal for picnicking, playing ball, canoeing, biking, paddleboating, and hiking. The park is protected from development, so it will always remain a beautiful spot in the midst of the beach area hubbub. Open daily. Admission charge. 3109 E. Sunrise Blvd. (phone: 564-4521).

John U. Lloyd Beach State Recreation Area – Many Ft. Lauderdale residents consider this to be *the* place for picnicking, swimming, fishing, canoeing, and other recreation. There are 244 acres of beach, dunes, mangrove swamp, and hammock. Park rangers lead nature walks during winter months. Open daily. Admission charge. 6503 N. Ocean Dr., Dania (phone: 923-2833).

Ocean World – All the requisite aquatic creatures — sharks, alligators, sea lions, turtles, and dolphins — are featured here in continuous 2½-hour water shows. Visitors enjoy watching the dolphins show off in Davy Jones's Locker, a 3-story circular tank or the more than 40 sharks, sea turtles, and fish in the Shark Moat. Boat tours and deep-sea fishing also are available. Open daily. Admission charge. 1701 SE 17th St. (phone: 525-6611).

Hollywood Broadwalk – A 2.5-mile, 24-foot-wide concrete ocean promenade bordered by a bicycle path and lined with inexpensive outdoor cafés often featuring contemporary music. Bikes may be rented at various sites on the Broadwalk, and there's often free music and dancing (jitterbug and polka are favorites) at the bandstand on Monday nights. This area has a French Canadian flavor — a preponderance of snowbirds and vacationers hail from Quebec — and half the promenade signs are in French. Lifeguard stations are manned all year from 10 AM to 4 PM.

Stranahan House – One of the area's oldest museums — the restored 1913 home and Indian trading post of early settler Frank Stranahan. It's hard to imagine the Ft. Lauderdale of those days, but a tour of this house provides some idea of the hardships early settlers had to endure against nature and the hostile Seminole. Open Wednesdays, Fridays, and Saturdays. Admission charge. 1 Stranahan Pl. at Las Olas Blvd. and the New River Tunnel (phone: 524-4736).

Bonnet House – Built in the 1920s as a family retreat, this 36-acre private estate is one of the few remaining wildlife areas on the oceanfront in South Florida. The 2-story house and grounds have been preserved. Tours are offered. Open from May through November. Admission charge. 900 N. Birch Rd. (phone: 563-5393).

International Swimming Hall of Fame – Many of the world's top swimming and diving competitions are held here, but its Olympic-size pools are open to the public when there's no meet scheduled. The adjoining museum, which also recently received a face-lift, houses unusual aquatic memorabilia from more than 100 countries. Open daily. Admission charge. 1 Hall of Fame Dr. (phone: 462-6536).

Topeekeegee Yugnee Park – With 40 acres, this is one of the area's larger parks. Visitors can enjoy all kinds of activities — swimming, boating, canoeing, picnicking, barbecuing, hiking, biking, and water sliding. Open daily. Admission charge on weekends and holidays. 3300 N. Park Rd., just off I-95, Hollywood (phone: 985-1980).

Seminole Indian Reservation – The Native Village includes a museum, gift shop for Indian arts and crafts, demonstrations of alligator wrestling, and snake and turtle shows. The museum gives an interesting glimpse into a little-known native group. The Seminole gave up their lands reluctantly and never did sign a treaty with the United States. Although bingo games for profit are not legal in Florida, they're allowed here on the reservation. The bingo hall holds up to 1,400 people, and often is full; winners have pocketed as much as $110,000 in a single game. There's an admission charge for the village and another for the bingo hall, which includes four bingo cards. Both are open daily. The village is at 3551 N. State Rd. 7, Hollywood (phone: 961-4519); the bingo hall is at 4150 N. State Rd. 7, Hollywood (phone: 961-3220). For more information, see *Tour 6: Cowboy and Indian Tour* in DIRECTIONS.

Goodyear Blimp – Though tourists may not go for a ride in the blimp (it's only for corporate clients), it's spotted so frequently in the skies above that most people are curious. You can, however, visit the "Spirit of Akron" at its hangar in Pompano Beach and see the 205.5-foot-long blimp up close. Call to see when it's berthed here. Open at varied times November to May. No admission charge. 1500 NE 5th Ave., Pompano Beach (phone: 946-8300).

■ **EXTRA SPECIAL:** To fully experience the tropical beauty and laid-back ambience that is Ft. Lauderdale, drive east on Las Olas Boulevard past its chic boutiques and palm-lined streets. Continue through the Isles of Las Olas area, which is laced with canals and filled with fancy homes nestled among royal palm trees. Large, luxurious boats are docked outside many of the homes. Look up and you may spot some of the red and blue parrots that nest here; some claim they're native to the area; others say that they were visitors who liked the neighborhood and stayed. Proceed on past the sailboat cove, where towering masts grope for the blue sky, and cruise over the small bridge to Route A1A, along the Atlantic Ocean. Drive north, and around 4 PM, stop at one of the hotel patio bars facing the ocean for a cocktail with the "end of the day" beach people. In an hour or so, the beach will become nearly deserted, yet the ocean is filled with the multicolored sails of boats returning to safe harbor, and cruise and cargo ships steaming out to distant corners of the world. Take off your shoes, walk along the sand at the water's edge — and let the images soak in.

LOCAL SOURCES AND RESOURCES

TOURIST INFORMATION: The Greater Ft. Lauderdale Convention & Visitors Bureau is in an easily accessible pink high-rise downtown (200 E. Las Olas Blvd.; Ft. Lauderdale, FL 33301; phone: 765-4466). Stop in or call for information on accommodations, activities, attractions, sports, dining, shopping, touring, and special events. The Broward County arts and entertainment hotline (phone: 357-5700) is updated weekly and provides recorded schedules of events and additional sources of information about visitor attractions. Contact the Florida state hotline (904-487-1462) for maps, calendars of events, health updates, and travel advisories.

Local Coverage – The *Fort Lauderdale Sun-Sentinel,* a morning daily, carries the following week's events in its Showtime section on Fridays; the monthly *South Florida* magazine lists cultural events and restaurants.

Television Stations – WPBS Channel 2–public television; WTVJ Channel 4–NBC; WCIX Channel 6–CBS; WSVN Channel 7–Fox; WPLG Channel 10–ABC.

Radio Stations – AM: WEAT 850 (easy listening); WINZ 940 (news/talk). FM: WTMI 93.1 (classical music); WZTA 94.9 (classic rock); WFLC 97.3 (soft rock); WKIS 99.9 (country); WLYF 101.5 (easy listening); WSHE 103.5 (album rock); WJQY 106.7 (easy listening).

TELEPHONE: The area code for Ft. Lauderdale is 305.

SALES TAX: The city sales tax is 6½%; there also is a 3% Broward County hotel tax.

GETTING AROUND: Bus – *Broward County Transit* serves most of the area. Weekly passes are available at hotels. For information, call 357-8400.

Car Rental – Ft. Lauderdale is served by all the major national firms, two of which have their corporate headquarters in the city: *Alamo* (110 SE 6th St.; phone: 522-0000) and *General Rent-A-Car* (2741 N. 29th Ave.; Hollywood, phone: 926-1700 or 800-327-7607). There also are several regional agencies; check the yellow pages. For more information on car rental, see GETTING READY TO GO.

Taxi – While you can hail a cab on the street, it's best to pick one up at a major hotel or restaurant, or to call for one. The major cab company is *Yellow Cab* (phone: 565-5400).

Tri-Rail – A double-decker train runs from West Palm Beach south through Ft. Lauderdale to Miami, and connects with Miami's *Metrorail/Metromover* and county and shuttle bus lines to deliver visitors to most of each city's major attractions. The train also travels to the airport in Broward (with a short shuttle ride), as well as the ones in Dade and Palm Beach counties, and schedules extra trains for games at *Joe Robbie* and *Orange Bowl* stadiums, the *Swap Shop, Bayside Marketplace,* and special events. At times, they schedule special sightseeing package tours. This is a convenient way to see a large part of South Florida and its attractions. Call for assistance in locating the stops nearest to the places you want to visit. Accessible to the handicapped (phone: 800-TRI-RAIL).

LOCAL SERVICES: Audiovisual Equipment – *Central Audio Visual,* 7212 S. Andrews Ave. (phone: 522-3796).

Baby-sitting – *Lul-A-Bye Sitters Registry* (phone 565-1222).

Business Services – *Professional Office Service, Inc.,* 4520 NE 18th Ave. (phone: 772-6520).

Dental Emergency – The *American Dental Association* maintains a 24-hour referral service (phone: 944-5668).

Dry Cleaner/Tailor – *Fashion Cleaners* (2427 W. Broward Blvd.; phone: 583-8225); *Lauderdale-by-the-Sea Cleaners* (4329 N. Ocean Dr., Lauderdale-by-the-Sea; phone: 776-0055).

Equipment Rental – *Kinko's,* at two locations, provides typewriters and computers for hourly rentals (6318 NW 9th Ave., Ft. Lauderdale; phone: 492-0006 and 3775 Hollywood Blvd., Hollywood; phone: 985-0411).

Limousine – *Airport Express* (phone: 527-8690); *Club Limousine Service* (phone: 522-0277).

Mechanics – *Ocean Exxon* (3001 N. Ocean Blvd.; phone: 561-3120), for American and foreign makes.

Medical Emergency – *Holy Cross Hospital* (4725 N. Federal Hwy.; phone: 771-8000); *North Beach Hospital* (2835 N. Ocean Blvd.; phone: 568-1000). For further information, see *Staying Healthy* in GETTING READY TO GO.

Messenger Service – *All Florida Messenger & Delivery,* open 24 hours (622 NW 20th Ave.; phone: 973-3278); *Sunshine State Messenger Service,* open 24 hours (6775 NW 15th Ave.; phone: 975-8100).

National/International Courier – *Federal Express* (phone: 484-4811 or 800-238-5355); *DHL Worldwide Courier Express* (phone: 791-7400 or 800-225-5345). For further information, see *Mail, Telephone, and Electricity* in GETTING READY TO GO.

Pharmacy – *Eckerd Drug Store* (154 N. University Dr.; phone: 432-5510) is open 24 hours. *Walgreen's Drugs* (3101 N. Ocean Blvd.; phone: 564-8424) is open 24 hours daily, with a pharmacist on call weekdays, 8 AM to 11 PM; weekends 9 AM to 9 PM..

Photocopies – *Copyright,* 969 W. Commercial Blvd. (phone: 491-2679) and *Kinko's* for standard and color copies (6318 NW 9th Ave., Ft. Lauderdale; phone: 492-0006 and 3775 Hollywood Blvd., Hollywood; phone: 985-0411).

Post Office – Located downtown at 330 SW 2nd St. (phone: 761-1172); the main office is at 1900 W. Oakland Park Blvd. (phone: 527-2070).

Professional Photographers – *University Studios* (phone: 772-6644); *Woodbury & Associates* (phone: 977-9000).

Secretary/Stenographers – *Alpha Temporary Services,* 1001 W. Cypress Creek Rd. (phone: 776-6030).

Teleconference Facilities – *Marriott's Harbor Beach* (3030 Holiday Dr.; phone: 525-4000); *Fort Lauderdale Marriott Hotel and Marina* (1881 SE 17th St.; phone: 463-4000). See *Checking In,* below, for more information on both.

Translators – *Berlitz Translation Services* (2455 E. Sunrise Blvd.; phone: 561-3935 or 800-523-7548) or *Master Translating Services* (1881 NE 26th St., Wilton Manors; phone: 563-2899).

Typewriter Rental – *A & J Business Machines* (306 W. Oakland Park Blvd.; phone: 563-0438). 1-week minimum.

Western Union/Telex – Many offices located around town (phone: 987-4061 or 800-325-6000).

 SPECIAL EVENTS: The *Seminole Indian Tribal Fair* at Flamingo Gardens, normally held during the first 2 weeks in February, is a showcase of Indian crafts, entertainment, and food. In March, the *Florida Derby Festival* hits town; activities include a beauty pageant, the *Derby Ball,* and parades, culminating in a thoroughbred race with a purse of $500,000. February 29 and March 1, the annual *Las Olas Festival,* hosted by the *Museum of Art,* attracts 205 juried artists, who display their work in Bubier Park; many of these artists don't exhibit elsewhere. Out in Davie, cowboys kick up their heels at the March *Orange Blossom Festival and Rodeo.* The *Honda Golf Classic,* one of the biggest PGA tournaments, is held in late February or early March at the *Weston Hills Country Club;* it attracts the PGA's top players. In April, seafood is king at the *Ft. Lauderdale Seafood Festival* at Bubier Park, where over 30 leading restaurants offer visitors samples of their house specialties. Anglers get to test their skills in May during the *Pompano Beach Fishing Rodeo and Seafood Festival,* where more than $250,000 in cash is awarded for the largest catches. *Oktoberfest* falls (naturally) in October and features lots of German food, drink, and music. The *Ft. Lauderdale Boat Show,* at the *Bahia Mar Yachting Center,* is the world's largest in-water display of all types and sizes of watercraft, held in November. Also in November is the *Promenade in the Park,* which showcases artwork, arts and crafts, food, and entertainment at Holiday Park, plus the *Greater Ft. Lauderdale Film Festival,* which shows more than 50 independent films, and the *Broward County Fair,* in Hallandale. The year's activities are capped by the month-long *Winterfest,* culminating in the Ft. Lauderdale and Pompano Beach boat parades, with processions of about 100 boats, festooned with colored lights and *Christmas* decorations, plying the Intracoastal Waterway, and a "Light up Lauderdale" laser show downtown on *New Year's Eve.*

MUSEUMS: The *Museum of Discovery and Science, International Swimming Hall of Fame,* and *Stranahan House* are described in *Special Places.* Other museums include the following:

Ft. Lauderdale Historical Society – Located in the historic district, the society conducts tours and hosts exhibits such as "South Florida's Mediterranean Revival Architecture." Open Tuesdays through Saturdays 10 AM to 4 PM and Sundays 1 to 4 PM. Admission charge. 219 SW Second Ave. (phone: 463-4431).

Museum of Art – Designed by Edward Larabee Barnes, this building houses 19th- and 20th-century European and American collections and mounts traveling exhibits, such as a collection of Audubon's bird watercolors. Open Tuesdays 11 AM to 9 PM, Wednesdays through Saturdays 10 AM to 5 PM, and Sundays noon to 5 PM. Admission charge; tours are included on Tuesdays, Thursdays, and Fridays at 1 PM. 1 E. Las Olas Blvd. (phone: 763-6464).

Young at Art Children's Museum – Primarily a hands-on museum, where young artists can develop their skills. Open Tuesdays through Saturdays 11 AM to 5 PM and Sundays noon to 5 PM. Admission charge, except for children under 2. 801 S. University Dr., Plantation (phone: 424-0085).

 MAJOR COLLEGES AND UNIVERSITIES: Broward Community College has three campuses (central, 3501 SW Davie Rd., Davie; north, 1000 Coconut Creek Blvd., Coconut Creek; and south, 7200 Hollywood Pines Blvd., Pembroke Pines; phone for all: 475-6500). Nova University is at 3301 College Ave., in Ft. Lauderdale (phone 800-541-NOVA). The University Tower (220 SE 2nd Ave.; phone: 355-5200) is a facility for graduate classes shared by Broward Community College, Florida Atlantic University, and Florida International University, whose main campuses are in Broward, Palm Beach, and Dade counties, respectively.

 SHOPPING: For a break from the beach (believe it or not, people do need that once in a while), visit one of the many shopping malls in the Ft. Lauderdale area. Here you can find anything your heart desires — malls are great for browsing and people watching as well.

Broward Mall – One of the South's largest shopping malls, with 130 specialty shops. Main stores are *Burdine's, Sears,* and *JC Penney.* Open Mondays through Saturdays 10 AM to 9 PM, Sundays noon to 5 PM. Broward Blvd. and University Dr., Plantation (phone: 473-8100).

Dansk Factory Outlet – For terrific buys on dynamic Danish-designed housewares. Open Mondays through Saturdays 10 AM to 5:30 PM, Sundays noon to 5 PM. At two locations: 2401 W. Atlantic Blvd. (phone: 973-7527) and 27 W. Hallandale Beach Blvd., Hallandale (phone: 454-3900).

Fashion Row – This is *the* place for bargain hunters. Long known as "Shmatte Row" (Yiddish for garments or rags), one section of discount dress and handbag shops runs along NE 1st Avenue off Hallandale Beach Boulevard; the other section is on NE 2nd Avenue between NE 3rd and NE 4th Streets. Open daily 10 AM to 5 PM; closed on Sundays in the summer.

Festival Marketplace – A gigantic, 400,000-square-foot indoor flea-market type of mall, with 755 vendors offering new merchandise (except for antiques and collectibles). Open Thursdays through Sundays from 9:30 AM to 5 PM. 2900 W. Sample Rd., Coconut Creek (phone: 979-4555).

Galleria – High-fashion clothes and home furnishings at this 3-story mall, featuring *Neiman Marcus, Saks,* and *Burdine's.* Open Mondays through Saturdays 10 AM to 9 PM, Sundays 12:30 to 5:30 PM. 2414 E. Sunrise Blvd. (phone: 564-1015).

Lord & Taylor Clearance Center – Clothing discounted 50% initially, with further reductions for special sales. Open Mondays, Thursdays, and Fridays 10 AM to 9 PM, Saturdays, Tuesdays, and Wednesdays 10 AM to 6 PM, and Sundays noon to 5 PM. 7067 W. Broward Blvd., Plantation (phone: 581-8205).

Maus & Hoffman – Upscale men's clothing. 800 E. Las Olas Blvd. (phone: 463-1472).

Sawgrass Mills – This alligator-shape, 2.2 million-square-foot shopping center is billed as the world's largest outlet mall (for more information, see *Special Places*). Open Mondays through Saturdays 10 AM to 9:30 PM, Sundays 11 AM to 6 PM. 12801 W. Sunrise Blvd., Sunrise (phone: 846-1000 or 800-FL-MILLS).

Sophy Curson – Open only in season, this store has high-fashion women's clothing. 1508 Las Olas Blvd. (phone: 462-7770).

Swap Shop – Indoor and outdoor booths beckon at this massive flea market with a wide variety of merchandise (for more information, see *Special Places*). There are two Broward locations: 3291 W. Sunrise Blvd. (phone: 791-SWAP) and 1000 N. State Rd. 7, Margate (phone: 971-SWAP).

Whispers – Designer clothes at a discount. 1507 Las Olas Blvd. (phone: 767-4606).

Zola Keller – Upscale fashions for women. 818 Las Olas Blvd. (phone: 462-3222).

 SPORTS: Baseball – Fans can watch spring training and pre-season games during March. The New York *Yankees* play at *Ft. Lauderdale Stadium* (5301 NW 12th Ave.; phone: 776-1921). A bit farther afield, West Palm Beach is the springtime home of the Atlanta *Braves* and Montreal *Expos.* The *Ft. Lauderdale Stadium* also hosts the *Mickey Mantle/Whitey Ford Fantasy Baseball Camp* in April, October, and November. Mantle, Ford, Hank Bauer, Mike Ferraro, and other former diamond biggies teach the over-thirtysomething crowd who wanted to be pros how to hit home runs. Contact Wanda Greer (PO Box 68, Grayson, KY 41143; phone: 606-474-6976; 212-382-1660 in New York). This year, South Florida's *Joe Robbie Stadium* becomes home to the National League's new team, the Florida *Marlins* (phone: 356-5848).

Diving – Diving is making a strong comeback in this part of Florida, due in large part to the practice of sinking freighters and other large objects into the sea to create artificial reefs. The most famous sinking in recent years was the *Mercedes,* which somehow landed on socialite Mollie Wilmot's terrace, but lots of other sunken wrecks also lure fish and coral. While many people say these manmade reefs can't replace nature's delicate work, colorful fish certainly congregate around the sunken ships off the beaches in Pompano and Ft. Lauderdale. Three tiers of coral reefs provide beautiful, more natural sights (see *Scuba Diving* in DIVERSIONS). Dozens of dive shops such as *Lauderdale Diver* (1334 SE 17th St. Cswy.; phone: 467-2822 or 800-654-2073) and *Pro Dive* (*Bahia Mar Yachting Center,* 801 Seabreeze Blvd.; phone: 761-3413 or 800-772-DIVE) operate in Broward; check the yellow pages or go directly to the boats that depart from Hillsboro Inlet in the northern part of the county, and from Port Everglades. Many operators offer package deals with hotels.

Fishing – There are lots of charter boat fishing operators at *Bahia Mar Yachting Center,* across A1A from the beach (801 Seabreeze Blvd.; phone: 525-7174) and at *Ft. Lauderdale Yacht Charters* at *Pier 66* (2301 SE 17th St. Cswy.; phone: 522-2712). A half-day charter costs about $400 for up to 6 anglers. Landlubbers fish 24 hours a day from the 1,080-foot Pompano Beach Fishing Pier, 2 blocks north of East Atlantic Boulevard, and Anglin's Fishing Pier (2 Commercial Blvd.; phone: 491-9403) for an admission charge. Freshwater fishing in the Everglades is possible from the pier or rented boats at Everglades Holiday Park (21940 Griffin Rd.; phone: 434-8111); from the pier or from rented boats at Quiet Waters Park (6601 N. Powerline Rd., Pompano Beach; phone: 360-1315); or from rented boats at Sawgrass Recreation Area (5400 US Rte. 27; phone: 389-0202).

Fitness Centers – *Nautilus Fitness Center,* with certified instructors, offers all the standard Nautilus exercise equipment, plus saunas. 1624 N. Federal Hwy. (phone: 566-2222).

Golf – There are more than 76 golf courses in the area. Among those open to the public are *American Golfers Club* (3850 N. Federal Hwy.; phone: 564-8760); *Bonaventure* (200 Bonaventure Blvd.; phone: 389-2100); *Rolling Hills* (3501 W. Rolling Hills Cir., Davie; phone: 475-3010); *Grand Palms* (110 Grand Palms Dr., Pembroke Pines; phone: 431-8800); *Weston Hills* (2603 Country Club Way; phone: 384-9422); and *Jacaranda* (9200 W. Broward Blvd., Plantation; phone: 472-5836). *Hole in One Golf,* a new service in Greater Ft. Lauderdale, arranges tee times, transportation, clubs, and lessons by pros at seven area courses (phone: 800-771-7888). Several resorts offer outstanding golf facilities (see *Great Golf* in DIVERSIONS).

Horse and Dog Racing – There's thoroughbred horse racing at *Gulfstream Park* (on US 1, Hallandale; phone: 454-7000), and harness racing at *Pompano Harness Track* (1800 SW 3rd St., Pompano Beach; phone: 972-2000). You can "go to the dogs" at *Hollywood Greyhound Track* (831 N. Federal Hwy., Hallandale; phone: 454-9400). Phone for racing dates.

Horseback Riding – There are many stables in the area. Among the larger ones are *Bar-B Ranch* for horse rentals (4601 SW 128th Ave., Davie; phone: 434-6175) and *Stride-Rite Training Center* for supervised rides (5550 SW 73rd Ave., Davie; phone: 587-2285). The county also operates stables at Tradewinds Park (3600 W. Sample Rd., Coconut Creek; phone: 968-3875).

Ice Skating – It seems incongruous in a tropical city, but Ft. Lauderdale residents love to ice skate. A favorite locale is *Sunrise Ice Skating Center,* 3363 Pine Island Rd. (phone: 741-2366).

Jai Alai – This Basque import is the area's most action-packed sport, with pari-mutuel betting adding spice. The season is year-round, except for 10 days in April and May. At *Dania Jai-Alai,* 301 E. Dania Beach Blvd., Dania (phone: 927-2841).

Nature Hikes – The Broward Parks & Recreation Department sponsors a different nature walk each Friday and Saturday, October through May. Call for a schedule (phone: 357-8101 or 536-PARK).

Rodeo – The "Wild West" can be found at the *Rodeo Arena* in Davie, where cowboys compete in bronco riding, calf roping, and other activities. Admission charge. 4201 SW 65th Way (phone: 797-1166). For more information see *Tour 6: Cowboy and Indian Tour* in DIRECTIONS.

Sailing – Fleets of boats are available for hire. For powerboats, try *Bahia Mar Yachting Center,* across A1A from the beach (801 Seabreeze Blvd.; phone: 525-7174), *Ft. Lauderdale Yacht Charters* at *Pier 66* (2301 SE 17th St. Cswy.; phone: 522-2712), or *Club Nautico* in Dania at the *Seafair* shopping complex (801 NE 3rd St., Dania; phone: 920-2796) or in Ft. Lauderdale (2301 SE 17th Cswy., Slip A19, Ft. Lauderdale; phone: 523-0033).

Swimming – The most crowded beach is along "The Strip," from Sunrise Boulevard to Bahia Mar. The Galt Ocean Mile is quieter, with an older crowd. Perhaps the quietest strand is the stretch between Galt Ocean Mile and NE 22nd Street, and if you search you may find small pockets of peace in John U. Lloyd Beach State Recreation Area (6503 N. Ocean Dr., Dania) or North Beach Park (3501 Ocean Dr., Hollywood). Deerfield Beach is a favorite of locals, from the border of Broward and Palm Beach counties south to SE 10th Street. This beach area has some of the best shower facilities around, and its huge boulders in the water create intriguing coves that invite exploration.

Tennis – Most major hotels have tennis courts. There also are numerous courts open to the public. Among them are *Holiday Park Tennis Center* (701 NE 12th Ave.; phone: 761-5378); *Dillon Tennis Courts* (4091 NE 5th Ave., Oakland Park; phone: 561-6180); *Pompano Beach Tennis Center* (900 NE 18th Ave.; phone: 786-4115); and *George W. English Park* (110 Bayview Dr.; phone: 566-0622). For resorts with excellent tennis facilities, see *Tennis* in DIVERSIONS.

 THEATER: The area's major theaters are *Parker Playhouse* (707 NE 8th St.; phone: 764-0700), which stars name actors in touring companies of Broadway productions, and *Sunrise Musical Theater* (5555 NW 95th Ave.; phone: 741-8600), which features touring Broadway musicals and individual stars in concert. Opened in early 1991, the $50-million regional *Broward Center for the Performing Arts* (624 SW 2nd St.; phone: 522-5334) stages opera, theatrical, ballet, and philharmonic productions. Theatrical and cultural events also are staged at the *War Memorial Auditorium* (800 NE 8th St.; phone: 761-5381) and *Bailey Hall* at Broward Community College, which also stages children's productions (3501 SW Davie Rd.;

phone: 475-6880). The playwright Vinnette Carroll, who wrote *Your Arms Too Short to Box with God,* opened a multi-cultural theater in a converted church, the *Vinnette Carroll Theater* (503 SE 6th St.; phone: 462-2424). For current offerings, check the newspapers.

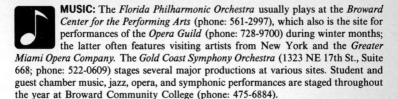

MUSIC: The *Florida Philharmonic Orchestra* usually plays at the *Broward Center for the Performing Arts* (phone: 561-2997), which also is the site for performances of the *Opera Guild* (phone: 728-9700) during winter months; the latter often features visiting artists from New York and the *Greater Miami Opera Company.* The *Gold Coast Symphony Orchestra* (1323 NE 17th St., Suite 668; phone: 522-0609) stages several major productions at various sites. Student and guest chamber music, jazz, opera, and symphonic performances are staged throughout the year at Broward Community College (phone: 475-6884).

NIGHTCLUBS AND NIGHTLIFE: Most hotels and larger motels offer music and/or comedy acts nightly. Growing in popularity are such comedy clubs as *The Comic Strip* (1432 N. Federal Hwy.; phone: 565-8887) and *The Comedy Stop* (3001 E. Commercial Blvd,; phone: 938-9033), which showcase New York and Los Angeles comics. The *Musician's Exchange Café* (729 W. Sunrise Blvd.; phone: 764-1912) is the place to go for jazz, blues, and rock. For dance music, try *Riverwatch Lounge* in the *Fort Lauderdale Marriott* hotel (1881 SE 17th St.; phone: 463-4000); *Confetti's* (2660 E. Commercial Blvd.; phone: 776-4080); *Shakers* (4000 N. Federal Hwy.; phone: 565-3555); *Café 66* and the *Pier Top Lounge* (2301 SE 17th St. Cswy.; phone: 728-3500); *Squeeze* (401 S. Andrews Ave.; phone: 522-2068); *Yesterdays* (3001 E. Oakland Park; phone: 561-4400). There's dancing and dinner for an older crowd at *Stan's* (3300 E. Commercial Blvd.; phone: 772-3777). A live band plays weekends at *Riverwalk Brewery* (111 SW 2nd Ave.; phone: 463-2337). *Chardee's* (2209 Wilton Dr., Wilton Manors; phone: 563-1800) attracts a gay crowd.

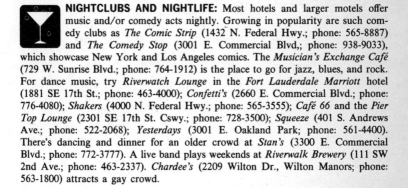

BEST IN TOWN

CHECKING IN: Ft. Lauderdale's busiest period is winter, when reservations should be made as far in advance as possible. In addition to the major hotels listed here, Ft. Lauderdale has hundreds of smaller chains (check the phone book for their toll-free 800 numbers) and family-operated hotels and motels. During high season, a double room listed in the very expensive range could run $180 to $300 per night; a room in the expensive range will cost $140 to $180; in moderate, $95 to $135; and $50 to $90 in inexpensive. In the summer, occupancy (and room) rates drop. Note that a 3% county tourist development tax and a 6½% state sales tax are added to all hotel bills. All telephone numbers are in the 305 area code unless otherwise indicated.

Marriott's Harbor Beach – The city's most expensive resort sits on 16 beachfront acres. Stunning public areas include 5 restaurants, 2 lounges, a pool bar, 5 tennis courts, and exercise facilities. There's also a tropically landscaped 8,000-square-foot free-form pool with a waterfall and 50 cabañas. By contrast, the 589 rooms are disappointing, especially in view of the rates. The 35 suites, however, are super. Free transport to the *Bonaventure Country Club* for golfers. Heavy meeting and convention clientele. Amenities include 24-hour room service, 29 meeting rooms, secretarial services, audiovisual equipment, and express checkout. 3030 Holiday Dr. (phone: 525-4000 or 800-228-9290; fax: 305-766-6152). Very expensive.

Palm-Aire – This is Ft. Lauderdale's original spa — over 1,500 acres with 191 rooms, 37 tennis courts, 1 executive and 4 championship golf courses, 3 pools, a jogging track, 2 racquetball courts, 1 squash court, and 4 dining rooms. Special packages of 3 and 7 days may be booked at the spa, whose programs include beauty, health, relaxation, and total spa experiences. See also *Great Golf* and *Sybaritic Spas* in DIVERSIONS. Other amenities include room service until 11 PM, a concierge, 16 meeting rooms, audiovisual equipment, and photocopiers. 2501 Palm-Aire Dr. N., Pompano Beach (phone: 972-3300 or 800-272-5624; fax: 305-968-2744). Very expensive.

Bonaventure – One of the most popular spas in town, this 1,250-acre resort, complete with waterfalls, offers 2 golf courses, 5 swimming pools, 24 tennis courts, 5 racquetball courts, a squash court, horseback riding, indoor roller skating, and bowling. The spa has a full range of health and nutrition programs in separate facilities for men and women. There's even a resident nurse. The 500 rooms and suites have been built in 4-story structures, along with 4 restaurants and 2 lounges. Amenities include room service until 2 AM, 24 rooms, a concierge, secretarial services, audiovisual equipment, photocopiers, and express checkout. 250 Racquet Club Rd. (389-3300 or 800-327-8090; fax: 305-384-0563). Very expensive to expensive.

Ft. Lauderdale Marriott – Located on the Intracoastal Waterway at the 17th Street Causeway, there are great views north and south from the 14-story tower and 2 low-rise sections. Most of the 580 recently renovated rooms have balconies and all have in-room safes and two telephones. The focus point of the property is a free-form pool, with pool bar, and the marina, with slips for up to 35 yachts. There are 4 tennis courts, a health club, sauna, outdoor Jacuzzi, gift shop, restaurants, and lounges. Business visitors have the use of 7 meeting rooms and 2 ballrooms, with audiovisual and secretarial services. A 24-hour computerized concierge service supplements the daytime personal service. 1881 SE 17th St. (phone: 463-4000 or 800-228-9290; fax: 305-527-6705). Very expensive to expensive.

Pier 66 – Alongside the Intracoastal Waterway, this 17-story octagonal tower was the city's first luxury high-rise. Multimillion-dollar expansion and refurbishing projects have greatly enhanced its appeal. There are 388 rooms, including 8 suites, all with balconies. Facilities include 2 tennis courts, 3 swimming pools with waterfalls, a 40-person Jacuzzi, a spa center, and 7 restaurants and lounges — including the revolving rooftop *Pier Top Lounge,* with heavenly views. A fleet of luxuriously furnished boats moored at the hotel's own marina is available for overnight lodging, business meetings, and sailing trips, and guests "rooming" aboard have full access to all the hotel's facilities. Amenities include 24-hour room service and a concierge. For business visitors, there are 19 meeting rooms, secretarial services, audiovisual equipment, and photocopiers. 2301 SE 17th St. (phone: 525-6666 or 800-327-3796; fax: 305-728-3541). Expensive.

Crown Sterling Suites – Formerly *Embassy Suites,* the chain's largest property in Florida offers 359 suites at prices equivalent to a standard hotel room. Facilities include a restaurant and lounge, pool, sauna, steamroom, and Jacuzzi. Breakfast and happy hour cocktails are free. Saluted by *Consumer Reports* magazine, the accommodations also feature a wet bar with refrigerator, microwave oven, coffee maker, and dining table. Complimentary beach shuttle service, parking, and 24-hour airport transportation also are available. Extra amenities include room service until 11 PM, 24 meeting rooms, audiovisual equipment, and express checkout. 1100 SE 17th St. Cswy. (phone: 527-2700 or 800-433-4600; fax: 305-760-7202). Expensive to moderate.

Ft. Lauderdale Marriott North – This 321-room property is adjacent to an 8-acre aquatic preserve in the burgeoning Cypress Creek area, north of the city. Facilities include an outdoor pool, a health club with saunas and lockers, a gift shop, and parking for 450 cars. The 16-story structure also features a restaurant, a lounge, the 5,082-square-foot Grand Ballroom, and 8 meeting rooms. Other amenities include room service until 11 PM, a concierge, secretarial services, audiovisual equipment, and express checkout. 6650 N. Andrews Ave., in the Cypress Park West business complex (phone: 771-0440 or 800-228-9290; fax: 305-771-7519). Expensive to moderate.

Hollywood Beach Hilton – Situated on the Intracoastal Waterway, with a pool complex — including children's pool and whirlpool bath — overlooking the waterway. The 306-room hotel offers a concierge floor, 2 tennis courts, 2 restaurants, a lounge, an outdoor bar, video gameroom, exercise room, and free supervised children's activities in season. 4000 S. Ocean Dr., Hollywood (phone: 458-1900 or 800-HILTONS; fax: 305-458-7222). Expensive to moderate.

Westin Cypress Creek – The Westin group's first foray into Florida, this 15-story, 293-room, luxury property overlooks a 5-acre lagoon that's spectacularly lighted at *Christmastime*. It features a health club, a large outdoor pool, and a lakeside pavilion; tennis and golf are a 5-minute drive away. There are 2 restaurants — one for fine dining, a second for casual food — and a bar complex. Two floors offer special concierge services. Other amenities include free parking, 24-hour room service, 20 meeting rooms, secretarial services, audiovisual equipment, and express checkout. 400 Corporate Dr., in the Radice Corporate Center (phone: 772-1331 or 800-228-3000; fax: 305-491-9087). Expensive to moderate.

Bahia Mar – This nautically oriented hotel and marina, at the Bahia Mar Yacht Basin at the southern end of "The Strip," has 300 rooms, 2 restaurants, the *Schooner's Lounge,* and 4 lighted tennis courts. There are 350 slips for fishing boats and pleasure yachts, and it is the home of the country's largest in-water boat show (in November). Amenities include room service until 11 PM, a concierge, 10 meeting rooms, secretarial services, photocopiers, and express checkout. 801 Seabreeze Blvd. (phone: 764-2233; fax: 305-524-6912). Moderate.

Grand Palms – A new resort that offers 137 rooms and suites developed around a golf course and lakes. So far, 18 holes have been built, with another 9 scheduled; there's also a pro shop and golf school (see *Great Golf* in DIVERSIONS. Other athletic facilities include 6 lighted clay tennis courts, an Olympic-size pool, and fitness center. A restaurant and lounge overlooking the golf course complete the picture so far. 110 Grand Palms Dr., Pembroke Pines (phone: 431-8800 or 800-327-9246; fax: 305-435-5988). Moderate.

Ramada Beach – All of its 220 rooms have balconies that overlook either the Atlantic or the Galt Ocean Mile, and some are beautifully decorated in soothing rose and mauve tones. Its *Ocean Café* offers a mostly continental menu, and the lounge features live music and dancing on weekends during the winter months. On the beach, it has a heated pool, a tiki bar for hors d'oeuvres and cocktails, and sailboat rentals. Other amenities include room service until 10 PM, a concierge, 4 meeting rooms, and photocopiers. 4060 Galt Ocean Dr. (phone: 565-6611; fax: 305-564-7730). Moderate.

Sheraton Yankee Clipper – "Moored" directly on the beach, its unusual architecture makes this landmark look like a ship, and the nautical theme — which provides a warm, clubby feeling — is carried through indoors, too. There are 505 rooms, 3 heated swimming pools, and a restaurant. Two lounges provide entertainment. Amenities include room service until 11 PM, concierge, 1 meeting room, and express checkout. 1140 Seabreeze Blvd. (phone: 524-5551; fax: 305-523-5376). Moderate.

Bahia Cabana – Small and unpretentious, nestled by the Bahia Mar Yacht Basin, this is an informal place and very Floridian. There are 116 rooms and apartments with kitchenettes, 3 swimming pools, a 36-person Jacuzzi, saunas, a dining room, and an outdoor patio bar/restaurant — a popular gathering spot for locals — overlooking the marina. Amenities include a concierge desk, photocopiers, and express checkout. 3001 Harbor Dr. (phone: 524-1555; fax: 305-764-5951). Inexpensive.

Riverside – Some 117 rooms in one of the city's oldest structures, this hostelry has a sedate ambience and cozy lobby, with chandeliers, armchairs, touches of wicker, and a fireplace. There's a restaurant, plus an intimate restaurant/lounge decorated with etched glass — and a swimming pool set amid tropical landscaping. Amenities include room service until 10:30 PM, 7 meeting rooms, limited secretarial services, audiovisual equipment, photocopiers, and express checkout. 620 E. Las Olas Blvd. (phone: 467-0671; fax: 305-462-2148). Inexpensive.

 EATING OUT: There are nearly 2,500 restaurants in Broward County. Many of these are well known, and most get quite crowded during the winter season, so it's always a good idea to make reservations. In fact, restaurant dining is such a part of the lifestyle that a recent *Restaurants & Institutions* magazine survey found Ft. Lauderdale restaurants second only to New York City as the country's busiest eating establishments. Casual dress is accepted at most restaurants, though a few of the more expensive ones prefer gentlemen to wear jackets. Expect to pay $75 or more for dinner for two in a restaurant listed in the very expensive range; $60 to $70 in the expensive range; $35 to $50 in the moderate range; and $25 or less for inexpensive. Prices do not include wine, drinks, or tips. All telephone numbers are in the 305 area code unless otherwise indicated and are in Ft. Lauderdale unless noted.

Plum Room – Located on the level above bustling *Yesterday's* restaurant (see below), it seems a world apart, serving beautifully prepared continental food in a luxurious, intimate setting. A harpist plays nightly. Oustanding entrées include Santa Rosa escargots encased in phyllo dough and veal medallions served with shrimp and crabmeat; for more adventurous diners there's also ostrich and Canadian elk on the menu. Outstanding wine list. Open from 6:30 to 11 PM Sundays through Thursdays, until midnight Fridays and Saturdays. Reservations advised. Major credit cards accepted. 3001 E. Oakland Park Blvd. (phone: 563-4168). Very expensive.

Casa Vecchia – Fine Northern Italian and Mediterranean food is served inside this lovely old house (built in the 1930s by the Ponds cold-cream family), tastefully decorated with lots of plants, ceramics, antiques, and wrought iron. Famed South Florida restaurateurs Leonce Picot and Al Kocab provide elegant atmosphere and excellent service, with a view of the Intracoastal Waterway from the *Greenhouse* dining room. The osso buco is a perennial favorite, but the veal piccata served with polenta or quail with figs and couscous is also hard to beat. Can be reached by water taxi. Open for dinner weeknights from 6:30 to 10 PM, Fridays and Saturdays to 10:30 PM, and Sundays to 9:30 PM. Reservations advised. Major credit cards accepted. 209 N. Birch Rd. (phone: 463-7575). Very expensive to expensive.

Le Dome – Atop a condominium building with views of Ft. Lauderdale, this dining spot offers rich, traditional fare for its mostly rich, traditional clientele. A pianist playing classical and show music adds to the elegant atmosphere. The lobster panache, with lobster meat overflowing a puff-pastry shell, boneless breast of duck, and chateaubriand are recommended. Open nightly from 6 PM to 10 PM; closed Mondays off-season. Reservations advised. Major credit cards accepted. 333 Sunset Dr. (phone: 463-3303 or 800-330 1721 outside Broward County). Very expensive to expensive.

Ruth's Chris Steak House – National chain known for its outstanding prime midwestern beef, never frozen. Open 5 to 11 PM Mondays through Saturdays, 5 to 10 PM Sundays. Reservations advised. Major credit cards accepted. 2525 N. Federal Hwy. (phone: 565-2338). Very expensive to expensive.

Armadillo Café – Serves Florida foods in a Southwest tradition, in the land of Florida's own cowboys. The café's black-and-white soup, contrasting semicircles of black-bean and Jack-cheese with jalapeño soups, is excellent. Favorites include Florida lobster quesadillas and grilled chicken with tomato and avocado salsas. Open Sundays and Tuesdays through Thursdays 5 to 10 PM, Fridays and Saturdays until 11 PM. Reservations necessary. Major credit cards accepted. 4630 SW 64th Ave., Davie (phone: 791-4866). Expensive.

Burt & Jack's – Owned by actor Burt Reynolds and partner Jack Jackson, this beautiful Spanish-style villa offers first-rate seafood and steaks and chops. Try for a window table so you can watch the cruise and cargo ships passing by. Open for dinner from 5 to 10 PM Sundays through Thursdays and until 11 PM Fridays and Saturdays; closed Mondays. Reservations advised; jackets required for men. Major credit cards accepted. Berth 23, Port Everglades (phone: 522-5225). Expensive.

By Word of Mouth – This European café–style spot in the heart of Ft. Lauderdale's industrial district serves some of the finest continental fare in the area. The owner has not advertised since opening the restaurant 10 years ago, but people hear about the abundant salads, hand-size portobello mushrooms stuffed with brie, duckling soaked in apricot brandy, and the pastries — a half-dozen chocolate choices, with brownie decadence followed closely by white chocolate mousse with raspberry sauce — the best. Open for lunch Mondays through Fridays 11 AM to 3 PM, for dinner Wednesdays and Thursdays 5 to 9 PM, and Fridays and Saturdays 5 to 10 PM. Reservations advised. Major credit cards accepted. 3200 NE 12th Ave. (phone: 564-3663). Expensive.

Café Max – This trendy, California-style eatery is credited with pioneering nouvelle American food in South Florida, under the direction of restaurateur Darrel Broek. Current chef (and co-owner) Oliver Saucy continues to win awards. Favorites include the duck and smoked mozzarella ravioli with sun-dried tomatoes, and the yellowfin tuna with three-peppercorn crust. The casual ambience and innovative menu are complemented by an excellent wine list emphasizing California bottlings, including many available by the glass. Open daily for dinner 6 to 11 PM. Reservations advised. Major credit cards accepted. 2601 E. Atlantic Blvd., Pompano Beach (phone: 782-0606). Expensive.

Christine Lee's Northgate – This is a branch of the popular Miami Beach restaurant serving Szechuan, Mandarin, and Cantonese dishes in a rich-looking setting of cyprus wood paneling and Oriental artifacts. Surprisingly, they also serve some of the best steaks in South Florida, and have recently added veal marsala and shrimp scampi to the menu. Open daily 5 to 11 PM. Reservations advised. Major credit cards accepted. 6191 Rock Island Rd., Tamarac (phone: 726-0430). Expensive.

Down Under – Another Leonce Picot/Al Kocab restaurant (the third is the elegant *Là Vielle Maison,* in Boca Raton), serving an eclectic menu of French, American, and seafood dishes. With a view of passing boats on the Intracoastal Waterway, the restaurant is, literally, under the approach to the waterway bridge. The atmosphere and decor are comfortable, with plants abounding. The brick walls are lined with old posters, and the large rooms are filled with tables placed rather closely together. Regulars favor the jumbo stone crabs and prime steaks. Excellent drinks and desserts. Open for lunch in season 11:30 AM to 2 PM Wednesdays, Thursdays, and Fridays, and for dinner daily 6 to 11 PM. Reservations advised. Major credit cards accepted. On the route of the water taxi. 3000 E. Oakland Park Blvd. (phone: 564-6984). Expensive.

Fulvio's – With its soft pink and white decor, this Italian dining spot is rich in atmosphere — and fine food. Fresh ingredients and last-minute preparation, from the herbs grown in the back-door garden to the salad tossed with dressing prepared just before leaving the kitchen, account for its culinary success. A stellar appetizer is the eggplant rollatini, sautéed eggplant slices rolled around ricotta cheese and topped with mozzarella cheese and chunky marinara sauce. Tender calamari *fra diavolo* and shrimp Fulvio also are first-rate. Open daily 4:30 to 11 PM. Reservations necessary; for Saturday nights, reserve a week in advance. Major credit cards accepted. 4188 SW 64th Ave. (Davie Rd. Extension), Davie (phone: 583-3666). Expensive.

Left Bank – The menu at this romantic spot near Las Olas Boulevard features French standards such as bouillabaisse and rack of lamb as well as innovative entrées, including escargot-stuffed chicken breast with Pernod cream sauce and red snapper filet encrusted with julienne potatoes. Open for lunch Mondays through Fridays 11:30 AM to 2:30 PM and dinner from 6 to 11 PM Sundays through Thursdays; until midnight Fridays and Saturdays. Reservations advised. Major credit cards accepted. 214 SE 6th Ave. (phone: 462-5376). Expensive.

Mai-Kai – For more than 35 years, this place has been a Ft. Lauderdale landmark, with its huge entranceway torches flanking a rattling plank-bridge entrance. Choose from the main dining room, where you can watch Polynesian dancing, smaller lavishly decorated dining rooms, or outdoor seating by a waterfall. The gardens are lush, with authentic South Seas statuary. The food and service are even better than the ambience, with exotic drinks, such as the famous Mystery Drink — a show in itself, and Polynesian, American, and Cantonese dishes (a specialty is Peking duck). The *Molokai Bar* is filled with old-time nautical memorabilia. The nightly Polynesian show (cover charge) is professional and highly entertaining. Open nightly 5 to 11 PM. Reservations advised. Major credit cards accepted. 3599 N. Federal Hwy. (phone: 563-3272). Expensive.

Martha's – Located on the Intracoastal Waterway, where the passing boat scene provides its own entertainment. The restaurant has a split personality — the glitzy downstairs serves dress-up types, while the second-floor deck is less formal, more tropical in flavor. The same courteous service and outstanding menu apply to both. Steaks, chops, and seafood are well prepared; fresh Florida snapper is offered eight different ways — the blackened version is perfectly cooked. Chicken gorgonzola with walnuts is also first-rate. Boat dockage available. Open daily for lunch 11:30 AM until 3:30 PM downstairs, until 4:30 PM upstairs, and for dinner Sundays through Thursdays 5 until midnight, Fridays and Saturdays until 1 AM. Sunday brunch served downstairs 11 AM to 3 PM. Reservations necessary Saturday nights, advised otherwise. Major credit cards accepted. 6024 N. Ocean Dr., Hollywood (phone: 923-5444). Expensive.

La Réserve – This French/continental dining place has a 2-tiered, beam-ceilinged, candlelit dining room with a sensational view of the Intracoastal Waterway. Adjoining it is *Ginger's*, the less formal bistro, available for private parties only. Open daily 6 PM to 11 PM. Reservations advised. Major credit cards accepted. Oakland Park Blvd. at the Intracoastal Waterway (phone: 563-6644). Expensive.

Silverado Café – A bit of the Napa Valley has been transplanted to the *University Park Plaza* shopping center, where good cooking and California wines prevail. Dine amid Victorian decor or in a small room designed to look like the gondola of a hot-air balloon. Appetizers include an outstanding black bean soup and lobster ravioli; fresh grilled fish or cashew chicken l'orange are tops for main courses. Open for lunch Tuesdays through Saturdays 11:30 AM to 2:30 PM, dinner 5 to 10 PM, and Sundays 5 to 9 PM; closed Mondays. Reservations advised. Major credit cards accepted. 3528 S. University Dr., Davie (phone: 474-9992). Expensive.

Yesterday's – An enormous, popular place on the Intracoastal Waterway, it features traditional steaks and seafood, such as beef Wellington and grilled swordfish. Open daily for dinner 5 to 11 PM, to midnight on Fridays and Saturdays. Reservations advised, especially for window tables. Major credit cards accepted. 3001 E. Oakland Park Blvd. (phone: 561-4400). Expensive.

Chart House – This branch of the chain offers the standard steaks and seafood with unlimited soup or salad, and fantastic mud pie for dessert. Its downtown Ft. Lauderdale location is a knockout. Housed in two homes (ca. 1904) on the New River, the window tables offer a passing show of pleasure craft and working vessels. Before or after dining, stroll along the 2 miles of the lushly landscaped Riverwalk to the *Broward Center for the Performing Arts.* Or take a water taxi back to your hotel. Open 5 PM to midnight Sundays through Thursdays, until 11 PM Fridays and Saturdays. Reservations advised. Major credit cards accepted. 301 SW Third Ave. (phone: 523-0177). Expensive to moderate.

L'Ile De France – A bistro that serves outstanding French fare prepared by chefs Remi Coulon, who worked aboard the Aga Khan's yacht, and his wife Sandra. Don't miss the excellent seafood ravioli, purses of shrimp and crabmeat swimming in chablis sauce, or the rib chop with champagne sauce and morel mushrooms. The papaya mousse pie with praline cream adds a welcome tropical influence. Open from 5:30 to 10 PM; closed Mondays. Reservations advised. Major credit cards accepted. 3025 N. Ocean Blvd. (phone: 565-9006). Expensive to moderate.

La Tavernetta – This 60-seat Italian eatery has been chef-owned and -operated for 14 years — for Florida, where restaurants come and go, that's saying something. Start with the hot antipasto platter. A favorite dish is shrimp paradiso with angel hair pasta, prepared tableside. Open Wednesdays through Sundays 5 to 11 PM. Reservations necessary. Major credit cards accepted. 8455 W. McNab Rd., Tamarac (phone: 722-1831). Expensive to moderate.

Brasserie Max – Noted restaurateur Dennis Max brought his touch to this affordable spot where the young and young-at-heart eat in a casual atmosphere. Food preparation and service are still tops. Creative pizza and pasta dishes are favorites, but the restaurant hits its peak with oak-grilled specialties such as salmon with candied walnut vinaigrette. The flourless chocolate cake might send chocoholics over the edge. Open Mondays through Thursdays 11:30 AM to 10 PM, Fridays and Saturdays until 11 PM, and Sundays noon to 9 PM. Reservations for five or more advised. Major credit cards accepted. 321 N. University Dr. (in *The Fashion Mall*), Plantation (phone: 424-8000). Moderate.

Charley's Crab – One of the best of Chuck Muer's six South Florida restaurants, it has a wonderful location on the Intracoastal Waterway, with tables inside and out. The passing water show ranges from a 110-foot Italian-designed yacht to a Labrador retriever, wearing life vest and sunglasses, skimming along in a Seadoo. Specialties include an excellent Martha's Vineyard salad, a wide range of fresh fish prepared almost every way imaginable, and a terrific apple tart with homemade cinnamon ice cream. Can be reached by water taxi. Open for lunch Mondays through Saturdays 11:30 AM to 3:30 PM and Sundays 11 AM to 3:30 PM; for dinner Sundays through Thursdays 5 to 10 PM and Fridays and Saturdays until 11 PM. Reservations advised. Major credit cards accepted. 3000 NE 32nd Ave. (phone: 561-4800). Moderate.

La Ferme – Marie-Paul Terrier welcomes guests with a smile, and closely watches over their well-being while husband Henri tends to the kitchen, whipping up traditional and nouvelle delights. The dining room is small and cozy, with French provincial food and decor set off by lace tablecloths. Open Tuesdays through Sundays 5:30 to 10 PM. Reservations advised. Major credit cards accepted. 1601 E. Sunrise Blvd. (phone: 764-0987). Moderate.

15th Street Fisheries – Located in a tin-roofed wooden building hung with fishnets and lobster traps, this eatery's view of boats plying the Intracoastal completes the nautical feel. But don't overlook the food. Even if you don't fancy fish, the homemade bread is reason enough to come here — along with the cheerful, friendly service. Try the sunshine salad, cold new potatoes with smoked salmon in a creamy dill dressing, or red snapper filet topped with ginger sauce. The most popular dish is the oddly named "bugs 'n pasta," linguine with a peppery cream sauce studded with Moreton Bay bugs (relax, they're Australian crustaceans, related to lobsters). Open weekdays 11:30 AM to 9:45 PM and Fridays and Saturdays from 10:30 AM to 9:45 PM. Reservations advised. Major credit cards accepted. 1900 SE 15th St. (phone: 763-2777 or 947-0808). Moderate.

Gibby's – An enormous eatery offering good value in a pretty setting, divided into several dining rooms with twinkling lights. A humongous salad is included with basic steaks and fish dishes and veal parmesan. Among the country's busiest restaurants, it serves about 1,500 dinners nightly in season. In the summer, the lobster specials are unbeatable. Open daily for lunch 11:30 AM to 2:30 PM and for dinner Mondays through Thursdays 5 to 10 PM, Fridays 5 to 11 PM, Saturdays 4:30 to 11 PM, and Sundays 4:30 to 10 PM. Reservations advised. Major credit cards accepted. 2900 NE 12th Ter. (phone: 368-2990). Moderate.

Pelican Pub – Downstairs, the casual, open-air eatery uses paper plates to serve food freshly plucked from the sea. Upstairs, the decor gets a bit fancier, but the food is just as fresh, with chicken and steaks added to the menu. Specialties of the house include a smoked fish spread and swordfish parmesan. Open daily 11 AM to 9:30 PM. Reservations advised for parties of more than six. Major credit cards accepted. 2635 N. Riverside Dr. (phone: 785-8550). Moderate.

La Perla – Good southern Italian cooking lures the dressy crowd. Regulars rave over pasta made fresh daily on the premises, with appreciative nods from the radicchio/oyster/mushroom crowd. Try the gnocchi and the osso buco. Open Sundays through Thursdays 5 to 10:30 PM and Fridays and Saturdays until 11 PM. Reservations advised. Major credit cards accepted. 1818 E. Sunrise Blvd. (phone: 765-1950). Moderate.

Ronieri's – Fine continental fare is featured in this western Broward County eatery tucked away in a shopping center. Specialties include raspberry chicken wings; veal *crustada*, a scaloppine stuffed with eggplant, mushrooms, mozzarella cheese, and pine nuts. The tiramisu is arguably the best in Florida. Calorie counters will appreciate the selection of freshly made Weight Watcher specials. Open from 5 to 10 PM; closed Mondays. Reservations advised. Most major credit cards accepted. 207 N. University Dr., Pembroke Pines (phone: 966-2233). Moderate.

Sea Watch – One of the few South Florida dining spots set on the Atlantic Ocean beach, this woodsy eatery has been here for almost 20 years. The fare is mostly fresh fish, including those famous stone crabs; oysters Rockefeller and Gulf garlic shrimp are also favorites. Open daily for lunch 11:30 AM to 3:30 PM; dinner from 5 to 10 PM Sundays through Thursdays and until 11 PM Fridays and Saturdays. Reservations advised for six or more. Major credit cards accepted. 6002 N. Ocean Blvd. (phone: 781-2200). Moderate.

Shooters – Located on the Intracoastal Waterway, where many guests arrive by boat (there's even a valet parking service for vessels), this is the place to get lots of fried pick-up goodies, burgers, or a Philly cheesesteak. A kiddie menu is available. This location gets a younger crowd than its North Miami counterpart. Open Sundays through Thursdays 11:30 AM to midnight, Fridays and Saturdays until 1 AM. No reservations. Major credit cards accepted. 3033 NE 32nd Ave. (phone: 566-2855). Moderate.

Bimini Boatyard – This place offers Bahamian decor and a view of the Intracoastal and features good food at reasonable prices. Specialties include conch fritters, grilled grouper, and jerk ribs — along with the wonderful Bimini bread. Open Mondays through Fridays from 11 AM to 11 PM, Saturdays and Sundays from noon to 11 PM. Reservations advised for parties of eight or more. Major credit cards accepted. 1555 SW 17th St. (phone: 525-7400). Moderate to inexpensive.

Manero's – Both locations of this family-run place are large, noisy, and crowded; the walls are adorned with autographed photos of many of the celebrities who have eaten here. Steaks and seafood are featured specialties. The older (Hallandale) branch, from 1954, is open Mondays through Fridays for lunch from 11:30 AM to 4 PM; dinner Mondays through Thursdays 4 to 10 PM, Fridays and Saturdays until 10:30 PM, and Sundays until 9:30 PM. No reservations. Major credit cards accepted. 2600 E. Hallandale Beach Blvd., Hallandale (phone: 456-1000). Margate branch open Tuesdays through Fridays for lunch 11:30 AM to 2:30 PM; dinner Tuesdays through Thursdays 5 to 9:30 PM, Fridays and Saturdays until 10 PM. Reservations advised. Major credit cards accepted. 5681 W. Atlantic Blvd., Margate (phone: 971-4995). Moderate to inexpensive.

Big Louie's – A line of people is perpetually waiting at the doors of these cheery, casual eateries that serve solid Italian food and pizza with a choice of 21 toppings. Open daily 11 AM to 11 PM in the Ft. Lauderdale locations and until 1 AM in the Sunrise spot. No reservations. Major credit cards accepted. Three locations: 1990 E. Sunrise Blvd. (phone: 467-1166), 2103 E. Commercial Blvd. (phone: 771-2288) and 3378 N. University Dr., Sunrise (phone: 572-2882). Inexpensive.

Brother's – This popular place offers bagels and lox and corned beef on rye, as well as roasted chicken dinners and the like, to droves of locals. Save room for the 7-layer cake. Open daily from 7 AM to 10 PM. No reservations. Major credit cards accepted. 1325 S. Powerline Rd., Pompano Beach (phone: 968-5881). Inexpensive.

Cap's Place – Marilyn Monroe, John F. Kennedy, and Winston Churchill ate in this wonderful, Old Florida island dining place. Founded during the 1920s, this old fishing shack once held many wild gambling parties and was the base for a healthy rum-running operation. Now it's strictly a seafood eatery. Diners are picked up by boat at NE 28th Court and taken for a 5-minute ride to Cap's Island, off Lighthouse Point. Open daily from 5:30 PM. Reservations advised. Major credit cards accepted. 2765 NE 28th Ct. (phone: 941-0418). Inexpensive.

Carlos & Pepe's – The clientele at this popular hangout is eager and hungry; the setting is crowded, but pleasant (light wood, green plants, and tile tables); and the menu is lighthearted Mexican (*fajitas, chimichangas,* and *chiles rellenos*). Open daily 11:30 AM to 11 PM. No reservations. Major credit cards accepted. 1302 SE 17th St. (phone: 467-7192). Inexpensive.

Ernie's Bar B Que – A local institution for 30 years, the ribs, chicken, pork, and beef are prepared in a special barbecue sauce that's famous throughout the area. For something different, try the fiery conch chowder. The decor has a rustic Key West style. Open Mondays through Thursdays 11 AM to 11 PM, Fridays and Saturdays until midnight, and Sunday noon to 11 PM. Reservations unnecessary. Major credit cards accepted. 1843 S. Federal Hwy. (phone: 523-8636). Inexpensive.

Lou's Pizza 'n Subs – For nearly 20 years owner Lou LoPrinzo and manager Lou Spinelli have served all kinds of pizza, subs, salads, and calzone with beer and wine. Intimate booths and tables, good food (including a super-large pizza), and courteous service make this place popular with both locals and tourists. At least one of the two Lous is usually on hand to see that guests are happy. Draft beer is 35¢ before 5 PM. Open from 11 AM to midnight, Fridays and Saturdays to 1 AM. No reservations. Major credit cards accepted. 1547 E. Commercial Blvd. (phone: 491-5600). Inexpensive.

Mario the Baker – Pasta and pizza are the specialties in this long-popular institution, but don't miss the greasy (but great) garlic rolls, washed down with beer or wine. Open from 11 AM to 11 PM Mondays through Thursdays, until midnight Fridays and Saturdays, and from noon to 11 PM Sundays. No reservations or credit cards accepted. 1313 Las Olas Blvd., Ft. Lauderdale (phone: 523-4990) and 2220 N. University Dr., Sunrise (phone: 742-3333). Inexpensive.

Moishe's – This is a good spot for spiritual revival after heavy-duty shopping. Some say the chicken soup is just like grandma used to make. Ditto for the dairy dishes, chopped liver, and brisket. Open daily from 11 AM to 9 PM. No reservations. MasterCard and Visa accepted. 1700 E. Hallandale Beach Blvd., Hallandale (phone: 454-1300). Inexpensive.

Papa Leone's – Papa Leone plays the organ every night at this small (only 18 candlelit booths and tables), old-fashioned, family-run, neighborhood Italian eatery. Closed Mondays. Reservations unnecessary. American Express accepted. Virtually invisible, it's next to *Publix* grocery store, at 2735 N. Dixie Hwy., Wilton Manors (phone: 566-1911). Inexpensive.

Pumpernik's – For 15 years, this enormous place has been supplying locals with corned beef on rye or blintzes with sour cream. They serve plenty of broiled fish and burgers, too. The restaurant boasts that it uses 4,000 eggs per week in season (definitely not for cholesterol watchers). Open daily from 7:30 AM to midnight. Reservations accepted for groups of ten or more. Visa and MasterCard accepted. 917 E. Hallandale Beach Blvd., Hallandale (phone: 454-6773). Inexpensive.

DIVERSIONS

For the Experience

Quintessential Miami

When people think of Miami, it's most often Don Johnson and "Miami Vice" that immediately come to mind — a land of sun, fun, and guns, pastel coated and complete with bronzed bodies tooling around in racy convertibles. But there's more to Miami than meets the television-viewing eye. It is a town of varied cultures — Cubans, Caribbeans, Seminole Indians, and retired Northerners are all here; colorful neighborhoods; great seafood; Art Deco design; the popular NFL *Dolphins* — and the beach. There are nightclubs for night owls, the nearby Everglades for those who are into gators and grasslands, and the Florida Keys for those looking for some respite from the mobs and some hints of Hemingway and Tennessee Williams. Below are some of the musts to put you in a Miami state of mind.

THE BEACH: *The* reason most vacationers choose Miami. Back in the 1920s, developer Carl Fisher raised the land that's now Miami Beach 5 feet above sea level by loading it with sand that he then secured with rows of large palm trees. Ever since, visitors have been flocking to Dade County's 15.5 miles of beaches to enjoy the mild air, plentiful sun, and warm, aqua-colored sea. Numerous restoration projects replenishing the sands (the latest in 1988) have made the beach even more beautiful than it was when Betty Grable and Robert Cummings romped here in the 1941 movie *Moon Over Miami.* Over the years, the beach has retained its glamour; oceans of movies — including *Goldfinger,* starring Sean Connery as James Bond — have been filmed on its glistening white sands. The most recent on-screen incarnation of Miami Beach was TV's "Miami Vice," whose shots of the beach, the Art Deco district, and the posh hotels introduced the city to a new generation of sun worshipers. The beach continues to attract filmmakers, and others who just come here to catch some rays are still apt to catch a glimpse of a celebrity or two.

The water, especially in the summer, is comfortably warm and inviting; in winter, diehard surfers can pit themselves against some respectable waves. At most points, the beach is a 300-foot-wide swath of clean white sand reached by boardwalks; the approach is fringed with a 65-foot-wide band of beach grass and sea grapes that protects the dunes and the beach from erosion (thanks to the Dade County Beach Vegetation Project). Those not staying at beachfront hotels can enjoy the sand and surf at numerous public beaches. (All Dade County beaches are open to the public; parking, however, may be difficult.) The beaches are considered so beautiful that a study done last year by a University of Maryland geographer found two of the nation's top ten beaches (after studying 650 candidates) to be located in southeast Florida: Crandon Park and Bill Baggs Cape Florida State Recreation Area, both public beaches on Key Biscayne. Perhaps the best spot at which to capture a vintage Florida tan while sampling the true flavor of a Miami beach is at the North Shore Recreation Area, a 40-acre state park that runs from 79th to 86th Streets in Miami Beach. For a nominal charge (50¢ for Florida residents, $1 for non-residents), beach lovers can sun and swim at a well-maintained, policed beach (entrances at 81st and 85th Sts., at Collins Ave.). Features include boardwalks, picnic tables and barbecue pits under palm trees, bicycle paths and bike rentals, bathrooms with lockers, outdoor showers, a playground area for tots, access ramps for the handicapped, a concession stand (at 83rd St.), and metered parking. There's also a Vita Course — a trail with marked stops with workout equipment and instructions for specific exercises. Open year-round, it's definitely earned its place in the sun.

ART DECO DISTRICT: This unique square-mile district, listed on the National Register of Historic Places, boasts the largest concentration of Art Deco resort architecture in the world. There are about 650 individual buildings in the area, designated by the National Registry as 5th to 22nd Streets, from Ocean Drive to Alton Road. Besides its historical value, the Deco district has become Greater Miami's hot, "in" place. Even the sidewalks are pastel delights — it's as if a mad Miamian scattered Necco wafers all over the ground! Tropical Deco combines buildings painted warm peach and turquoise or lavender teamed with pink with stylized nautical motifs (mermaids, waves, and flying porpoises). Quintessential expressions of Miami, these buildings abound with features such as porthole windows and metal railings, juxtaposed against palm trees from the coconut plantation that once stood on the white strand across the street.

The "art" in Art Deco extends far beyond the architecture, however; the human street scene is an artwork in its own right. With a backdrop of wonderfully, whimsically restored buildings built between the 1920s and 1940s (earlier buildings were destroyed by a hurricane in 1926), a young man wearing bike shorts and sporting a live snake draped around his neck roller-skates by, beautiful blonde fashion models from Germany drape themselves in front of archways as cameras click away, tables chockablock with patrons line newly widened sidewalks; an old woman shuffles along, wearing three sweaters and gloves in the 80F heat, and a Japanese tourist looks perplexed. The photogenic potential of such contrasts appealed to "Miami Vice" producer Michael Mann, who opted for the realism of shooting here rather than on a Hollywood set. Local authorities admit gratitude for the publicity — and resultant tourist dollars — the show generated. In fact, the area is so much in demand for photographic shoots for fashion magazines and fashion catalogues that seven modeling agencies have sprung up here.

The popularity of this district has undergone some changes over the decades. In the 1920s and 1930s, hotel guests and residents here were largely Jews, who were restricted to living south of 15th Street and east of Washington Avenue; beyond those boundaries, developer Carl Fisher enforced the "Caucasian Clause" of his predecessors' real-estate contracts, and denied Jews and blacks the opportunity to stay in his hotels or to buy real estate. This area, also known as South Beach, was then developed by the Lummus brothers, who admitted Jews but prohibited blacks. Over the years, the area fell into decline, and the former hotels became homes for the elderly living on Social Security; in a few instances, they still can be seen sitting on their porches in rocking chairs.

In 1980, many emigrés from Cuba's famous Mariel boatlift settled here. Some of the hotels that remain have small rooms and unit air conditioners, but provide very inexpensive accommodations. A few, like the *Beach Paradise* hotel, stand out (see "Checking In" in *Miami,* THE CITIES); it's a good base for exploring the region. While not as whimsical-looking as other buildings, the hotel's white stucco walls and flamingo-pink trim, the lobby's original fireplace, and the pecky cypress ceiling are hallmarks of its Art Deco design. A 90-minute guided tour, led by a historian who regales visitors with fascinating anecdotes, leaves the *Miami Design Preservation League* office (661 Washington Ave.; phone: 305-672-2014) every Saturday at 10:30 AM; admission charge. Reservations unnecessary. Additional tours are available during *Art Deco Weekend* in January, with juried artists, culinary booths, stage concerts, and the *Moon Over Miami* ball. Those driving will find inexpensive, safe parking at Lincoln Road Mall Parking near the *Theater of the Performing Arts (TOPA)* and the *Miami Beach Convention Center.* For more information see *Tour 1: Art Deco District* in DIRECTIONS.

LITTLE HAVANA: With Cuba off-limits to most of us, this enclave of Cuban and Nicaraguan immigrants is the next best thing to experiencing a slice of Havana life firsthand. The neighborhood now called Little Havana was primarily a Jewish community until about 35 years ago. Cuban immigrants then began arriving in droves, especially once Castro took power. Now a stroll down Calle Ocho can evoke images of the Havana many remember from the classic film versions of Hemingway's *The Old Man and the Sea* and Graham Greene's *Our Man in Havana.* The sounds of samba and rumba music can be heard wafting out of apartment windows and bars; the smells of *plátanos* (plantains), chicken and rice, black beans, and grilled pork strips comingle in the air, while street vendors sell vegetables and other wares. Mothers and their children attired in brightly colored, ruffled dresses sit together on steps and watch the tourists watching them. Men in *guayaberas* (tieless, embroidered shirts often worn in Latin American countries) gather in doorways or in Máximo Gomez Park (SW 8th St. and SW 15th Ave.) to play dominoes or chess and smoke cigars (no cursing, gambling, or women allowed!). The air is alive with activity accented with the vibrant colors of the Latin world — oranges, reds, and yellows.

Eateries with grill-fronted windows that open onto the street dispense strong *café con leche* and guava *pasteles;* stores sport signs in Spanish and, if you can't speak any, you may have problems communicating; vendors in open-air markets hawk sugarcane stalks and green coconuts complete with straws for drinking the coconut milk. For a taste of Cuba, try a Cuban sandwich (ham, cheese, pickles, and mustard on crispy Cuban bread) at *El Pub* (SW 16th Ave.). For a complete Latin meal, try *Málaga* (740 SW 8th St.) or *Versailles* (3535 SW 8th St.) for roast pork with rice and black-bean sauce, then flan (a custard covered with caramel syrup) for dessert. Cuban products even can be seen being made at various spots in the neighborhood. At *El Crédito* (1106 SW 8th St.), watch cigars being made at Miami's largest hand-rolled cigar factory, a business that was launched here in 1969, but began in Havana in 1907. Peek in at the *Botánica la Abuela* (1122 SW 8th St.); besides the handmade dolls and a few *piñatas,* shelves bear such items as leaves and roots used for *santería* rituals, an Afro-Cuban mixture of voodoo and Catholicism. A few blocks away, *La Casa de las Piñatas* (1756 SW 8th St.) sells wonderful *piñatas.* The standard paper donkeys from Mexico are moderately priced (about $25), but prices go up for the fantastic creations suspended from the ceiling, such as a 4-foot-high Big Bird, which sells for $179; others are priced as high as $500 (squawk!). A more somber note prevails at the Brigade 2506 Memorial (at SW 13th Ave.), built to commemorate those who fell in the ill-fated Bay of Pigs invasion. But the Hispanic fervor really erupts each year for *Carnaval Miami,* a 10-day-long celebration in early March featuring a *paseo,* an 8-km run, and folkloric entertainment; it culminates in *Calle Ocho: Open House,* the country's largest street festival. Begun in 1978 as a block party, this event now includes 23 blocks of 50 stages featuring 200 musical groups and 500 vendors selling everything from hot dogs to paella — with plenty of samples. More than 1 million people participate. For information, contact the *Kiwanis Club of Little Havana* (phone: 305-644-8888). But if it's the sultry sensuality of a Latin night that you seek, pick a dimly lit table for two at one of the local restaurants, order up some Cuban chow, make sure the salsa music is well within earshot, and then close your eyes — you might almost forget for a moment that you're in Miami!

FOOTBALL FEVER: From September to January, this town goes nuts over football — collegiate and professional. Frequent NFL-division champions, the Miami *Dolphins* play at *Joe Robbie Stadium* in Greater Miami North (2269 NW 199th St.; phone: 305-620-2578; fax: 305-620-6596). Dan Marino — *Dolphins* quarterback and *Pro Bowl* choice — has brought the local football fanaticism to new heights. The competitive national college football power, the University of Miami *Hurricanes,* toss the pigskin at the *Orange Bowl Stadium* (1501 NW 3rd St.; phone: 305-358-5885 for tickets, 305-643-7100 for other *Orange Bowl* information; fax: 305-643-7115). The world-famous Federal Express *Orange Bowl Football Classic,* pitting the Big Eight collegiate conference champion against another nationally ranked team, is played at the *Orange Bowl Stadium* on *New Year's* night (phone: 305-642-5211). It's preceded by the *King Orange Jamboree Parade,* a lavish procession downtown on Biscayne Boulevard on *New Year's Eve* (phone: 305-642-1515). In response to this craziness, the *King Mango Strut* parade developed a few years back; it winds its way through Coconut Grove a few days in advance — a socially satirical poke at much that is considered "holy" these days (phone: 305-441-0944). Top-ranked collegiate teams go head-to-head at the *Block-buster Bowl* at *Joe Robbie Stadium* during the last weekend in December (phone: 305-620-2578; fax: 305-620-6596).

EARLY-BIRD DINNERS: The classic joke is that Florida's state tree is the sabal palm and the state bird is the "early bird." Early-bird dinners are a regular topic of conversation around pools, on golf courses, and in lines at the supermarket; dining out is a favorite South Florida activity and early-bird specials afford a full dinner at less money than the same meal will cost later in the evening. To spread business over a longer dinnertime (especially in season, when long lines are frequently the norm), restaurateurs provide incentives to dine early by lowering prices before peak hours (sometimes people have their evening meal as early as 4 PM). Some eateries, though, offer their early-bird hours as late as 6 PM or so. Experienced early birds know what is the latest possible time to get in line and still qualify as an early bird. For the rest of us, it's best to check the local papers for times. That way, you too can enjoy the same tropical decor, attentive service, scenic views, and first-rate fare that will be served a few hours later at up to twice the price. An example is *Charley's Crab* (see "Eating Out" in *Ft. Lauderdale,* THE CITIES), where diners from 5 to 5:45 PM daily can choose from a menu that is limited but still features fresh fish and the noteworthy Martha's Vineyard salad — all for about $10 — while enjoying the same waterfront entertainment as later diners. Or try a restaurant as elegant as *Dominique's* (see "Eating Out" in *Miami,* THE CITIES), where you can savor the wonderful lobster ravioli and the beef tournadoes with sauvignon sauce. An elegantly served three-course dinner costs $20 from 5:30 to 7 PM. Be aware that early-bird meals sometimes masquerade as "sunset specials," "twilight dinners," or the like. If you don't mind eating early, be sure to ask restaurants if they offer such a deal. A better-kept secret is the summertime bargain. Since business falls off drastically when the "season" ends — usually about April or May — some restaurateurs have trouble retaining and paying their staffs over the summer. To drum up business, they provide specials such as two meals for the price of one. *Gibby's* (see "Eating Out" in *Ft. Lauderdale,* THE CITIES) features dinners with two Maine lobsters and other accoutrements for the cost of a chicken meal during season — $17. The outdoor *Pelican Bar* at *Pier 66* (see "Eating Out" in *Miami,* THE CITIES) has a lobster dinner with salad and a drink for $10. Never mind the worm; here it's definitely the early bird that catches the inexpensive lobster.

JOE'S STONE CRAB: A Miami Beach institution for 8 decades, famous for its stone crabs (a local delicacy) and creamy mustard sauce, this eatery, run by Joe Weiss's family, is open only when stone crabs are in season, mid-October to mid-May (grand-daughter JoAnn is now president). The tasty crustaceans are trapped in Florida waters in much the same way as lobsters are caught, except that fishermen only pull off one of the claws and throw the crabs back in to regenerate for the next harvest. No reservations are accepted, the wait for dinner is sometimes hours long, and the service rushed, but regulars swear it's worth the inconvenience. Business types lunch here when it's less frenetic. Other foods served include lobster and fresh fish, killer hash brown potatoes, delicious cole slaw, and a mean Key lime pie. If you don't want to fight the crowds, pick up a picnic lunch from the restaurant's take-out section and head for the beach. An allied company, *Joe's Stone Crabs Inc.,* supplies stone crabs and that wonderful Key lime pie to other restaurants. 227 Biscayne St., Miami Beach (phone: 305-673-0365 or 800-780-CRAB).

Best Hotels

 Miami is a hotel town, welcoming tourists by the droves every winter as they escape the cold northern climes. Below we list the cream of the crop — those establishments where first-rate service, facilities, and atmosphere make for a memorable vacation experience. Reservations should be made well in advance during the busy season (winter). Come and enjoy the luxury and the balmy weather — the only place you can ski here is on the water.

COLONNADE: Built in the 1920s, this European-style Coral Gables hostelry incorporates an original Spanish Renaissance façade and a 2-story, marble-floored rotunda with traditionally furnished accommodations. Luxurious details include carved mahogany furniture, late-19th-century decor with European elegance, king-size beds, armoires, marble vanities, and gold bathroom fixtures. No-smoking rooms are available. Upon arrival, guests are greeted with champagne and orange juice in the intimate lobby; once settled in, they can expect complimentary coffee and the daily newspaper with wake-up calls, and a room-service breakfast can be delivered to outdoor tables set among lovely gardens at the rooftop pool and Jacuzzi that overlook Coral Gables. Information: *Colonnade,* 180 Aragon Ave., Coral Gables, FL 33134 (phone: 305-441-2600 or 800-533-1337; fax: 305-445-3929).

DORAL COUNTRY CLUB: It is well-nigh impossible to accurately pick the centerpiece here: the world class golf (5 championship courses and a par 3 practice course), 15 tennis courts, an equestrian center, virtually unlimited access (and free transportation) to its sister property, the *Doral Ocean Beach* resort, or the *Doral Saturnia International Spa* resort. *Saturnia* is the spa everyone's talking about (see *Sybaritic Spas*), a luxurious $33-million facility modeled after the *Terme di Saturnia* in Italy. Guests live in posh spa suites, indulging in everything from *fango* (volcanic mud) treatments to workouts — all in European grandeur. Taking into account the availability of facilities at all the *Dorals,* virtually no physical or spiritual need is left unattended. Information: *Doral Resort and Country Club,* 4400 NW 87th Ave., Miami, FL 33178 (phone: 305-592-2000; 800-22-DORAL; fax: 305-594-4682).

GRAND BAY: Everything about this consistent winner of top Florida and US hotel awards is done in high style. Strains of Mozart and Mendelssohn fill the elegantly appointed, European-style lobby; lavish fresh flower arrangements are everywhere. All of its 181 spacious rooms (most have private balconies) overlook Biscayne Bay; suites are decorated in a theme — Italian terra cotta, French country, Japanese, and Olde English. Michael Jackson's suite — available when he's not in town — has its own dance floor and some suites have baby grand pianos. Attention to individual needs is paramount; details even extend to the placement of a mat beside your bed so your bare feet needn't touch the carpet. This also is home of the fashionable *Régine's* nightclub and 3 restaurants, including the famed *Grand Café* (see "Eating Out" in *Miami,* THE CITIES). Information: *Grand Bay,* 2669 S. Bayshore Dr., Coconut Grove, FL 33133 (phone: 305-858-9600 or 800-327-2788; 800-341-0809; fax: 305-859-2026).

TURNBERRY ISLE: Set on a verdant, 300-acre island, this complex of 3 hotels — each with its own distinct personality — offers a total of 361 rooms and suites. The

Country Club is a stunner; its palatial lobby/lounge has gleaming marble floors, classically designed upholstered sofas, and Oriental jardinières filled to overflowing with colorful floral arrangements. Its *Veranda* restaurant (see "Eating Out" in *Miami,* THE CITIES), with more beautiful flowers and French elegance, serves innovative dishes such as rum-glazed shrimp with passion-fruit sauce, plantain-crusted salmon filet, and fire-roasted ranch veal chops. The hotel's exterior has a Mediterranean accent, with barrel-tile roofs, fountains, and tile inserts. Beautifully decorated guestrooms boast 3 dual-line telephones, marble countertops, and whirlpool baths. Even the meeting rooms are brighter and airier than most, with windows opening onto the golf course. Located on the marina, the *Yacht Club* attracts those who revel in things nautical. Museum-quality ship models enhance the decor; there's even a musty, but appealing, shipboard scent. Vacationers can charter *Miss Turnberry,* a 140-foot yacht, for $12,000 per day. The adjacent spa (see *Sybaritic Spas*), an impressive facility geared to the exercise-oriented, features beauty and stress-management programs as well. Beside it sits the *Marina* hotel, favored by such notables as Bill Cosby and Elton John for its no-lobby privacy. The hotel is designed in a Mediterranean-style decor with marble and tile. The spa is contemporary with all modern facilities. The complex, linked by a complimentary shuttle, offers 9 restaurants and lounges, 2 Robert Trent Jones, Sr. golf courses, 25 tennis courts, 5 pools, a spa, marina, private beach club, 24-hour room service, and a concierge. Information: *Turnberry Isle,* 19999 W. Country Club Dr., Aventura, Turnberry Isle, FL 33180 (phone: 305-932-6200 or 800-327-7028; fax: 305-932-9096).

■**Worth A Short Detour:** Just 30 minutes north of Ft. Lauderdale, the elegant *Boca Beach Club* is definitely worth a visit. You know you're entering a special place from the moment you arrive: Cozy armchairs and a goblet of champagne or a flagon of fresh orange juice are offered even before you check in, and registration is accomplished at lovely antique desks attended by a smiling, attentive staff. The rooms are large and well furnished, and the club's site on a spit of land between the Intracoastal Waterway and the Atlantic guarantees a watery vista no matter where your room is. The best rooms in the house, however, are those on the ground floor: They offer lanais for lounging and direct access to the beach on the Atlantic side. There also are 2 large pools, and guests have access to the numerous tennis courts, the golf course, and the considerable other amenities of the sprawling 1,000-room *Boca Raton Resort and Club.* The resort itself, however, has seen better days; we recommend only the *Club.* Information: *Boca Raton Resort and Club,* 501 E. Camino Real, Boca Raton, FL 33431-0825 (phone: 407-395-3000 or 800-327-0101).

Best Restaurants

Eating out is a major-league sport in South Florida. While there are those who say that dining here doesn't compare with Manhattan or San Francisco, the variety of restaurants — everything from an impressive range of sophisticated dining places to more casual ethnic eateries — can tempt (and amply satisfy) a visitor's tastebuds. Since eating out is such a popular social activity, be prepared for long lines during the winter season (December through April), when snowbirds swell the ranks of regulars. Sample the seafood, and don't be timid about trying some Cuban specialties: this is probably as close to Havana as you'll get for some time.

ARAGON CAFÉ: The *Colonnade* hotel's outstanding dining spot features Old World European decor, with mahogany trim and crystal chandelier. The menu includes a blue crab cake appetizer and an enormous veal chop with polenta. Delicious details include the sweet-potato mousse that accompanies entrées, and specialty dessert soufflés, which must be ordered at the beginning of dinner. (The pistachio soufflé with chocolate chips in a bed of vanilla sauce makes diners think they've gone to heaven.) Service is impeccable, without being condescending. Open for dinner from 6 to 11 PM Mondays through Saturdays. Information: *Aragon Café,* 180 Aragon Ave., Coral Gables (phone: 305-441-2600 or 800-533-1337).

BRASSERIE LE COZE: On the theory that you can't have too much of a good thing, owners Gilbert and Maguy Le Coze of New York City's *Le Bernardin* have brought their impressive culinary talents to the South. This newest entry to the Miami dining scene had its roots in Paris (*Le Bernardin* was one of Paris's three-star restaurants) and later moved its headquarters to New York City. In this Florida addition the Le Cozes offer an appealing ambience in a setting of hand-painted Portuguese and French tiles, leather booths, and terrace doors that open onto sidewalk tables. The fare is first-rate and the menu is as diverse as the surroundings. Dining choices run the gamut from grouper with aioli (garlic) sauce to duck *confit* cassoulet. Also try the shellfish, priced by-the-piece for oysters and clams. It's not the Faubourg St.-Honoré or West 51st Street, but it's close. Open Thursdays through Sundays, serving lunch noon to 2:30 PM and dinner from 6 PM to midnight. Information: *Brasserie Le Coze,* 2901 Florida Ave., Coconut Grove (phone: 305-444-9671).

BY WORD OF MOUTH: The focus is on food at this less-than-posh but oh-so-delicious Ft. Lauderdale dining place, where the day's dining options are displayed in a refrigerated glass case. Don't miss the Acapulco shrimp salad, outrageous sun-dried tomato and pesto pie, or mussels with red pepper vinaigrette. To top off the meal, there are mouth-watering desserts such as alpine cake filled with chocolate mousse and raspberry preserves. Open for lunch Mondays through Fridays 11 AM to 3 PM; for dinner Wednesdays and Thursdays 5 to 9 PM; and Fridays and Saturdays 5 to 10 PM. Information: *By Word of Mouth,* 3200 NE 12th Ave., Ft. Lauderdale (phone: 305-564-3663).

CAFÉ CHAUVERON: Transplanted many years ago from New York City to Bay Harbor without the slightest disturbance to its delirious desserts, this French dining place exudes elegance with its rich decor, dark wood paneling, and crystal chandelier. The dining room is divided into two levels; the lower level boasts a wall of windows looking out onto Indian Creek. It's a good place for spotting Miami's famous and infamous. Everything is beautifully prepared, from stone-crab ravioli and Dover sole to the famous mile-high soufflés, including Grand Marnier with raspberry *coulis* and *crème fraîche.* Docking space is provided if you arrive by boat. Open daily 6 to 10:30 PM, but closed from June through early October. Information: *Café Chauveron,* 9561 E. Bay Harbor Dr., Bay Harbor Island, Miami Beach (phone: 305-866-8779).

CAFÉ MAX: This simply decorated eatery in the Pompano Beach strip shopping center focuses on great food. And though it's not an elegantly styled room, the dishes created here are on the cutting edge of new American cooking; many have been recipients of major awards, their recipes written up in such food publications as *Food & Wine* magazine. Created by restaurateur Dennis Max and chef Mark Militello (who now owns *Mark's Place;* see below), owners now are Darrel Broek and Oliver Saucy, who also is executive chef. Each presentation is a visual masterpiece. For example, oysters are dipped in ground pistachios and fried, then replaced in their shells atop a bed of corn and tomato salsa and surrounded by a mound of red and green curly lettuce, enoki mushrooms, lemon grass, and a nasturtium blossom. The Peking pork with honey-sesame glaze, and white chocolate mousse pie with raspberry sauce and a white chocolate truffle, attest to the chef's melting-pot inventiveness. Open daily for dinner 6 to 11 PM. Information: *Café Max,* 2601 E. Atlantic Blvd., Pompano Beach (phone: 305-782-0606).

CHEF ALLEN'S: Allen Susser is the chef/owner who has won deserved national acclaim for his culinary achievements. (Susser was voted one of the country's Best New American Chefs by *Food & Wine* magazine.) Featured here is regional South Florida cooking, using local produce and fresh-caught yellowtail, tuna, and snapper (Norwegian salmon also is served here with its own caviar) in a sophisticated atmosphere — lacquered furniture and colorful lights. Even the salad of field greens is beautifully presented, with tiny confetti-like squares of colorful peppers. Carrot timbale enhances the entrées, and the white chocolate bombe is as rewarding to the eyes as to the taste buds. Many creative "spa cuisine" dishes are also featured. Open daily for dinner from 6 to 10:30 PM, until 11 PM Fridays and Saturdays. Information: *Chef Allen's,* 19088 NE 29th Ave., North Miami Beach (phone: 305-935-2900).

FISH MARKET: Far more elegant than its name implies, this hotel dining room (actually, there are two rooms) gleams with marble and mirrors. Considered the best seafood place in the area, it's known for its grilled fish, which may be ordered with a choice of sauces; the kitchen also does delicious specialties such as sole filets stuffed with Florida lobster, mussels, and wild mushrooms or scallops and medallions of lobster served with *risotto milanese* (i.e., with saffron). Garden vegetables are combined with a taste-tantalizing corn flan. And for a special treat, try the pâté of tropical fruits and berries with passion-fruit sauce for dessert. Open for lunch 11:30 AM to 2:30 PM Mondays through Fridays, and for dinner 6:30 to 11 PM Mondays through Saturdays. Information: *Fish Market,* in the *Omni International Hotel,* 1601 Biscayne Blvd., Miami (phone: 305-374-4399).

GRAND CAFÉ: On Queen Elizabeth's 1991 visit to Miami, it was this eatery's Chef Suki who conferred with the royal chefs regarding local foods; moreover, *Grand Café* provided the hors d'oeuvres for her fete at the *Vizcaya* mansion (see *Memorable Museums*). It has an elegantly European dining room, attentive service, and wonderful creations including such international innovations as duck smoked over Texas pecan shells and topped with ginger-flavored passion-fruit sauce. Also try Suki's famous black linguine (made with squid ink). Open daily for breakfast 7 to 11 AM, plus Sunday brunch 11:30 AM to 3 PM; for lunch 11:30 AM to 3 PM Mondays through Saturdays; dinner daily 6 to 11 PM. Information: *Grand Café,* in the *Grand Bay Hotel,* 2669 S. Bayshore Dr., Coconut Grove (phone: 305-858-9600).

JOE'S STONE CRAB: For the ultimate Miami dining experience, this place offers the best stone crabs around, along with scrumptious home fries, delectable coleslaw, and to-die-for Key lime pie. Diners often have to wait hours to be seated and service can be rushed and sporadic, but devoted fans say it's well worth the wait and inconvenience. Besides the crabs, lobster and fresh fish also are served. Picnickers can buy lunch from the restaurant's take-out section and avoid the lunacy in the dining room. Information: *Joe's Stone Crab,* 227 Biscayne St., Miami Beach (phone: 305-673-0365 or 800-780-CRAB).

MARK'S PLACE: The modern interior — dramatized by vibrant contemporary Venetian glass sculptures — serves as an exciting backdrop for this Miami "in" spot. Chef Mark Militello whips up such imaginative dishes as grilled yellowtail snapper with Mediterranean salsa, West Indian pumpkin, and hearts of palm, or salmon with couscous, fried onion strips, and nasturtiums. The rich desserts include a terrific pear tart. Open for lunch weekdays noon to 2:30 PM; for dinner Mondays through Thursdays 6:30 to 10:30 PM, Fridays and Saturdays 6 to 11 PM, and Sundays 6 PM to 10:30PM. Information: *Mark's Place,* 2286 NE 123 St., North Miami Beach (phone: 305-893-6888).

PAVILLON GRILL: For diners seeking creative cookery in elegant surroundings, here is top American food with a decidedly nouvelle bent: Everglade frogs' legs cakes with chilled vermouth mayonnaise, grilled venison medallions with cassis sauce, and duck "in two acts" (sautéed breast and duck confit). The *crème brûlée,* filled with fresh berries, is a visual and gustatory sensation. The setting is stylishly formal, with beveled mirrors and green granite; the food magnificently prepared, and the service faultless. Dinner only from 6 to 10 PM Mondays through Thursdays, until 11 PM Fridays and Saturdays; closed Sundays. Information: *Pavillon Grill,* in the *Inter-Continental Hotel,* 100 Chopin Plaza, Miami (phone: 305-577-1000).

PLUM ROOM: One of South Florida's most romantic, intimate rooms, it features beautifully prepared and presented continental food as a harpist plays in the background. There are classic dishes, including sole Veronique and beef Wellington; don't miss the cream of mushroom soup, made with shiitake, enoki, and white mushrooms — and exotica such as ostrich and elk. There's also an extensive — and impressive — wine list. Open from 6:30 to 11 PM Sundays through Thursdays, until midnight Fridays and Saturdays. Information: *Plum Room,* 3001 E. Oakland Park Blvd., Ft. Lauderdale (phone: 305-563-4168).

Shopping Spree

Even the most dedicated sun worshipers need a break from the beach sometimes, so when the sun gets too strong, or, heaven forbid, it *rains,* visitors and residents alike head to the many shopping malls in the Miami area. You can find anything your heart desires at the various malls and shopping areas listed below; many have lovely outdoor restaurants and there are benches at which to rest your shop-weary feet — or to park your shop-weary companion.

AVENTURA MALL: This Spanish-style shopper's haven, one of South Florida's largest, has 200 shops on 2 levels and a large food court. Department stores include *Lord & Taylor* and *Macy's.* Open daily 10 AM to 9:30 PM. 19501 Biscayne Blvd., North Miami Beach (phone: 305-935-1110).

BAL HARBOUR SHOPS: With its splashing fountains and colorful gardens, this charming shopping area is a pleasant spot for buyers and browsers alike. Fashionable stores include *Saks Fifth Avenue, Neiman Marcus, Cartier, Brooks Brothers,* and *F.A.O. Schwarz.* Among the five outdoor eateries are *Ms. Grimble, American Way,* and *Coco's.* Open Mondays, Thursdays, and Fridays 10 AM to 9 PM; Tuesdays, Wednesdays, and Saturdays 10 AM to 6 PM; and Sundays noon to 5 PM. 9700 Collins Ave., Bal Harbour (phone: 305-866-0311).

BAYSIDE MARKETPLACE: Designed by the same folks who gave Boston *Faneuil Hall,* this outdoor, tropical-looking complex of 150 shops and 32 eateries boasts emporia including *Exit Shops* and *Brookstone,* plus outdoor pushcarts hawking Central and South American crafts. Located at Miami's Biscayne Bay, within walking distance of cruise-ship docks. Parking available; also served by public transportation and trolleys. Open Mondays through Saturdays 10 AM to 10 PM, Sundays noon to 8 PM. 401 Biscayne Blvd., Miami (phone: 305-577-3344).

BROWARD MALL: An ultramodern mart, it attracts young families and seniors alike with its 130 specialty shops (more than any mall in Florida) and mainstay merchandise marts, including *Burdine's, Sears,* and *JC Penney.* Open Sundays noon to 5 PM, other days 10 AM to 9 PM. Broward Blvd. and University Dr., Plantation, Ft. Lauderdale (phone: 305-473-8100).

DADELAND MALL: One of southern Miami's most popular shopping venues, it's got Florida's largest *Burdine's,* along with *Saks Fifth Avenue, Lord & Taylor* and 170 other shops. Open Mondays through Saturdays 10 AM to 9 PM, Sundays noon to 6 PM. 7535 N. Kendall Dr., Miami (phone: 305-665-6226).

DANSK FACTORY OUTLETS: For discounted Danish-designed housewares, featuring seconds and overstocks on stainless flatware, wood serving pieces, and well-designed Scandinavian tableware. Open Mondays through Saturdays 10 AM to 5:30 PM and Sundays noon to 5 PM. 27 W. Hallandale Beach Blvd., Hallandale (phone: 305-454-3900) and 2401 W. Atlantic Blvd., Pompano Beach (phone: 305-973-7527).

FALLS SHOPPING CENTER: A pretty, woodsy setting of upscale stores and restaurants among splashing waterfalls. The 60 shops include Miami's only *Bloomingdale's*. Open Mondays through Saturdays 10 AM to 9 PM, Sundays noon to 5 PM. 8888 Howard Dr., Miami (phone: 305-255-4570).

FASHION ROW: Long known as "Shmatte Row" (Yiddish for garments or rags), this region near the railroad tracks has been luring bargain hunters for years. Along NE 1st Avenue off Hallandale Beach Boulevard is one section of discount dress and handbag shops (look for *Sheila's* and *Bags 'n Things*); the other section is on NE 2nd Avenue between NE 3rd and NE 4th Streets (don't miss *Michael's* and *Vera* for lingerie). Open daily 10 AM to 5 PM; closed on Sundays in the summer. Stop at *Barnett's* (around the corner), chock-full of everything for the home at discount prices. 100 E. Hallandale Beach Blvd., Hallandale (phone: 305-456-0566).

FESTIVAL MARKETPLACE: A 400,000-square-foot indoor flea-market-type mall in western Ft. Lauderdale, where 755 vendors offer brand-new merchandise as well as antiques and collectibles. Try the *Rodeo Drive Boutique* for designer clothing. There also are 8 movie theaters, an amusement arcade, and an international food court. Many items are discounted. Future plans call for a farmers' market reminiscent of those in the Pennsylvania Dutch country. Open Thursdays through Sundays from 9:30 AM to 5 PM. 2900 W. Sample Rd., Coconut Creek (phone: 305-979-4555).

GALLERIA: High fashion for the body, specialty shops include *Ann Taylor, Cartier, Brooks Brothers,* and *Sharper Image* plus retail giants *Neiman Marcus, Saks, and Burdine's*. Open Sundays 12:30 to 5:30 PM, other days 10 AM to 9 PM. 2414 E. Sunrise Blvd., Ft. Lauderdale (phone: 305-564-1015).

SAWGRASS MILLS MALL: Touted as the world's largest outlet mall, this bright and airy alligator-shape discount shopping complex is located 9 miles west of Ft. Lauderdale. Boasting anchor stores including *Sears, Marshalls, Macy's, Saks Fifth Avenue, Spiegel's,* and *Phar-Mor* — it has 200 other retail and discount shops, among them *Benetton, Guess?, Dexter Shoes, American Tourister, Lillie Rubin,* and *Van Heusen*. Some stores offer valid savings of 20% to 60%; others push products so old and shopworn it's hard to believe someone would pay hundreds of dollars for them. This mall is for Olympic-caliber shoppers; it's important to know what things sell for elsewhere. Several restaurants and two food courts provide respite. An 18-plex movie theater, billed as the largest east of the Mississippi, completes the picture. Open Mondays through Saturdays 10 AM to 9:30 PM, Sundays 11 AM to 6 PM. 12801 W. Sunrise Blvd., Sunrise (phone: 305-846-1000 or 800-FL-MILLS).

SWAP SHOP: There are bargains galore at this mostly outdoor flea market, the South's largest, where 2,000 vendors hawk everything from blue jeans to tapes, paintings to cucumbers. (It claims to be Florida's second-largest tourist attraction after *Walt Disney World*.) Free concerts by the likes of Marie Osmond and Loretta Lynn are presented; there's also a daily circus. Open daily from 7:30 AM to 7:30 PM; Saturdays and Sundays to 6:30 PM; outdoor stalls close an hour earlier. 3291 W. Sunrise Blvd., Ft. Lauderdale (phone: 305-791-SWAP). A second branch with 550 booths is open Tuesdays, Saturdays, and Sundays from 6 AM to 3 PM. 1000 State Rd. 7, Margate (phone: 305-971-SWAP).

For the Body

Great Golf

 Its almost constant sunshine, balmy breezes, and picturesque fairways make Greater Miami a dream for golfers most of the year — witness the preponderance of golf tournaments held here. Several resorts boast excellent golf courses, and many that lack their own links provide access to other clubs. It's usually necessary to call ahead for reservations, especially during the winter season.

Many other courses (approximately 76 in all) are open to the public. For information in Miami, call the following Parks and Recreation Departments: Metro-Dade County (phone: 305-579-2968); City of Miami Beach (phone: 305-673-7730); or City of Miami (phone: 305-575-5256). In Ft. Lauderdale, call the Parks and Recreation Division of Broward County (phone: 305-357-8100).

The *Honda Golf Classic* is one of the major US events on the PGA circuit, played in March at the private *Weston Hills Country Club* in Coral Springs. You might spot such pros as Nick Faldo, Tom Watson, or Greg Norman attempting a birdie here (phone: 305-755-4220). The $1.4-million *Doral-Ryder Open* is held annually on the championship *Blue Monster* course at the *Doral Resort & Country Club* in Miami in late February or early March. A Ladies PGA event is held each February at *Inverrary,* former home of the *Jackie Gleason Inverrary Golf Classic.*

Here are a few of our favorite greens.

BONAVENTURE: Two championship 18-hole courses lure golfers to this 504-room resort. The east course is considered one of Florida's top ten, and the waterfall hole is certainly challenging. There's also a driving range, putting green, and pro shop. Moonlight golf adds to the standard tee-off times. Special plans combine spa and golf vacations. Pro is Rick Weber. Information: *Bonaventure,* 250 Racquet Club Rd., Ft. Lauderdale, FL 33326 (phone: 305-389-2100 or 800-327-8090; fax: 305-384-0563).

DORAL: At the moment, this 650-room resort stands like the grande golfing dame of the Miami–Miami Beach tourist axis. The *Doral*'s superb golf facilities (five 18-hole layouts, plus a par 3 executive course) thus far remain unassailed, and the fabled championship *Blue Monster* is still one of the most formidable challenges in the state; it is the site of the annual $1.4-million *Doral-Ryder Open.* And the *Gold* course offers little diminution in challenge. Touring pro: Peter Jacobsen. Information: *Doral Resort & Country Club,* 4400 NW 87th Ave., Miami, FL 33178 (phone: 305-592-2000, 800-327-6334, or 800-22DORAL; fax: 305-594-4682).

PALM-AIRE: Courses here have hosted the *Florida Open, US Open* qualifying matches, and the Florida PGA's tournament. The resort is part of a 1,500-acre hotel and residential development, with four 18-hole championship golf courses and an 18-hole executive course. The *Cypress, Palms,* and *Oaks* courses are considered among Florida's toughest 20. Instruction available, combination spa and golf packages possible. Director of golf at the *Cypress* and *Oaks* is Jerry Sehlke (phone: 305-978-1737); touring pro at the *Palms* is Tom Malone (phone: 305-968-2775). Information: *Palm-*

Aire, 2601 Palm-Aire Dr. N., Pompano Beach, FL 33069 (phone: 305-972-3300 or 800-272-5624; fax: 305-968-2744).

TURNBERRY ISLE: Boasting two Robert Trent Jones, Sr., courses, its golf inducements include daily lessons and clinics and three pro shops. Set on a 300-acre island, the complex also features 3 hotels, a first class spa, and a marina with a private beach club. Director of golf and touring pro is Raymond Floyd, former *US Open* and *Masters'* champion. Information: *Turnberry Isle,* 19999 W. Country Club Dr., Aventura, FL 33108-2402 (phone: 305-932-6200 or 800-327-7028; fax: 305-932-9096).

Tennis

Mild and sunny weather make South Florida ideal for year-round tennis, as attested to by residents Gabriella Sabatini and Steffi Graf. Most major resorts have tennis courts, and public courts are available throughout the region — over 550 courts in metropolitan Dade County parks alone (phone: 305-579-2676). In Ft. Lauderdale, contact the Broward County Parks and Recreation Division (phone: 305-357-8100). Call ahead to check on availability.

The 10-day *Lipton International Players Championships* is one of the world's largest tennis happenings, with such top players as Boris Becker and Ivan Lendl on hand in March. For information, contact the *International Tennis Center,* 7300 Crandon Blvd., Key Biscayne, FL 33179 (phone: 305-361-5252) or 2 Alhambra Plaza, Coral Gables, FL 33134 (phone: 305-446-2200).

Don't be intimidated by the pros. There are lots of fine courts where you can ace it with the best of them.

BONAVENTURE: The 504-room resort offers 24 tennis courts, most nightlit; 18 are clay. There also are 5 indoor air conditioned racquetball and squash courts, and a pro shop. Combination tennis and spa packages are available. Information: *Bonaventure,* 250 Racquet Club Rd., Ft. Lauderdale, FL 33326 (phone: 305-389-3300 or 800-327-8090; fax: 305-384-0563).

DORAL: A veritable city of a resort, this 2,400-acre establishment offers just about any diversion (including five 18-hole championship golf courses and one 9-hole course), except a beach of its own. But there's one just 15 minutes away at its sister property, the *Doral Ocean Beach* resort (along with a swimming pool, 3 restaurants, and a cocktail lounge with dancing). Tennis facilities: 15 well-kept clay and hard-surface courts; backboard and ball machines; court reservations; private lessons and group clinics. Arthur Ashe is director of tennis. It's managed by *Peter Burwash Clinics.* Information: *Doral Resort & Country Club,* 4400 N.W. 87th Ave., Miami, FL 33178 (phone: 305-592-2000, 800-327-6334, or 800-22DORAL; fax: 305-594-4862).

FISHER ISLAND: This exclusive resort's tennis program, directed by Gardnar Mulloy, has 3 grass courts and 14 clay courts, all lit. You might bump into a well-known movie star or millionaire working on his serve. A video camera may be used for private lessons and weekly clinics and round robins help pick up your game. Information: *Fisher Island,* 1 Fisher Island Dr., Fisher Island, FL 33109 (phone: 305-535-6000 or 800-624-3251; fax: 305-535-6008).

INTERNATIONAL TENNIS CENTER: The site of the annual *Lipton International Players Championship,* it is available for play year-round, offering 17 hard and 7 clay courts, a pro shop, racquet rentals, and lessons. Information: *International Tennis Center,* 7200 Crandon Blvd., Key Biscayne, FL 33149 (phone: 305-361-8633 or 305-361-9725).

SHERATON ROYAL BISCAYNE BEACH: The courts at this resort, off the Miami shore, draw locals as well as vacationers; you can almost always find a tennis partner. Facilities include 10 Laykold courts (4 lighted); video replay and ball machines; private and group lessons. Court reservations are necessary. Information: *Sheraton Royal Biscayne Beach,* 555 Ocean Dr., Key Biscayne, FL 33149 (phone: 305-361-5775 or 800-325-3535).

SONESTA BEACH: This deluxe resort is located on Key Biscayne. In addition to its 10 tennis courts (3 of which are lighted), it also features 5 miles of white sandy beach, an Olympic-size pool, water sports, a fitness center, bicycling, and a championship golf course nearby. Information: *Sonesta Beach,* 350 Ocean Dr., Key Biscayne, FL 33149 (phone: 305-361-2021 or 800-SONESTA; fax: 305-361-3096).

TURNBERRY ISLE: This resort hosts major Pro-Am tournaments, such as the *Barbara Sinatra Classic* and *Barry Gibb's Love and Hope* tournaments. There are 24 tennis courts (18 lighted), including 4 Hydro Court, 4 Deco-Turf, 5 Har-Tru, and 11 hard courts. Teaching staff is under the guidance of Fred Stolle, winner of *Wimbledon,* and the *French, US,* and *Australian Opens.* Information: *Turnberry Isle,* 19999 W. Country Club Dr., Aventura, FL 33180-2401 (phone: 305-932-6200 or 800-327-7028; fax: 305-932-9096).

Horsing Around

 Most people don't think of southern Florida as the Wild, Wild West, but horse country is within closer range than may be expected. Out west (western Ft. Lauderdale, that is), cowboy country awaits in Davie (see *Tour 6: Cowboy and Indian Tour* in DIRECTIONS), with many stables in the area offering trail rides and horse rentals. Among the larger ones are *Bar-B Ranch* for horse rentals (4601 SW 128th Ave., Davie; phone: 305-434-6175) and *Stride-Rite Training Center* for supervised rides (5550 SW 73rd Ave., Davie; phone: 305-587-2285). Broward County also operates stables at *Tradewinds Park* (3600 W. Sample Rd., Coconut Creek; phone: 305-968-3875).

For those who'd rather sit in the stands than in the saddle, thoroughbred racing can be seen at *Calder* racecourse, with the country's only all-weather racing track, on Saturdays and Sundays. For family fun, visitors to Breakfast at Calder can see the thoroughbreds exercise and chat with trainers and jockeys on Saturdays from September to January, 7 to 9 AM. Or try Family Days on Saturdays from May to mid-December, with games, face painting, and a petting zoo. *Calder Race Course,* North Miami next to *Joe Robbie Stadium* (phone: 305-625-1131 in Dade, 305-523-4324 in Broward).

They're also running at *Gulfstream Park* from mid-January to May (but closed Wednesdays); it's also the site of the *Breeder's Cup* (in November). Hallandale Beach Blvd. and US Highway No. 1, Hallandale (phone: 305-944-1242).

Hialeah Park has introduced racing again after a 2-year layoff, in the park noted for its beautiful grounds and pink flamingos. Races daily except Mondays in late autumn. Dining, live music, and kids' attractions also available. 2200 E. 4th Ave., Hialeah (phone: 305-885-8000 or 800-442-5324).

And Florida's only harness racing takes place at *Pompano Harness Track,* beginning early October and running through May, Mondays through Saturdays. 1800 SW 3rd St., Pompano Beach (phone: 305-972-2000).

Biking

Almost every day, cyclists, many looking like contenders in the *Tour de France,* take to the more than 100 miles of bicycle paths in the Miami area, pedaling along tree-shaded lanes through Coconut Grove, Coral Gables, and public parks.

A self-guided bicycle tour of Key Biscayne originates in Crandon Park. The 3.5-mile multipurpose path begins at the park's south end and passes the palm tree–lined beach. Bikers continue through the woods, passing hammocks crafted of trees and cane grass, as well as softball and soccer fields. The path ends at the park's north end, at the marina. Dade County Parks & Recreation has more information (phone: 305-579-2676).

Another favorite spot for cyclists and runners is scenic Tropical Park. The 2-mile path winds through a wooded area, along North Lake and a fishing lake, past a football stadium and boxing and tennis centers. Pick up a map at the park office (open Mondays through Fridays 8 AM to 5 PM; phone: 305-226-8315) or the tennis center (open daily 9 AM to 8 PM; phone: 305-223-8710).

Bicycle rentals are available throughout the Greater Miami area. A few to try:

Cycles on the Beach: 713 Fifth St., Miami Beach (phone: 305-673-2055).

Dade Cycle Shop: 3216 Grand Ave., Coconut Grove (phone: 305-443-6075).

Hun-Fun Scooter & Bicycle Rentals: 220 Sunny Isles Blvd., North Miami (phone: 305-940-3889).

Key Biscayne Bicycle Rentals: 260 Crandon Blvd., Key Biscayne (phone: 305-361-5555).

Miami Beach Bicycle Center: 923 W. 39th St., Miami Beach (phone: 305-531-4161).

Fishing

Anglers of every ilk will find their special brand of fishing within reach here. The Miami shores and inland lakes have attracted such personalities as George Bush, Ernest Hemingway, Theodore Roosevelt, and Winston Churchill. Surf and offshore saltwater fishing is available year-round. Fishing seasons offshore vary by location, as do regulations on kinds and sizes of fish you're allowed to catch. The *Florida Fishing Handbook* is available at no charge by writing to the Florida Game and Fresh Water Fish Commission (620 S. Meridian St., Tallahassee, FL 32399-1600; phone: 904-488-1960). The boardwalks on the Rickenbacker, MacArthur, and Venetian causeways are popular fishing spots; landlubbers with fishing poles can be seen on every bridge and overpass.

The Keys have numerous charter boat services, and there is a sport fishing and shrimping fleet in Key West. Licenses are required for both freshwater and saltwater fishing, and can be obtained from bait and tackle stores as well as *K-Mart* stores. A saltwater fishing license is $30 for non-residents, and $12 for residents. Long-term licenses are also available.

For 24-hour ocean fishing (with an admission charge), try the following:

Anglin's Fishing Pier: 2 Commercial Blvd., Lauderdale-by-the-Sea (phone: 305-491-9403).

Fisherman's Wharf of Pompano Beach: 222 N. Pompano Beach Blvd., Pompano Beach (phone: 305-943-1488).

Haulover Beach Fishing Pier: 10800 Collins Ave., Miami Beach (phone: 305-947-3525).

Holiday Inn Newport Pier: 16701 Collins Ave., Miami (phone: 305-949-1300).

For deep-sea fishing, dozens of party boats are listed under "Fishing" in the yellow pages of the Miami and Ft. Lauderdale telephone books. Charter boats in Miami offer a half day and full day of deep-sea fish, snapper, grouper, yellowtail, pompano, and mackerel trips. Expect to pay about $400 for a half day for up to 6 anglers.

Deep-sea fishing venues include the following:

Bahia Mar Yacht Basin: Across A1A from the beach. 801 Seabreeze Blvd., Ft. Lauderdale (phone: 305-525-7174).

Beach Boat Rentals: Offers 18-footers and speedboats, with or without captains. 2380 Collins Ave., Miami Beach (phone: 305-534-4307).

Castaways Dock: Rents 60-foot and larger fishing boats with captain, mate, bait, and tackle. 16485 Collins Ave., Miami Beach (phone: 305-949-2278).

Club Nautico: Powerboats for charter by the hour, half day, or full day with docks in Miami (phone: 305-371-4252), Miami Beach (phone: 305-673-2502), Coconut Grove (phone: 305-858-6258), North Miami (phone: 305-945-3232), Dania (phone: 305-920-2796), and Ft. Lauderdale (phone: 305-523-0033).

Crandon Park Marina: Fishing boats, powerboats, and sailboats are all available for rental. 4000 Crandon Blvd., Key Biscayne (phone: 305-361-1281).

Ft. Lauderdale Yacht Charters: At *Pier 66.* 2301 SE 17th St. Cswy., Ft. Lauderdale (phone: 305-522-2712).

Great Escape Yachts: Charter fishing boats and dive cruises complete with captains and mates. Speedboats and overnight cruises also available. 3191 Mary St., Coconut Grove (phone: 305-936-0111).

Haulover Marina: 10800 Collins Ave., Miami Beach (phone: 305-947-3525).

There's also plenty of freshwater action in canals and backwaters, including the Everglades and Florida Bay. A favorite strip is along Alligator Alley (Rte. 84), between Ft. Lauderdale and Naples. Bass and bluegills take the bait, especially at low tide. Information: *Naples Area Chamber of Commerce,* US 41, Naples, FL 33940 (phone: 813-262-6141). Freshwater fishing in the Everglades is available from the pier or rented boats at Everglades Holiday Park (21940 Griffin Rd., Ft. Lauderdale; phone: 305-434-8111), Sawgrass Recreation Area (1005 US Rte. 27, Ft. Lauderdale; phone: 305-389-0202), and Quiet Waters Park (6601 N. Powerline Rd., Pompano Beach; phone: 305-360-1315).

Competitive fisherman may want to enter the *Greater Miami Billfish* tournament in April. The event attracts more than 500 anglers vying for South Florida's richest fishing purse (phone: 305-754-0710).

Sailing

After the sunshine, the water is one of South Florida's greatest draws. The year-round good weather is a major plus, and Biscayne Bay and the surrounding waters are sheltered, so there's little chance of large waves. The US Corps of Engineers has eliminated most of the shoal areas and maintains navigational aids. There's also the proximity of the National Marine Sanctuary at Key Largo, with its coral reef and attendant marine life. Oceans of options await sailors. Private and public marinas provide virtually every type of boat for rent:

Cat Ppalu **and** *Pauhana:* These two 49-passenger catamarans are available for charter or sunset tours. *Bayside Marketplace,* 8396 NW S. River Dr., Medley, FL 33166; phone: 305-888-3002).

Club Nautico: This international company rents powerboats in Miami (phone: 305-371-4252), Miami Beach (phone: 305-673-2502), Coconut Grove (phone: 305-858-6258), North Miami Beach (phone: 305-945-3232), Dania (phone: 305-920-2796), and Ft. Lauderdale (phone: 305-523-0033).

Dinner Key Marina: Offers sailboats. 3400 Pan American Dr., Coconut Grove (phone: 305-579-6980).

Easy Sailing: Rents sail- and powerboats, along with windsurfers and Hobie Cats (some with free instruction), on Key Biscayne. 3360 Pan American Dr. (phone: 305-858-4001).

Florida Yacht Charters: Large and small sailboats with or without captains are available for long- or short-term rentals. 1290 5th St., Miami Beach (phone: 305-532-8600).

For landlubbers who don't want to get wet but enjoy the excitement of watching sailboat races, you can't beat the 2-day *Columbus Day Regatta* held in June in Biscayne Bay, attracting more than 600 entrants (phone: 305-858-1733).

Scuba Diving

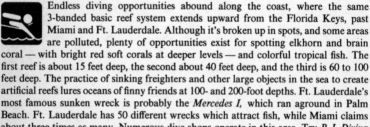

Endless diving opportunities abound along the coast, where the same 3-banded basic reef system extends upward from the Florida Keys, past Miami and Ft. Lauderdale. Although it's broken up in spots, and some areas are polluted, plenty of opportunities exist for spotting elkhorn and brain coral — with bright red soft corals at deeper levels — and colorful tropical fish. The first reef is about 15 feet deep, the second about 40 feet deep, and the third is 60 to 100 feet deep. The practice of sinking freighters and other large objects in the sea to create artificial reefs lures oceans of finny friends at 100- and 200-foot depths. Ft. Lauderdale's most famous sunken wreck is probably the *Mercedes I,* which ran aground in Palm Beach. Ft. Lauderdale has 50 different wrecks which attract fish, while Miami claims about three times as many. Numerous dive shops operate in this area. Try *R.J. Diving Ventures* (15560 NE 5th Ave., North Miami Beach; phone: 305-940-1182), *Great Escape Yachts* (3193 Mary St., Coconut Grove; phone: 305-936-0111), *Team Divers* (1290 Fifth St., Miami Beach; phone: 305-673-0101), *Lauderdale Diver* (1334 SE 17th St. Cswy., Ft. Lauderdale; phone: 305-467-2822 or 800-654-2073) or *Pro Dive Charters* (*Bahia Mar Yachting Center,* 801 Seabreeze Blvd., Ft. Lauderdale; phone: 305-761-3413 or 800-772-DIVE). Check the yellow pages for others. Expect to pay about $30 for a half day.

Day Cruises

A favorite activity of vacationers and Floridians alike is taking a 1-day cruise. This provides an introduction to the sea for novices, but also is popular among many frequent cruisers. Some people may simply want a day off from the world — a tasting of the Bahamas, or a little gambling — without changing their "home base." Cruises may be booked in advance directly through a cruise company or through a travel agent, risking no-refunds if the weather's amiss. It's also possible to wait until the chosen day, arriving early to stand in line for a vacant spot. Prices, as on longer cruises, include meals on board, activities, nightclub entertainment (tips and alcoholic drinks are extra), and access to casinos, which don't open until ships pass the 3-mile limit. High rollers are frequently seen queuing up outside closed casino doors. Kids under 11 usually sail free on all ships; inquire when making reservations.

DISCOVERY: This is the largest cruise liner hereabouts, debarking from Port Everglades, Ft. Lauderdale. It offers daytime and evening "cruises to nowhere" or to Freeport, the Bahamas. Buffet dining is included; à la carte dining is an additional charge. Information: *Discovery Cruises,* 1850 Eller Dr., Ft. Lauderdale, FL 33316 (phone: 305-525-7800 or 800-937-4477).

SCANDINAVIAN DAWN: The *SeaEscape* sails from Port Everglades, Ft. Lauderdale. It has daytime and evening "cruises to nowhere" or to Bimini or Freeport, the Bahamas. Buffet dining or à la carte at no additional charge. Information: *SeaEscape Cruises,* 8751 W. Broward Blvd., Suite 300, Plantation, FL 33324 (phone: 800-432-3939 in Florida or 800-826-6842 elsewhere in the US).

SCANDINAVIAN SUN: This day cruiser from Miami offers "cruises to nowhere" and to Bimini or Freeport, the Bahamas. Buffet dining or à la carte dining at additional charge. Information: *SeaEscape Cruises,* 8751 W. Broward Blvd., Suite 300, Plantation, FL 33324 (phone: 800-432-3939 in Florida or 800-826-6842 elsewhere in the US).

TROPIC STAR: The newest entry in the day-cruising market sails to Bimini, the Bahamas, from Miami; it also offers evening cruises to nowhere Thursdays through Saturdays. Buffet-style meals are included in the fare; à la carte dining is available at additional charge. Children 2 to 15 sail at a reduced rate. Information: *Starlite Cruises,* 1007 N. America Way, Miami, FL 33312 (phone: 305-539-3500 in Dade County; 800-354-5005 elsewhere).

Sybaritic Spas

 With several resorts featuring health and fitness spas, there is an abundance of opportunities to be pampered and pummeled throughout Miami and Ft. Lauderdale. Although sun worshiping with abandon is no longer in vogue, these spots provide new ways to care for your health and appearance. In addition to skin-care programs, massages, and facials, diet and stress-management plans help visitors to care better for their bodies — and their minds.

Many clients of these spas are show business and *Fortune* 500 executive types who slip down to Florida for stays lasting from a day to a few months. Happily, facilities are not always at the high end of the scale (although some — especially ones like *Bonaventure* — can make a major dent in your pocketbook), making them affordable for most vacationers. And remember, even the more costly spas include all meals and most activities in their rates. So relax. It's time to do something nice for yourself — you've earned it.

BONAVENTURE: Frequently judged among the country's best, attractions are hot and cold plunge pools, aerobic and water aerobic exercise classes, massage options (Swedish, shiatsu, and reflexology), aromatherapy, herbal and sea kelp body wraps, thermal back treatments, and nutrition consultation. There is an executive wellness program in conjunction with the Miami Heart Institute. The resort's beautiful grounds feature 5 swimming pools, 24 tennis courts, two 18-hole championship golf courses, racquetball, and squash courts. The spa dining room has a varied menu; smoking is prohibited. Information: *Bonaventure,* 250 Racquet Club Rd., Ft. Lauderdale, FL 33326 (phone: 305-389-3300 or 800-327-8090; fax: 305-384-0563).

DORAL SATURNIA: Based on the *Terme di Saturnia* in Tuscany, Italy, where restorative volcanic waters have supposedly helped sojourners for thousands of years, this complex lures those interested in health and fitness, diet control, and stress management. Recently judged the top North American spa by "Lifestyles of the Rich and Famous," its facilities include 4 exercise studios (with 30 daily exercise classes), a weight room with cardiovascular equipment, large outdoor pool with hot tub, outdoor lap pool, indoor exercise pool, hydrotherapy tubs, saunas, indoor track for walking and jogging, and an outdoor quarter-mile par-course and exercise stations. There are assessments, cholesterol- and blood pressure–reduction programs, dance classes, cellulite-reduction programs, collagen-repair facials, personal trainers, a beauty salon, cooking demonstrations, and take-home programs. Guests may use facilities at the adjoining *Doral Resort and Country Club* (5 championship golf courses and 15 tennis courts) and the beachfront *Doral Ocean Beach.* Information: *Doral Saturnia,* 8755 NW 36th St., Miami, FL 33178 (phone: 305-593-6030, 800-331-7768, or 800-22DORAL; fax: 305-591-9266).

FISHER ISLAND: The spa *internazionale* on fabulous Fisher Island, with its Spanish-style architecture, offers several programs for beauty, fitness, and relaxation treatment: thalassotherapy and aromatherapy, hydromassage, Swedish massage, herbal wraps, facials, computerized fitness assessment, and personal training. Other novelties include an indoor lap pool with retractable roof, a Jacuzzi with cold plunge pool, an outdoor Roman waterfall, a large aerobics studio for classes, a beauty salon, and a café serving spa food. The ultimate experience is "The Perfect Day," renting the luxurious marble and tile VIP Private Suite for a half- or full-day program of customized fitness and/or beauty treatment. The resort has 17 tennis courts and a 9-hole golf course. Information: *Fisher Island,* 1 Fisher Island Dr., Fisher Island, FL 33109 (phone: 305-535-6030 or 800-624-3251; fax: 305-535-6008).

FONTAINEBLEAU HILTON: The Spa Pavilion, with 130 rooms, features a South Florida motif. Enticements include massage therapy, mineral baths, Nautilus machines and free weights, aerobics classes, and cellulite treatment. The Adrien Arpel Salon offers facials and makeup lessons. The Mount Sinai Sports Institute provides fitness evaluation and training. There also are some spa items on hotel menus. Information: *Fontainebleau Hilton,* 4441 Collins Ave., Miami Beach, FL 33140 (phone: 305-538-2000 or 800-HILTONS; fax: 305-534-7821).

HARBOR ISLAND: This moderately priced, family-owned facility, off John F. Kennedy Causeway, includes a lounge, 3 nightlit tennis courts, 2 pools, and aerobics and aquatics classes, in addition to Nautilus machines, massages, facials, and diet or non-diet meals. Information: *Harbor Island Spa,* 7900 Larry Paskow Way, North Bay Village, FL 33141 (phone: 305-751-7561 or 800-SPA-SLIM; fax: 305-754-6244).

LIDO: Long-established, this inexpensive spa on Belle Island offers medical supervision, 2 pools, a sauna, diet or individually planned meals, and daily massages. Closed in May. Information: *Lido Spa,* 40 Island Ave., Venetian Cswy, Miami Beach, FL 33139 (phone: 305-538-4621 or 800-327-8363; fax: 305-534-3680).

PALM-AIRE: Stars such as Elizabeth Taylor, Billy Joel, and Liza Minnelli often shape up here. The 25-year-old spa is part of a 1,500-acre hotel and residential development sporting 5 golf courses and 7 tennis courts. Spa facilities include aerobic and water exercise classes, outdoor and private indoor whirlpool baths, saunas, massage choices (Swedish, shiatsu, and reflexology), aromatherapy, thalassotherapy, facials, herbal wraps, and a solarium. The spa dining room features delicious calorie-controlled meals, plus take-home books and instruction. Information: *Palm-Aire,* 2601 Palm-Aire Dr. N., Pompano Beach, FL 33069 (phone: 305-972-3300 or 800-327-4960; fax: 305-968-2744).

PIER 66 FT. LAUDERDALE: The full-service *Spa LXVI* at this Intracoastal resort offers Nautilus machines, sauna and steamroom, loofah and Swedish-Esalen massage, herbal wraps, and more. There are 2 swimming pools, an outdoor hydrotherapy spa, and 2 lit tennis courts. Information: *Pier 66 Ft. Lauderdale,* 2301 SE 17th St. Cswy., Ft. Lauderdale, FL 33316 (phone: 305-525-6666 or 800-327-3796, 800-432-1956 in Florida; fax: 305-728-3541).

TURNBERRY ISLE: This marina/golf/tennis complex also offers a health- and beauty-oriented spa with Finnish sauna, Turkish steamrooms, cold plunge pool, indoor and outdoor whirlpool baths, Nautilus equipment, racquetball courts, aerobics classes, and more. Diet plans are supervised by a staff physician and a nutritionist. Resort options include 2 championship golf courses and 24 tennis courts. Information: *Turnberry Isle,* 19999 W. Country Club Dr., Aventura, FL 33180 (phone: 305-932-6200 or 800-327-7028; fax: 305-937-0528).

For the Mind

Memorable Museums

 People think of Miami as a beach-oriented resort, or as one restaurant after another. However, there's also food for the mind here. Museums, some housing world class exhibitions, others a bit far-fetched, do serve those with specific interests or merely afford a place to spend a few hours if it's raining.

AMERICAN POLICE HALL OF FAME AND MUSEUM: A relative newcomer to Miami, this museum previously was located in Sarasota County. A marble monument commemorates more than 3,400 slain officers. Exhibits in the 3-story building include law enforcement vehicles and equipment — such as a guillotine and an electric chair. At a mock crime scene, visitors are encouraged to solve a murder. Open daily from 10 AM to 5:30 PM. Admission charge; free to police officers and families of slain officers. Information: *American Police Hall of Fame and Museum,* 3801 Biscayne Blvd., Miami (phone: 305-573-0070).

BASS MUSEUM OF ART: The building itself is listed on the National Registry of Historic Places for its classic Art Deco keystone design, influenced by French Art Deco. The small museum counts several gems in its permanent collection: two 17th-century Flemish tapestries, and works by Botticelli, Ghirlandaio, Rembrandt, and Rubens plus architectural and Oriental collections. Changing exhibitions, lectures, and a classic film series complete the picture. Open 10 AM to 5 PM Tuesdays through Saturdays and 1 to 5 PM Sundays. Admission charge. Information: *Bass Museum of Art,* 2121 Park Ave. (off Collins Ave.), Miami Beach (phone: 305-673-7533).

CENTER FOR THE FINE ARTS: Designed by Philip Johnson as part of the lovely complex at *Metro-Dade Cultural Center,* it hosts major traveling exhibitions of artists such as Pablo Picasso and Jasper Johns. Signs are in English and Spanish. There also is a small gift shop. Open from 10 AM to 5 PM Tuesdays, Wednesdays, Fridays, and Saturdays, and until 9 PM Thursdays; noon to 5 PM on Sundays. Admission charge; voluntary contributions on Tuesdays. Information: *Center for the Fine Arts,* 101 W. Flagler St. at 1st Ave., Miami (phone: 305-375-1700).

CUBAN MUSEUM OF ARTS AND CULTURE: Changing exhibitions here promote the cultural heritage of Miami's growing Cuban community. Open weekdays from 10 AM to 5 PM, Saturdays and Sundays from 1 PM. Admission charge. Information: *Cuban Museum of Arts and Culture,* 1300 SW 12th Ave. (phone: 305-858-8006).

HISTORICAL MUSEUM OF SOUTH FLORIDA: This museum on the graceful plaza at *Metro-Dade Cultural Center* boasts excellent exhibitions on the histories of the various groups that have settled here. Numerous displays, including a *chickee* hut, depict Indian life, while the Spanish exploration period comes alive through 17th-century maps and a mock-up of a fort kids can climb. Maritime history displays include artifacts from treasure fleets, like a gold ear pick. There's also a full-size trolley car that was used in Miami in the 1920s. Ongoing contributions made by the settling Cubans, blacks, and Jews bring it up to date; a sign points out that only "30 years ago, Jews and blacks were barred from part of Dade County." Signs and recorded messages are in both English and Spanish. A fine gift shop sells books and colorful accessories. Open Mondays through Saturdays from 10 AM to 5 PM; Thursdays until 9; Sundays noon to 5 PM. Admission charge. Information: *Historical Museum of South Florida,* 101 W. Flagler St. at 1st Avenue, Miami (phone: 305-375-1492).

LOWE ART MUSEUM: A permanent collection of Renaissance and baroque art, Spanish masterpieces, Asian and African art, and furniture and paintings from the Kress Collection of Renaissance and baroque art, plus visiting exhibits. Open Tuesdays through Saturdays from 10 AM to 5 PM; Sundays from noon to 5 PM; closed Mondays. Admission charge. Information: *Lowe Art Museum,* 1301 Stanford Dr., on the University of Miami campus in Coral Gables (phone: 305-284-3535).

MIAMI MUSEUM OF SCIENCE AND SPACE TRANSIT PLANETARIUM: Kids love the hands-on exhibits and mini-shows on Florida natural life. Observatory open weather permitting. The planetarium features multimedia astronomy and laser shows. (Call 854-2222 for show schedules.) Open daily 10 AM to 6 PM; closed *Christmas* and *Thanksgiving.* Admission charge. Information: *Miami Museum of Science and Space Transit Planetarium,* 3280 S. Miami Ave., Coconut Grove (phone: 305-854-4247).

MIAMI YOUTH MUSEUM: Hands-on exhibits are fun for the kids and guided tours are in both English and Spanish. The new permanent Kidscape exhibit is a miniature neighborhood with Dr. Smile's dental office, a fire station, and a supermarket. Also popular is the ecologically themed "Recycle Mania" exhibit. Open daily until 5 PM, from 10 AM weekdays and from 11 AM Saturdays and Sundays; closed holidays. Admission charge. Information: *Miami Youth Museum,* Bakery Centre, 5701 Sunset Dr., South Miami (phone: 305-661-3046).

MUSEUM OF ART: This new 63,800-square-foot museum, housed in a building designed by Edward Larabee Barnes, features 19th- and 20th-century American and European art. The collection includes more than 2,000 paintings, 5,000 prints, and West African, pre-Columbian, and American Indian art. Traveling exhibits are housed in three galleries, and there's a sculpture garden and auditorium. Open Tuesdays 11 AM to 9 PM, Wednesdays through Saturdays 10 AM to 5 PM, and Sundays noon to 5 PM. Admission charge (tours are included in the price on Tuesdays, Thursdays, and Fridays at 1 PM). Information: *Museum of Art,* 1 E. Las Olas Blvd., Ft. Lauderdale (phone: 305-763-6464).

MUSEUM OF DISCOVERY AND SCIENCE: One lure of Ft. Lauderdale's second new museum (85,000 square feet) is the 5-story IMAX screen, housed in a theater that will seat 300. Among other exhibits are walk-through simulated Florida habitats, a manned maneuvering unit space ride, a laser pinball, and a KidScience display. Tours also are offered of the *King-Cromartie House,* a restored turn-of-the-century residence replete with antiques and set on the New River. There's a cafeteria and museum store on the premises. Across from the *Broward Center for the Performing Arts.* Closed Mondays. Admission charge. Information: *Museum of Discovery and Science,* 431 SW 2nd St. Ft. Lauderdale (phone: 305-462-4115).

VIZCAYA: This mansion was the 70-room winter residence of International Harvester magnate James Deering, who harvested enough cash to build a Venetian palace and furnish it with museum-quality antiques. Dazzlers in the elegant 1916 building include Roman sculpture, 17th-century Italian marble tables, and a Chinese snuff-bottle collection. There are 10 acres of formal gardens with fountains, grottoes, and statuary comparable to that found in an Italian palazzo. Not surprisingly, this is the site of annual *Italian Renaissance Festival.* Guided tours available. Open daily, except *Christmas Day,* from 9:30 AM to 5 PM; the gardens remain open until 5:30 PM. Admission charge. Information: *Vizcaya Museum and Gardens,* 3251 S. Miami Ave., Coconut Grove (phone: 305-579-2708).

WEEKS AIR MUSEUM: For those who wish they had wings, this museum is dedicated to aircraft from its beginnings through the end of the World War II era. Displays of 35 aircraft, along with engines and propellers in hangars and on the field, delight airplane buffs. Open daily 10 AM to 5 PM. Admission charge. Information: *Weeks Air Museum,* 14710 SW 128th St., Kendall-Tamiami Airport (phone: 305-233-5197).

Historic Churches

Although Miami's history only goes as far back as the late 1800s (the city was incorporated in 1896, when the railroad came to town), there are a few historical churches of note. The oldest is an ancient church, built in 1141, that was imported from Segovia, Spain. Most of the other older buildings fall into one of two basic architectural categories, either bearing the Spanish mark, with capped steeples, hand-carved wooden doors, and stone exteriors, or the Art Deco influence, with stucco exteriors, rounded corners, and spires. All welcome wanderers and worshipers alike.

CORAL GABLES CONGREGATIONAL CHURCH: Dating from 1923, its Spanish design has a barrel-tile roof, pews carved from native cypress, and 16th-century furnishings. The bell tower, like that at the *Biltmore* hotel, is based on Spain's Giralda Tower. Information: *Coral Gables Congregational Church,* 3010 DeSoto Blvd., Coral Gables (phone: 305-448-7421).

PLYMOUTH CONGREGATIONAL CHURCH: This 1917 Spanish-style limestone church boasts a 375-year-old hand-carved walnut door from a Spanish monastery. Call to arrange a visit. Information: *Plymouth Congregational Church,* 3400 Devon Rd., Coconut Grove (phone: 305-444-6521).

SPANISH MONASTERY OF ST. BERNARD: The western hemisphere's oldest building was not erected in Florida, but built in 1141 in Segovia, Spain. William Randolph Hearst had it shipped in pieces to America in the 1920s. Twenty-five years later, Miami developers rebuilt it on this site. It is a functioning Episcopal church, and it's worth visiting for its collection of ancient art and furnishings. Open daily 10 AM to 5 PM, Sundays noon to 5 PM. Admission charge. Information: *Spanish Monastery of St. Bernard,* 16711 W. Dixie Hwy., North Miami Beach (phone: 305-945-1461).

TEMPLE BETH JACOB: Miami's oldest synagogue, its two cream-colored stucco buildings, both on the National Register of Historic Places, house an Orthodox congregation. The copper-domed building is the older, dating from 1922. The stained glass windows, marble pulpit, huge brass chandelier, and sconces are period Deco. Information: *Temple Beth Jacob,* 311 Washington Ave., Miami (phone: 305-672-6150).

TEMPLE EMANU-EL: Built in 1948 (although the congregation dates from 1938), the temple is important for its size and its cultural activities (guest performers and lecturers have included the late Isaac Bashevis Singer, Norman Schwarzkopf, and Itzhak Perlman, among others). Of white stucco with a silver dome over the sanctuary, and seating 2,000, the Conservative synagogue is the place of worship for 1,300 families. Information: *Temple Emanu-El,* 1701 Washington Ave., Miami Beach, near the Art Deco district and the Miami Beach Convention Center (phone: 305-538-2503). For tours featuring unusual synagogues and colorful stories of Jewish heritage, contact Dr. Sam Brown, Newport S, Apt. 4086, Deerfield Beach 33441 (phone: 305-421-8431).

TRINITY EPISCOPAL CATHEDRAL: Home of Miami's oldest congregation, the white neo-Romanesque church, known for its beautiful rose window, is now the seat of the South Florida Episcopal Archdiocese. Information: *Trinity Episcopal Cathedral,* 464 NE 16th St., Miami (phone: 305-374-3372).

Theater

 Professional drama, music, and ballet performances fill the stages primarily during the "season," while repertory and dinner-theaters fill the gap at other times. Check the papers and *South Florida* magazine for performance schedules.

In Greater Miami, the *Jackie Gleason Theater of the Performing Arts,* referred to locally as *TOPA,* offers touring plays and musicals, including some pre- and post-Broadway shows (1700 Washington Ave.; phone: 305-673-8300). The *Gusman Cultural Center* (174 E. Flagler St.; phone: 305-374-2444) and the *Dade County Auditorium* (2901 W. Flagler St.; phone: 305-545-3395) book theatrical and cultural events year-round. The *Coconut Grove Playhouse* (3500 Main Hwy.; phone: 305-442-4000) imports New York stars for its season of classics from October to May.

In Broward County, the area's major theaters are *Parker Playhouse* (707 NE 8th St.; phone: 305-764-0700), which stars name actors in Broadway productions, and *Sunrise Musical Theater* (5555 NW 95th Ave.; phone: 305-741-8600), which features Broadway musicals and individual stars in concert. A $50-million regional *Broward Center for the Performing Arts* (624 SW Second St.; phone: 305-522-5334) opened in early 1991, with high-tech staging and lighting and performances to match. Theatrical and cultural events also are staged at *War Memorial Auditorium* (800 NE 8th St.; phone: 305-761-5381) and *Bailey Hall* at the Broward Community College (3501 SW Davie Rd.; phone: 305-475-6880). The playwright Vinnette Carroll, who wrote *Your Arms Too Short to Box with God,* opened a multi-cultural theater with its own resident repertory company in a converted church, the *Vinnette Carroll Theater* (503 SE 6th St.; phone: 305-462-2424).

There's also lots of fine music in the air. Visiting orchestras and artists perform in Miami at the *Gusman Cultural Center* (174 E. Flagler St.; phone: 305-374-2444) and at *Dade County Auditorium* (2901 W. Flagler St.; phone: 305-545-3395), or in Miami Beach at the *Theater of the Performing Arts* (1700 Washington Ave.; phone: 305-673-8300). The *Greater Miami Opera Association* (1200 Coral Way; phone: 305-854-7890) stages a full complement of major productions in the winter season, as does the *New World Symphony,* an advanced training orchestra for gifted young musicians directed by conductor Michael Tilson Thomas (101 E. Flagler St.; phone: 305-371-3005). Pop stars such as Madonna, Gloria Estefan and the *Miami Sound Machine,* and Billy Joel often appear at the *Miami Arena* (721 NW First Ave.; phone: 305-530-4400) or the *Orange Bowl* (1501 NW Third St.; phone: 305-371-3351).

In Ft. Lauderdale, the *Florida Philharmonic Orchestra,* under the direction of James Judd, usually plays at the *Broward Center for the Performing Arts* (201 SW Fifth Ave., Ft. Lauderdale; phone: 305-561-2997), which also is the site for performances of the *Opera Guild* (phone: 305-728-9700) during winter months. The latter often features visiting artists from New York and the *Greater Miami Opera Company. Gold Coast Symphony Orchestra* (1323 NE 17th St., Suite 668; phone: 305-522-0609) stages several major productions at various sites. Student and guest chamber music, jazz, opera, and symphonic performances are staged throughout the year at Broward Community College (phone: 305-475-6884).

For ballet, the *Miami City Ballet* (905 Lincoln Rd., Miami Beach; phone: 305-532-7713), headed by Edward Villella, is one of the country's best young companies, and performs a full season beginning each fall. Touring companies such as the *American Ballet Theatre* often visit in season, and there are numerous performances of *The Nutcracker* throughout the region around *Christmastime.* The *New World School of the*

Arts Dance Ensemble spotlights high school and college students, and combines ballet, modern jazz, Spanish, new wave, and Afro-Caribbean influences.

Antiquing

Not everybody in Greater Miami lives among glass and lucite. Many traditionalists prefer antiques, and lots of estate sales keep the suppliers going. Check the yellow pages for dealers in Miami and Coconut Grove.

Those who love to prowl among things old may find a bonanza at the *Coconut Grove Antique and Jewelry Show* in August at the *Coconut Grove Convention Center* (phone: 305-579-3312).

"Antique Row" runs along the 100 block of Federal Highway (US 1) between North First Street and Dania Beach Boulevard in Dania, and spills into several of the side streets. The 150 stores and stalls deal in old china, furniture, books, jewelry, and assorted "chatchkes." Most are open Mondays through Saturdays 10 AM to 5 PM. The following are worth a look:

> *English Accent Antiques:* 53 N. Federal Hwy., Dania (phone: 305-923-8383).
> *House of Hirsch Antiques:* 75 N. Federal Hwy., Dania (phone: 305-925-0818).
> *Maxine's Antiques:* 8 N. Federal Hwy., Dania (phone: 305-920-0588).
> *Rose Antiques:* 17 N. Federal Hwy., Dania (phone: 305-921-0474).
> *Treasure Chest:* 6A N. Federal Hwy., Dania (phone: 305-923-0999).

Seaport

Bayside Marketplace, developed by the same people who brought you Boston's *Faneuil Hall Marketplace* and Baltimore's *Harborplace,* is a tropical waterside complex of 182 shops and eateries. Many bear the same names as in other similar developments, but the accent is definitely more salsa-fied here. While dining alfresco, watch the boats docking at the adjacent Miamarina. (Charter boats may be hired here, or you can catch a delightful sightseeing ride aboard the *Nikko* to see Biscayne Bay from a fish's-eye view or sail to Ft. Lauderdale; phone: 305-945-5461 or 305-921-1193). Stroll the 2-story peach-tinted buildings housing folk art displayed on pushcarts and at upscale boutiques. The kids will be entertained by jugglers and larger-than-life cartoon characters. Or nosh your way through the food court — with more of a Latin flavor than in other similar complexes throughout the country. Board the HMS *Bounty* (admission charge), built for the 1960 film *Mutiny on the Bounty,* open April through October. *Bayside* is open Mondays through Saturdays 10 AM to 10 PM and Sundays noon to 8 PM; restaurants other than those in the Food Arcade often remain open later. Visitors may arrive by *Metrorail*'s PeopleMover, public bus, *Old Town Trolley,* car (parking available), or by boat. 401 Biscayne Blvd., Miami (phone: 305-577-3344).

A Shutterbug's View

With all its pastels, seascapes, and picturesque neighborhoods, Miami is a very photogenic city. There is architectural variety: Art Deco is juxtaposed with modern, ornate with ordinary, and a skyline bristling with the temples of modern commerce with the seashore reaching to meet it. There also is natural variety: Flowers embroider a park footpath, a palm tree waves in the breeze, and a sunrise sparks the horizon over the ocean. There's human variety as well: Immigrants exchange the latest news from the Old Country in Spanish, ruddy fishermen return with their catch, and beachcombers flaunt their tans on the boardwalk. The thriving city, the shimmering sea, the parks, the people, and traces of rich history make Miami a fertile stomping ground for shutterbugs. Even a beginner can achieve remarkable results with a surprisingly basic set of lenses and filters. Equipment is, in fact, only as valuable as the imagination that puts it into use.

Don't be afraid to experiment. Use what knowledge you have to explore new possibilities. At the same time, don't limit yourself by preconceived ideas of what's hackneyed or corny. Because the Art Deco district has been photographed hundreds of times before doesn't make it any less worthy of your attention.

In Miami, as elsewhere, spontaneity is one of the keys to good photography. Whether it's a sudden shaft of light bursting through the clouds and hitting the waves just so, or fishermen unloading their catch as dawn creeps over the pier, don't hesitate to shoot if the moment is right. If photography is indeed capturing a moment and making it timeless, success lies in judging just when a moment worth capturing occurs.

A good picture reveals an eye for detail, whether it's a matter of lighting, of positioning your subject, or of taking time to frame a picture carefully. The better your grasp of the importance of details, the better your results will be photographically.

Patience is often necessary. Don't shoot a view of a windsurfer if a cloud suddenly dims the shot. A rusted old Volkswagen in the center of your Art Deco scene? Reframe your image to eliminate the obvious distraction. People walking toward a scene that would benefit from their presence? Wait until they're in position before you shoot. After the fact, many of the flaws will be self-evident. The trick is to be aware of the ideal and have the patience to allow it to happen. If you are part of a group, you may well have to trail behind a bit in order to shoot properly. Not only is group activity distracting, but bunches of people hovering nearby tend to stifle spontaneity and overwhelm potential subjects.

The camera provides an opportunity, not only to capture Miami's varied and subtle beauty, but to interpret it. What it takes is a sensitivity to the surroundings, a knowledge of the capabilities of your equipment, and a willingness to see things in new ways.

LANDSCAPES, SEASCAPES, AND CITYSCAPES: Miami's populated beaches and historic buildings are most often visiting photographers' favorite subjects. But the city's greenspaces and waterways provide numerous photo possibilities as well. In addition to the historic hotels, churches, and the Art Deco district, be sure to look for natural beauty: at the Fairchild Tropical Gardens, the well-manicured plots of flowers in the public parks, and the rolling waves of the Atlantic.

Color and form are the obvious ingredients here, and how you frame your pictures can be as important as getting the proper exposure. Study the shapes, angles, and colors that make up the scene and create a composition that uses them to best advantage.

Lighting is a vital component in landscapes and seascapes. Take advantage of the richer colors of early morning and late afternoon whenever possible. The overhead light of midday is often harsh and without the shadowing that can add to the drama of a scene. This is when a polarizer is used to best effect. Most polarizers come with a mark on the rotating ring. If you can aim at your subject and point that marker at the sun, the sun's rays are likely to be right for the polarizer to work for you. If not, stick to your skylight filter, underexposing slightly if the scene is particularly bright. Most light meters respond to an overall light balance, with the result that bright areas may appear burned out.

Although a standard 50mm to 55mm lens may work well in some landscape situations, most will benefit from a 20mm to 28mm wide-angle. The Ft. Lauderdale skyline from the top of the *Pier 66* resort, for example, is the type of panorama that fits beautifully into a wide-angle format, allowing not only the overview, but the opportunity to include people or other points of interest in the foreground. A fruit stand, for instance, may be used to set off a view of a street in Little Havana; or people can provide a sense of perspective in a shot of a café in the Art Deco district.

To isolate specific elements of any scene, use your telephoto lens. Perhaps there's a particular carving in a historic building that would make a lovely shot, or it might be the interplay of light and shadow on the façade of an old Spanish church. The successful use of a telephoto means developing your eye for detail.

PEOPLE: As with taking pictures of people anywhere, there are going to be times in Miami when a camera is an intrusion. Your approach is the key: Consider your own reaction under similar circumstances, and you have an idea as to what would make others comfortable enough to be willing subjects. People are often sensitive to having a camera suddenly pointed at them, and a polite request, while getting you a share of refusals, will also provide a chance to shoot some wonderful portraits that capture the spirit of the area as surely as the scenery does. For candids, an excellent lens is a zoom telephoto in the 70mm to 210mm range; it allows you to remain unobtrusive while the telephoto lens draws the subject closer. And for portraits, a telephoto can be used effectively as close as 2 or 3 feet.

For authenticity and variety, select a place likely to produce interesting subjects. The *Bayside Marketplace* is an obvious spot for visitors, but if it's local color you're after, visit the boardwalk in Ft. Lauderdale, Little Havana, or Coconut Grove. Aim for shots that tell what's different about Miami. In portraiture, there are several factors to keep in mind. Morning or afternoon light will add richness to skin tones, emphasizing tans. To avoid the harsh facial shadows cast by direct sunlight, shoot in the shade or in an area where the light is diffused.

SUNSETS: While the sun doesn't set over the ocean in Miami, there are days when the last golden rays reflect off a lone sailboat, or when a fiery light hits the *Adrian* hotel's pink and turquoise façade, crowned with magical clouds of pink and lavender, purple and red.

When shooting sunsets, keep in mind that the brightness will distort meter readings. When composing a shot directly into the sun, frame the picture in the viewfinder so that only half of the sun is included. Read the meter, set, and shoot. Whenever there is this kind of unusual lighting, shoot a few frames in half-step increments, both over and under the meter reading. Bracketing, as this is called, can provide a range of images, the best of which may well be other than the one shot at the meter's recommended setting.

Use any lens for sunsets. A wide-angle is good when the sky is filled with color-streaked clouds, when the sun is partially hidden, or when you're close to an object that silhouettes dramatically against the sky.

Telephotos also produce wonderful silhouettes, either with the sun as a backdrop or against the palette of a brilliant sunset sky. Bracket again here. For the best silhouettes, wait 10 to 15 minutes after sunset. Unless using a very fast film, a tripod is recommended.

Red and orange filters are often used to accentuate a sunset's picture potential. Orange will help turn even a gray sky into something approaching a photogenic finale to the day, and can provide particularly beautiful shots linking the sky with the sun reflected on the ocean. If the sunset is already bold in hue, the orange will overwhelm the natural colors. A red filter will produce dramatic, highly unrealistic results.

NIGHT: If you think that picture possibilities end at sunset, you're presuming that night photography is the exclusive domain of the professional. If you've got a tripod, all you'll need is a cable release to attach to your camera to assure a steady exposure (which is often timed in minutes rather than fractions of a second).

For situations such as evening concerts or nighttime harbor cruises, a strobe does the trick, but beware: Flash units are often used improperly. You can't take a view of the skyline with a flash. It may reach out as far as 30 feet, but that's it. On the other hand, a flash used too close to a subject may result in overexposure, resulting in a "blown out" effect. With most cameras, strobes will work with a maximum shutter speed of 1/125 or 1/150 of a second. If you set the exposure properly and shoot within range, you should come up with pretty sharp results.

CLOSE-UPS: Whether of people or of objects such as Art Deco spires, close-ups can add another dimension to your photography. There are a number of shooting options, one of which is to use a 70mm or a 210mm lens at its closest focusable distance. Unless you're working in bright sunlight, a tripod will be worthwhile. If you are very near your subject and there is a good deal of reflective light, it may pay to underexpose a bit in relation to the meter reading.

If you do not have a telephoto lens, you can still shoot close-ups using a set of magnification filters. Filter packs of one-, two-, and three-time magnification are available, converting your lens into a close-up lens. Even better is a special macro lens designed for close-up photography.

It's tough to get broad perspectives in Miami, where the highest elevations are bridges — not a hill in sight. But that doesn't stop anybody, as you'll notice by all the professional photographers toting heavy equipment around. Below, a few of Miami's most photogenic places.

A SHORT PHOTOGRAPHIC TOUR

THE BEACHES: Best views of the beach are anywhere on Miami Beach, but standing slightly elevated on the boardwalk that runs between 21st and 46th streets affords a better perspective.

SOUTH BEACH: Stroll along the ocean side of Ocean Drive rather than trying to snap pictures from a moving car in the Deco district. Colorful spots are at 13th Street, where you'll see the *Carlyle* hotel on the south corner with its buff and mauve exterior and green-trimmed "eyebrows" and the *Cardozo* on the north corner, bedecked in white and peach with brownstone pillars and "eyebrows." Or at 8th Street, you can shoot the pink and turquoise *Adrian* and include the *Tudor* (down the street at Collins Avenue), with its rounded entry and neon-lighted finial. Approaching from the west by car, you may be able to capture the three signature tall hotels, with their unique towers, in one shot around 17th Street: from north to south, the *Ritz Plaza*, the *Delano*, and the *National*.

CRUISE SHIPS: For a fantastic view of a half-dozen cruise ships with Miami skyscrapers in the background, drive across MacArthur Causeway (A1A) between Miami and Miami Beach and pull in at the sign for *Chalk's Flights*. There are parking spots, and it's much safer than parking along the narrow roadside. The largest number of ships are docked on Saturdays and Sundays. Catch them pulling out in the late afternoon, decks lined with smiling and waving passengers. Just remember not to shoot directly into the sun.

DOWNTOWN: For terrific views of downtown Miami, including *Bayside*, visit the *Inter-Continental* hotel's fifth-floor pool area or jogging track (100 Chopin Plaza; phone: 305-577-1000, or 800-327-3005).

HISTORIC MIAMI: To see Florida as it once was, drive to the southern tip of Key Biscayne. Out on the palm-studded beach, where it juts into the Atlantic Ocean, stands the Cape Florida Light, built of red brick in 1825. There's an admission charge to the *Bill Baggs Cape Florida State Recreation Area* (see THE CITIES).

FT. LAUDERDALE: The best view of Ft. Lauderdale is atop the *Pier 66* resort (2301 SE 17th St. Cswy, Ft. Lauderdale; phone: 305-525-6666) in the *Pier Top Lounge*. The tower's top revolves once every 66 minutes, providing wonderful vistas of ocean, Intracoastal Waterway, and canals.

DIRECTIONS

Introduction

Mention Miami and the first image that comes to mind is miles and miles of beach. True, Miami Beach boasts a splendid swath of white sand that seems to stretch from here to tomorrow, but for those who can pry themselves away from the shoreline, there's a whole other Miami just waiting to be discovered. This other Miami — small neighborhoods, historic churches and landmarks, and picturesque cafés and shops — is best explored on foot; other vistas cover a broader area and require a car.

Whether you're walking or driving, pay careful attention to names of streets; it makes a big difference whether the "20th" you're seeking is a street or an avenue, or you'll find yourself in the completely wrong spot. The first tour begins in the Deco district at the southern tip of Miami Beach. From there we proceed west, back to the mainland, then to South Miami and over to Key Biscayne before heading to the Cubanized area of Calle Ocho. To its west is the lovely suburb of Coral Gables, and farther south lies Coconut Grove, Florida's oldest and most bohemian neighborhood. Just for fun, we've thrown in a Cowboy and Indian tour in Ft. Lauderdale before moving north to luxurious Palm Beach for a glimpse at the lifestyles of its rich and often famous (or infamous) residents.

And for those who'd like to journey farther, there are visits to the secluded, but oh-so-beautiful, Florida Keys and to the almost otherworldly, farthermost reaches of the Everglades. As we said, Miami is much more than just another pretty beach.

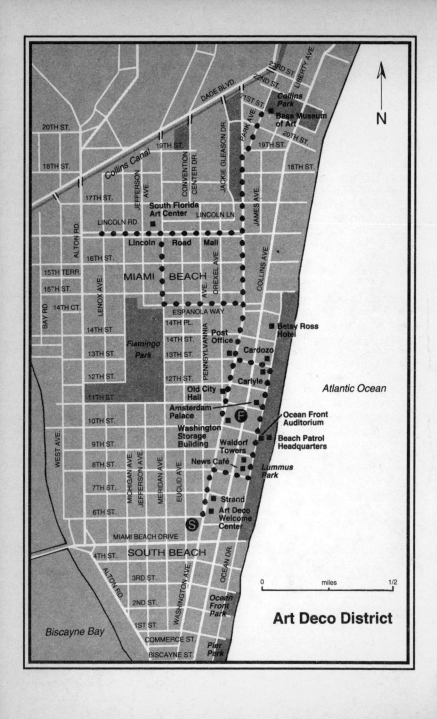

N

20TH ST.
18TH ST.

Collins Canal

19TH ST.

17TH ST.

JEFFERSON AVE.

CONVENTION CENTER DR.

DADE BLVD.

JACKIE GLEASON DR.

PARK AVE.

23RD ST.
22ND ST.
21ST ST.

LIBERTY AVE.

Collins Park

■ Bass Museum of Art

20TH ST.
19TH ST.
18TH ST.

South Florida Art Center ■

LINCOLN RD.

LINCOLN LN.

JAMES AVE.

ALTON RD.

Lincoln   Road   Mall

16TH ST.

MIAMI   BEACH

15TH TERR.
15TH ST.

LENOX AVE.

DREXEL AVE.

COLLINS AVE.

BAY RD.
14TH CT.

Espanola Way

14TH PL.

14TH ST.

Flamingo Park

14TH ST.
13TH ST.
12TH ST.
11TH ST.

PENNSYLVANNIA

Post Office

13TH ST.

■ Betsy Ross Hotel

■ Cardozo

Carlyle ■

Old City Hall

Amsterdam Palace

Washington Storage Building

WEST AVE.

10TH ST.
9TH ST.

MICHIGAN AVE.
JEFFERSON AVE.
MERIDAN AVE.
EUCLID AVE.

Waldorf Towers

News Café

Ⓕ

Atlantic Ocean

■ Ocean Front Auditorium

■ Beach Patrol Headquarters

Lummus Park

8TH ST.
7TH ST.
6TH ST.

Ⓢ

■ Strand
■ Art Deco Welcome Center

MIAMI BEACH DRIVE

SOUTH BEACH

4TH ST.

ALTON RD.

3RD ST.

2ND ST.

WASHINGTON AVE.

OCEAN DR.

Ocean Front Park

1ST ST.

Biscayne Bay

COMMERCE ST.

BISCAYNE ST.

Pier Park

0   miles   1/2

Art Deco District

Tour 1: Art Deco District

One of the earliest Miami Beach neighborhoods is again in the limelight. Miami Beach originally was developed as a coconut plantation, and although the enterprise failed, many beachfront coconut palms remain. In the 1920s, Carl Fisher began developing the beach as a vacation area for well-heeled sun worshipers. He dredged the mosquito-ridden mangrove swamps and built the first bridge to the mainland. (Above 15th Street, Fisher enforced the "Caucasian Clause," which prohibited blacks and Jews from buying property or staying in hotels. He made some notable exceptions, however, permitting Bernard Gimbel, the department store founder, to stay at his *Flamingo* hotel, and John Hertz, founder of the Yellow Cab Company, to buy land.)

Most of the construction in this area occurred just after World War I. But Miami's first attempt to gain a place in the sun failed miserably. An initial building boom went bust, the Hurricane of 1926 struck, destroying what had been built, and the Depression followed. Undaunted, Miami tried again in the late 1930s — and this time, for a while at least, it succeeded. During this latter era, the first of two major periods of Art Deco construction and design was prevalent. Classical Art Deco, based on the French decorative movement, was characterized by elaborately designed fountains and rich surface ornamentation, but used tropical themes — palm trees, flowers, dolphins, flamingos — and soft pastels to adorn and reflect its resort setting. The second period, known as Art Moderne, followed, until World War II brought all frivolous construction to a halt. Influenced by industrial design, Art Moderne was characterized by minimal ornamentation, rounded corners, and cantilevered window shades called "eyebrows." Following the sleek designs of cars and planes from the Art Moderne period, the tropical element in Miami's version of the design movement evolved in the form of ocean liner motifs.

When Miami got back to building after the war, it was the softer, more decorative, classic themes that prevailed. Most buildings were originally painted white, with warm pink and yellow trim. Today, however, many have been daubed with ice-cream-soda colors of raspberry pink, banana yellow, and blueberry blue. Beth Dunlop, *Miami Herald* architecture critic, claims the experiment began here in the 1980s, and the imaginative coloration then spread throughout South Florida. Much credit for this renaissance is given to "Miami Vice" producer Michael Mann and the visibility the series gave to Miami's whimsical heritage.

The Art Deco district, referred to by locals as South Beach and increasingly as SoBe, is once again enjoying a rebirth. Thanks to the efforts of preservationists, spearheaded by the late Barbara Baer Capitman (who founded the Miami

Design Preservation League), many buildings were saved from the wreckers' ball — although some were lost because of opposition by developers who wanted to tear down the older buildings to replace them with modern structures. The area was officially designated as the Art Deco district in 1979 and placed on the National Register of Historic Places — it's the country's largest collection of Art Deco architecture in one area.

About 650 important buildings are within a walkable square mile, bordered by the ocean on the east and Flamingo Park on the west, and running from 5th to 23rd Streets. The Deco district today, though, is more than a collection of historic buildings. The hotels and restaurants have become fashionable, with nightspots open until the wee hours. Groups of high-fashion models and photographers fly in from New York, Paris, and Frankfurt to do shoots for magazines and clothing catalogues. There's an excitement here that sometimes leaves the resident senior citizens shaking their heads in wonder.

If you're driving in from the west, be sure to look up and see the three signature high-rise hotels around 17th Street and Collins Avenue: the *Ritz Plaza,* the *Delano,* and the *National.* Streetside parking may be a problem, with few metered spots; try the municipal parking lot near *TOPA,* Lincoln Road Mall Parking.

Start your tour at the Art Deco Welcome Center (661 Washington Ave.; phone: 305-672-2014); open Mondays through Fridays 10 AM to 6 PM and Saturdays 10 AM to 2 PM. You can go at your leisure or join the 90-minute walking tour offered Saturday mornings at 10:30 (admission charge), with colorful anecdotes spicing up the history. You'll see the *Cardozo* hotel (where Frank Sinatra filmed the 1959 movie *Hole in the Head*) and Española Way (where — legend has it — Desi Arnaz made the rumba a dance craze). Pick up maps and books here, too, including the *Miami Beach Art Deco Guide* by Keith Root ($10), which has six self-guided tours and a glossary of architectural terms. Or proceed on your own, remembering to look up to spot the characteristic parapets and finials.

Remember that streets progress logically, with numbered streets running east-west; street addresses reflect the closest numbered cross street. Walk north on Washington past the *Strand* (No. 671), former home of the *Famous* restaurant, and featuring a ziggurat parapet and pelican capitals. On the corner of 8th Street, a rounded building that originally was built for — and until recently housed — *Friedman's Bakery.* The 1934 building — which appeared on the cover of *Progressive Architecture* — looks like a pink- and lilac-frosted wedding cake, with stepped back "layers" and a parapet for the bride and groom.

Proceed east 2 blocks to Ocean Drive. Here the majority of hotels line the street facing palm-studded Lummus Park and the beach. Walk north on Ocean Drive's recently broadened sidewalks; building after building, it's an Art Deco–phile's delight. Some structures have been turned into chic hotels and stylish eateries, others are home to senior citizens, and still others are undergoing renovation. There also are a few shops selling funky clothes and beach articles; please note that here and elsewhere in the Deco district, clothing shops may not open until late morning (11 AM), but remain open into the evening (until 9 or 10 PM). Plan to have breakfast or lunch at one of the popular outdoor places such as the *News Café* (800 Ocean Dr.).

At No. 860, the 1937 *Waldorf Towers* sports Art Deco "eyebrows" to shield the sun, and a unique rooftop tower. Notice the *Breakwater*'s vertical neon sign and racing stripes (No. 940). A pool links this hotel and the *Edison* (No. 960), which shows Mediterranean Art Deco Revival influence.

If you've resisted strolling over to the beach until now, detour to the Beach Patrol Headquarters behind the auditorium at 10th Street. The building resembles a ship, typical of the Nautical Moderne style. Its seaside face, with porthole windows and metal ship railings, recalls the *Normandie,* the Art Deco *French Line* cruise ship.

The *Amsterdam Palace* (1116 Ocean Dr.) looks a bit out of place architecturally, with its arched entrance and windows, barrel-tile roof, and wrought-iron balconies. In fact, it was built in 1930 in a Mediterranean Revival style, modeled after the colonial Alcázar de Colón, home of Diego Columbus (Chris Columbus's brother) in the Dominican Republic. Not open to the public, its exterior is still well worth noting.

At the corner of 13th Street stand two Deco landmarks — on the south side is the *Carlyle,* painted buff and mauve with green-trimmed eyebrows. On the north side is the white and peach *Cardozo,* with brownstone eyebrows and porch pillars, and a terrific-looking lobby/dining room (see *Eating Out* in *Miami,* THE CITIES).

Most of the 15 or so restaurants along this stretch are popular among locals who sit either at tables on the broad sidewalk or in the slightly more formal indoor dining rooms. Despite their pleasant ambience, the culinary creations are often pedestrian. One of the more recent restaurants to open, *A Mano* in the *Betsy Ross* hotel (1440 Ocean Dr.; phone: 305-531-3934), has been winning praise from critics both locally and nationally. Chef Norman Van Aken bills his fare as "New World Cooking," the style favored by South Florida's best chefs, using classical techniques married to local and Caribbean ingredients. Try the grilled grouper with mango relish and plantains or the outrageous venison with porcini. *Stars & Stripes Café,* the hotel's less formal sister restaurant, serves such continental fare as risotto with Indian River clams and duck *confit* ravioli (phone: 305-531-3310).

Turn west on 13th Street. At Collins Avenue, you'll see the peach-colored Mediterranean Revival *Alamac,* with barrel-tile roof. At the northwest corner of 13th and Washington Avenue sits the still-functioning 1937 main post office, with a lantern finial crowning its dome. Climb the pink marble steps and enter through the brass doors for a peek into the impressive rotunda lobby.

Continue north on Washington, veering northeast on Park Avenue (it begins at 19th Street). At the corner of 21st and Park is the *Bass Museum of Art,* built in 1930 of Key stone (taken from the Florida Keys). Outside adornments include carved seagulls on the roof and bas-relief panels with nautical themes over doorways. Housed here are two enormous 17th-century Flemish tapestries, along with works by Botticelli, Ghirlandaio, Rembrandt, and Rubens. The architectural and Oriental collections have recently been expanded. Open 10 AM to 5 PM Tuesdays through Saturdays and 1 to 5 PM Sundays; admission charge.

At the corner of 21st and Park is the *Plymouth;* though it's now a run-down residential hotel, it's worth taking a look into the lobby to see the 1939

Rousseau-esque mural, depicting an idyllic tropical land with visions of skyscrapers rising in the background. Return to Washington Avenue.

Go south on Washington; between 17th and 16th Streets is *Lincoln Road Mall.* Built by Carl Fisher as an artery to the island's first commercial area, the road is still lined with many Art Deco buildings. In 1960, the city hired Morris Lapidus, the architect who designed the *Fontainebleau* hotel, to design new landscaping for the now pedestrians-only street. Today, many of the once fashionable stores along here are closed, but the west end is enjoying a retail revival. Walk west to the Miami Beach Community Church (500 Lincoln Rd.); built in 1921, it is the city's first church. Pass the headquarters for the *New World Symphony* (541 Lincoln Rd.) to Meridian Avenue (the 800 block). Between it and Lenox Avenue, about 100 artists work in studios and galleries. The *South Florida Art Center* (810 Lincoln Rd.) owns three buildings housing a gallery and rotating exhibits, and leases space to artists. Also here are the home of the *Miami City Ballet* (909 Lincoln Rd.); a branch of *Books & Books* (933 Lincoln Rd.), selling (what else?) books and offering a film series; plus about ten restaurants, from fine Italian dining spots to casual cafés. Several, including *South Beat* and *Expresso Bongo,* offer live music as well.

Turn south on Meridian Avenue; between 15th and 14th Streets is Española Way. Turn east and stroll to the block between Drexel and Washington Avenues, known as the Spanish Colony. This block has been refurbished, bringing to life the coral-painted Spanish Renaissance–style buildings with their iron balconies, red-tile roofs, and gaslight streetlamps. Band leader Desi Arnaz supposedly started the US rumba craze on this street. Today it's home to art galleries and vintage clothing and furniture stores. On the corner of Washington Avenue is the *Clay Hotel and International Youth Hostel* (phone: 305-534-2988), where young travelers can often find lodging. At 1445 Washington Ave., the 1938 *Cameo* theater hosts rap and reggae performers. Resume the tour here.

If you haven't sidetracked to the *Bass Museum* and Española Way, continue south on Washington Avenue. On the west side (at No. 1130) sits the 9-story Old City Hall, dating from 1927. The Mediterranean-style building boasts barrel-tile roofs and Corinthian columns. Peek inside, where the Justice Center and University of Miami School of Continuing Education hold forth, to see the lobby's moldings and old brass fixtures. Another worthwhile stop is the *Grille* restaurant (also at No. 1130; phone: 305-532-0006); try their grilled seafood specialties.

On the east side (at No. 1001) stands the Washington Storage Building. Built in 1927 for summer storage serving winter visitors, it features ornate carved relief bands in the Spanish baroque style; it's now being restored by the Wolfson Foundation. In 1995, the building will open as a museum and study center of the decorative and propaganda arts — intended to illustrate the destructive side of human nature — housing part of the Mitchell Wolfson, Jr., Collection of 50,000 objets d'art and rare books.

Return to the Welcome Center, or hop in your car to continue touring the area.

Tour 2: South Miami by Car

From Miami Beach's South Beach, drive across MacArthur Causeway (Rte. 395). To the right, on the turquoise waters of Biscayne Bay, sit the private islands of Star, Hibiscus, and Palm, with their spectacular private homes and equally spectacular yachts. The rest of us can't get past the guard houses, but from Watson Island you can get a pretty good view. On the left pass the ferry to the plush Fisher Island resort. Still on the left, note the string of cruise ships lined up at the Port of Miami, the world's busiest cruise port. Since the increase of terrorism a few years back, security has been tightened so that visitors can no longer board the ships. However, visitors can pull over at the sign to *Chalk's Flights* (a charter seaplane company), park the car, relax beneath the trees, and watch the huge cruise ships maneuver in and out of port. About 3 million passengers disembark from here annually on one of the 17 ships that call this port home and regularly call here. On weekends, you may see eight or so mammoth floating hotels sailing in or out at once, including some of the world's largest, such as *Royal Caribbean Cruise Line*'s *Sovereign of the Seas, Norwegian Cruise Line*'s *Norway,* and *Carnival*'s *Celebration.*

Continue west to Route 1 (Biscayne Blvd.) and go south through downtown Miami. Notice the pink Freedom Tower (No. 600) on the right, a Spanish Renaissance–style building dating from 1925 and replicating Spain's Giralda Tower. Built for the *Miami News,* it received its nickname when it was used as the Cuban Refugee Emergency Center in 1962. Rescued from the wrecker's ball, it now houses offices.

On the left is the *Bayside Marketplace* (8396 NW S. River Dr.), where shoppers and diners can spend several hours. The Rouse-developed complex of 185 shops and eateries harbors many of the same shops as in New York City's *South Street Seaport* or *Riverwalk* in New Orleans. But being able to sit and sup while watching a 1,035-foot ship trying to fit into a tight parking space is a distinctly Florida experience. And the food is definitely more Latin in flavor than in any other US place.

Continue south on Biscayne, and follow the signs to US 1 South. Note the downtown commercial area to the right, with additional skyscrapers constantly changing the skyline. Notice in particular I.M. Pei's International Tower, formerly Centrust Tower (100 SE 2nd St.), three graduated ellipses of glass that, when lit at night, look like a glowing waterfall. Pass the *Hyatt Regency* hotel (400 SE 2nd Ave.) on the right and immediately cross the Miami River — that is, unless the bridge is open, which can hopelessly back up traffic in this bustling business zone. Passing over the bridge, look to the

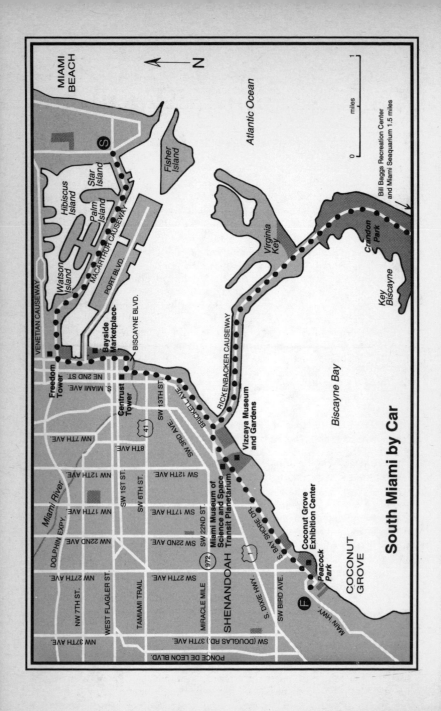

South Miami by Car

right. Alongside the elevated track carrying *Metrorail* trains is *Miami Line,* a multicolored, neon, 300-foot, public sculpture by Rockne Krebs; it's particuluary striking at night.

On the other side, US 1 becomes Brickell Avenue. The area from SE 15th Street to SE 5th Street looks more like Wall Street with palm trees; more than 2 dozen imaginatively designed buildings house several US and Latin Amercan international bank headquarters. Unlike Wall Street, however, these sparkle with marble and mirror; some even have palm trees poking their tufted tops through the atria.

Continue south on Brickell past the pricey condominiums on the left, many boasting striking architecture. Villa Regina (1581 Brickell Ave.), an Isamu Noguchi–designed condominium building, has a rainbow-hued exterior decorated by Israeli artist Yaacov Agam. Another is the Atlantis (2025 S. Brickell Ave.), seen in opening shots of "Miami Vice," with its 5-story-high central courtyard housing a curved red staircase, full-size palm tree, and a hot tub. The latter was designed by the progressive architecture firm named Arquitectonica.

If you're visiting sometime during mid-May through June, detour 1 block west of Brickell to South Miami Avenue, between SW 15th Road and SW 25th Road; the 4-lane, malled street is lined with huge royal poinciana trees which, during that time, form a canopy of huge orange blossoms. (To check on blooming times, call the Fairchild Tropical Garden; phone: 305-667-1651.)

At the end of Brickell, you can go left across the Rickenbacker Causeway to Key Biscayne (see below) to see Crandon Park, Bill Baggs State Recreation Area, and the *Miami Seaquarium,* with its numerous displays of fish from the Atlantic and Caribbean, including a 10,000-pound killer whale, sea lions, and dolphins.

Or follow the signs to Bayshore Drive, past *Vizcaya Museum and Gardens* (3251 S. Miami Ave.; phone: 305-579-2813) on the left. The opulent 1916 Italian Renaissance–style villa was the winter home of International Harvester Company's James Deering. Fronting on the bay, it rivals any mansion in Newport, Rhode Island. The 34 rooms are bursting with antique European furniture — including 17th-century Italian and French pieces, and artworks such as the Greek *Torso of Aphrodite* from the 2nd century BC. Magnificently manicured plants and fountains comprise 10 acres of formal outdoor gardens. Gift shops and a café are on the premises. Guided tours are available. The grounds annually host the *Italian Renaissance Festival* during the third weekend in March (this year March 19–22). The festival simulates a 16th-century marketplace, complete with costumed vendors, chamber trios, troubadours, jesters, and a *Living Chess Tournament* (with real people as the chess pieces). Open daily from 9:30 AM to 5 PM; gardens open until 5:30 PM; admission charge.

On the right is the *Miami Museum of Science and Space Transit Planetarium* (3280 S. Miami Ave., Coconut Grove; phone: 305-854-4247). The science museum offers live demonstrations of scientific phenomena, 150 hands-on exhibits, and an aviary and wildlife exhibit. The planetarium presents daily star shows and multimedia laser shows. Open daily 10 AM to 6 PM; closed *Christmas* and *Thanksgiving;* admission charge.

Continue south on Bayshore Drive past a high-rent condominium area. On the right, note *The Windward,* the large red sculpture by Alexander Leiberman, resting in front of the *Grand Bay* hotel (at 27th Ave.), Florida's only Mobil 5-star property. On the left, with colorful nautical flags painted on its exterior, is the new Coconut Grove Exhibition Center. Here sailboat masts seem to sprout like trees in a forest; the bay plays a major role in life hereabouts. Stop in at *Monty's* for a casual lunch on the deck, and stroll the dock at the marina to see the boats. Soon the road curves in front of Peacock Park (named for early settlers Charles and Isabella Peacock, who built the first hotel on South Florida's mainland), a small park with assorted ball courts. Continue to the next traffic light and make a hard left onto Main Highway, the heart of Coconut Grove.

FARTHER SOUTH: KEY BISCAYNE

From the southern end of Brickell Avenue, or from US Route 1 exiting at SE 26th Road, follow the signs eastbound to Rickenbacker Causeway to Key Biscayne (a key is a low island, or reef). Key Biscayne is a large island — once a coconut plantation — that's winter home to the rich, famous, and infamous (including actor Andy Garcia, businessman Charles "Bebe" Rebozo, and, formerly, President Richard Nixon); it's the site of the annual *Lipton Tennis Tournament* and two large public parks.

Cross the first bridge to a small island known as Windsurfer Beach. A good spot for windsurfing (what else?), aficionados bring their own gear or rent on the spot from *Sailboats Miami* (phone: 305-361-SAIL or 305-361-3870). There are picnic facilities, public bathrooms, and parking; the beach isn't much by Miami standards, but, in addition to windsurfers, it also attracts fisherfolk, who cast their lines from the bridge.

Continue across William Powell Bridge to Virginia Key. On the right is the *Miami Seaquarium* (4400 Rickenbacker Cswy.; phone: 305-361-5705). Six daily shows feature Flipper (not the original trained dolphin of TV fame; he's long since gone to the aquarium in the sky) in the original lagoon set, a 10,000-pound killer whale, sharks, and sea lions. Reef tanks display native sea life from the Atlantic and Caribbean. Plan to spend several hours. There's a cafeteria on the premises. Open daily from 9 AM; closing time varies with the season. Admission charge. For more information see "Special Places" in *Miami,* THE CITIES.

From here, drive over the next bridge onto Key Biscayne; you'll be on Crandon Boulevard. Pass the Crandon Marina (with charter boats available for half- or full-days). Plan on lunch or cocktails at *Sundays on the Bay,* a delightful spot with a dockside deck where diners can watch the boating scene while enjoying anything from a snack to first-rate continental fare (phone: 305-361-6777).

The road continues through a natural area of palmettos and sea grapes; this is Crandon Park (more about the park below). If you don't detour to the park, drive 1.5 miles from the *Seaquarium* to the *International Tennis Center* (phone: 305-361-8633) on the right. The Dade County facility offers 17 courts (6 night-lit) with an additional 7 clay courts expected to be completed this year. There's a pro shop with racquet rentals, and lessons with the pro ($40 per hour) or assistant ($30 per hour). Open daily 8 AM to 10 PM; court fees are $2 per person per hour, $3 at night.

This is the site of the annual *Lipton Tennis Tournament* (phone: 305-446-2200) in March, which draws almost 200,000 fans and top-ranked players from around the world.

Controversies have arisen over the 67,500-seat stadium at the *International Tennis Center,* which is slated for completion this year; much of the flack has come from the Matheson family heirs, whose antecedents donated the land to Crandon Park in 1940. They claim the intention was to leave the area in its natural state and have fought to reclaim it.

Pass through the center of Key Biscayne and turn right at the next traffic light onto Harbor Drive. Go 1.4 miles onto Mashta Island. (Developed by Dr. William J. Matheson in 1902, his daughter named the island for the Egyptian word "mashta," meaning "home on resting spot by the sea." Circle around to the right to see the stunning residences, especially those on the northwest side; located right on Biscayne Bay, they enjoy a magnificent view of downtown Miami.

Return to Crandon Boulevard and turn right. Continue to the road's end and the entrance to the 900-acre Bill Baggs State Park (1200 Crandon Blvd.; phone: 305-361-5811). Here are 1¼ miles of beaches, playgrounds, walking and bike trails, fishing for snapper and bonefish, concession stands, and showers. There's a red brick lighthouse (ca. 1825), built before the Seminole War. There are guided tours of the lighthouse and the keeper's dwelling. Several spots offer views of Stiltsville, private homes suspended by stilts above the bay and accessible only by boat (the water-based dwellings were memorialized in Carl Hiaasen's novel *Skin Tight*). Open daily from 8 AM until sunset (the lighthouse is closed Tuesdays); admission charge.

Leaving the park, drive 1.4 miles to an entrance to the 960-acre Crandon Park Beach (4000 Crandon Blvd.; phone: 305-361-5421). To enjoy the 3⅓ miles of beaches, visitors may rent cabañas on a daily or weekly basis. Other activities include baseball, golf, tennis, walking and biking paths, boating, and fishing (boat rentals are available). There also are concession stands, barbecue pits, and picnic areas; covered picnic pavilions may be reserved (in person) at 4000 Crandon Blvd., Parking Lot No. 3. Open daily 8 AM to sunset. Parking charge.

Continue west to the *Miami Marine Stadium* (3601 Rickenbacker Cswy; phone: 305-361-6730 or 305-361-6732), a 6,500-seat roofed stadium hosting outdoor pop concerts, fireworks displays, and the annual 3-day *Budweiser Unlimited Hydroplane Regatta* in early June, purportedly the world's largest.

On the right are more beaches; most have jet ski rentals, and all afford a fabulous view of downtown Miami's business skyline, South Miami's colorful condos, Dodge Island with its large ships and, if the night cooperates, a different view of that moon over Miami.

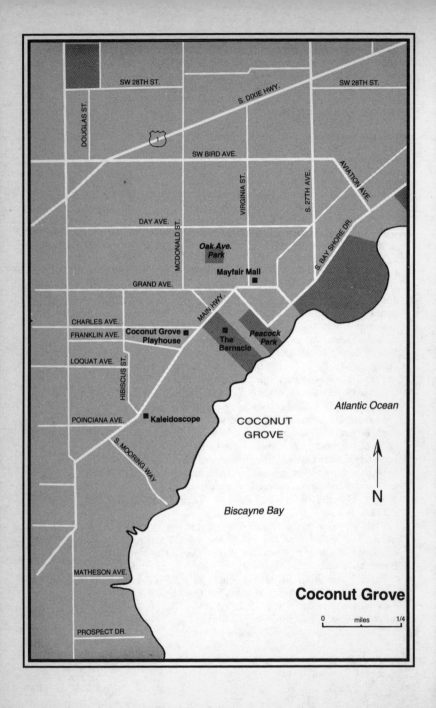

SW 28TH ST.

S. DIXIE HWY.

SW 28TH ST.

DOUGLAS ST.

SW BIRD AVE.

VIRGINIA ST.

S. 27TH AVE.

AVIATION AVE.

DAY AVE.

McDONALD ST.

Oak Ave. Park

S. BAY SHORE DR.

GRAND AVE.

Mayfair Mall

MAIN HWY.

CHARLES AVE.

FRANKLIN AVE.

Coconut Grove Playhouse

The Barnacle

Peacock Park

LOQUAT AVE.

HIBISCUS ST.

Atlantic Ocean

POINCIANA AVE.

Kaleidoscope

COCONUT GROVE

S. MOORING WAY

N

Biscayne Bay

MATHESON AVE.

Coconut Grove

0   miles   1/4

PROSPECT DR.

Tour 3: Coconut Grove

Park your car and continue on foot. Coconut Grove is Florida's answer to New York City's Greenwich Village, complete with shops selling high fashion and funky duds, elegant restaurants, and droves of casual eateries with tables spilling out onto the sidewalks. It's fun to stop at an outdoor café, nurse an ice cream cone or a beer, and watch the passing parade. Kids with punk hairdos flit by on skateboards, and seniors shop for antiques and paintings. Plenty of arty and intellectual types live in this area, along with descendants of early Bahamian settlers; at almost any time of the day or night, it's a great place to people watch or participate in an impromptu sing-along. Musicians serenade on the street.

The *King Mango Strut Parade,* Coconut Grove's own organized festival, takes place each December. Developed as an answer to those who take the *Orange Bowl Parade* seriously, this is a major tongue-in-cheek event. Marching groups may include strutters decked out as characters off the label of Fruit of the Loom underwear, transformed into bunches of grapes by purple and green balloons; there's always someone offering a spoof of the current president or mayor.

Art lovers come together in February, when the *Coconut Grove Arts Festival* draws hundreds of thousands to its juried outdoor exhibits. For more information, call the Chamber of Commerce (phone: 305-444-7270).

Stroll along Main and up and down the short side streets, peeking into boutiques and galleries. Sidewalk cafés offering light meals and snacks line every sidewalk. For more serious food, *Kaleidoscope* offers fine dining in a romantic enclosed garden, a balcony, or in air conditioned indoor dining rooms (see "Eating Out" in *Miami,* THE CITIES). Favorite dishes include grilled swordfish and roasted red snapper with honey-mustard glazed bananas.

On nearby Grand Avenue, *CocoWalk* is a recently opened shopping center vying for visitors' bucks, with lots of trendy boutiques and eateries such as *Café Tu Tu Tango* and *Big City Fish* (see *Eating Out* in *Miami,* THE CITIES); unfortunately, the formerly upscale *Mayfair Mall* has lost numerous tenants, including its *Burdine*'s anchor store. Residents are hopeful of a turnaround.

On the east side of Main is The Barnacle, one of Dade County's oldest homes (Coconut Grove is South Florida's oldest settlement). Dating from 1891, the wood building in a wooded setting has historical merit as an example of early settlers' homes, with authentic Victorian-era furnishings. (The roof is barnacle-shaped.) Operated as a state park, daily tours are available. The boathouse, where owner Commodore Ralph Munroe designed all and built some of his nationally renowned Presto-type sailboats, may also be toured. Open Thursdays through Mondays 9 AM to 4 PM; admission charge. 3485 Main Hwy. (phone: 305-448-9445).

Diagonally across the street is the 1927 *Coconut Grove Playhouse,* which has produced such plays as the American premiere of *Waiting for Godot.* The theater also often plays host to pre-Broadway try-outs. Recent offerings include *Fame: The Musical, Run for Your Wife,* and *Matador.* The playhouse also has a children's theater. 3500 Main Hwy. (phone: 305-442-4000).

On Charles Avenue are the original wood-frame houses built by the black Bahamians who emigrated here to work in the nearby coconut groves late in the last century; homes in the area, comprising Miami's first black settlement, date from 1889.

From Coconut Grove follow the next route in nearby Coral Gables, or head back to the beach and save it for another day.

Tour 4: Cruising through Coral Gables

George Merrick developed this prime residential area in the 1920s, as part of his innovative concept of a perfectly designed city, patterning it on ancient communities with curving boulevards (which also make it very easy to get lost), and four grand entrances to the city built with Spanish-style spiral pillars. Merrick built more than 600 homes, and donated land for the city's first church, library, and what would become the University of Miami. Unfortunately, inflated land values wreaked havoc financially; the Hurricane of 1926 did the rest.

Today, however, the 12-square-mile city remains an area of great beauty, with lovely homes set among spacious gardens. Canals leading to Biscayne Bay run alongside it, and docked boats bob in the water. Many of the original buildings remain, and ongoing restoration projects are returning many buildings to their former grandeur. Coral Gables also is home to a number of multinational business offices, as well as numerous sophisticated restaurants.

Start the drive at the Chamber of Commerce building (50 Aragon Ave.; phone: 305-446-1657). Go west on Aragon for 3 blocks to Le Jeune Road, then south on Le Jeune 1 block to the Miracle Mile (Coral Way). Make a half-right turn onto Biltmore Way. (Don't look for street signs above eye level in most of the Gables; they're discreetly placed in whitewashed cornerstones on the ground.) Stop at the 1928 City Hall (405 Biltmore Way; phone: 305-446-6800), built of Key stone (oolitic limestone from the Florida Keys), with its curved, colonnaded façade. Peek inside to see some of the original fixtures, furnishings, and paintings.

Go west 2 blocks on Biltmore Way to Segovia Street and turn left. Then drive 3 blocks to Sevilla Avenue and turn right; proceed 4 blocks to De Soto Boulevard. At No. 2701, stop at the Venetian Pool, the only swimming pool listed in the National Register of Historic Places. Recently restored to its former splendor, it was originally a limestone quarry; the 800,000-gallon pool is fed by underground artesian wells. The setting also boasts coral caves, a palm-fringed island, bridges, fountains, and painted gondola poles. Movie stars such as Esther Williams, queen of water ballet, and Johnny "Tarzan" Weismuller once backstroked here, and Paul Whiteman's orchestra provided background for dancers. A photo exhibit chronicles beauty pageants and celebrities' visits. Visitors may swim here (amenities include swimming, scuba, and snorkeling lessons, lockers, and a café), but the pool is extremely crowded during the summer, when kids from local camps come here to splash

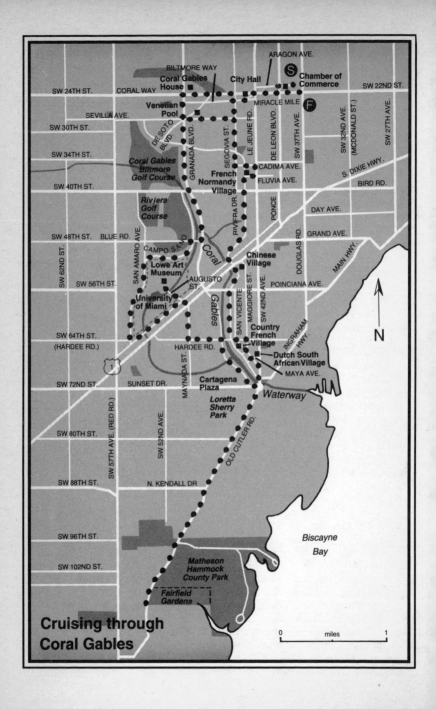

Cruising through Coral Gables

ARAGON AVE.
BILTMORE WAY
Coral Gables House
City Hall
S Chamber of Commerce
SW 24TH ST.   CORAL WAY
MIRACLE MILE
F
SW 22ND ST.
Venetian Pool
SEVILLA AVE.
SW 30TH ST.
SW 34TH ST.
DE SOTO BLVD.
GRANADA BLVD.
SEGOVIA ST.
LE JEUNE RD.
DE LEON BLVD.
SW 37TH AVE.
SW 32ND AVE. (MCDONALD ST.)
SW 27TH AVE.
Coral Gables Biltmore Golf Course
CADIMA AVE.
French Normandy Village
FLUVIA AVE.
S. DIXIE HWY.
BIRD RD.
SW 40TH ST.
Riviera Golf Course
RIVIERA DR.
PONCE
DAY AVE.
SW 48TH ST.   BLUE RD.
CAMPO SANO
Coral
GRAND AVE.
Chinese Village
DOUGLAS RD.
MAIN HWY.
SAN AMARO AVE.
SW 62ND ST.
Lowe Art Museum
AUGUSTO ST.
SW 56TH ST.
Gables
MAGGIORE ST.
SAN VICENTE
SW 42ND AVE.
POINCIANA AVE.
University of Miami
SW 64TH ST. (HARDEE RD.)
HARDEE RD.
Country French Village
INGRAHAM HWY.
Dutch South African Village
1
MAYNADA ST.
MAYA AVE.
SW 72ND ST.   SUNSET DR.
Cartagena Plaza
Waterway
Loretta Sherry Park
SW 57TH AVE. (RED RD.)
SW 52ND AVE.
OLD CUTLER RD.
SW 80TH ST.
SW 88TH ST.   N. KENDALL DR.
SW 96TH ST.
Biscayne Bay
SW 102ND ST.
Matheson Hammock County Park
Fairfield Gardens

N

0   miles   1

around. Open year-round Tuesdays through Fridays 11 AM to 4:30 PM and Saturdays and Sundays 10 AM to 4:30 PM. Admission charge.

Circle back via Sevilla to Segovia Street; turn right and continue south 8 blocks to University Drive and turn left; immediately bear right into Cadima Avenue; notice the large banyan or Indian fig trees, deep setbacks, and unobtrusive low metal street lamps throughout the area. Proceed 3 blocks and turn right onto Le Jeune. In this area, developer George Merrick created a residential district featuring "villages," each with a distinct architectural style. On the right, on Viscaya Court, are some of the occupied remains of his experiment. Here is the French Normandy Village, designed in a French architectural style with white stucco houses, wooden beams, and shuttered windows. Circle back to Le Jeune, go 1 block south to Fluvia Avenue and turn right; proceed 1 block to Riviera Drive and turn left. Follow Riviera for 15 blocks, and cross US 1 (South Dixie Hwy.) to Menendez Avenue, the next street on the left. Here is the Chinese Village, the most bizarre of Merrick's sections, with blue-and-yellow-tile upturned roofs and doorways painted red and yellow. Circle around the village and return to Riviera Drive. Go south .65 miles to Hardee Road, then turn left. Go 1 block to San Vicente Street, where there are examples of the Country French Village on the left, with its red tile roofs and stucco façades with wooden beams. Continue 1 block to Maggiore Street and turn right, then go 2 blocks to San Vicente and turn left. At the third corner on the left, at Maya Avenue, stands the Dutch South African Village, with homes of white stucco with curlicued gables.

Circle around it, returning to Le Jeune, and turn right. Go 2 blocks, passing over the canal. Park at the tiny Loretta Sherry Park on the right. Here are some lovely, large homes (and equally lavish yachts), typical of the upscale residential area.

Continue around the circle (Cartagena Plaza) to Old Cutler Road. Go south 2 miles. On the left is the entrance to the Matheson Hammock County Park. Walk along its winding trails through native forest to a manmade lagoon overlooking Biscayne Bay, where you can take a dip. Facilities include a beach, picnic area, snack bar, and showers. Open sunup to sundown; parking charge (phone: 305-666-6979).

About a half-mile farther south on Old Cutler Road, on the left side, are Fairfield Gardens, where something's always in bloom, such as red-edged impala lilies or red silk cotton trees. The 83-acre grounds, supposedly the largest tropical botanical garden in the continental US, afford visitors hours of beauty and tranquillity. Along with one of the world's largest collections of palms, there's also a rain forest and a rare plant house. Stroll leisurely around the 11 lushly landscaped lakes, with benches for contemplation thoughtfully provided. Guided walking tours are available at no charge; tram tours for a small fee. Other features include a snack bar open on weekends, and a bookstore focusing on horticulture. Open daily 9:30 AM to 4:30 PM; closed *Christmas*. Shirts and shoes must be worn; admission charge (phone: 305-667-1651).

Return 2.2 miles on Old Cutler Road to Cartagena Plaza. Circle it to the first right, which is Sunset Drive, and take the first right after that, Granada Boulevard. Follow it for .7 miles to Hardee. Go .3 miles west on Hardee, passing a section between Cellini and Leonardo Streets where a new French-looking community mimics Merrick's older experiment. Proceed to Maynada Street and turn right. Continue for .35 miles to Augusto Street. Follow Augusto across US 1 and Ponce de León Boulevard, known locally as just Ponce. On the right is the *Lowe Art Museum,* on the University of Miami campus (1301 Stanford Dr.; phone: 305-284-3536), displaying a permanent Renaissance art collection and changing displays. (Open Tuesdays through Saturdays 10 AM to 5 PM and Sundays noon to 5 PM; closed major holidays; no admission charge.)

Leaving the museum, you'll still be on the campus of the University of Miami, a major university with a large undergraduate enrollment and graduate schools in law, the Rosenstiel School of Marine and Atmospheric Science, and the highly regarded University of Miami/Jackson Memorial Medical Center — not to mention the famed *Hurricanes* football team. Return to Ponce, turn right, and proceed to the third traffic light, San Amaro Avenue. Turn right, keeping your eyes peeled for one of those famous *Hurricanes,* and go .9 miles to Campo Sano. Turn right and proceed east for .5 miles to University Drive. Go north (left) and, at the next corner, turn right on Blue Road. Cross the canal; the first light is Granada Boulevard. Turn left and continue north for 1.5 miles to Coral Way.

Turn right on Coral Way. In the first block, on your left, is the Coral Gables House (No. 907), built in 1907 as the Merrick family home. Built of oolitic limestone, the interior still boasts many of its original furnishings from the 1920s. Other pieces reflect the varied history of the city. Open Sundays and Wednesdays, 1 to 4 PM, or by appointment (phone: 305-460-5360). Admission charge.

Continue east on Coral Way; turn right at Segovia (the next traffic light). The next corner on the left is Biltmore Way. Take it back into Coral Way. The area between Le Jeune Road and Douglas Road is known as the Miracle Mile, although parts of it are somewhat less than a miracle today; nevertheless, it's an attractive pedestrian thoroughfare with 160 shops and eateries. Some upscale specialty shops are already in place and plans are afoot to lure additional European retailers.

While in the shopping mode, pop into *Books & Books* around the corner at 296 Aragon Avenue. Owner Mitch Kaplan regularly schedules readings and lectures by such well-known writers as Susan Sontag (the late Isaac Bashevic Singer was also a speaker here), plus photographic art exhibits.

Coral Gables boasts several fine restaurants. The two listed below serve both lunch and dinner. *St. Michel* (162 Alcazar Ave.; phone: 305-446-6572) is a bistro in a charming 1926 bed and breakfast establishment. Specialties include blue crab cake on black-pepper linguine and grilled, herb-crusted swordfish. Open for breakfast weekdays; lunch and dinner weekdays 11 AM to 11 PM, until 1 AM Fridays and Saturdays; dinner Sundays from 5 to 11 PM. Live music accompanies Sunday brunch 11 AM to 2:30 PM. *Yuca* (177 Giralda Ave., Coral Gables; phone: 305-444-4448), another fine neighborhood eatery (its name is an acronym for Young Upscale Cuban-Americans, as well as the name of the starchy vegetable often used in Cuban cooking, both of which symbolize the food here). The menu (in English and Spanish) features nouvelle creations of Cuban standards. Don't miss the plantain-coated dolphin (fish). A braille menu also is available. Open noon to midnight Mondays through Thursdays, noon to 2 AM Fridays, and for dinner 5 PM to 2 AM on Saturdays, 5 PM to midnight on Sundays.

Little Havana

El Credito

Botanica
la Abuela

SW 11TH AVE.

SW 12TH AVE.

SW 12TH CT.

Cuban Museum of
Art and Culture

Brigade 2506
Memorial

Ⓢ

LL.

Los Pinarenos

CUBAN MEMORIAL BLVD.

SW 8TH ST.

SW 13TH CT.

LITTLE HAVANA

McDonald's

CALLE OCHO

SW 12TH ST.

SW 14TH AVE.

N

Maximo
Gomez
Park

SW 9TH ST.

SW 10TH ST.

SW 11TH ST.

SW 11TH TERR.

SW 13TH ST.

SW 15TH AVE.

SW 16TH AVE.

El Pub

Little Havana

0   1/8
    miles

SW 17TH AVE.

Tour 5: Little Havana

From downtown Miami, drive south on Biscayne Boulevard, following signs around to Brickell Avenue (Rte. 1). Cross the Miami River and continue to SE 7th Street. Turn right and proceed to SW 13th Avenue and park. Walk 1 block south to the corner of SW 8th Street (Calle Ocho, the heart of Little Havana) and SW 13th Avenue, where you'll find the Brigade 2506 Memorial. This monument to those who died in the unsuccessful 1961 Bay of Pigs invasion of Cuba symbolizes the political outlook of many who settled here in the 1950s. (For a thorough background, read Joan Didion's *Miami.*)

Earlier called Shenandoah, this neighborhood was mainly a middle class Jewish community until the 1950s, although a large Hispanic group had settled here before the refugees from Castro's reign arrived. Many of the Jewish shops gradually became Hispanic, although some of the older signs still are visible; a grocery selling pork is the former site of a kosher butcher. Today, many of the original middle class Cuban residents have moved on to more affluent neighborhoods, and other Hispanic groups have settled here. Now more Nicaraguans live here than Cubans, and the area long known as Little Havana increasingly is called the Latin Quarter.

From the monument, walk west along Calle Ocho. Here is *Los Pinareños,* an open-air market (1334 SW 8th St.) selling sugarcane stalks, *plátanos* (tiny bananas), and green coconuts. As you stroll, look down and notice the red-brick sidewalk, dubbed the Hispanic Walkway of Stars. Squares are dedicated to various Hispanic stars, such as Gloria Estefan, María Conchita Alonso, and Julio Iglesias.

At the corner of SW 14th Avenue, note the *McDonald's* restaurant. Because new buildings must adhere to the Spanish architectural style, this one has a red-tile roof and blue tiles on its stuccoed exterior. It may be the only *McDonald's* that serves *café con leche.*

At the corner of SW 15th Avenue, in Máximo Gomez Park, elderly men in *guayaberas* sit at outdoor tables under roofed areas playing dominoes and chess. Hispanic music fills the air. Although this is a city park, visitors can enter only with a membership card and they must be males above age 55.

For an inexpensive lunch, pop into *El Pub* (SW 16th Avenue). Pick up a shot glass of coffee at the window or be seated at an inside table. Try a Cuban sandwich consisting of ham, cheese, pickles, and mustard on Cuban bread. Or a cup of *café con leche,* so strong that the spoon you mix it with may come out bent. (Stand in the same line for coffee and lottery tickets.)

SW 17th Avenue is the boundary of Little Havana (after this it becomes Little Managua); cross the street and retrace the route on the opposite side. The *Dunkin Donuts* at 16th was the first in the country to serve *café con leche;* it also bakes guava doughnuts. *La Casa de Los Trucos,* between 13th and 14th, does big business in satin and sequinned costumes — especially at *Halloween.*

Stop in at *Botánica la Abuela* (No. 1122) There are a few *piñatas* and dolls here, but the stock of candles, roots, and oils used for *santería* purposes is even more fascinating — it's a religion combining voodoo and Catholicism. An Amazonian Indian is on hand, with feathers and other paraphernalia piercing his ears and nose.

At 11th Avenue, stop at *El Crédito* and watch cigars being made at Miami's largest hand-rolled cigar factory (1106 SW 8th St.; phone: 305-858-4162). The business began in Havana in 1907, and opened here in 1969. Today, the tobacco is imported mainly from the Dominican Republic and Mexico. Closed Saturdays and Sundays.

Return to your car and drive to SW 13th Street (Ronald Reagan Ave.) on 12th Avenue to visit the *Cuban Museum of Arts and Culture.* Originally designed to showcase Cuban heritage, it now focuses on the entire Hispanic community, with 200 paintings and drawings in its permanent collection. Open Mondays through Fridays 10 AM to 5 PM, Saturdays and Sundays 1 to 5 PM. Admission charge (1300 SW 12th Ave.; phone: 305-858-8006).

Take SW 12th Avenue north to SW 7th Street. Turn left and proceed to SW 19th Avenue, then left to SW 8th Street and turn left. On your right is a wonderland of *piñatas* at *La Casa de Las Piñatas* (1756 SW 8th St., 2nd floor; phone: 305-649-4711). The standard Mexican paper donkeys are available, but hanging throughout are fantastic creations such as a Ninja Turtle *piñata* holding five of the creatures, or a tableau of a beauty pageant, complete with beauty queen, emcee, and television cameraman. These decorations are swung in the air and then hit with long sticks so the candy inside spills out — a tradition at children's parties, especially at *Quinces,* the often lavish parties thrown for 15-year-old girls (akin to a "Sweet 16" party). *Piñata* prices range from $25 to $500. The store is busiest in summer and is closed for *Christmas.*

Try a typical Cuban meal — spiced pork, paella, or *arroz con pollo,* and flan for dessert — at *Málaga* (740 SW 8th St.; phone: 305-858-4224) or *Versailles,* open daily till the wee hours (3555 SW 8th St.; phone: 305-445-7614).

Tour 6: Cowboy and Indian Tour

For a change from the sun and surf of South Florida, head west to the land of cowboys and Indians — just south of Ft. Lauderdale. Here the Seminole Tribe of Hollywood (Florida) have a reservation. The tribe is a fairly recent arrival historically, having relocated here in the early part of the 18th century. An amalgamation of the Creek, Oconee, and other tribes, the confederation took the Creek word "is-te-seminole," meaning "wild people," to differentiate themselves from other Florida Indians who had become tolerant of white settlers. Today, they too have intermarried with other area residents.

Many residents have developed industries appealing to tourists. Some seem tacky, but despite the kitsch, they offer insights into earlier lifestyles. The year's major event is the *Seminole Indian Tribal Fair* (held in late February), featuring Native American food, art, and tribal dancing from all over North America. For information, call 305-583-7112.

From US 1 or I-95, drive west on Sheridan Street (State Rd. 822) in Hollywood to US 441 (also called State Rd. 7) and turn north. After about 10 blocks, be on the lookout for the Native Village, a commercial enterprise (3551 N. State Rd. 7; phone: 305-961-4519) on the right; it's run by Bobbie Billie, the chief's wife. After passing through the gift shop, wander through a jungle-like setting of small lakes, waterfalls, and dripping foliage. Tropical birds call out, a roar blasts from three caged Florida panthers — a protected, endangered species — and in the snake pit, a trainer approaches a rattlesnake — very carefully. The man describes the various venomous snakes slithering about, and then provokes a non-venomous type into biting him. But the most excitement is generated at the alligator wrestling exhibit. The trainer enters the pit, describing the native animal's characteristics, and then pries his mouth open to reveal 80 large teeth. The trainer's hand darts in and out of the huge mouth and the animal snaps his jaws shut — usually *after* the trainer's hand has been withdrawn. Open Mondays through Saturdays from 10 AM to 4 PM. Admission charge.

On the west side of the street is the *Seminole Bingo Hall.* Although high-stakes bingo is illegal elsewhere in Florida, it's permitted here because the land is a federally protected Indian reservation. The enclosed hall, seating 1,400, attracts players hopeful of winning $100,000 jackpots. Open daily 11:45 AM to 6 PM and 7:15 PM to 5 AM; admission charge. 4150 N. State Rd. 7 (phone: 305-961-3220).

A few blocks north is a complex of *chickee* huts, including an open-air haircutting salon. Stop in at the *Anhinga Indian Museum and Art Gallery* (5791 S. State Rd. 7) for nicely crafted pottery, colorful appliquéd Indian skirts and jackets, and beaded jewelry.

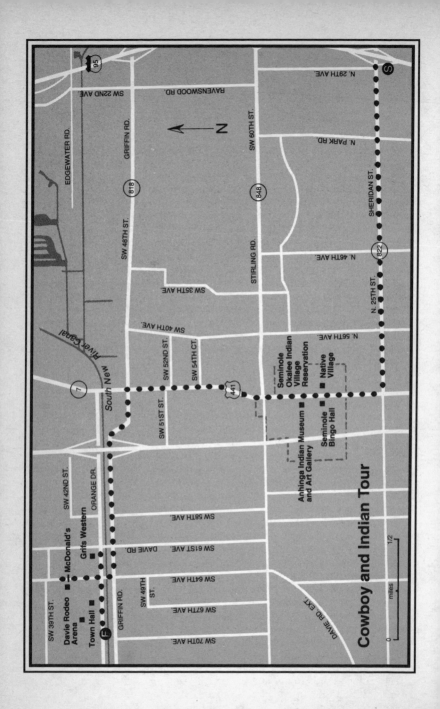

Cowboy and Indian Tour

Continue north to Griffin Road and turn west. Drive along the South New River Canal to Davie Road (SW 64th Ave.) and you're in cowboy territory. When the area was developed in the early part of the 20th century, it was dotted with orange plantations, sugarcane fields, and dairies where cattle were raised. The cattle herders evolved into cowboys, and others who love horsing around followed suit.

Today, visitors can still spot many equestrians, usually clad in cowboy-cut jeans and Stetson hats, riding their steeds through the streets. Shops advertise boot and saddle repairs, and shopping centers are designed to look like porches at a ranch. *Boot Barn* (7138 Stirling Rd.; phone: 305-435-BOOT) carries such brands as Tony Lama, with handmade boots made of snake, alligator, lizard, buffalo, elk, and elephant. Ranches abound where horses are boarded, and riders can rent mounts by the hour or by the day. The region's heritage leaps to life during the annual *Orange Blossom Festival* held in late March, a week-long celebration featuring rodeos, food, and music.

Turn right on Davie, cross over the canal, and immediately turn right on Orange Drive. Stop at *Grifs Western,* a 20,000-square-foot emporium featuring saddles, hats, western shirts, and seemingly miles of boots, priced from $80 to $600. There are hitching posts out front for those arriving on horseback. 6211 SW 45th St. (phone: 305-587-9000).

Return to Davie and turn right. On the left, at SW 41st Street, stands a ranch-style *McDonald's.* Out back, riders park their horses at hitching posts in the Golden Arches' corral, where the nags slurp from water troughs while their riders put on the feedbag inside.

Retrace the path on Davie to Orange Drive and turn right. On the right is the Town Hall, a western-style complex of rough-hewn cedar. (The fire and police stations down the road bear the same façades.) In back of Town Hall is the new covered *Davie Rodeo Arena,* where 5,000 folks can watch cowboys compete in bareback riding, calf roping, steer wrestling, tie-down roping, bull riding, and girls' barrel racing every Thursday night at 8 PM and the second Friday and Saturday nights of each month at 8 PM. The *Five Star Pro Rodeo* monthly series features professional rodeo cowboys from around the country, and points for the events go toward the *National Finals Rodeo* in Las Vegas. The *Florida State Championship Rodeo* takes place here each December. 4201 SW 65th Way (phone: 305-437-8800).

If you can't wait to get in the saddle yourself, mosey up to one of the area stables. You can rent horses at the *Bar-B Ranch* (4601 SW 128th Ave., Davie; phone: 305-434-6175) or join a supervised ride at the *Stride-Rite Training Center* (5550 SW 73rd Ave., Davie; phone: 305-587-2285).

Those in the area at dinnertime who wish to sample authentic southwestern food (not the standard Tex-Mex, fast-food variety) should stop in at the *Armadillo Café.* The chefs have created original drama using southwestern influences. Outstanding dishes are the black and white soup (a combination of black-bean soup with jack-cheese soup) and smoked duck with orange juice and wildflower honey sauce. Open 5 to 10 PM Tuesdays through Thursdays and Sundays; 5 to 11 PM Fridays and Saturdays. 4630 SW 64th Ave., Davie (phone: 305-791-4866).

For an experience unique to South Florida, an easy visit to the Everglades awaits. Continue west on Griffin Road about 25 miles to US 27 (it's 18 miles west of I-95, a half-hour drive from 441) and the Everglades Holiday Park. A narrated airboat ride skims guests over the sawgrass through the park that conservationist Marjorie Stoneman Douglas termed a "River of Grass." Visitors will probably spot snoozing live alligators (sometimes a nest of babies), and flocks of 2-legged tropical denizens such as red-legged gallinules. There's an alligator wrestling show and wildlife exhibit, plus Seminole crafts sold in a straw hut. Learn about Native American food and clothing, as well as the Indian uprisings. Park open for wandering, fishing, and 45-minute airboat tours daily, 9 AM to 5 PM. Admission charge for tours. 21940 Griffin Rd. (phone: 305-434-8111). Another option is the Sawgrass Recreation Area, where fishing boats can be rented for $33 for 4 hours; guided airboat tours cost $11.50 for adults, $6.50 for children under 12, including a stop at an Indian village. Nature walks and a store also are available. Open daily 6 AM until dusk, with airboat rides from 9 AM to 4:30 PM. 5400 US Rte. 27 (phone: 305-389-0202). For more information see *Tour 9: Everglades National Park,* below.

Tour 7: Palm Beach

Another day might be spent viewing the area where the rich, famous, and infamous winter in Palm Beach. There also are several interesting sights along the way. (It's an easy drive north to Palm Beach; just be sure to avoid I-95 during rush hours.)

Take I-95 North (for those in the western region of South Florida, Florida's turnpike is less heavily trafficked). For a short diversion, exit at Palmetto Park Road (Exit 38) and go east for 2 miles to Federal Highway (Route 1). Turn left and pass one traffic light. On the right, turn into Mizner Park, a stunning complex of pink buildings with orange barrel-tile roofs, green balconies, brick roads, and splashing fountains. Visitors might want to browse among boutiques and outdoor cafés in this new multi-use center. Among its "cultural" amenities is the *Museum of Cartoon Art,* relocated here after spending 18 years in Rye Brook, New York; the new location also houses the world's only Cartoon Hall of Fame, and boasts 100,000 original works of cartoon art, a 10,000-book library, and a theater for viewing its 100 hours of videotape and film. 200 Plaza Real, Boca Raton (for information, contact the Boca Raton Chamber of Commerce at 407-395-4433).

Return to I-95 North and continue to Southern Boulevard, Route 98 (Exit 50). Those traveling with children, or who simply love animals, should go west 18 miles to *Lion Country Safari.* Occupants remain in their cars and drive through more than 500 acres, where they pass prides of lions and herds of antelope in re-creations of African areas such as the Serengeti Plains and Skukuza Veldt.

As you stop, a rhinoceros may lumber alongside the car. As a pickup truck deposits a load of sapling trees for the African elephants' lunch, adult elephants protectively circle around their babies. Paddleboat and kiddic rides, plus a snack bar, are available on the premises. Plan to spend several hours. Southern Blvd. W., West Palm Beach (phone: 407-793-1084). Open daily from 9:30 AM, with the last cars admitted at 5:30 PM; admission charge.

After the safari, return to Southern Boulevard and go east for 19.2 miles. Follow the Southern Boulevard Bridge across the Intracoastal Waterway; note the winter waterfront mansions on the left. The closest one, with a pink 75-foot Moorish tower, is Mar-A-Lago, the estate currently owned by Donald Trump, but originally built for the late Majorie Merriweather Post, heiress to the Post cereal fortune. The 118-room mansion is listed on the National Register of Historic Places. You're now on the island of Palm Beach, one of the barrier beaches along South Florida's east coast. Proceed around the traffic circle, following signs for Route A1A North.

Continue north on South Ocean Boulevard past Mar-A-Lago (don't turn left where A1A continues). The ocean is on the right. On the left, the strip is dotted with elegant mansions owned by members of European royalty or

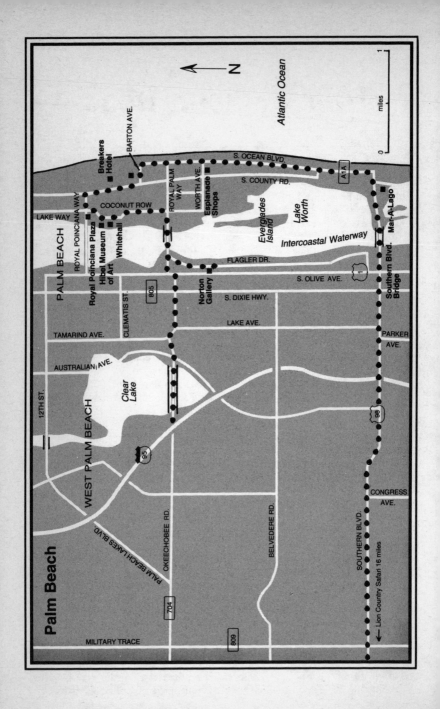

giants of American industry. The mansions' architecture — in Spanish, French, and Italian styles — recalls the landscape along the Riviera.

At 1.65 miles from the traffic circle, look to the left for the street sign marked Worth Avenue. This famed street is well worth a visit. If there are no vacant parking meters, there's a parking lot (with valet parking) in the *Esplanade Shops* about half a block down on the left, just east of *Saks Fifth Avenue*. (Or try the outdoor lot a few blocks away on Peruvian Avenue.)

Whether you're a world class shopper or just the window-shopping type, these few blocks along Worth Avenue should not be missed. The 200 glamorous stores — and the elegantly dressed shoppers who frequent them — are reminiscent of Beverly Hills' Rodeo Drive, although one recent visitor from Beverly Hills noticed more Rolls-Royces here in a day than he ever spotted back home. In addition to its pricey shops, Worth Avenue's architectural beauty is worthy of note.

Basically, the 4-block-long street is lined with 1- and 2-story shops built by 1920s architect Addison Mizner, in the Spanish Revival style he thought the region's history and climate demanded. Mizner was responsible for many grand homes throughout the area as well, for families such as the Vanderbilts and the Phippses. Buildings are white stucco with orange barrel-tile roofs, dripping with cerise bougainvillea. Arched galleries face miniature royal palm trees; and everything is spotless and subdued. At the eastern end, the 2-story *Esplanade Shops,* with their Spanish tiles and water fountains, add further charm to the scene.

One of the top restaurants for a fashionable lunch or dinner is award-winning *Café L'Europe* (150 Worth Ave.; phone: 407-655-4020) on the second floor of the *Esplanade,* serving French and continental fare (such as sautéed capon with wild mushrooms and leeks) in an elegant setting of rich woods, leaded glass, heavy lace curtains, and crystal. There is a caviar bar (with five varieties of caviar) and champagne botttles in silver top-hat wine buckets. Open for lunch 11:30 AM to 3 PM Mondays through Saturdays and dinner 6 to 10 PM daily.

Don't miss the "vias," charming side courtyards off the street hosting additional shops and eateries, with gurgling fountains and lush flower beds.

High-fashion shops include *Martha's, Sara Fredericks, Valentino Boutique, Polo by Ralph Lauren, Brooks Brothers, Salvatore Ferragamo, Sonia Rykiel,* and *Saks Fifth Avenue.* Leather goods are at *Gucci* and *Mark Cross.* Jewelry can be purchased at *Cartier* and *Van Cleef & Arpels.* Artworks can be found at *Wally Findlay Galleries* and *Holsten Gallery.* High-priced toys are at *F.A.O Schwarz.* There's also a thrift shop where you just might find a cast-off sequin gown formerly owned by a society czarina.

When you've had your fill of shopping and staring, head east along any of the streets, returning to Ocean Boulevard. Continue north as far as it goes (Barton Avenue). Ahead is a white-pillared house that belongs to cosmetics magnate Estée Lauder. Local lore has it that if the guards stand at the dooorway, she's in residence. Beyond that lies the Kennedy compound, which isn't visible from the street. (Don't expect to approach any of these well-guarded private homes.)

Follow Barton left to South County Road (the first traffic light) and turn right. At the second light (Breakers Row), turn right into the *Breakers* hotel and park near the fountain. This 528-room stucco hotel, built in 1926 (after two former wooden incarnations burned down), is reminiscent of a European palace with its Italian Renaissance–style antique furniture and hand-painted ceilings. Notice the 15th-century tapestries in the lobby. If your visit coincides with the "season," you may spot one or several of the many movie stars and heads of government who stay here. Have lunch in the *Beach Club,* overlooking the ocean, or in the *Fairways Club,* overlooking the golf course (1 S. County Rd., Palm Beach; phone: 407-655-6611).

Once refreshed, return to your car. Go back on South County Road to the next light, Royal Poinciana Way, and turn right. At the next light (Coconut Row), turn left. On the right pass *Royal Poinciana Plaza,* a low-key complex housing the *Royal Poinciana Playhouse,* stores, and restaurants. In the "famous-for-all-the-wrong-reasons" category is *Au Bar* (336 Royal Poinciana Way; phone: 407-832-4800), the supposed rendezvous spot in the 1992 William Kennedy Smith rape trial. (Smith was acquitted and, despite the notoriety, *Au Bar* is a good watering hole.) Those who prefer a quick snack might opt for *Too-Jay's,* serving New York–style delicatessen sandwiches, unusual salads, and fantastic pastries such as the killer chocolate cake (phone: 407-659-7232). The *Hibel Museum of Art* mounts the works of 75-year-old artist Edna Hibel — original oils, lithographs, bronze sculptures, and collectible plates. The first female artist to be awarded the medal of honor by Pope John Paul II, Edna Hibel also has been honored with a fellowship to the World Academy of Art and Science. Open Tuesdays through Saturdays 10 AM to 5 PM, Sundays 1 to 5 PM; no admission charge. 150 Royal Poinciana Plaza (phone: 407-833-6870).

Exit the *Royal Poinciana Plaza;* shortly ahead on the right is the 73-room *Henry Morrison Flagler Museum.* Called "Whitehall," the mansion was the home of Henry Morrison Flagler, a co-founder of the Standard Oil Company who brought what is now the *Florida East Coast Railroad* south through Florida, down to Key West. (He subsequently opened resorts throughout Florida, and is credited with establishing Palm Beach and aiding development of Miami Beach and Key West.) He built this home in 1901 for his third wife, who was 38 years his junior. (One of his tokens of affection was a pearl necklace with a clasp enhanced by a 12-carat diamond.)

A vacation home like those in Newport, Rhode Island, it cost $2.5 million to build and $1.5 million to furnish. (In 1993 dollars, that would run over $70 million to build and over $42 million to furnish.) Its 110-foot-long foyer is decorated in seven kinds of marble. Features include gilded moldings, ceiling murals, museum-quality furnishings, enormous Baccarat crystal chandeleirs, columns, fireplaces, and artworks. Children will enjoy the doll room with its antique doll collection. There are costume collections dating from 1895 to 1915, and other collections, including lace and silver. Allow about 1½ hours for a tour. Open Tuesdays through Saturdays from 10 AM to 5 PM, Sundays from noon to 5 PM; closed *Christmas* and *New Year's.* Admission charge. Coconut Row, Palm Beach (phone: 407-655-2833).

Continue south on Coconut Row and turn right on Royal Palm Way (towering royal palms line both sides of this especially striking street); continue over Royal Palm Bridge. Exit the bridge and turn left onto Flagler Drive. Proceed .3 miles to Diana Place on the right, site of the 1-story, buff-colored *Norton Gallery,* with its permanent collection of French Impressionist, Chinese, and American art, plus traveling exhibitions. Open from 10 AM to 5 PM Tuesdays through Saturdays and 1 to 5 PM Sundays; closed Mondays. Donation requested. 1451 S. Olive Ave., West Palm Beach (phone: 407-832-5194).

Return north on Flagler to the bridge (Lake View Avenue) and turn left. Staying on the right side of the road as it crosses Dixie Highway (US 1), the road curves right and then continues straight as Jessamine Street. Continue west across the railroad tracks, and straight ahead (after the third light from the bridge) note the recently built $52-million *Kravis Center for the Performing Arts.* Offerings include opera and ballet performances, such as the *Bolshoi Ballet,* plus national companies of Broadway shows. For information, call the Palm Beach County Convention and Visitors Bureau (phone: 407-471-3995).

At this point, Lake View Avenue has turned into Okeechobee Boulevard. From the corner of Okeechobee and Tamarind Avenue, continue west on Okeechobee for 1 mile, until you see the signs for I-95 southbound. Now, retrace the route back to your hotel, or perhaps stay and sample the elegance of the *Breakers* at dinner. Its *Florentine* dining room, where diners sit beneath 25-foot-high, frescoed, beamed ceilings patterned after the Palazzo Davante in Florence, also is open to non-guests. Sample the famed wine list and dance to live orchestra music. Men are required to wear jackets. Open daily 6 to 10 PM. 1 S. County Rd. (phone: 407-659-8480).

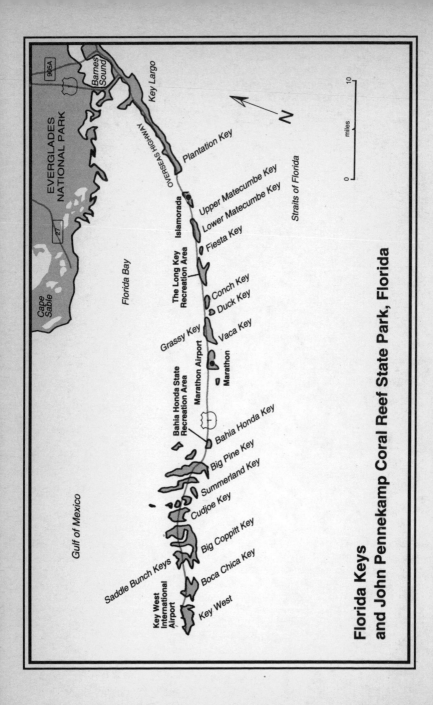

Florida Keys
and John Pennekamp Coral Reef State Park, Florida

Tour 8: Florida Keys and John Pennekamp Coral Reef State Park

Curving 150 miles out into the Gulf of Mexico from the southern tip of mainland Florida, the Florida Keys dot the waters like an ellipsis following a phrase. And in many ways this archipelago is an afterthought to that great landmass above, centered around Miami, with its glittering nightlife and crowded swimming beaches. The 45 principal islands that make up the Keys are generally tucked soundly away by 11 PM, have very few swimming beaches despite the availability of water (the shallow waters, coupled with fierce coral, discourage swimming), and few glamorous resorts. A local hotel with 5 stories — a midget by Miami standards — is a skyscraper hereabouts. The Keys are an easy day trip from Miami; for those who would like to stay overnight, our choice of hotels is listed below.

What the Keys do have, however, are some of the finest seascapes around — the blue waters of the Atlantic to the east and south and the green seas of the Gulf of Mexico on the northwestern side. As you drive along the Overseas Highway (US 1), a toll-free highway that spans the islands with 43 bridges (some only 100 feet long, one stretching more than 7 miles), you are surrounded by sea and sky on all sides. Even on the Keys themselves, many of which are only a few hundred yards wide, you can see through the mangroves, Caribbean pine, and silver palmetto to the sea, which is the overwhelming presence here. And though you can't see it from a car, the view is even more dramatic below the water's surface.

The Keys are surrounded by an offshore coral reef. There are dive shops all along the route, indicated by the red-and-white-striped divers' flags, which arrange private or group snorkeling expeditions to nearby reefs where you stalk (swim after) your prey. The best section of the reef can be seen close up at the John Pennekamp Coral Reef State Park in Key Largo. It is a slightly hallucinogenic underwater scene, as bright blue and green tropical fish move in and out of the sculptured reefs of white, pink, and orange coral.

The story of the Overseas Highway is interesting. During the late 1880s, Henry Flagler, an associate of John D. Rockefeller, aimed to establish a "land" route to Cuba by extending the *Florida East Coast Railroad* line to Key West. From there he planned a ferry shuttle for the final 90 miles to Havana. He invested some $20 million in the construction of tracks, but the 1929 crash destroyed his project. Six years later, the *Labor Day* hurricane of 1935 wiped out most of what remained of the tracks and roadbed. At that point, the government stepped in and began building the Overseas Highway along the same route. In 1982, 37 bridges were replaced with wider, heavier spans, including the well-known Seven-Mile Bridge at Marathon.

Of the 45 keys linked by the highway, several are major islands with accommodations, restaurants, shops, and their own unique characteristics. Much of this local flavor has to do with the natives of the area. They're Floridians, but they call themselves Conchs. Descended from London Cockneys who settled in the Bahamas, the Conchs also incorporate Cuban, Yankee sailor, and Virginia merchant blood. Conchs always have been people of the sea — fishermen, boatsmen, spongers (they dive for sponges), and underwater salvagers. (They hardly could be otherwise, living as they do, surrounded by water.) And when you are in their territory, you can easily share their pleasures.

Fishing is king in these parts, with over 300 varieties of fish in the surrounding waters. Besides the challenges to anglers, the availability of fresh fish has stimulated Keys chefs to dream up such creations as conch chowder and, in their land-bound flights of fancy, Key lime pie — which must be yellow, not green, to be genuine.

Key Largo is the first of the keys and the longest, but what is most interesting here is underwater. Running parallel to the Key for 21 miles is the country's only underwater state park, and the largest living coral reef in the continental US. The park is a snorkeler's and scuba diver's heaven, encompassing 165 square miles of the Atlantic Ocean, hundreds of species of tropical fish, and 55 different varieties of coral. Laws forbid taking anything from the water so that the area will be preserved for others to see.

To get an overview of the reef and surrounding sea, take a glass-bottom boat tour operated by *Coral Reef Park* (phone: 305-451-1621), which sails three times daily (cost is $14 for adults, $7.50 for children under 12). It provides valuable insights on the ecological balance of the reef and journeys several miles out onto the high seas to the reef's most spectacular section, where you'll see beautifully colored coral formations and other marine life, including barracuda, giant sea turtles, and sharks, from a dry vantage point.

You also can venture into the water for snorkeling and scuba diving tours of the reef. Gear can be rented at one of Key Largo's many dive shops or at park headquarters.

Closer to shore, water trails for canoeing in the mangrove swamp offer alternatives for those who want to stay above water. For those who want to go in, the swimming beach has a roped-off area that is good for a dip or some casual skin diving.

There are 47 campsites, all with tables, charcoal grills, electrical hookups, and water. Reservations for the sites should be made up to 60 days in advance — the park is a very popular destination. Stop by the visitors' center. Reservations and information: *John Pennekamp State Park*, PO Box 487, Key Largo, FL 33037 (phone: 305-451-1202; for concession and equipment rental information call 305-451-1621).

Islamorada, in Upper Matecumbe Key, is a sport fishing center in an area that's famous for fishing; its many coral reefs in the surrounding shallow waters attract scuba and skin divers as well. The Underwater Coral Gardens, two colorful coral deposits and the wreck of a Spanish galleon, offer underwater exploration and photography and can be reached by charter boat.

Also stop at Long Key for some underwater hunting (in season) of crawfish — lobster-like crustaceans without the pincers. The Long Key State Recreation Area features 60 campsites, picnic areas with tables, barbecue grills, fresh water, and nature trails through the mangrove swamps. Long Key Park, 67.5 mile, Long Key (phone: 305-664-4815).

Marathon, the large key midway down the archipelago, has been developed as a tourist center and has an airport and an 18-hole golf course. Nevertheless, Marathon retains much of the original character of a fishing town. There are over 80 species in the gulf and ocean waters which can be taken with rod and reel or nets from charter boats or the key's bridges. For information on the many fishing contests held throughout the year, write to the Chamber of Commerce (3330 Overseas Hwy., Marathon, FL 33050; phone: 305-743-5417). The competition is tough and the fish are smart. *Hall's Diving Center* (1994 Overseas Hwy.; phone: 305-743-5929) is a good place to rent gear.

Big Pine Key, the largest of the Lower Keys, contains 7,700 acres thick with silver palmetto, Caribbean pine, and cacti. Tiny Key deer were thought to be extinct until they reappeared here, and it also is possible to spot the endangered great white heron.

At Bahia Honda Key, the 740-acre Bahia Honda State Recreation Area (5 miles east on US 1) has 80 campsites, 6 cabins, boating, picnicking, and coral-free swimming (phone: 305-872-2353).

And last, but not least, Key West, the southernmost community in the US and the point closest to Cuba (a 90-mile swim), combines Southern, Bahamian, Cuban, and Yankee influences in a unique culture that can be seen in its architecture, tasted in its often quirky food, and felt in its relaxed, individualistic atmosphere. Traditionally, fishermen, artists, and writers have been drawn to this tranquil slip of sand and sea. Ernest Hemingway, among its early devotees, lived here during his most productive years, when he wrote *To Have and Have Not, For Whom the Bell Tolls, Green Hills of Africa,* and one of his greatest short stories, "The Snows of Kilimanjaro." His Spanish colonial–style house of native stone, surrounded by a lush garden of plantings from the Caribbean, is now a museum with many original furnishings and Hemingway memorabilia, along with descendants of Hemingway's pet cats (907 Whitehead St.; phone: 305-294-1575). Among others who have been attracted to Key West are John James Audubon, Tennessee Williams, John Dos Passos, Robert Frost, and President Harry S. Truman, who established a "Little White House" here. It is now a museum filled with Truman's original furniture and artifacts (open daily from 9 AM to 5 PM; admission charge; 111 Front St.; phone: 305-294-9911).

To get your bearings, take the *Conch Tour Train,* a 90-minute narrated tram ride that covers 14 miles, passing all the local highlights. The train leaves from Mallory Square and North Roosevelt Boulevard, next to the Welcome Center (phone: 305-294-5161). Purchase tickets at the bright yellow kiosk on the corner of Duval and Front Streets. Since Key West is best for strolling, you can later visit the places that sounded most interesting — for example, the wooden gingerbread architecture influenced by Bahamian settlers and

New England sea captains — or walk to the galleries, craft, and shell shops.

The area also has the dubious distinction of having more T-shirt shops per square foot than anywhere else in the Miami/Ft. Lauderdale area. Another great orientation is provided by *Old Town Trolley Tours.* The narrated tours pick up passengers at 14 stops; 1 price ($12) permits full-day on-again, off-again privileges until the loop is completed (phone: 305-296-4444 or 800-284-4482). For water viewing, *Discovery Tours'* boat leaves from Lands End Marina (phone: 305-293-0099). Unlike glass-bottom boats, *Discovery* craft have a below-deck viewing room where passengers look through eye-level windows lining the hull. Twice-daily trips visit the coral reef, while a sunset cruise stops at the reef, then sails to Mallory Dock in time to watch the sun go down. In fact, the main tourist attraction in these parts is the *Sunset Celebration* at Mallory Square. Locals and visitors watch as the sun sinks, hoping to spot the green flash. Artisans, jugglers, and flame swallowers add to the color as shrimp boats head home. Numerous glass-bottom boats ply the water as well. A favorite is the long-established *Fireball,* with two boats that sail daily from the foot of Duval Street (phone: 305-296-6293).

The *Lighthouse Museum* (open daily; admission charge; Truman Ave. and Whitehead St.; phone: 305-294-0012) has many military displays. The *Audubon House* (open daily; admission charge; 205 Whitehead St.; phone: 305-294-2116), where the artist worked on paintings of Florida Keys wildlife in 1831 and 1832, has a complete set of his *Birds of America* engravings. Restored by the philanthropic Wolfson family who hail from these parts, *Audubon House* also encompasses the home and belongings of a wealthy 19th-century sea captain and wrecker. Wrecking was an important industry among early "conchs", and it's explained through talks and pictures at the *Wreckers Museum.* The oldest house in Key West (dating from 1829 and owned by a sea captain), it harbors furniture, documents, and ship models (open daily 10 AM to 4 PM; admission charge; 322 Duval St.; phone: 305-294-9502). More treasures await at *Mel Fisher's Treasure Exhibit,* housed in the dark former navy warehouse. It displays loot salvaged from the Spanish ships *Atocha* and *Santa Margarita,* sunk in a 1622 hurricane. On view are hoards of silver bars, gold chains, and emerald and diamond jewelry (open daily 9:30 AM to 5 PM; admission charge; 200 Green St.; phone: 305-296-9936).

Fishing dominates sports here as elsewhere in the Keys. In addition to fishing, there is a collection of local marine life at the *Municipal Aquarium* (open daily 10 AM to 6 PM; admission charge; Whitehead St. on Mallory Sq.; phone: 305-296-2051). For snorkeling and scuba diving around the coral reefs, the *Key West Pro Dive Shop* sponsors trips and rents gear (1605 N. Roosevelt Blvd., PO Box 580, Key West, FL 33040; phone: 305-296-3823). Information: *Key West Chamber of Commerce,* 402 Wall St., Key West, FL 33040 (phone: 305-294-2587). Area information: *Florida Keys Visitors Bureau,* PO Box 1147-PR, Key West, FL 33041 (phone: 800-FLA-KEYS).

Antonia's (615 Duval; phone: 305-294-6565) is considered one of Key West's best restaurants. Outstanding meals also are served at *Louie's Backyard,* either inside or on the large deck under a huge banyan tree, overlooking the ocean (700 Waddell Ave.; phone: 305-294-1061), and at the *Pier House Restaurant* (1 Duval St.; phone: 305-294-9541), where the Key lime pie may be the best anywhere. And Hemingway fans never miss a pilgrimage to *Sloppy Joe's* (phone: 305-294-5717), the Duval Street bar once frequented by the writer himself; current regulars are not of the literary persuasion.

Below are some suggested overnight stays in the Keys.

Cheeca Lodge, Islamorada – Its low-key elegance makes this 27-acre seaside hideaway a romantic pleasure. There are 64 villas, 49 guestrooms, and a penthouse. Other amenities include a dining room and open-air grill, 2 swimming pools, a manmade lagoon with a sand beach and waterfalls, 6 lighted tennis courts, and a 9-hole, par 3 golf course designed by Jack Nicklaus. Water activities — such as fishing, snorkeling, and parasailing — also are available. Marker 82, PO Box 527, Islamorada, FL 33036 (phone: 305-664-4651 or 800-327-2888).

La Concha Holiday Inn, Key West – In the heart of Old Town, this 160-room, 7-story Art Deco hotel in Old Town first opened in 1926 and has been recently restored. Chenille bedspreads, four-poster beds, lace curtains, and antique furnishings abound, although plumbing and electronic equipment are modern. There's a restaurant, as well as 3 bars, boutiques, and a pool. There's a daily sunset celebration (weather permitting) at the rooftop bar. 430 Duval St., Key West, FL 33040 (phone: 305-296-2991 or 800-HOLIDAY; fax: 305-294-3283).

Little Palm Island, Little Torch Key – On a secluded island just off Key West is this charming hideaway, a member of the prestigious Relais & Châteaux group. There are 30 private cottages with thatch roofs and rustic but elegant furnishings, a swimming pool, and a fine restaurant. Tennis and golf facilities are nearby. Rte. 4, Box 1036, Little Torch Key, FL 33042 (phone: 305-872-2524; fax: 305-872-4843).

Curry Mansion Inn, Key West – This impeccably and authentically restored Victorian mansion features 15 rooms in an antiques-filled main house, as well as an L-shape guesthouse enclosing the pool and patio, where homemade breakfast is served and cocktail parties are held each evening. Guests have beach privileges at the *Pier House* (see below). 511 Caroline St., Key West, FL 33040 (phone: 305-294-5349 or 800-253-3466; fax: 305-293-4093).

Hyatt Key West, Key West – With its own private beach and marina, this 4-story, 120-room hostelry close to town offers a pool and a Jacuzzi. 601 Front St., Key West, FL 33040 (phone: 305-296-9900 or 800-233-1234; fax: 305-292-1038).

Marriott's Casa Marina, Key West – Built in 1921 by Henry Flagler, this full-service resort with its own beach has 312 rooms, 2 restaurants, a pool, a whirlpool bath, 3 lighted tennis courts, a health club, and water sports. 1500 Reynolds St., Key West, FL 33040 (phone: 305-296-3535 or 800-228-9290; fax: 305-296-4633).

Ocean Reef Club, Key Largo – Originally a private fishing camp and now a posh tropical paradise, this 300-room exclusive — and expensive — resort boasts good golf, terrific fishing, and 4,000 acres of park and wildlife preserve. It is now offering accommodations to "potential members." Amenities also include 7 restaurants and 5 lounges. If you're into high-style living and have the pocketbook to back it up, this is the place for you. 31 Ocean Reef Dr., N. Key Largo, FL 33037 (phone: 305-367-2611 or 800-741-REEF; fax: 305-367-2224).

Pier House, Key West – In the heart of the restored Old Town area, this 142-room property has 5 dining areas (the *Pier House* restaurant is first-rate), a health spa, a manmade sand beach, a pool, and a deck for sunset watchers. 1 Duval St., Key West, FL 33040 (phone: 305-296-4600; 800-432-3414 in Florida; 800-327-8340 elsewhere in the US; fax: 305-296-7569).

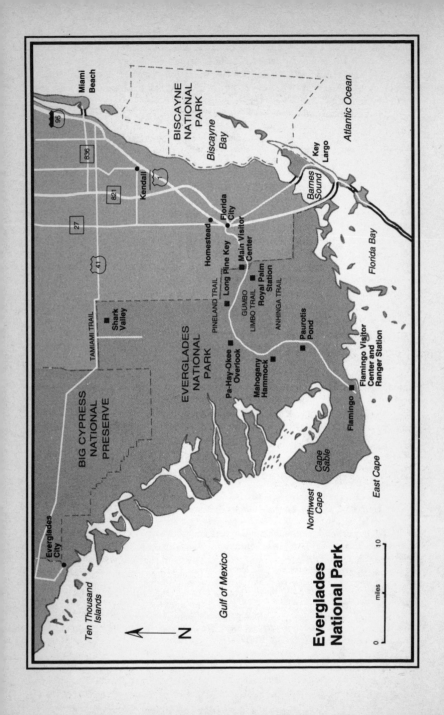

Tour 9: Everglades National Park

If you've had your fill (for a while, at least) of sea and sand, venture 21 miles (about a half hour along the Tamiami Trail) from Miami to Everglades National Park.

In most of America's national parks there's little more to do than arrive and open your eyes to be impressed. The Everglades is far more demanding. Here you must know something about ecology, and something about what you're looking at, to appreciate the full splendor of this magnificent swamp wilderness.

The Everglades is America's only subtropical wetlands. Fed by the waters of southern Florida's huge Lake Okeechobee, the entire southern tip of the state was once more or less as the Everglades is today — a huge tract of mangrove swamps, seas of sawgrass, hammocks of hardwood trees, and millions of birds, fish, snakes, alligators, and insects (especially mosquitoes). As southern Florida developed, the slow-draining waters of Okeechobee were channeled for irrigation and the swamps drained. Bit by bit, southern Florida dried out.

In 1947, alarmed by the destruction of these unique wetlands, the federal government set aside 1.5 million acres 30 miles southwest of Miami as Everglades National Park. Despite various (and continuing) environmental threats, the park remains. It's the third-largest of America's national parks — 2,350 square miles of the world's most delicate ecological system, stretching to Florida's southern and western Gulf coasts. Although the Everglades is considered one of the nation's most threatened natural areas, there is reason to be optimistic about its future. The Everglades Expansion Act of 1989 added more than 107,000 acres of the East Everglades to the park. South Florida's water management system of canals, levees, and dams is being modified to restore natural water flow and marsh conditions to this critical wildlife habitat. Water entering the park will be cleansed of pollutants as it passes through filtration marshes being created north of the park.

You must understand the delicacy of the Everglades to enjoy its understated pleasures. It is actually a freshwater river (its Indian name is Pa-Hay-Okee, "River of Grass") 100 miles long, 50 miles wide, and just inches deep. This strange stream travels along an incline of only 3 inches a mile, moving so slowly that a single drop of water takes years to reach the Gulf from Lake Okeechobee. The slow river provides nourishment for a vast and complex system of life, and is a perfect laboratory in which to see the interdependence and sensitivity of an ecosystem. Where the earth rises as much as 3 inches, the plant life in the Everglades changes from sawgrass to hardwood forest.

Where ripples appear in a pond, a small fish is eating mosquito larvae; a large fish, a bream perhaps, will dine on the larvae-eater; bass hunt the bream; gar will feed on the bass; and the gar is fodder for the alligator who originally made (or deepened) this pool by digging in with his tail during the winter.

About 200 miles north of the Tropic of Cancer, the Everglades is the meeting point of subtropical and temperate life forms. In this, it is unique in the US: Here you see mangrove, West Indian mahogany, and the poisonous manchineel tree, and in a nearby hammock rising from the sawgrass, pine and hardwood trees. Alligators, crocodiles, and white-tailed deer share the same stomping ground.

Plan to visit the Everglades during the winter, just about the only time to avoid being consumed by mosquitoes. Indeed, in summer, some areas are so infested by these offensive insects that a pleasant visit is nigh impossible. Always carry insect repellent, regardless of the time of year.

The main entrance to the Everglades is on Route 9336, about 10 miles southwest of Homestead; admission charge. Route 9336 ends at the park entrance; from here follow the main park road for a 38-mile journey through the park to Flamingo, on Florida Bay. There are several ways to see the 'glades: By car, drive to various stops along the road; on foot, follow trails into the heart of things (with or without ranger guides); by small outboard or canoe, follow the water routes. In any case, the first stop is the visitors' center at the park entrance to see exhibitions on park wildlife and ecology and pick up information on guided tours, "swamp tromps" (more about these later), and park activities and rules.

The next stop is the Royal Palm Visitor Center (about 2 miles beyond the center), where you can follow boardwalks over the sawgrass and watch for animal life. ("Sawgrass" is actually a misnomer; it is not a grass but a fine-toothed sedge. Despite its delicate appearance, it has mean, serrated edges on three sides that chew clothes or flesh with equal ease, so be careful.)

Beyond Royal Palm, the road runs through pine forests to Long Pine Key, a good picnicking and camping spot. Note the pines. They manage to survive only because they are sturdily fire resistant. You may see a number of them with fire-blackened trunks. In both summer and winter, fires often sweep through parts of the 'glades. Many trees are killed, but pines burn only on the outside; their corky bark protects them. In summer, the saltwort marshes that flank many of the forests dry out and are torched by summer lightning, but since it is the rainy season, when water levels are relatively high, these fires do little damage. It is the fires during the winter dry season — usually caused by man — that do the most harm.

Pa-Hay-Okee, the next stop along the route, provides some of the best views and bird watching in the park. From here you have access to a high platform and boardwalks that overlook Shark River Slough, where alligators and fowl gather. The alligators form an important link in the chain of life in the Everglades. During the dry season — autumn through spring — they settle into sloughs and dig deep holes with their tails. In late winter, as the marshes dry out, fish get caught in these 'gator-holes, which become teeming pools of fish life. This is crucial for the wading birds, which nest near these ample sources of food and are assured a food supply.

Seven miles beyond Pa-Hay-Okee is Mahogany Hammock, the largest stand of mahoganies in the US. Boardwalks allow you to wander into it. A bit farther is Paurotis Pond, where you encounter the first mangrove trees. Here salt and fresh water begin to mix, and the mangrove is the only tree that thrives in salt water. It is a great colonizer and lives in a constant drama of creation and destruction all along the Gulf shore. It settles into the swampy salt water of the coast, and as it drops seeds and throws out breathing roots it captures material and actually begins "building" earth bulwarks against the sea. As seagulls and other sea birds collect around it, dropping guano, this earth becomes rich and fertile. Then hurricanes sweep the coast, and everything is ripped out of the swampy ground and thrown inland.

The main park road ends at Flamingo, where you'll find another visitor center, a hotel, campgrounds, and boats for hire (including houseboats) for excursions into portions of the 'glades accessible only by waterway.

Serious visitors should plan to spend most of their time out of their cars, on marked foot trails or on a "swamp tromp" into the very heart of the marshes. For the less hardy, foot trails are a comfortable way to have an intimate experience in the 'glades. (There also is a tram ride available at Shark Valley off Route 41, which skims the northern border of the park.)

Gumbo Limbo Trail begins at Royal Palm and explores the interior of Paradise Key, where exotic air plants and hardwood trees grow; also at Royal Palm, Anhinga Trail is a likely route to spot a number of alligators and a variety of birds from an elevated walkway. You might just be lucky enough to spot some of the delicate Virginia white-tailed deer along the Pineland Trail (beginning about 2 miles from Long Pine Key area). These little deer are the prey of the Florida panther, which, sadly, lives in dwindling numbers here in the Everglades. At the Pa-Hay-Okee Overlook, there is a perspective of the expanse of sawgrass that makes up Shark River Slough.

For the more intrepid who would like to meet nature's challenge, there are the frequent "slough slogs" or "swamp tromps" from December through March — walking expeditions led by park naturalists which really get you into things — quite literally. You'll need old clothes and shoes that you don't mind getting muddy and wet. And be sure to have plenty of mosquito repellent handy. There are several possible destinations: out to a 'gator hole, a tree island, or a major mangrove stand. Ask for schedules at the visitors' center.

The Wilderness Waterway is just about the most challenging test the Everglades can cook up for an outdoors person. It is a 99-mile water trail that corkscrews through the Ten Thousand Islands area. Although the water lanes are well marked, there is sufficient room for error that travelers are asked to take all precautions when undertaking this journey. By powerboat it is quite possible to complete the course in about 6 hours. However, any serious nature observer will opt for the canoe and the serenity it offers en route. There are minimally outfitted campsites, each wryly nicknamed, along the water lanes: "Hell's Bay" ("hell to get into and hell to get out of"); "Onion Key," the bare-bones remains of a 1920s land developer's dream; and a crude pit outhouse and fireplace campsite known as "the Coming Miami of the Gulf." Shorter canoe trails, equipped with overnight camping, are also available. Overnight stays require a backcountry use permit issued at no charge by

Everglades City (Everglades City Ranger Station, Drawer D, Everglades City, FL 33929; phone: 813-695-4217) or Flamingo Ranger Station (PO Box 279, Homestead, FL 33030; phone: 813-695-3101, ext. 182). The waterways begin at Everglades City and extend to Flamingo.

The somewhat less athletic and daring boater might prefer to take a guided boat cruise. One such cruise departs every evening from Flamingo to tour Florida Bay; this is a good opportunity to view Florida's blazing sunsets and watch the indigenous birds returning to roost for the evening. There also are daily cruises from Everglades City to explore Upper Chokoloskee Bay. But the craft most visitors associate with the Everglades is the airboat. Though banned from Everglades National Park (the noise and gas fumes disturb the fragile environment), airboats may be operated outside the park. Near the Shark Valley entrance, airboat rides are offered at Everglades Safari Park (Rte. 41, about 9 miles west of Krome Ave.; phone: 305-226-6923).

Another way to explore the wilderness is by kayak. *Ibis Tours* (5798 Sun Point Cir.; Boynton Beach, Fl 33437; phone: 800-525-9411) offers guided trips by sail-equipped sea kayaks (which are more stable and easier for first time kayakers). The 5-day journey starts in Everglades City; travelers paddle their way through the Ten Thousand Islands area and continue to the Gulf of Mexico, camping out on various secluded keys along the way. En route, there will be plenty to see: dolphins and manatees in the water and herons, eagles, and ospreys in the skies above. It's a great way to get acquainted with nature up close.

The not-so-visible members of the Everglades family run the gamut from the lowly and much-hated mosquito all the way to the signature 'gator, who is most often spotted when his eyes break water while the rest of him hides beneath the surface. Fish are tropical and abundant, each with a role in the food cycle that maintains the chain of life in the Everglades. Schools of dolphin can sometimes be spotted from the coastal shorelines. Recreational fishing is permitted, but all plants and animals are protected by law from any molestation or harm by man. Information: *Superintendent, Everglades National Park,* PO Box 279, Homestead, FL 33030 (phone: 305-242-7700).

For an overnight stay that doesn't involve camping out, try the *Flamingo Lodge* in Flamingo, the only place to stay right in the Everglades, with simple, rustic accommodations in 24 cottages and 101 motel rooms. There's a screened-in swimming pool, too. On Florida Bay, 38 miles from the entrance of Everglades Park (PO Box 428, Flamingo, FL 33030; phone: 305-253-2241); restaurant and gift shop closed May through October. And in the morning, after you've scraped the mud off your shoes, climb back in your car. From darkest jungle to sunlit sand, have we got a beach for you!

INDEX

Index